McDougal Littell

# Alabama Citizenship Course
## Workbook

TEACHER'S EDITION

McDougal Littell
A DIVISION OF HOUGHTON MIFFLIN COMPANY

Copyright © by McDougal Littell, a division of Houghton Mifflin Company.
All rights reserved.

Permission is hereby granted to teachers to reprint or photocopy in classroom quantities the pages or sheets in this work that carry a McDougal Littell, a division of Houghton Mifflin Company copyright notice. These pages are designed to be reproduced by teachers for use in their classes with accompanying McDougal Littell material, provided each copy made shows the copyright notice. Such copies may not be sold, and further distribution is expressly prohibited. Except as authorized above, prior written permission must be obtained from McDougal Littell, a division of Houghton Mifflin Company to reproduce or transmit this work or portions thereof in any other form or by any other electronic or mechanical means, including any information storage or retrieval system, unless expressly permitted by federal copyright law. Address inquiries to Supervisor, Rights and Permissions, McDougal Littell, a division of Houghton Mifflin Company P.O. Box 1667, Evanston, Illinois 60204

ISBN 0-618-60097-3

Printed in the United States of America.

1 2 3 4 5 6 7 8 9—MDO—08 07 06 05

# Table of Contents

Note to the Teacher................................................................. iv
Correlations ........................................................................... v

## Civics in America Workbook

| | | | |
|---|---|---|---|
| 1. | American Citizenship ................................................. | T1 | 1 |
| 2. | The Foundations of American Government ............... | T4 | 6 |
| 3. | The Constitution ......................................................... | T7 | 10 |
| 4. | Bill of Rights ............................................................... | T9 | 13 |
| 5. | The Living Constitution ............................................. | T11 | 16 |
| 6. | The Legislative Branch ............................................... | T13 | 19 |
| 7. | The Executive Branch ................................................. | T15 | 22 |
| 8. | The Judicial Branch .................................................... | T17 | 25 |
| 9. | State Governments ..................................................... | T19 | 28 |
| 10. | Local Government ...................................................... | T22 | 35 |
| 11. | How Our Political System Works .............................. | T24 | 38 |
| 12. | Public Opinion and Interest Groups ......................... | T26 | 41 |
| 13. | Law and Our Legal System ....................................... | T28 | 44 |
| 14. | The American Justice System .................................... | T30 | 48 |
| 15. | Economics and the American Economy .................... | T32 | 51 |
| 16. | Government's Role in the Economy .......................... | T35 | 56 |
| 17. | United States Foreign Policy ..................................... | T37 | 62 |
| 18. | Global Issues ............................................................... | T39 | 65 |

## Consumer Economics and Personal Finance Text and Workbook

| | | | |
|---|---|---|---|
| 19. | Making a Budget ........................................................ | T41 | 68 |
| 20. | Handling Your Money ............................................... | T43 | 84 |
| 21. | Using Credit Wisely ................................................... | T45 | 97 |
| 22. | Becoming a Wise Consumer ...................................... | T47 | 114 |
| 23. | Smart Shopping on the Internet ................................ | T49 | 129 |
| 24. | Smart Shopping for Food ........................................... | T51 | 136 |
| 25. | Smart Shopping for Clothing ..................................... | T53 | 145 |
| 26. | Smart Shopping for Health Care ............................... | T55 | 156 |
| 27. | Making a Home .......................................................... | T57 | 171 |
| 28. | Getting Around .......................................................... | T59 | 187 |
| 29. | How Insurance Can Protect You ............................... | T61 | 205 |
| 30. | How to Invest for Your Future .................................. | T63 | 220 |

## Copy Masters

Application for Employment ................................................. T65
Monthly Budget ...................................................................... T66
Check Front & Back ................................................................ T67
Check Register ........................................................................ T68
Grocery List ............................................................................. T69

Answer Key ............................................................................. 231

# Note to the Teacher

The Citizenship Course Workbook is tailored specifically for the seventh grade Alabama Citizenship student and teacher. Chapters 1–18 of the student book are designed as a workbook to accompany the *Civics in America* NexText book.

*The Consumer Economics and Personal Finance* section (chapters 19–20) primarily addresses standard 8 of the Alabama Citizenship Course of Study. This portion of the book includes the full text of each chapter before the workbook pages.

This Teacher's Edition includes all student pages plus a teacher's resource section consisting of objectives, background information, further resources, objectives, vocabulary, review and critical thinking questions, and class activities to aid planning each chapter. The teacher pages are grouped in front of the student workbook and are tabbed for distinction from the rest of the book. The Teacher's Edition also includes copy masters and the answer key.

The table of contents in the teacher's edition lists the teacher resource section pages followed by the student workbook pages for each chapter.

Please note that the standards in the correlation (page v) have been modified. General bullet points were converted to subpoints (a, b, c, etc.) for more efficient reference to correlations throughout the book.

McDougal Littell
# Civics in America, a NexText Coursebook and the Alabama Citizenship Course Workbook
correlated to the
## Alabama Course of Study
### SEVENTH GRADE
### Citizenship

| Standard | Civics in America | Alabama Citizenship Course Workbook |
|---|---|---|
| 1. Describe the influences of ancient Greece, the Magna Carta, and the Mayflower Compact on the government of the United States. | 10, 11, 16–17, 19–20, 21–22, 23, 26–27, 31, 32, 69, 221–223, 255 | T1–T2; 1–9 |
| 1.a Identifying essential characteristics of the Declaration of Independence, the Constitution, and the Bill of Rights as the foundation of the government of the United States AHSGE II.2 | 10, 11, 16, 26–30, 31, 38–49, 50, 51–56, 58–65, 67, 69–79, 80–85, 87, 96–101, 103, 105–111, 113–120, 122–133, 135–138, 140–148, 149–156, 158, 177, 220–223, 232–234, 255 | T1–T5, T7–T32; 1–55 |
| 1.b Describing the influence of John Locke AHSGE II.1 | | T6; 31–34 |
| 1.c Explaining essential characteristics of the political system of the United States *Examples: organization and functions of political parties, process of selecting political leaders* AHSGE II.1 | 18, 28–30, 31, 42–49, 51–56, 58–65, 67, 87–95, 96–101, 103–111, 113–120, 122–133, 135–138, 140–148, 149–156, 158, 174–185, 186–191, 206–209, 220–221 | 6–45 |
| 2. Compare the government of the United States with other governmental systems. *Examples: monarchy, limited monarchy, oligarchy, dictatorship, theocracy, pure democracy* | 7, 15, 23–24, 25–26, 31, 66, 107, 243, 267, 268–270, 276–279, 283–288, 290–294, 298–303 | T1–T6, T15–T16, T32–T40; 1–9, 22–24, 51–67 |
| 3. Describe essential characteristics of state and local governments in the United States. | 5, 8, 15, 140–147, 149–156, 158–159, 161, 163–172, 179, 202–203, 258–267 | T1–T3, T19–T27; 1–5, 28–43 |
| 3.a Identifying major offices and officeholders of state and local governments | 140, 142–145 | 32–34 |

v

| Standard | Civics in America | Alabama Citizenship Course Workbook |
|---|---|---|
| 3.b Explaining the historical background of the 1901 Constitution of Alabama and its impact on state and local governments<br>*Examples: lack of home rule* | | T21; 33 |
| 3.c Describing how local and state governments are funded | 159–160, 171 | T22–T23; 35–37 |
| 4. Compare the duties and functions of members of the legislative, executive, and judicial branches of local, state, and national governments. | 87–97, 98–101, 103–114, 115–120, 122–124, 126, 135–138, 158–159, 161, 163–169, 179, 278–279 | T13–T38; 19–64 |
| 4.a Identifying the geographic and political districts of the legislative, executive, and judicial branches of national, state, and local governments | 88–95, 125, 127–133, 145–146, 149–156, 158 | T13–T23; 19–37 |
| 4.b Describing the organization and jurisdiction of courts within the judicial system of the United States at the local, state, and national levels | 21, 31, 38, 49, 50, 55, 64, 65, 67, 87, 111–112, 122–125, 127–133, 134–138, 145–146, 148, 149–156, 161–163, 166–169, 188, 207, 208, 217–219, 225–230, 232–234, 237, 245, 271, 281 | T4–T34; 6–55 |
| 4.c Explaining the concepts of separation of powers and checks and balances among the three branches of state and national governments | 44, 45, 49, 50, 96–97, 101, 103, 109–112, 122–124 | T7–T8, T13–T18, T28–T29, T37–T38; 10–12, 19–27, 44–47, 62–64 |
| 5. Explain the importance of juvenile, adult, civil, and criminal laws within the judicial system of the United States. | 211–220, 225–234, 236–240 | T28–T31; 44–50 |
| 5.a Explaining the rights of citizens under the Constitution<br>*Examples: due process, right to keep and bear arms, private property right, right to privacy, equal protection, religious expression, habeas corpus* | 11, 52–56, 58–65, 67, 70–79, 80–85, 148, 211, 213, 225, 230 | T1–T12; 1–18 |

| Standard | | Civics in America | Alabama Citizenship Course Workbook |
|---|---|---|---|
| 5.b | Explaining what is meant by the term rule of law | 211 | |
| 5.c | Understanding consequences of breaking the law | 211, 215–219, 225, 230, 232–236 | T28–T31; 44–50 |
| 5.d | Contrasting juvenile and adult laws and their respective court systems | 225, 236–240 | T30–T31; 48–50 |
| 5.e | Identifying laws that most affect youth at home, school, and in the community | 212–216, 221 | |
| 6. | Describe how people organize economic systems for the production, distribution, and consumption of goods and services to address the basic economic questions of what goods and services will be produced, how they will be produced, and who will consume them. | 242–250, 251–256, 258–267, 268–270, 272–274 | T26–T36; 41–61 |
| 6.a | Using economic concepts to explain historical and current developments and issues in global, national, or local contexts<br>*Examples: increase in oil prices resulting from supply and demand* | 242, 258, 261–267, 268–270, 272–274, 290–294, 296–303 | T32–T40; 51–67 |
| 6.b | Analyzing the distribution of urban areas to determine how they are linked together<br>*Examples: using distribution maps to examine population flows among cities, suburbs, and small towns* | 9 | T3; 3–4 |
| 7. | Describe the relationship between the consumer and the marketplace in the economy of the United States regarding scarcity, opportunity cost, trade-off decision making, characteristics of a market economy, and supply and demand. | 242–250, 251–253, 258–267 | T26–T36; 41–61 |

| Standard | | Civics in America | Alabama Citizenship Course Workbook |
|---|---|---|---|
| 7.a | Describing the influence of the stock market upon individuals and the economy | 252–253 | T32–T36; 51–61 |
| 7.b | Analyzing distribution and production maps to determine patterns of supply and demand | 246, 248, 249, 253–254, 255 | T43; 54–55 |
| 7.c | Describing the effects of government policies on the free market | 248, 249, 253–254, 255, 259–274 | 59–61 |
| 7.d | Identifying laws protecting the rights of consumers and avenues of recourse when those rights are violated | 228 | T30–T36; 48–61 |
| 8. | Apply principles of money management to the preparation of a personal budget that addresses housing, transportation, food, clothing, medical expenses, and insurance as well as checking and savings accounts, loans, investments, credit, and comparison shopping. | 242 | Budget: chapter 19, housing: chapter 27, transportation: chapter 28, food: chapter 24, clothes: chapter 25, medical expenses: chapter 26, insurance: chapter 29, checking/savings/loans: chapters 20, 21 & 30, investments: chapter 30, credit: chapter 21, comparison shopping: chapters 22–23 |
| 9. | Identify individual and civic responsibilities of citizens of the United States. *Examples: individual responsibilities—respect for rights of others, self-discipline, negotiation, compromise; civic responsibilities—respect for the law, patriotism, participation in the political process* | 1, 12–14, 15, 211, 222, 235–236 | T1–T3, T28–T29, T30–T31; 1–5, 44–47, 48–50 |
| 9.a | Describing differences in rights, privileges, duties, and responsibilities between citizens and noncitizens | 6, 15, 24, 31, 69, 74–79, 80–85, 211 | T1–T3, T4–T6, T11–T12; 1–5, 6–9, 16–18 |
| 9.b | Explaining how United States citizenship is acquired | 2–4, 14, 15 | T1–T2; 1–5 |

| Standard | | Civics in America | Alabama Citizenship Course Workbook |
|---|---|---|---|
| 9.c | Interpreting an immigration map | 8–9 | T3; 4–5 |
| 9.d | Identifying character traits that are beneficial to individuals and to the republic of the United States<br>*Examples: honesty, courage, compassion, civility* | 215–216 | T28–T29; 44–47 |
| 10. | Describe changes in social and economic conditions in the United States during the twentieth and twenty-first centuries.<br>*Examples: social — family values, peer pressures, educational opportunities; economic — career opportunities, disposable income* | 271–274 | T35–T36; 56–61 |
| 10.a | Describing the impact of print and electronic media and the Internet on the American way of life<br>*Examples: fashion trends, consumer spending, increased debt, speed of communication, changes in language and social skills* | 183, 193–201, 204, 206–209, 279–282 | T24–T27, T37–T38; 38–43, 62–64 |
| 11. | Describe examples of conflict, cooperation, and interdependence of groups, societies, and nations using past and current events. | 16, 26, 31, 194–201, 202–203, 204, 208–209, 215–216, 276–287, 288–294, 298–303, 304–310 | T4–T6, T26–T29, T37–T40; 6–9, 41–47, 62–67 |
| 11.a | Tracing the political and social impact of the modern Civil Rights Movement from 1954 to the present, including Alabama's role | 80–82 | T26–T27; 41–43 |

| Standard | Civics in America | Alabama Citizenship Course Workbook |
|---|---|---|
| 12. Explain how the United States can be improved by individual and collective participation and by public service. | 11–12, 148–149, 179, 187, 310 | T1–T2, T19–T21, T24–T25; 1–5, 28–34, 38–40 |
| 12.a Identifying options for civic and community action<br>*Examples: investigating the feasibility of a specific solution to a traffic problem, developing a plan for the construction of a subdivision, using maps to make and justify decisions about the best location for facilities* | 64, 94, 148–149, 187, 201, 235, 254, 282 | T19–T21, T24–T25, T32–T34; 28–34, 38–40, 51–56 |
| 12.b Participating in the political process<br>*Examples: writing letters, being involved in political campaigns and issues* | 11–12, 148–149, 174, 179, 187, 193–201, 202–203, 204–209, 235, 282 | T1–T2, T19–T43, T30–T31, T37–T38; 1–5, 28–43, 48–50, 62–64 |
| 12.c Identifying ways adults participate in the political process<br>*Examples: voting, running for office, serving on a jury* | 11–12, 75–79, 80–83, 129, 148–149, 174, 179, 186–187, 190–191, 193, 202–203, 282 | T1–T2, T11–T12, T17–T27, T37–T38; 1–5, 16–18, 25–43, 62–64 |
| 12.d Applying a problem-solving model to a community project, including constructing a policy statement, budget, and an action plan to achieve one or more goals related to an issue of public concern | 254, 310 | T32–T34; 51–55 |

# 1. American Citizenship

## Objectives
- what citizenship means
- why we have government
- what values the citizens of the United States hold
- the duties and responsibilities of United States citizens

## Vocabulary

| | | | |
|---|---|---|---|
| allegiance | civics | government | monarchy |
| anarchy | coup | immigrant | native |
| baby boomers | democracy | inalienable | natural rights |
| census | dictatorship | jury | naturalize |
| citizen | diverse | loyalty | society |

## Background

In this chapter, students learn about the nature and meaning of citizenship, particularly in relation to a citizen's fundamental agreement with the government. They also examine our values as American citizens and the specific duties and responsibilities that come with living in a free, secure, and diverse nation.

By examining the Pledge of Allegiance and the Oath of Allegiance, students begin by seeing more clearly that citizenship is essentially a "contract" whereby the citizen pledges his or her loyalty to the government in exchange for the promise of governmental protection. They also learn how a person becomes a citizen, either as a native-born American or as a newly naturalized immigrant.

In explaining the "contract of citizenship," the text goes on to detail how the government upholds its end of the agreement by serving the public through the protection and maintenance of: the nation's security, law and order, public services, and other key service institutions. To improve their understanding through comparison, students learn about different types of governments—monarchies, dictatorships, and democracies—and their effects on citizens' rights.

Students move on to gain a more in-depth view of the kinds of factors that unite America, like the universally held ideal of the "American Dream;" our nation's rich history of racial and cultural diversity; and the values of equality, freedom, and justice that serve as a basis of our government and legal system.

Finally, students examine their end of the citizen contract, which includes such duties as obeying laws, defending the nation, paying taxes, serving on juries, and attending school. They also learn of their responsibilities that involve protecting each other's rights, voting, and helping to make society better by volunteering or through other pursuits.

### Further Resources

Kimmel, Barbara Brooks, and Lubnier, Alan M. *Citizenship Made Simple: An Easy to Read Guide to the U.S. Citizenship Process.* Chester, NJ: Next Decade, Inc., 2002.

Smith, Roger M. *Civic Ideals: Conflicting Visions of Citizenship in U.S. History.* New Haven, CT: Yale University Press, 1997.

## Review

1. Besides loyalty to your country, what are three other characteristics of citizenship?

2. What are the basic requirements to become a naturalized citizen?

3. What are some of the reasons for establishing a government?

4. What citizens' rights does the American justice system work to protect?

## Critical Thinking

1. What does U.S. citizenship mean to you? Support your answer with examples.

2. Who do you think values their citizenship more: native citizens or newly naturalized ones? Why?

3. What are your views on whether illegal aliens should receive social services like schooling and health care? Explain.

4. What do you think life would be like in a society living under anarchy? What negative and positive aspects would there be? Explain.

5. Do you think that all citizens in U.S. society today fully participate in the traditional American values and ideals of equality, freedom, and justice? Why or why not? Give examples.

## Activities

1. **Examining the Oath of Allegiance**
   Divide the class into groups and have each review the Oath of Allegiance on page 2. Ask each group to break down the oath into specific responsibilities that are asked of all U.S. citizens. Encourage students to weigh the fairness of the "contract" and whether they are personally willing to fulfill the terms if necessary. Using different scenarios, have the class as a whole debate what should happen if a citizen chooses not to or is unable to meet one of his or her duties.

2. **Our Government's Side of the Contract**
   Divide the class into four groups representing the four main service areas the government provides as part of the citizenship contract: (1) national security, (2) law and order, (3) public services, and (4) service institutions. Ask each "governmental area" to examine and explore its public function before discussing its role in society with the class. Then have each area explain the kinds of goals, problems, and daily issues it must pursue in order to support the citizens of the nation.

3. **Internet: The Immigrant Experience**
   Divide the class into pairs, directing each group to search the Internet for web sites that document the American immigration experience. Have students write a report giving their impressions and explaining how this American tradition has evolved from the early 1800s to the present.

4. **Special Sources: Living under a Dictatorship**
   In groups or individually, have students search the library for information about daily life in a nation under the rule of a dictator, either past or present. Have them write a report or give a presentation explaining how the dictator came to power, the effects on society and basic civil rights, and how these effects compare to life in the U.S.

# Immigration and Urban Distribution

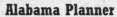

**Alabama Planner**

Citizenship Course of Study
9.c, 6.b

Learning Objectives:
- Interpreting an immigration map
- Analyzing the distribution of urban areas to determine how they are linked together

## Background: State Population of Alabama

From fast food businesses to high-tech industry, immigrants are essential to keeping the American economy strong. They fill an intrinsic need in the labor force in Alabama and in this nation.

The Census Bureau estimates that in July 2003 Alabama's population had increased by an annual average of about 16,943 residents since 2000 (to 4,500,752 residents). An annual average of about 4,910 (or 26.8%) of that increase was directly due to net international migration (more immigrants arriving than leaving). During the same period there was an annual average population loss of about 3,125 residents from net domestic migration (more native-born residents leaving than arriving).

The 2000 Census found 4,447,100 persons resident in Alabama. This was an increase of 406,513 persons above the 1990 Census. The rate of increase (10.1%) was the 25th largest in the country, and the amount of increase was the 25th largest in the country.

The 2000 population report includes about 4,000 more persons than the Census Bureau had expected to find in the state in 2000 when it issued its most recent state population projections in 1996. The significance of this is that the Census Bureau has concluded that much of the shortfall in their population estimates during the 1990s was due to an underestimation of the illegal alien population.

Many immigrants, both legal and illegal, make the United States their home. They have profound impact on population growth, employment, and wages. The immigrant population is growing 6.5 times faster than the native-born population. The 31.1 million immigrants found in the 2000 Census is unparalleled in American history. It is more than triple the 9.6 million in 1970 and more than double the 14.1 million in 1980. Although the absolute size of the foreign-born population is at an all-time high, the foreign-born comprise just over 11 percent of the population—significantly below the 15 percent recorded in the early 20th century.

### Source References

http://www.census.gov/Press-Release/www/documentation/2002/dp_comptables.html

http://www.prcdc.org/summaries/immigrationupdate02/immigrationupdate02.html

### Discussion Question

Why do so many immigrants (legal and illegal) come to live in the United States?

### Possible Answers

People come to the United States for many different reasons, but mainly for better opportunities for themselves and their families: better jobs, a better life, to join family, to escape war, and for freedom.

For pages 4 and 5 in the workbook, graph information was provided by:
Federation for American Immigration Reform
1666 Connecticut Avenue, NW, Suite 400
http://www.fairus.org/About/AboutMain.cfm

# 2. The Foundations of American Government

## Objectives

- the roots of our government
- how the American colonies were governed
- why the colonies moved toward independence
- how our nation's early governments worked

## Vocabulary

Articles of Confederation
bail
charter

city state
common law powers
confederation

direct democracy
due process

Enlightenment
executive powers

## Background

In this chapter, students get an in-depth view of the roots and evolution of the government system in America—from the ways in which the colonies were governed to the historical ideas and events that led to independence and formal establishment of our nation's early government system.

Students begin by examining the classic ideas and historical developments that guided the Founding Fathers in creating America's new government. These included two classic ideas of government—direct democracy and republic—and four key developments in English history—the Magna Carta, the English Bill of Rights, England's unwritten constitution, and England's use of common law.

Students move on to learn about developments in government during the colonial era that became influential, like the Mayflower Compact of 1620 and the formation of the House of Burgesses, which served as a model for the kind of representative system that we rely on today. Reviewing other aspects of colonial government (charter, legislature, and use of governors) and the basic rights that were extended to many (voting, religion, and press) help students draw connections between differences in public life in the colonies and the present-day.

As the chapter explores the critical events that led the colonies to fight for the independence from Britain, students learn about Britain's taxing Stamp Act, the protest that led to Boston Tea Party, the coercive Intolerable Acts, and the growing and united rebellion that led to the convening of the First and Second Continental Congresses, the war for independence, and the Declaration of Independence.

Next, students are guided through how the colonies became states (and the varied approaches each took in creating its new constitution). Students learn how the Second Continental Congress created the Articles of Confederation in an effort to strike a balance between forming a central government that did not take away from state sovereignty. Students then learn how the Articles created a weak central government and created a number of problems that took a farmer's rebellion to readdress and resolve.

### Further Resources

Boorstin, Daniel J. *The Americans: The Colonial Experience.* New York: Random House, 1995.

Green, Jack P. *Political Life in Eighteenth-Century Virginia.* Williamsburg, VA: Colonial Williamsburg Foundation, 1986.

# For Discussion

## Review

1. What were four important developments in English history that shaped the way that England ruled and governed?

2. What were the three basic rights that many of the colonies provided to their citizens?

3. What were four laws that became known as the Intolerable Acts?

4. What were the six crucial problems with the Articles of Confederation?

## Critical Thinking

1. What kind of leadership qualities do you look for in a representative? Would you prefer one who voted on bills by following personal conscience or the wishes of his or her constituents? Why?

2. Why do you think the Founding Fathers started putting all state and national constitutions in writing?

3. If you were a woman in the early colonies, what freedoms could you expect to exercise? Why?

4. Why is the more-prank-than-protest Boston Tea Party such a noteworthy event in American history? Explain.

5. What kinds of issues, events, or personal fears led the Second Continental Congress to pass the Articles of Confederation?

# Activities

1. **Let's Form a State Government!**

   Divide the class into 13 groups of "delegates," if possible, each representing one of the former colonies. With or without the use of their textbooks, have each team of delegates map out their specific plans for forming a state government, including constitutional plans, how powers will be divided between the government and people, and any other ideas, values, or rights they feel should be a part of their new government. Have them present their plans before the class for discussion.

2. **Debate: Taking a Closer Look at Shays's Rebellion**

   Provide the class with more detailed information about Shays's Rebellion and the alarm it sounded on the weakness of the Articles of Confederation. Have students examine Shays's motivation in leading the armed protest and debate about whether he was an unjustified, violent radical or a justified victim of an ineffective government system. How should he and others like him who break laws to protest a possible wrong be regarded historically?

3. **Internet: Reading the Declaration of Independence**

   Either individually or in pairs, have students search the Internet for a copy of the Declaration of Independence. Ask them read, take notes, and record their reactions about the language, aims, and spirit of this historic document. Have the class discuss their impressions and the significance of the Declaration to Americans of the Revolutionary era and today.

4. **Special Sources: England's Influence on U.S. Government**

   Divide the class into groups of four with each representing the Magna Carta, the English Bill of Rights, its unwritten constitution, or its use of common law. Have each group research library materials for in-depth information on their topic and discuss as a class how their document or legal tradition took form, changed people's lives, influenced America's new government, and impact their lives today.

# The Influence of John Locke

**Alabama Planner**

Citizenship Course of Study
1.b

Learning Objectives:
- Describing the influence of John Locke

AHSGE: II.1

## Background

According to the writings of John Locke, there are rules of "natural law" or "the laws of nature" that are inborn and entitled to everyone. He wrote, "No one ought to harm another in his life, health, liberty, or possessions."

Locke asserted that no government can exist until it has been created and the people have given their consent to be ruled by it. Therefore, government gets its right to govern from the consent of the people. Thomas Jefferson included Locke's idea in the Declaration of Independence when he wrote that "Governments are instituted among men, deriving their just powers from the consent of the governed . . ."

Locke also believed that since the people give the power to the government, the people have the right to take it away if the government does not serve purposes for which it was formed. He and the Founders agreed that the people have the right to create a new government (a right of revolution) if it fails them. This was also incorporated in the Declaration of Independence which states that "Whenever any Form of Government becomes destructive of these ends, it is the Right of the People to alter or to abolish it, and to institute new Government . . ."

The Constitution was ratified by the minimum number of states in 1788 which gave explicit consent of the people to the new government. Anyone who is born in America and remains here implies consent by remaining in this country and living under its laws. One also affirms consent by taking the Pledge of Allegiance, participating in an election, or participating in other civic activities.

## Discussion Question

Why did Locke and other Founders agree that people within a government have the right to take the power away from a government? Students may discuss the government of Iraq as an example.

## Answer

If a government fails to protect the people and enforce laws on behalf of the people, Locke and other Founders believed that the people within the government have a right to create a new government.

## References

Reill, Peter Hans and Ellen Judy Wilson, Encyclopedia of the Enlightenment. Facts on File, 1996.

http://www.archives.gov/national_archives_experience/charters/declaration_transcript.html

# 3. The Constitution

## Objectives

- how a meeting to revise the Articles of Confederation became the Constitutional Convention
- what principles of government were built into the Constitution
- how the Founding Fathers structured the Constitution
- how the Constitution can be amended

## Vocabulary

| | | | |
|---|---|---|---|
| amendment | convention | House of Representatives | proportional representation |
| amendment process | delegate | imports | ratify |
| Anti-Federalist | executive branch | judicial branch | Senate |
| Bill of Rights | exports | legislative branch | Supreme Court |
| checks and balances | federalism | nationalists | Virginia Plan |
| confederationists | Federalist | New Jersey Plan | |
| Constitution | Founding Fathers | popular sovereignty | |
| constitutional convention | freeholders | preamble | |

## Background

In this chapter, students learn how the Constitutional Convention of 1787 came to be and the painstaking efforts our Founding Fathers made to create a new plan of government that, among other things, empowered the people by limiting governmental authority. An in-depth review of the issues, principles, and structure of the Constitution is given.

Students begin by learning how the Constitutional Convention emerged out of a meeting to revise the Articles of Confederation. The delegates—who would become the Founding Fathers—decided that a new plan for government was needed to strengthen the national government. Students are given some insights about the founders—which included George Washington, James Madison, and Benjamin Franklin—and of the basic rules that governed the secretive proceedings. The key aspects of the Virginia and New Jersey plans are explored, as are the key compromises that helped to resolve the strife between nationalists and confederationists. Students are then able to see how basic powers are divided among the three branches of government, before learning of the serious struggle it took to get the new Constitution ratified by the 13 states.

Students move on to examine the governing principles that underlie the Constitution: popular sovereignty, limited government, federalism, separation of powers, and checks and balances. The Preamble is considered before the seven Articles of the Constitution are broken down so students can see how their government is organized and functions. The chapter closes by reviewing how federal and state governments propose and ratify amendments to the Constitution.

### Further Resources

Berkin, Carol. *A Brilliant Solution: Inventing the American Constitution*. New York: Harcourt, 2002.

Bradford, M.E.E. *Founding Fathers*. Lawrence, KS: University Press of Kansas, 1994.

# For Discussion

## Review

1. What were the three basic rules of the Constitutional Convention?

2. What five basic principles served as a basis of the U.S. Constitution?

3. What are the three branches of the U.S. government?

4. What are the six goals for the U.S. government, as listed in the Preamble?

## Critical Thinking

1. Had the convention been open to the public and press, what problems would have occurred? Could a final plan for government have been made under these circumstances? Why or why not?

2. Why was proportional representation such a threat to smaller states? Do you think it is fair to have a national government solely based on this form of representation? Why or why not?

3. What is your opinion of the Three-Fifths Compromise and how the issue of slavery was addressed in the Constitutional Convention?

4. What would have happened if the Constitution had not been ratified? Why? Explain.

5. Do you agree with the U.S. Supreme Court that a person should have the right to burn the American flag in public on the Fourth of July?

# Activities

1. **The Great Debate: The Virginia v. New Jersey Plans**

   Divide the class into two groups: nationalists and confederationists. Have each side discuss and further research their positions, as if they are the founders at the Constitutional Convention. Then have each side debate the merits of each plan and their concerns over the role of a stronger central government and other related issues like representation, slavery, and commerce.

2. **You and Your Three Branches of Government**

   Divide the class into three main groups that represent the federal, legislative, and judicial branches of government. In an open class discussion, have each team take turns discussing things like (1) what its basic powers and functions are, (2) how the system of checks and balances among the branches works, and (3) how they might work together under different, difficult scenarios, as with an impeachable president or an unconstitutional law.

3. **Internet: Visiting the Constitutional Convention**

   Have students, in pairs, explore the Internet for websites that document all aspects of the convention. Have each team come up with a list of interesting insights or facts about the figures or events surrounding the convention, and then have the class as a whole discuss these elements in order to create for everyone a fuller picture of this critical period in U.S. history.

4. **Special Sources: Getting to Know Our Founding Fathers**

   Have students, either in pairs or individually, choose one of the 55 convention delegates, or Founding Fathers, to research in the library or on the Internet. Then have them give a presentation on their subject that recounts interesting personal and professional developments in the figures' lives, particularly about any special positions or roles they might have taken at the 1787 convention.

# 4. Bill of Rights

## Objectives
- why additions were made to the original Constitution
- how constitutional amendments protect the rights of citizens
- what rights and freedoms are protected by the Bill of Rights

## Vocabulary

| | | | |
|---|---|---|---|
| double jeopardy | incriminate | petition | slander |
| eminent domain | indictment | probable cause | treason |
| grand jury | militia | publish | warrant |
| impartial jury | | | |

## Background

In this chapter, students learn about the Bill of Rights, and that the Constitution might never have been ratified without the basic rights and freedoms this document guarantees for all American citizens. Students explore how the Bill of Rights first came into being and then each of its ten amendments.

Students begin by learning how some early government leaders refused to ratify the Constitution without a "bill of rights," still remembering the serious abuses to civil rights that the colonists endured under the British. Students see how Virginia delegate George Mason's Declaration of Rights of 1776 was influential in the writing of the Bill of Rights and how the First Congress of the U.S. ratified 10 of the proposed 12 amendments to the Constitution in 1791.

The chapter goes on to give students an in-depth and detailed look at each of the ten amendments that make up the Bill of Rights that we enjoy today:

The First Amendment guarantees and protects five basic freedoms: religion, speech, the press, assembly, and petition. The Second Amendment discusses the right to bear arms. The Third Amendment prohibits the government from forcing people to house and feed soldiers in their homes. The Fourth Amendment protects citizens from unreasonable searches and seizures. The Fifth Amendment guarantees that a person accused of a crime will not be denied the right to life, liberty, or property without due process of law. The Sixth Amendment guarantees the right of an accused person to trial by jury, representation by an attorney, and a speedy trial. The Seventh Amendment guarantees citizens the right to a trial by jury in civil cases. The Eighth Amendment protects accused persons against imprisonment or punishment that is excessive. The Ninth and Tenth Amendments are included to protect the rights and freedoms not specifically mentioned in the Constitution and to prevent the government from taking powers that belong to the states and the people.

## Further Resources

Dolan, Edward F., Jr. *Protect Your Legal Rights: A Handbook for Teenagers*. New York: Julian Messner Publishing, 1983.

McCuen, Gary E. *Secret Democracy: Civil Liberties vs. the National Security State*. Hudson, WI: Gem Publications, 1990.

# For Discussion

## Review

1. What are the five specific rights that are guaranteed under the First Amendment?

2. What are the five major protections guaranteed under the Fifth Amendment?

3. What are the four ways the Sixth Amendment protects people accused of crimes?

4. What are the two protections extended to people accused of crimes under the Eighth Amendment?

## Critical Thinking

1. What would your life be like without the Bill of Rights? Support your answer using examples.

2. Which of the amendments in the Bill of Rights do you think are the most important? Why?

3. Do you think prayer should be allowed in public schools? Why or why not? Under what circumstances, if any, should religious expression be allowed?

4. Which freedom under the First Amendment helps to limit government corruption? Why? Explain.

5. How do you feel about the Second Amendment, which provides the right to bear arms? If the founders were alive today, do you think they would still favor this amendment or consider it outdated? Why?

# Activities

1. **Debate: Wearing Uniforms in Public Schools**

   Divide the class into two groups—those who favor wearing public school uniforms and those who do not. Before having each team debate their cause, have them develop their arguments as a team and/or perform background research on their topic in the library or on the Internet. While each team argues for or against, have them spell out all the positives and negatives of wearing uniforms and explore issues like the school administration's purpose in implementing such a program.

2. **Interview: Judges, Lawyers, Police**

   Ask students if they are related to or know anyone who is a judge, lawyer, or policeperson, or serves in another occupation dealing with upholding and interpreting the Bill of Rights on a daily basis. Divide the class into groups and have them compile a list of questions to ask such people about the importance and fundamental challenges of their work, as well as the ways in which they regard and use the Bill of Rights. Discuss findings in class.

3. **Internet: Countries without a Bill of Rights**

   Have the class as a whole come up with a list of countries that they think are without a bill of rights or personal freedoms in general. Then divide the class into pairs, and have each team pick one of the countries to research on the Internet to gain an in-depth view of the kinds of limits, barriers, or abuses its citizens endure without the kinds of freedoms Americans exercise every day. Have each team report their findings when finished.

4. **Special Sources: Court Cases and the Bill of Rights**

   Using the library and the Internet, have students research important past Supreme Court cases that played an important role in either upholding or redefining the limits of the amendments from the Bill of Rights. Have students present their cases to the class, and discuss important arguments, developments, and how it affected the way we live or how we interpret the amendment.

# 5. The Living Constitution

## Objectives
- why we have constitutional amendments
- how and why the voting rights of Americans have changed
- how changes in society affect how our Constitution is interpreted

## Vocabulary

| | | | |
|---|---|---|---|
| abolitionist | Emancipation Proclamation | racial profiling | segregation |
| affirmative action | ordinance | reverse discrimination | suffrage |
| Confederacy | poll tax | secede | suffragists |
| discrimination | quota | | |

## Background

In this chapter, students see that the Constitution is a living document designed to be changed as the nation develops. They review the 17 amendments added since 1787 and how these changes have been critical to the advancement of our country.

Students begin by learning that constitutional change is made possible by Article V. They then examine how the Founders were unable to address the injustice of slavery constitutionally without sacrificing national unity. Key slavery-related events are then described—the Northwest Ordinance of 1787, the Missouri Compromise of 1819, and the Dred Scott case of 1857—each marking a major point along America's descent into civil war and the passing of critical amendments to the Constitution. These included the abolition of slavery (Thirteenth) and the extending of citizenship and civil rights to former slaves and all citizens (Fourteenth).

Students then explore voting rights, including giving voting rights to all citizens (Fifteenth), allowing the public to directly elect their senators (Seventeenth), and the arduous suffrage movement which earned women the right to vote (Nineteenth). Students are also made aware of key voting amendments passed during the 1960s and 1970s: the right of citizens in the District of Columbia to vote in national elections (Twenty-third), as well as the elimination of poll taxes (Twenty-fourth) and how the baby boomers and young soldiers lowered the voting age to 18 (Twenty-sixth).

Finally, students see how changes in public attitudes and ethnicity of America have brought constitutional changes. The obstacles to the civil rights movement show students how discrimination made amendments difficult to implement socially. Students learn of the movement's key leaders, events, and court cases, and how they were necessary to bring about the freedoms promised, particularly in the South. Students also see how new groups (senior citizens, the disabled) and programs (affirmative action) are a visible part of America's ongoing effort to test and expand the rights of the people.

### Further Resources
Gurko, Miriam. *The Ladies of Seneca Falls: The Birth of the Woman's Rights Movement*. New York: Delacorte, 1974.

Williams, Juan. *Eyes on the Prize: American Civil Rights Years, 1954–1965*. New York: Viking, 1987.

# For Discussion

## Review

1. What are three important parts of the Fourteenth Amendment, which granted citizenship and civil rights to all citizens, regardless of race or religion?

2. Who were three important suffragist leaders of the late 19th and early 20th centuries?

3. What were some of the rights guaranteed to minorities under the Civil Rights Act of 1964?

4. What are some cases where new groups in society have won recognition and expanded rights?

## Critical Thinking

1. If you could amend the Constitution with a measure that would improve the quality of life in America, what would it be? Why?

2. Which of the 17 additional amendments to the Constitution do you think was the most important? Why?

3. What do you think would have happened to America had the Founding Fathers abolished slavery as part of the new Constitution in 1787? Explain.

4. If proposed, do you think a "Seventh Generation Amendment" seeking to protect the environment for future generations would ever be passed by Congress? Why or why not?

5. Do you support affirmative action policies? For example, do you think the use of quotas is fair and just? Why or why not? Support your answer using examples.

# Activities

1. **Addressing Affirmative Action**

    Research a recent court case involving affirmative action. Then divide the class into three groups representing the plaintiff, defense, and the U.S. Supreme Court. Provide the class with basic details surrounding the case so that they may argue, defend, and finally pass judgment on the case. Once your classroom "justices" have rendered a verdict and opinion, inform the class of the actual outcome of the case and discuss at length.

2. **Interview: Women and Equal Rights**

    Individually or in pairs, have students interview an older woman who they think would be a good person to talk to about women's fight for equality, both past and present. Have them compile a list of questions that touches on women's heritage (suffrage), personal feelings and struggles for equality, and any present or future issues that serve as barriers for women in America.

3. **Internet: From Emancipation to the Civil Rights Movement**

    Have students choose an important leader, court case, or incident that impacted the African-American struggle for equality in our nation's history. Ask students to research web sites that provide credible and insightful information on their subject and report to the class how this person or event was significant in this ongoing American effort.

4. **Special Sources: Examining Our Amendments**

    Divide the class into pairs, assigning each one of the 17 amendments to research in the library and/or on the Internet. Have students find out the key figures, events, and circumstances that helped to bring about this critical change in our Constitution. Have students present their findings to the class and discuss the importance of the change.

# 6. The Legislative Branch

## Objectives
- the functions of Congress
- the members of Congress
- how Congress makes laws
- the powers given to Congress by the Constitution

## Vocabulary

| | | | |
|---|---|---|---|
| bicameral | Elastic Clause | majority party | standing committee |
| bill | *ex post facto* law | minority party | whip |
| bill of attainder | floor leader | president pro tempore | writ of *habeas corpus* |
| conference committee | joint committee | select committee | |
| Congressional district | legislation | Speaker of the House | |

## Background

In this chapter, students take an in-depth look at the workings of Congress, particularly the way it is structured, organized, and empowered by the people under the Constitution to pass laws and help govern the nation. Congressional powers and the process of making laws are reviewed in detail.

Students review the fact that Congress is divided into the House of Representatives and the Senate. They evaluate the duties, terms, and qualification differences between members of these houses, including the size of the House and the longer senatorial term limits. Students are then made familiar with the varied rules, procedures, and precedents that govern how Congress considers and passes laws. Next, they learn how each chamber is broken down into majority and minority parties, revealing the kind of power dynamic that controls the chambers and the types of laws that are considered.

Students then examine how Congress is organized in terms of leadership. They learn that a "new Congress" is elected every two years, that a Speaker of the House leads the Representative chamber, and that the vice president presides over the Senate. The critical roles of party floor leaders and whips help students see how parties align and function to prioritize the laws they favor. Students also come to learn the purposes and roles of congressional staffs and the four types of committees that study different kinds of laws: standing, joint, select, and conference.

Students then examine both the expressed and implied powers granted to Congress under the Constitution. They see that certain powers, as part of the checks and balances system, are shared while others are not. Students also learn of instances where Congress is restricted from passing certain laws. Finally, students learn the lengthy and complicated process of turning a bill into a law.

### Further Resources

Cheney, Timothy D. *Who Makes the Law: The Supreme Court, Congress, the States, and the People*. Upper Saddle River, NJ: Prentice Hall, 1997.

Sinclair, Barbara. *Unorthodox Lawmaking: New Legislative Processes in the U.S. Congress*. Washington D.C.: Congressional Quarterly, 1997.

# For Discussion

## Review

1. How are congressional proceedings governed?

2. What are the four types of committees that serve in Congress?

3. What are the three main roles of congressional committees?

4. As specified in the Constitution, what are three types of laws that Congress cannot pass?

## Critical Thinking

1. Do you support term limits for senators? Why or why not? If not, what kind of change would you propose? Support your answer.

2. Would you ever consider running for public office, like the Congress or Senate? Why or why not?

3. Do you think it is fair for a state like California to have upwards of 52 representatives while states like Alaska have only one? Should people reconcile this big difference? Why or why not?

4. Do you think members of Congress or elected officials in general should be able to accept gifts? Why or why not? What limits, if any, do you think should be established?

5. What is your impression of the extensive legislative process involved in passing a law? Why do you think our lawmaking system is organized this way?

# Activities

1. **Hey, What's an Elastic Clause?**

   Divide the class into groups of three. Have each group's members take turns creating questions and quizzing each other on all aspects of the legislative branch they have learned in this chapter—from the members and functions of Congress to their constitutional powers and lawmaking processes. Optional: the winners of each group can face-off with other winners to find out who knows the material and their nation's legislature the best.

2. **Activity: Passing Laws in Your Classroom**

   First, have the class come up with five bills it would like to have introduced to Congress. Then, using the flowchart on pages 98 and 99 as a basis, divide the class into different groups representing bill-passing phases: Congress, its various committees, and the President. Have each of the bills introduced and have each group or phase discuss the merits of the bill and why it should approve or "kill" the bill before it becomes a law.

3. **Internet: Contacting Your Representatives**

   Ask students whether they or their parents have ever contacted their federal, state, or local representatives. Then have students search the Internet for the web sites of their federal representatives to gather information about them and where they stand on key issues and legislation. Ask students to review the information and offer their opinions about their representative(s) in an open class discussion. You may also decide to have students write them about particular issues about which they feel strongly.

4. **Special Sources: Controversial Bills**

   Have students, in pairs, use the library and the Internet to research controversial bills of the last 20 years that either "died" in Congress or became laws after the president's veto was overcome by Congress. Have students present the bill/law to the class and discuss.

# 7. The Executive Branch

## Objectives
- how to become president or vice president of the United States
- what powers the president has
- how the executive branch is organized

## Vocabulary

| | | | |
|---|---|---|---|
| ambassadors | civil service | execute | pension |
| amnesty | commission | executive privilege | presidential succession |
| bureaucracy | diplomat | foreign policy | private sector |
| bureaucrats | duties | licensing | regulator |
| Cabinet | Electoral College | pardon | |

## Background

In this chapter, students examine the organization and function of the executive branch, the many departments and agencies it encompasses, and the roles and powers of the president and vice president. Students learn about the qualifications and special benefits of the jobs of president and vice president. They also find out that the Electoral College plays a big role in determining who wins a presidential election.

Students move on to become better aware of the many powers and roles of the president. They learn that the president has executive, emergency, budgetary, and policy-making powers. They find out that he or she can grant pardons to people who've committed crimes and that executive privilege gives him or her the option of making some types of independent decisions. Examining further, students see that the president's position also includes responsibility for making speeches, appointing high level officials, communicating with foreign leaders, signing or vetoing bills, and meeting with business and labor leaders.

Students gain more insight through a diagram that breaks down the organization of the executive branch and that includes more than 200 independent groups like Amtrak, the Food and Drug Administration, the FBI, the Internal Revenue Service, and Immigration and Naturalization Services. Students further analyze the Executive Office, which comprises, among others, the Council of Economic Advisors and the National Security Council.

Finally, students learn that most of the government's work is done by the 14 executive departments (the heads of which are among the president's cabinet). They discover that these departments cover areas like agriculture, defense, education, justice, health and human services, and transportation. The chapter explains to students that, although some complain that the federal bureaucracy is too large (about three million people), few would want to relinquish the services it provides because these are necessary and important to the American people.

### Further Resources

Hart, John. *The Presidential Branch: From Washington to Clinton.* New York: Chatham Publishers, 1995.

Landau, Elaine. *The Executive Branch (How Government Works).* Minneapolis, MN: Lerner Publishing Co., 2003.

# For Discussion

## Review

1. What are the other benefits the president receives in addition to his salary?

2. What are the two main duties the job of vice president requires?

3. How much space should be taken up by each section of a yearbook?

4. What are the few specific powers that the Constitution lists as the president's powers?

## Critical Thinking

1. There already are three qualifications needed to be elected president. What would you add to that list? Explain your answers.

2. How do you feel about the Electoral College? Do you think the individual vote is adequately recognized? Explain.

3. Do you think it is important that Congress be able to keep the office of the president from becoming too powerful? What do you think could happen if the office wasn't kept in check?

4. Of the 14 different executive departments, which one would you prefer to work in? Explain.

5. What do you think it would be like to have the job of president of the United States? What positive and negative aspects would there be? Explain.

# Activities

1. **Write a Letter to the President**

   Divide students into teams of two. Ask them to write a letter to the president about something specific, such as the economy, foreign relations, or an issue about lawmaking. They should choose one topic and research it well enough to pose informed questions or give informed opinions. Have them bring their letters to class for a discussion and then mail them to the president.

2. **The Presidential Roles**

   Divide students into groups of four. Ask each group to choose a role of the president, as listed beginning on page 113. Ask each group to put on a 3–5-minute skit for the class, depicting a scenario in which their role is exercised. The skit should be creative and convey information to the class about the role and what it entails.

3. **Internet: The 14 Executive Departments**

   Divide students into pairs. Have them use the Internet to find the home pages of the 14 executive departments. Have students create on poster boards illustrations and descriptions of the 14 departments. Have them briefly describe what they learned about each department on their site. Have them bring their finished project to class for a discussion.

4. **Special Sources: History of Laws**

   Divide students into groups of four. Have them research the history of laws and how they've changed. What were some of the first laws and legal codes? Why were they enacted? How have laws changed? How does that parallel with how society has changed? Have students bring their findings to class for a discussion.

# 8. The Judicial Branch

## Objectives

- how the federal court system works
- what the U.S. District Courts and Courts of Appeal do
- how the United States Supreme Court protects the Constitution
- why the Supreme Court has changed

## Vocabulary

| | | | |
|---|---|---|---|
| amicus curiae | dissenting opinion | judiciary | prosecuting attorney |
| appeal | district courts | jurisdiction | Rule of Four |
| appellate jurisdiction | exclusive jurisdiction | magistrate | special courts |
| brief | impeachment | majority opinion | trial courts |
| concurrent jurisdiction | judicial activism | mandatory sentences | |
| concurring opinion | judicial restraints | opinion | |
| courts of appeals | judicial review | original jurisdiction | |

## Background

In this chapter, students see the importance of the Constitution in relation to our legal system. They examine the Supreme Court and the federal court system, including the lower courts. Students learn that these courts were created to protect the rights and freedoms of all Americans. Students find that the integrity of the court is ensured by its independence.

Students also learn about the jurisdictional differences in the courts. The Constitution gives federal courts power to hear cases that deal with issues such as laws and treaties, maritime laws, or disputes in which the U.S. is being sued.

Students move on to examine the lower courts, which consist of district courts and courts of appeal. Among the district courts are trial courts that hear criminal and civil cases in both bench trials and jury trials. The chapter explains that, if a trial needs to be reheard, the U.S. Courts of Appeals may be called upon to and decide whether to uphold the judge's ruling. Other courts, called special courts, hear cases with specific types of controversies, like tax cases and veterans' claims on their benefits.

Finally, students see that the job of the Supreme Court is immense and detailed. The process used to choose a Supreme Court justice is lengthy and involves both the legislative and executive branches.

Students also learn about the history of the Court and its landmark decisions, such as the 1954 case that outlawed segregation in public schools.

### Further Resources

Hall, Kermit L. *The Least Dangerous Branch: Separation of Powers and Court Packing.* New York: Garland Publishers, 2000.

Jost, Kenneth. *The Supreme Court A to Z.* Washington, D.C.: Congressional Quarterly, Inc., 1998.

# For Discussion

## Review

1. What are the two ways that the Constitution protects the judiciary from the influence of the other two branches of government?

2. What are the two types of trials in district court?

3. Once justices have decided to hear a case, attorneys may be asked to do what two things?

4. In the Supreme Court, what three types of opinions may be written by the justices after the court has reached a decision on a case?

## Critical Thinking

1. In your opinion, how important is it that the judicial branch be independent of the other two branches?

2. How do you feel about the fact that federal judges do not need to meet any special qualifications, that their terms are for life, and that they can only be removed through impeachment?

3. What are your views on the fact that Supreme Court Justices serve life terms and don't have to retire at any specific age? What negative and positive aspects might there be to this situation?

4. How do you think the mandatory sentences argument can be resolved?

5. In your opinion, which one of the landmark rulings of the Supreme Court on page 137 is the most significant to Americans today? Explain your answer.

# Activities

1. **Article III of the Constitution**

   Divide students into teams of two. Ask them to look at Article III of the Constitution and to write an analysis of it. What is their interpretation of the article? How might it be written today? What would they change about it?

2. **Our Court System**

   Divide students into four groups representing the four courts depicted on page 127: (1) Supreme Court, (2) Appellate Courts, (3) Trial Courts, and (4) Special Federal Courts. Assign each group a court to research. Have students review what their court's duties are and become familiar with the types of cases heard, as well as the process by which the courts go about preparing and hearing cases.

3. **Internet: The U.S. Supreme Court Landmark Rulings**

   Divide students into 12 groups. Assign each group a landmark ruling from the list on page 137. Ask them to research the ruling on the Internet. When did it occur? What was the social atmosphere at the time? How did the ruling change things? What negative and positive results came from this ruling?

4. **Special Sources: Compare Our System**

   Divide students into teams of two. Ask each team to choose a country other than the U.S. and research that country's court system and compare it with our court system. Do other countries have the equivalent of our Supreme Court? Do they have several types of courts like ours? Do they have a way to appeal a decision? Ask students to bring the information to class for a discussion.

# 9. State Governments

## Objectives

- how the Constitution divides power between the federal government and the state governments
- what services state governments provide
- how state governments are organized

## Vocabulary

| | | | |
|---|---|---|---|
| appropriations | concurrent powers | initiative | proposition |
| censured | criminal cases | interstate commerce | recall |
| certification | delegate | lower courts | referendum |
| civil cases | exclusive powers | misdemeanor | reprieve |
| clemency | extradition | parliamentary procedure | reserved powers |
| committee | felony | parole | supremacy clause |
| commute | general trial courts | polls | |

## Background

In this chapter, students learn how the Constitution divides power between the federal and state governments, what services are offered by state governments, and how they are organized.

Students begin by learning that the powers of the federal and state governments originated with the Constitution and that the states share some powers with the federal government. State and federal governments must cooperate in order for things to run smoothly, and that states offer services like holding elections and providing educational facilities.

Students move on to examine the state legislative branch. They learn that legislators have the power to make laws but have executive and judicial powers as well. Students find out that a governor has many roles. As chief of state, he or she acts as the spokesperson for the state's goals and values. As head of the executive branch, one of his or her jobs is to manage the people that run the executive branch. The governor also has the power to sign or veto laws. In the judicial area, the governor can grant clemency to people convicted of crimes. Students learn about the roles of lieutenant governor, secretary of state, and attorney general, among others.

Finally, students examine the judicial branch, which encompasses the state's court system. The court system interprets the law for citizens, and it handles various disputes. Students learn that not all court systems are the same, but that many include the state supreme court, the appeals court, general trial courts, and lower courts.

### Further Resources

Adrian, Charles R., and Fine, Michael R. *State and Local Politics*. Belmont, CA: Wadsworth Publishing Co., 1999.

Martinez, John, and Libonati, Michael E. *State and Local Government*. Cincinnati, OH: Anderson Publishing Co., 2000.

# For Discussion

## Review

1. What are the exclusive powers given to the national or federal government?
2. What are some of the services that states provide to their citizens?
3. What are some of the ongoing issues that standing committees approach?
4. What are some of the important state agencies?

## Critical Thinking

1. If you could choose your state's flag, motto, and symbols representing the history or interests of the state, what would you choose?
2. What is your view about having term limits for people in office?
3. What do you think life would be like in a state that did not have any laws?
4. What kind of new law would you like to propose as a citizen, using the initiative process?
5. How do you feel about the fact that, as of 2001, there had been only two governors of African-American descent?

# Activities

1. **Study State Constitutions**

   Assign two states to each student. Ask each student to compare and contrast the constitutions of the two states. Discuss the results in class.

2. **Survey on Graduated Licenses**

   Divide students into teams of two. Ask each team to take a survey of an equal number of adults and students their own age (about 20 of each). Ask the people surveyed how they feel about graduated licenses. Write down their answers. What is the difference between the adults' answers and the students' answers?

3. **Internet Search on State Legislatures**

   Divide students into teams of two. Ask each team to choose a state legislature to research on the Internet, including that of their own state. What size legislature does that state have? How big is the state? What is going on right now in that state's legislature?

4. **Special Sources: Library Research on Executive Officials**

   Ask students to individually research at the library the executive officials that are listed, starting on page 151. Ask them to get an idea of what each job entails and then write a brief paper on which of those jobs they would like to have and why.

# State and Local Governments: How Does it Work in Alabama?

**Alabama Planner**

Citizenship Course of Study
3.b, 3.c

Learning Objectives:
- Identifying major offices and office-holders of state and local governments
- Explaining the historical background of the 1901 Constitution of Alabama and its impact on state and local governments

AHSGE: II.2

## Background

A constitution should serve as a guide defining the authorities, responsibilities and relationships of a government. At the same time, it should maintain flexibility to meet changing conditions and needs. Our federal constitution is so well designed that it has been amended only twenty-six in more than 200 years. Alabama's constitution, however, has been amended more than 740 times. Looking back on state history, many note that the legislature spent so much time on local bills that subjects of statewide interest were often neglected. Rather than grant the counties increased home rule, local matters were kept in the hands of the legislature. As a result, hundreds of amendments have been added making Alabama's constitution the longest in the United States.

The Alabma Constitution of 1901 was developed under the governorship of William J. Samford. He was born in Georgia, but moved to Auburn, Alabama as a young boy. At age 17 he enlisted in the Confederate Army, and was later captured and made a prisoner of war. When the war was over, Samford practiced law in Opelika and held several public offices. He became a member of the constitutional convention in 1875. Samford was nominated for governor by the Democratic party and won the election. He was inaugurated in December 1900, but his term was cut short. Samford died on June 11, 1901, after just six months in office.2 William D. Jelks was president of the senate when Governor Samford died so he automatically became Samford's sucessor as governor. After completing Samford's term, Jelks was elected by the people and served for four more years.

The 1901 constitution writers, generally fearful of the misuse of power, saw the state constitutions as restrictions of power. One of the main the reasons for the Alabama's 1901 Constitutional Convention was to ostroracize African-American people through new laws. The Constitution of 1901 was similar to those of previous years, with the addition of unfair voting rquirements such as literacy tests and property ownership. Such limiting restrictions made it nearly impossible for African-Americans to have voting rights unless they could read or they owned land—priveledges most did not have.

Although many outrageous features of the Alabama state constitution have been corrected through amendments and court actions, most of Alabama's thorniest governmental problems still have their roots in this document. One complaint about the 1901 Constitution is that it is more like a code of laws than a framework for government. The Alabama Constitution provides only two methods whereby it may be revised:
1) by amendment initiated in the legislature or
2) by a convention of elected delegates, also initiated in the legislature. Many Alabamians believe the 1901 Constitution of Alabama is still in great need of revision.

### Online Resources

HTTP://WWW.GOVERNOR.STATE.AL.US/
http://www.legislature.state.al.us/ALISHome.html
Alabama Judicial System Online—
http://www.judicial.state.al.us/
http://www.archives.state.al.us/ts.html
http://en.wikipedia.org/wiki/History_of_alabama

# 10. Local Government

## Objectives
- the services provided by local governments
- the authority of local governments
- how city, county, town, township, and special district governments work
- challenges faced by local governments

## Vocabulary

| | | | |
|---|---|---|---|
| alderman | Dillon's Rule | mayor-council plan | strong-mayor plan |
| commission plan | grant | metropolitan area | township |
| council | home rule | municipality | trustees |
| council-manager plan | manager | property assessment | weak-mayor plan |
| county | mayor | special district | zoning |

## Background

In this chapter, students learn about the authority of local governments; what they provide; how city, town, township, and special district governments work; and the problems faced by local governments.

Students begin by learning that services that they receive—like police and fire protection, safe drinking water, education, and so on—are services provided by their local government and paid for, in part, by citizens through their taxes. Students also analyze the spending and income pie chart to get a better idea of how money is used within the government. Students move on to examine the authority of their local government, beginning with Dillon's Rule, established in response to corruption in the local government, which in turn led to the home rule of government.

Students continue to examine the various forms of governments in cities, including the widely used mayor-council plan, the less effective council-manager, and the commission plan. Students move on and learn about county governments, whose widely used forms of government are called commission, commission-administrator, and council-executive.

Finally, students examine town, township, and village governments, special districts, and problems in government. They learn that villages and towns are usually governed by a board of elected officers and that townships provide many services that the county would normally provide. The most common form of local government is the special district, which is governed by an elected board and provides specific services that the local government does not—such as water, fire, park, library, and insect control districts. Students also learn about some of the problems faced by local governments.

### Further Resources

Adrian, Charles R., and Fine, Michael R. *State and Local Politics*. Belmont, CA: Wadsworth Publishing Co., 1999.

Martinez, John, and Libonati, Michael E. *State and Local Government*. Cincinnati, OH: Anderson Publishing Co., 2000.

# For Discussion

## Review

1. What are the six broad categories of services that are generally provided by local governments?
2. What are the three organizational plans on which most city governments are based?
3. What are the three forms that county governments can take?
4. What kinds of services are special districts set up to provide if local governments do not provide them?

## Critical Thinking

1. Before reading the chapter, from where did you think the basic services that are provided by your local government came? Explain.
2. If you could divide the pie charts on page 160 yourself, how would you do it?
3. What is your opinion of the Supreme Court case detailed on page 161? With which ruling do you agree?
4. Do you think it is fair to others that a town can put limits on its growth? How would you feel as a person who wanted to move in and could not? How would you feel as a current resident?
5. Would you rather have lower taxes and fewer services or higher taxes and more services? Explain.

# Activities

1. **County Officials**

   Divide students into six groups. Assign each group a job from the list on page 167. Ask each group to research the job and make a presentation to the class about it, including what it entails day to day and how citizens benefit from the services.

2. **Three City Government Organizations**

   Divide students into three groups, each representing one of the three city government organizational plans listed on page 163: the mayor-council plan, the council-manager plan, and the commission plan. Ask each group to research its plan and why it is or is not effective for use in local government. Have groups compare their findings in class.

3. **Internet: Look at Your Local Government**

   Divide students into teams of two. Assign each team a local government's web site to view. What does the site look like? Is it user friendly for citizens? Does the site list the government's services? Does the site give details about government spending? What other information does the site offer to citizens?

4. **Special Sources: Dillon's Rule, Home Rule, and Corruption**

   Divide students into three groups. Ask one group to research Dillon's Rule, another group to research home rule, and the third to look at local government corruption in the 1800s. Ask all three groups to look for connections to the other topics when researching. Come together as a class to discuss the three topics.

# 11. How Our Political System Works: Parties, Politics, and Participation

## Objectives
- why we have political parties
- election campaigns
- how voting and elections work

## Vocabulary

| | | | |
|---|---|---|---|
| absentee ballot | Federal Election Commission (FEC) | political party | public policy |
| ballot | nominate | political platform | recount |
| caucus | nonpartisan | polling place | registration |
| debate | political convention | precinct | runoff election |
| election campaign | | primary election | split ticket |

## Background

In this chapter, students learn about our political system, political parties, election campaigns, and how our voting system works. Students begin by becoming familiar with American political parties. Those parties are formed because people share beliefs that they want recognized. If they can get enough people in office that share their views, then they can have more control in the government. Students also learn about the history of these political parties, party platforms, the importance of third parties, and the structure and organization of our political parties.

Students move on to examine our election campaigns. They learn how candidates are chosen through self-nomination, caucus, write-ins, nominating petitions, or conventions. Students learn about the many aspects of elections, beginning with the primary elections, running the campaign, preparation and organization, getting the word out to voters, and financing a campaign. Students learn that political parties get the money from many sources, both private and public, including a fund for citizens to donate money through their income tax. They also learn the importance of the issue of campaign finance reform as it pertains to how special interest groups may be influencing politicians.

Finally, the chapter goes on to detail the voting and election processes. It lists the requirements to vote, including that one must be an American citizen, at least 18 years old, and a resident of the state in which one votes. Students learn about elections and that there are two ways to vote—by secret ballot and absentee ballot—but that the final vote in national elections is decided by the Electoral College.

## Further Resources

Sifry, Micah L. *Spoiling for a Fight: Third-Party Politics in America*. New York: Routledge, 2000.

Ware, Alan. *Political Parties and Party Systems*. Oxford, England: Oxford University Press, 1997.

# For Discussion

## Review

1. What are the seven things that political parties do?

2. What are three main changes that have been seen in recent years in the role of political parties?

3. What are some of the methods used to influence and persuade voters to vote for candidates?

4. What are the four important sources of private funding?

## Critical Thinking

1. As a citizen, how do you feel the politicians in office have or have not represented your point of view? Explain.

2. What is your opinion of the two sides depicted in the chart on page 178 entitled "Comparing Party Platforms"? Which point of view do you agree with and why?

3. How do you feel about groups who contribute large sums of money to campaigns? Do you think they are trying to influence candidates?

4. How do you feel about the responsibility of voting even if you don't like the choice of candidates?

5. What is your opinion of the Electoral College as it is depicted on page 189?

# Activities

1. **Ask Your Caregivers about Politics**

   Ask students to interview their caregivers about what they have seen occurring over the years in politics. What choices have they had in terms of candidates? Which political parties have been in power since they have been old enough to vote? Do they see any trends? What changes have they seen?

2. **Running for Office**

   Divide students into teams of two. Ask each team to choose one person to "run" for the presidency and the other to be his or her vice president. Ask each team to choose a party and an important current issue. Ask them to research that issue and prepare a speech about it (as though running for office) and present it to the class.

3. **Internet: Third-Party Politics**

   Divide students into teams of two. Ask each team to choose a third party or a third-party candidate to research online. If they choose a party: What does the party represent? Why was it originally formed? How many people are involved in the party? How much has it grown? If they choose a candidate: what issues does he or she focus on? For what offices has he or she run? How did the voting turn out? How much money and support did the candidate have?

4. **Special Sources: The History of Politics**

   Divide students into four teams. Assign each team one of the following four topics to research the history of at the library: political parties, political issues, politicians, and voter turnout. Ask students to begin their research in the mid-1800s and to look for patterns and changes in these topics. What changes have taken place and why?

Alabama Citizenship Workbook   T25

# 12. Public Opinion and Interest Groups

## Objectives

- how public opinion is shaped and measured
- how propaganda is used to influence public opinion
- what special interest groups are and how they influence government

## Vocabulary

| | | | |
|---|---|---|---|
| approval rating | grassroots support | name-calling | special interest group |
| conglomerate | hard money | opinion polls | spin |
| enculturation | lobby | political action committees (PACs) | testimonials |
| euphemisms | lobbyist | propaganda | transfer |
| factions | mass media | public opinion | |
| generalities | muckraking | soft money | |

## Background

In this chapter, students learn how public opinion is influenced and measured, that propaganda is used to impact public opinion, and what special interest groups are and how they affect government.

Students begin by seeing that propaganda plays a big role in influencing the public. There are many types of propaganda used, from name-calling to glittering generalities to exaggeration. Students learn that public opinion is shaped by public officials, mass media, and special interest groups. Legislators and the executive in office also can use the media to reach the public. Media conglomerates are formed and spin is used in the media to make incidents or views look positive. The public's views can be determined through the use of opinion polls and election results.

Students move on to examine special interest groups. Whether they're big or small, these groups can impact the opinions of many. There are many different kinds of groups—economic, political, professional, and civil rights groups, to name a few. Students learn that interest groups organize the means they're going to use to get their views publicized, whether through lobbyists who are hired to influence legislators or grassroots campaigns. Political action committees are groups that raise money to help get a candidate elected.

Finally, students find out that interest groups help make government work more effectively by getting issues out to the public, by helping support their members, by supporting candidates, and by using the court system. There is concern over the power that interest groups may have. There are controls put into place for lobbyists and political action committees so that things don't get out of control.

### Further Resources

Chomsky, Noam. *Media Control: The Spectacular Achievement of Propaganda*. New York: Seven Stories Press, 2002.

Grossman, Gene M., and Helpman, Elhanan. *Special Interest Politics*. Cambridge, MA: MIT Press, 2001.

# For Discussion

## Review

1. What are some of the factors that shape what you and other citizens think and believe?

2. What do public opinion polls determine?

3. What are the four methods used by interest groups to accomplish their goals?

4. What are the four broad ways in which interest groups help make governments work more effectively?

## Critical Thinking

1. Other than those listed on page 194, what political or social issues do you feel can be addressed through a public opinion poll?

2. What is your opinion of your government's and other institutions' use of propaganda?

3. Do you agree with the arguments for or against investigative reporting of candidates? Explain.

4. If you could be involved with a special interest group, which one would you choose? Explain.

5. Besides those listed on page 207, what do you think are some of the "destructive decisions" that SADD may be referring to?

# Activities

1. **Types of Propaganda**

   Divide students into groups of four. Ask each group to make up examples of the ten types of propaganda listed on pages 195–196. Have students gather as a class and play a game called "guess the propaganda," in which groups take turns giving examples of the types of propaganda and other students guess which types they are.

2. **Looking at Mass Media**

   Ask students to look at different forms of media—television, newspapers, radio, magazines, books, film, audiotapes, CDs, DVDs, and the Internet—for different ways that they are used to shape public opinion. Have each student choose five forms of media and get at least one example from each form. Discuss results as a class.

3. **Internet: Interest Groups**

   Assign each student a specific interest group from pages 202–203 to research. Have them gather information from their groups' web sites. What is the group's purpose? How many members do they have? What kinds of things do they do as an interest group? Have students record their findings and present them to the class.

4. **Special Sources: Research Lobbyists, Grassroots Campaigns, and PACs**

   Divide students into three groups. Assign each group one of the following: lobbyists, grassroots campaigns, and political action committees. Encourage students to subdivide each topic within their group. Ask each group to analyze the success or failure of each type of organization, as well as its roots, and its ability to draw members and supporters. Use examples.

# 13. Law and Our Legal System

## Objectives
- how law is related to society
- what types of laws exist
- what the sources of American law are
- what basic rights come with responsibilities

## Vocabulary

| | | | |
|---|---|---|---|
| administrative law | conscientious objector | Justinian Code | property |
| civil disobedience | copyright | law | Ten Commandments |
| civil law | criminal law | legal code | |
| Code of Hammurabi | enforce | minor | |
| common good | injunction | precedent | |

## Background

In this chapter, students learn about America's laws and legal system and how they protect society. The chapter begins with why laws are needed—to keep order, ensure safety, and protect property, freedoms, and the common good. The issue of protecting property is brought into focus when students consider the questionable practice of downloading copyrighted music (or "swapping").

The chapter then moves on to the concepts of laws, morals, and civil disobedience. Students learn about the universal moral definitions that shape laws and punishments. Students find out about the characteristics of "good laws," i.e., that they be fair, reasonable, understandable, and enforceable. An example of a "bad law" is also discussed.

Students then survey the various types of laws that exist. Criminal law is distinguished from other laws by three main characteristics: the overall impact on society, how the government enforces the law, and the serious punishments that could result. Civil laws are different from criminal laws in that their limited impact on society leaves individuals to settle their cases—sometimes with a judge and/or jury involved. Constitutional law ensures a balance of power in government, a division of power between federal and state authorities, and protection of individual rights.

In the last part of the chapter, students learn about the sources of American law and their own rights and responsibilities as citizens. The main sources of American law include the Ten Commandments, the Code of Hammurabi, Roman law (the Justinian Code), and English law. Students will also be asked to think about their responsibilities as American citizens.

### Further Resources

Feinman, Jay M. *Law 101: Everything You Need to Know About the American Legal System*. Oxford, England: Oxford University Press, 2000.

Fine, Tony M. *American Legal Systems: A Resource and Reference Guide*. Cincinnati, OH: Anderson Publishing Co., 1997.

# For Discussion

## Review

1. What are the four main reasons that we need laws?
2. What are the four characteristics of good laws, and what do they mean?
3. Explain the three main ways that civil law differs from criminal law.
4. What is constitutional law and what are the three main things it protects?

## Critical Thinking

1. Some laws are more controversial than others. What do you think the laws should be concerning capital punishment, war, and assisted suicide?
2. Why do you think someone would intentionally break a law and suffer the punishment?
3. How do moral laws provide a foundation for society's laws upon which most citizens can agree?
4. How do taxes help support the common good?
5. What is your view of Muhammad Ali's refusal to obey the law and fight for a war in which he didn't believe? What kind of citizen do you think he is?

# Activities

1. **Developing and Debating New Laws**

   Some laws are more controversial than others. Ask students to list three laws that they would like to change or stop. Ask them to present them, to support their choices, and to present one of their arguments to the class for discussion.

2. **Classroom Trial**

   Create a classroom trial by choosing a judge, jury, defendant, and two opposing legal teams. Choose or create a controversial school rule that many students may not like—for example, a rule that punishes students for being late. Choose a defendant to pretend he or she is accused of the crime of being late. Ask the defense to argue against the law's fairness. For example, "things happen in life;" therefore it is unfair to expect their client always to be on time. The prosecution may suggest that the law is fair because people generally can plan ahead and that order needs to be maintained. The jury can decide the rest.

3. **Internet: Debating Music-File Swapping**

   Divide the class into two groups for a debate. Assign one group the task of arguing against music-file swapping on the Internet; ask the other group to argue for the practice. Allow each side to collect information online to support their arguments. This might include statistics, copyright laws, online swapping-service practices, and the like.

4. **Special Sources: Famous Cases in American History**

   Have students, in groups or individually, search the library for information about famous (perhaps noncriminal) law trials in American history. Ask them to prepare reports detailing how the law succeeded or failed in its aim for a just decision. Examples of famous cases include the Dred Scott decision, *Rowe* v. *Wade*, and cases concerning Big Tobacco.

# 14. The American Justice System

## Objectives

- the purpose of civil law
- what happens in a civil lawsuit
- the purpose of criminal law
- how a crime is prosecuted
- the juvenile justice system

## Vocabulary

| | | | |
|---|---|---|---|
| arraignment | domestic-relations laws | parole | rehabilitation |
| compensated | equity | plaintiff | remedy |
| contract | evidence | plea bargain | restitution |
| defendant | indictment | pleadings | tort |
| delinquent | juvenile | probation | warrant |

## Background

In this chapter, students learn about the American justice system. The first topic covered is civil law, the part of law that deals with personal, noncriminal disputes. On the whole, people who file such suits are seeking a remedy to a problem. A remedy can include a monetary payment (compensation), a fair way to settle the dispute (equity), or both. Students will also learn the five basic types of civil cases. These include (1) contracts and private agreement disputes, (2) personal injury or property damage issues, (3) property disputes, (4) consumer protection issues, and (5) domestic relation disputes.

Students then move on to civil procedures and the ways they may be settled. Civil procedures normally begin with court pleadings, followed by the gathering of evidence and the trial itself. Unlike in criminal cases, the jury must only be 51 percent convinced that the plaintiff is correct. Lawsuits can also be settled through mediation and arbitration.

The chapter then moves on to how criminal law differs from civil law in the way it defines elements like punishment, proof of guilt, and victim. It then discusses types of crimes and their penalties before covering the criminal justice system and what happens when one is arrested. After arrest the accused is quickly brought before a judge, arraigned, and then may plea bargain or face trial.

The chapter then details the various ways the corrections system punishes offenders. Students then learn about the different elements and objectives of the juvenile justice system—including its history and modern goals and processes. Finally, the chapter provides the opposing arguments for and against trying juvenile offenders as adults.

### Further Resources

Humes, Edward. *No Matter How Loud I Shout: A Year in the Life of Juvenile Court.* New York: Touchstone Books, 1997.

# For Discussion

## Review

1. Describe the two ways that a civil suit can be remedied. Provide an original example of each.

2. What are the five general categories of civil cases?

3. Explain the three broad areas in which criminal law differs from civil law.

4. Describe the five ways in which the corrections system punishes offenders.

## Critical Thinking

1. What is your view of the fact that a person can sue another person for damaging his or her image or reputation?

2. What is a plea bargain? Do you think justice is served when prosecutors "limit the risk and expense" this way?

3. Many states punish felons by taking away their right to vote, serve on juries, and hold particular jobs. Do you think this is fair? Support your view.

4. What is an innocence project and why does it exist?

5. What do you think causes juvenile crime?

# Activities

1. **Crime Prevention and Enforcement**

   If students were in charge, how would they prevent crime? Ask students to split into two "think tanks." Ask one think tank to brainstorm new, realistic ways to prevent crime in the community. Ask the other think tank to suggest new, realistic ways for police to improve the accuracy and application of police enforcement. Have each group present its results to the class.

2. **Life on the Outside**

   Many convicted felons find it difficult to turn their lives around once they are released. Many don't have a proper education, marketable work skills, and other elements needed to "go straight" and earn a good wage. Ask students to discuss the high rate of recidivism—repeat offenders returning to jail. Pose the question: If jail is so bad, why are so many criminals returning? Next, what kind of programs would they suggest to help ex-convicts adjust to life on the outside?

3. **Internet: How Ridiculous Can Civil Suits Get?**

   Divide the class into as many groups as you have computers with Internet access. Ask students to use search engines to find famous and infamous lawsuits. For example, note the case of the woman who successfully sued a national restaurant chain because she bought coffee there—and then spilled it on herself in the car. She blamed her burns on the restaurant, sued them, and won a large sum of money. Ask students to search for other unusual lawsuits.

4. **Special Sources: National Crime**

   Have students, in groups or individually, search for information about trends in national crime rates. Ask students to determine and graph the changes in different types of violent and non-violent crime rates. Ask them also to research the national figures for juveniles in the same categories and share them with the class.

# 15. Economics and the American Economy

## Objectives
- how the United States economy is structured
- how different economic systems distribute resources
- the operation of a free-market economy
- how businesses in the United States are organized
- the factors that drive basic economic decisions

## Vocabulary

| | | | |
|---|---|---|---|
| barter | demand | land | profit |
| bonds | distribution | liability | resources |
| capital | economy | market | scarcity |
| capitalism | factors of production | market economy | socialism |
| command economy | free enterprise | mixed economy | sole proprietorship |
| communism | free market | monopoly | stocks |
| consumer | interest | not-for-profit organization | supply |
| consumption | labor | partnership | |
| corporation | laissez-faire | production | |

## Background

In this chapter, students learn about economics and the American economy. The chapter begins with a description of basic economic freedoms in the United States. Students then learn about scarcity and the law of supply and demand.

The chapter then discusses different kinds of economic systems. First, the barter system is described as the equal exchange of goods and services. In a command economy, the central government makes most of the country's economic decisions. In a market economy, natural market forces control the economy. Finally, a mixed economy mixes some government control and natural market forces. Students also learn about how U.S. businesses are organized and managed.

Next, the chapter explains the three main factors of production—capital (money, property, and machinery), land (natural resources and land itself), and labor (human work and employed people). Finally, the chapter describes economic decision-making factors.

### Further Resources
Foss, Murray F., and Stein, Herbert (eds.). *The Illustrated Guide to the American Economy*. Washington, D.C.: AEI Press, 2000.

# For Discussion

## Review

1. What general economic system is the U.S. economy based on? What basic economic freedoms does it allow?

2. Describe the three economic systems that have replaced the barter system in most nations today.

3. What are the four different types of U.S. business organizations?

4. Describe the three main factors of production.

## Critical Thinking

1. Do you think it's fair to set the price as high as people are willing to pay? Explain your view.

2. What is the danger of a monopoly and how is a mixed economy like the U.S. likely to deal with it?

3. U.S. businesses are organized in four different ways. If you were to start a business, what would it be and how would you organize it?

4. What do the ups and downs of the stock market mean?

5. How healthy is your local economy? Is business busy where you live or are there a lot of empty stores and people out of work? Can you use what you've learned to guess the causes?

# Activities

1. **Start a Student Business**

    Ask students to choose a fun activity or reward that they would like to do as a class. Suggest that they brainstorm ideas for a school-based business they can start to fund that activity. This may include selling something at lunch, cleaning teachers' chalkboards, etc. They should elect key organizers and plan ahead for success.

2. **Volunteer for a Not-for-Profit**

    Many not-for-profit organizations were started to help the community without profiting monetarily from their work. Ask students to research a local not-for-profit and volunteer for at least a day. Ask them to share their experiences with the class. Some students may enjoy the experience and choose to continue to volunteer indefinitely.

3. **Internet: Choose and Follow an Investment**

    Divide the class into as many groups as you have computers with Internet access. Ask them to choose a company to follow on the stock market. Then, ask them to research the basics of the stock market. What is the company symbol on the stock exchange? At what price are the shares trading today? Have each student follow the stock for a week and prepare a line graph to be shown to the other "investors" in the class.

4. **The Fall of the Soviet Union (U.S.S.R.)**

    For many older Americans, the Cold War between the communist Soviet Union and the United States was a struggle of nuclear and economic foes. Ask students to split into two groups to study the rise and fall of the Cold War. Have one group focus on political milestones (especially the arms race); have the other group focus on the Soviet economy. Have students discuss how both the economy and politics brought down the powerful communist nation.

# Supply and Demand

> **Alabama Planner**
>
> **Citizenship Course of Study**
> 7.b, 7.c
>
> Learning Objective:
> - Analyzing distribution and production maps to determine patterns of supply and demand
> - Describing the effects of government policies on the free market

## Background

Alabama, a state that had never produced an automobile prior to 1997, is expected to become the third-largest automobile producing state in the South by 2005. A study by the Alabama Automotive Manufacturing Association in December 2002 shows that Alabama currently ranks sixth among eight southern states in automobile production capacity at 230,000 vehicles a year. The Southern states include: Alabama, Kentucky, Tennessee, Georgia, Texas, Virginia, Louisiana, and South Carolina.

By 2005, Alabama will reach a capacity of 760,000 vehicles per year, trailing only Kentucky and Tennessee in vehicle production capacity in the South and capturing nearly 17 percent of the region's total capacity.

# 16. Government's Role in the Economy

## Objectives
- how the government tries to maintain economic stability
- what business cycles are
- how government manages businesses and the banking system
- how government protects consumers and workers

## Vocabulary

| | | | |
|---|---|---|---|
| antitrust laws | deflation | Gross Domestic Product (GDP) | picket |
| budget deficit | depression | inflation | recession |
| budget surplus | discount rate | labor | reserve requirement |
| business cycles | economic indicators | labor union | strike |
| collective bargaining | expansion | national debt | trust |
| Consumer Price Index (CPI) | government securities | peak | unemployment rate |

## Background

In this chapter, students learn about government's role in the economy. Students first find out that the government does try to guide the overall economy. The Constitution grants the government certain powers—like collecting taxes—but government also insures that free-enterprise businesses pay taxes, compete fairly, and refrain from harming consumers. As students continue, they learn that the government also tries to use taxing and spending to grow or shrink the economy. Such efforts increase the stability in an economy that may cycle through four stages of economic change: expansion, peak, recession, and depression.

The chapter then discusses how the government measures and controls economic performance. The government uses the Gross Domestic Product (GDP) and the Consumer Price Index (CPI) as economic indicators. The government also watches for monthly changes in the indexes of inflation, deflation, and unemployment, and uses fiscal and monetary policy to improve the health of the economy. Students next examine the balancing of the budget and the national debt.

Students learn about the Federal Reserve System and how government regulates business by protecting fair competition, consumers and workers, and the environment. Government protects fair competition by "trust busting" and protects consumers with (1) the Consumer Product Safety Commission, (2) the Food and Drug Administration, and (3) the Department of Agriculture.

### Further Resources

Dubofsky, Melvyn, and Dulles, Foster R. *Labor in America*. Wheeling, IL: Harlan Davidson, 1999.

Woodward, Bob. *Maestro: Greenspan's Fed and the American Boom*. New York: Simon & Schuster, 2000.

# For Discussion

## Review

1. What economic powers does the Constitution give to Congress?

2. Describe the four stages through which business may cycle.

3. Name five economic indicators that government uses to measure economic performance.

4. What are the four main duties of the Federal Reserve?

## Critical Thinking

1. What was the Great Depression?

2. Why do you think they call the Federal Reserve chairman the "second-most-powerful person in the world"?

3. How did Standard Oil form an unfair trust?

4. What does the Federal Trade Commission do?

5. Consider the arguments for and against the actions of unions. Do you think that unions damage businesses by raising costs and protecting incompetent workers, or do their happier workers work harder and make businesses more profitable?

# Activities

1. **Debate: Government Influencing the Economy**

   Ask students to split into two groups for a debate. Ask one group to gather evidence and prepare to debate the benefits of more government control of the economy. Ask the other group to prepare and argue against more government control.

2. **Business vs. Labor**

   Ask students to break up into two groups. One group can represent a business that must negotiate with striking workers. The workers want a 10 percent raise, more vacation time, better working conditions, and more personal leave time. Assume that the business is barely breaking even at the time and that every day of work stoppage is costing money. Can they negotiate an acceptable deal in which both sides benefit?

3. **Internet: Trust Busting?**

   Divide the class into as many groups as you have computers with Internet access. Ask them to use the Internet to investigate and report on government trust busting. What were the circumstances before and after the government's efforts? Have them present their findings to the class.

4. **The Great Depression**

   For many older Americans, The Great Depression was a very difficult time when many people were out of work and hungry. Have students use the library to learn more about different elements of the time period. These may include the stock market, businesses, farmers, the WPA, etc.

# 17. United States Foreign Policy

## Objectives

- what foreign policy is
- who decides foreign policy
- about the tools used in making foreign policy
- the history of America's foreign policy
- what U.S. foreign policy is today

## Vocabulary

| | | | |
|---|---|---|---|
| alliance | containment | embassy | political asylum |
| boycotting | diplomacy | intelligence | sanctions |
| Cold War | domestic | isolationism | treaty |

## Background

In this chapter, students learn about American foreign policy, past and present. They first learn about America's foreign policy goals, which include (1) protecting American citizens, (2) working for peace in the world, (3) supporting democracy, and (4) providing humanitarian assistance. Different entities influence foreign policy. These are the executive branch, Congress, and groups outside of government. Private citizens also have a few ways to influence foreign policy.

Students then find out about the tools of American foreign policy, which include diplomacy, alliances, foreign aid, and intelligence. They then move on to the history of American foreign policy, including its beginnings and the periods of isolationism leading up to the end of World War II. The period following World War II, the Cold War, and the birth of the United Nations are discussed. Students learn more about the structure of the UN, as well as its peacekeeping and humanitarian work. The other international organizations that exist outside of the UN are then presented and discussed.

Next, students explore the challenges of today's foreign policy. Some general challenges include dealing with ethnic conflicts, the rise of developing nations, trade competition, obtaining resources, and the threat of hostile groups and nations. In the Middle East, American foreign policy interests include the trade of oil, the Arab-Israeli conflict, and the countries of Iraq and Iran. African concerns include the country of South Africa and the civil wars that occur between ethnic groups on the continent. In the Americas, American foreign policy concerns include the North American Free Trade Agreement (NAFTA), Cuba, the export of illegal drugs, poverty, and political instability. In Asia and the Pacific Rim, American foreign policy is focused on issues in countries like China, North Korea, and Japan.

### Further Resources

Kissinger, Henry. *Does America Need Foreign Policy?* New York: Simon & Schuster, 2001.

Meisler, Stanley. *United Nations: The First Fifty Years.* New York: Atlantic Monthly Press, 1997.

# For Discussion

## Review

1. What are the four goals of United States foreign policy?

2. On what four executive departments does the president rely for help in making foreign policy decisions?

3. What four responsibilities does Congress have in making foreign policy?

4. What are the four goals of the UN charter?

## Critical Thinking

1. Do you think the creation of new weapons is a strength that protects the U.S. and promotes peace, or is it something that "increases world danger"?

2. Describe the War Powers Act. Why is it in place?

3. Do you think the mass media's treatment of an issue can change public opinion—and therefore foreign policy? Explain.

4. In what ways can a citizen influence foreign policy?

5. What are the four tools of foreign policy?

# Activities

1. **Senior Advisor to the President of the United States**

   Ask students to prepare a report for the president advising on how to use his or her power to gain world peace. What methods would they suggest? How realistic are their suggestions? What are the benefits versus the costs to the U.S.? Ask students to present their ideas to the class for discussion.

2. **Debate: Arms for Peace?**

   Ask students to split into two groups. Ask one group to prepare to argue for the idea that making and exporting arms protects the United States and its allies. Ask the other group to argue the opposite view: that making and exporting arms is certain to bring about more conflict.

3. **Internet: Current Events**

   Divide the class into two groups. Ask them to use the Internet to investigate and report on the most recent foreign policy topic in the news. Ask one group to report the U.S. view of the topic. Ask another group to present the opposing side's view. Afterward, have the class discuss the issue. How could it be solved with both views in mind?

4. **The History of U.S. Foreign Policy**

   Many older Americans remember U.S. isolationism, fear of foreigners, the need to go to war in foreign nations, and more. Ask students to select an important topic in the history of U.S. foreign policy and research it in the library. Have them present their reports to class.

# 18. Global Issues

## Objectives

- how the global economy works
- why environmental issues are important
- that terrorism is not a new threat
- what nations can do about world health and human rights
- how citizens can make a difference

## Vocabulary

closed market
developing countries
fossil fuels
global warming

industrialized countries
infrastructure
literacy rate
nonrenewable resource

open markets
refugees
renewable resource
terrorism
transnational companies

## Background

In this chapter, students learn more about global issues. They begin with the world's division into two groups: the wealthier, more developed, industrialized nations and the poorer, developing countries. Sometimes transnational companies will set up offices in other countries, but this can sometimes lead to a "culture clash" of sorts between Western consumerism and the more traditional values of developing nations.

Students then learn about American citizens and world trade. The effects of tariffs and open markets are introduced, as well as environmental issues like natural resources and pollution.

The chapter then moves on to the subject of terrorism. Students find out that terrorism is nothing new and that it is an historical occurrence both in the United States and around the globe. This leads to the discussion of ways to keep and maintain world peace.

Next, the chapter discusses world health. Hunger and nutrition challenges include (1) the growth of population vs. food production, (2) food distribution, and (3) the way land is used. Disease is also a challenging world issue. HIV, Hepatitis C, and cholera are spreading, mostly in developing nations. Students then learn the many terrible effects of drug abuse.

Finally, the chapter introduces the subject of human rights. Many nations practice prejudice, violate human rights, and refuse to give the people a democratic voice in who governs them. Refugees and their host countries face difficult challenges themselves. Students learn that the efforts of individuals can still make a difference in combating these complicated global issues.

### Further Resources

Gilpin, Robert, and Gilpin, Jean. *Global Political Economy: Understanding the International Economic Order.* Princeton, NJ: Princeton University Press, 2001.

Lappe, Frances Moore, et al. *World Hunger: Twelve Myths.* New York: Grove Press, 1998.

# For Discussion

## Review

1. Describe the main divisions of the world economy. How many countries are in each category?
2. What are the three main things a transnational company expects from a host country?
3. What three things do terrorists threaten most?
4. The United Nations and individual countries have focused on what three health issues?

## Critical Thinking

1. What do you think of life in America's industrial economy? Do you think Americans are "happier" than people in developing nations? Explain.
2. What are four general factors that affect American citizens and world trade?
3. What important fuels are nonrenewable and how many years' supply do we have left?
4. What problems can the presence of refugees create in host countries? What do you think host countries should do about refugees?
5. In what way would you like to "make a difference" and change the world? What could you do now to help make that happen?

# Activities

1. **Local Environmental Issues**

   Ask students to split into three groups that will research and present a report on the state of pollutants in the local environment. The first group can focus on air quality, the second on land-based pollution, and the third on water quality. Ask students to use different resources or even personal observation to find and report possible polluters.

2. **Debate: Civil Liberties and Domestic Terrorism**

   Ask students to split into two groups. Ask one group to prepare to argue for the view that government needs broader powers to effectively combat terrorism. These may include wire-tapping, broader search warrant rights, and other powers. Ask the other group to argue that such powers open the door for the abuse of individual rights. After the debate, ask the groups to discuss the best way to combat terrorism.

3. **Internet: Study a Developing Nation**

   Divide the class into two groups. Select a developing nation somewhere in the world. Ask group one to use the Internet to research the country from a business perspective, as if asking, "What kind of business might be best suited for this country's resources and infrastructure?" Ask group two to study the people and their quality of life. This should include education rates, human rights, leadership, nutrition, etc.

4. **World Health**

   The world has historically suffered many devastating health challenges. Ask students to use the library to choose and report on a specific world health issue. The report can include current health issues (HIV, cholera, etc.) or historic challenges such as the bubonic plague or smallpox.

# 19. Making a Budget

## Objectives
- developing a budget
- keeping records
- paying taxes

## Vocabulary

budget
credit rating
deductions
discretionary expenses
expenses
fixed expenses
flexible expenses
gross wages
income
net wages
paycheck stub
Social Security
taxes

## Background

In this chapter, students find that budgeting, organizing their records, and learning about taxes will help them achieve their financial goals. They learn about choosing financial goals wisely by deciding on them, making a plan, and sticking to it. Students also learn about setting financial priorities and how to make a budget. In addition, they find new ways to keep track of their expenses and learn to distinguish between the many expenses they will incur.

When students start to work, they will find that they have to divide their paychecks so that all their expenses are covered: housing, food, clothes, health care, recreation, transportation, bills, and savings. They will also find out that making a budget and living with it are two different things. The reality of what they like to spend their money on (the non-essentials) ultimately affects their budgeting. The idea of sticking to a budget might be difficult for students, but they find helpful tips in the chapter to support their efforts. Students may find that they need to revise their budgets because of changes in their lives and will find a three-step plan for doing this. Organization is important in handling finances, and students will find ample information on record keeping, sorting receipts, and organizing personal records.

The amount that they thought they were getting paid is not the actual amount that they will see on their paycheck. After taxes and other deductions are taken out, they will see a difference between their gross and their net incomes. Taxes are taken out to pay for services and other benefits to citizens. They also will see deductions on their paychecks for other payments. Their paycheck stubs give them information on what these things are.

When students understand that they will be paying taxes, they also learn about filing procedures and the forms they need to use to file their taxes.

To supplement this material, you will find a blank budget copy master on pages T-66 of this text. You may wish to make a copy on acetate to use on an overhead projector.

## Further Resources

Bijlefeld, M., and Zoumbaris, S.K. *Teen Guide to Personal Financial Management.* New York: Greenwood, 2000.

# For Discussion

## Review

1. What are three things to do when choosing financial goals?

2. What are two things you need to know before preparing a budget?

3. What are the two factors that affect the amount of taxes that is taken out?

## Critical Thinking

1. Under what circumstances can you envision your own mismanagement of your money creating a problem in your life? Give examples.

2. If one of your goals was to buy a car a year from now, how would you go about achieving that goal? What other expenses would you have to consider?

3. Besides payroll taxes, what are some additional required or voluntary deductions?

# Activities

1. **Activity: An Older Person's Budget**

   Ask students to ask a grandparent or any retired person if they can make a sample budget for him or her, based on whatever figures the individual gives them. These figures needn't be their own. These should include income from Social Security, retirement accounts, pensions, and savings. They should also include real circumstances that an older retired person has to deal with, e.g., medical expenses or long-term-care insurance.

2. **Survey: Student Budgets and Income**

   Divide students into teams of two. Ask them to interview their peers around school and in their neighborhood about budgeting and income. What do they expect their incomes to be when they reach adulthood? What are their priorities? What are their goals? What kinds of expenses do they expect to have? What kind of plans, if any, do they have for their future financial situation? Ask students to present their findings to the class.

# 20. Handling Your Money

## Objectives
- banks and other financial information
- checking and savings accounts

## Vocabulary

bank
certificate of deposit
check register
cooperative
credit union

deposit
depositor
endorse
interest
interest rate

money market account
payee
profit
transactions

## Background

In this chapter, students learn about banks, banking, and other financial institutions. Students find out about government and community banking, checking accounts, and savings accounts. Students discover that, before they open their first checking account, they need to research different accounts at different banks. The chapter shows them how to write a check and record it, how to balance their checkbooks, and how to read a bank statement.

At some point, students will make errors in their checkbooks. The list of common errors in the chapter prepares students for this inevitable occurrence. Savings accounts may not be used as often, so students will likely make fewer mistakes with their savings. The chapter explains three types of savings vehicles: standard savings, money market accounts, and certificates of deposit.

To supplement this material, you will find blank check and check register copy masters on pages T67–T68 of this text.

### Further Resources

Lee, R.S., and M.P. *Coping with Money*. New York: Rosen, 1988.

# For Discussion

## Review

1. What are the two main ways banks make money?

2. What are three steps one should follow when writing checks?

3. What are the minimum six pieces of information that a bank statement includes?

## Critical Thinking

1. How do you feel about using a checkbook and a check register, and balancing your checkbook?

2. What are some of the difficulties you might have in maintaining a savings account?

# Activities

1. **Banking**

    Divide students into pairs. Have the class prepare a brief questionnaire for bankers. Ask them to phone local banks and make appointments for brief interviews with the bankers. What kinds of loans do they offer? What are the current interest rates? What are the different rates and what do they mean? What are the purposes of the different fees? Discuss their findings in class.

2. **Interview: Parents and Their Checking Accounts**

    Ask students to ask their parents 10 questions about their checking accounts. For example, why do you have one? Is it difficult to balance it? Do you sometimes forget to put information into the register? What happens if you do? Have students discuss their findings in class.

# 21. Using Credit Wisely

## Objectives
- understanding credit
- keeping a good credit rating
- avoiding getting into debt

## Vocabulary

annual percentage rate (APR)
bankruptcy
capacity
capital
cash advance
character
charge back
charge card

commercial credit
cramming
credit
credit bureau
credit history
credit limit
credit report
credit score

delayed gratification
down payment
equity
finance charge
grace period
home equity loan
identity theft
immediate gratification

mortgage
overextended
personal credit
principal
revolving credit
sales finance companies

## Background

In this chapter, students learn about the definition of credit, immediate and delayed gratification, commercial and personal credit, how credit is used, and its advantages and disadvantages. Information on rates and fees and what lenders look for in a borrower will be useful for students. Students discover information on loans: where to get a loan, and the types of loans for which one can apply, as well as dishonest loan offers of which they should be wary.

Credit cards will be a major draw for students when they can acquire them. Having a credit card involves responsibility. A credit limit will help keep them from spending too much. Students also need to watch out for credit card fees. Since fees vary, choosing the right card will be something students can research. Students may be tempted to get cash advances on their charge cards, but will pay dearly for it. After learning about debit cards, they may see the advantage of using their debit cards over their credit cards for smarter budgeting. Students will also get tips on how to live within their means, and how to avoid credit card fraud by credit card companies, fraud by sellers, and fraud by other people.

Students may be surprised to learn that their spending and payment habits are noticed by creditors. When they establish credit, they will eventually receive a credit score, based on their employment and income, housing, assets, and credit history. Their score will go on a credit report. Students learn how to keep a good score and what to do if they overextend themselves or possibly go into bankruptcy. Finally, they learn how to stay free of credit problems altogether.

## Further Resources

Hegeman, William R., and Whinnery, Alice J. *Teen Talk: Money: How to Get It . . . Keep It . . . Avoid Getting Ripped Off!* New York: Financial Education Services, 1994.

# For Discussion

## Review

1. What are the "three Cs of credit"?
2. What are the three types of credit card fraud?
3. Your credit score comes from information related to which four areas?
4. What possible financial problems can occur if you become overextended?

## Critical Thinking

1. When it comes to making purchases, are you an immediate- or delayed-gratification type of person? Why?
2. Do you ever find yourself falling for ads that are too good to be true? Give examples.
3. How do you think it might feel to have the responsibility of a family, a mortgage, a car loan, and so on?
4. What are the advantages and disadvantages of owning a credit card?
5. What are the tips on living within your means? Could you follow them?

# Activities

1. **Ads**

   Ask students to look through the ads that are in newspapers and magazines. Ask them to cut out the ones that appear truthful to them and the ones that appear to be dishonest. What makes the honest ones look legitimate? Why don't they trust the other ones? Have them bring the ads to class for comparison and discussion.

2. **Interview: A credit card company.**

   Ask students to call at least two credit card companies. Tell them to ask questions about their fees, interest rates, credit limits, and so on. Compare findings in class.

3. **Internet: Credit Bureaus**

   Divide students into pairs. Ask them to look on the Internet for information on credit bureaus. What do they do? What do they offer? Discuss research results in class.

4. **Special Sources: Bankruptcy**

   Divide students into groups of three. Ask them to use library materials to look up issues on bankruptcy. What happens when someone files for bankruptcy? What do the courts say? How long before they can get a bankruptcy taken off their record? Ask them to write short papers on their findings.

# 22. Becoming a Wise Consumer

## Objectives
- what influences your buying decisions
- how to be a smart shopper

## Vocabulary

| | | | |
|---|---|---|---|
| advertising | fraud | need | warranty |
| affordable | hierarchy | peers | |
| comparison shopping | market research | want | |

## Background

This chapter can be useful to students in a number of ways. It can help them understand themselves better as consumers learn how and where to buy. Students have the opportunity to analyze their own motivations as consumers. They discover that there are reasons for buying that are based on psychological, sociological, and economic influences.

Students look at need versus want in the world of buying. Maslow's hierarchy of needs explains this further. Students learn not to be fooled by advertising for a product and come to understand that advertisers can use manipulation and deception (but not outright lies) to get their attention, make them want a product, and get them to purchase it. Students also are encouraged to look at their own spending habits and influences from peers.

There are many tips available to students interested in becoming smart shoppers. Being well organized is a key. Once they decide what they want to buy, research the product, and gather information through various consumer-friendly sources, they can price shop and comparison shop and be on their way to better spending. Students learn where to buy a product, and gain information on warranties and contracts as well.

Students receive information on the long-term care of products and other things such as how not to become a victim of fraud and what to do if that happens. Also, they learn what to do if they get a defective product.

### Further Resources

Menhard, Francha Roffe. *Teen Consumer Smarts: Shop, Save, and Steer Clear of Scams.* New York: Enslow Publishers, Inc., 2002.

Moses, Elissa. *The $100 Billion Allowance: How to Get Your Share of the Global Teen Market.* New York: John Wiley & Sons, 2000.

## For Discussion

### Review

1. Why we buy what we buy is the result of a mixture of what three influences?
2. What are the four common special offers?
3. What are the five types of fraud?
4. What are the four rights in the "Consumers' Bill of Rights"?

### Critical Thinking

1. Do you think your needs outweigh your wants, or vice versa? Give examples.
2. What is your opinion of the law that says that an advertisement can be "deceptive," but cannot lie? In your opinion, what is the difference?
3. Have you ever bought a product out of brand loyalty? What was the product and why? If not, would you?
4. What do you think about ordering products online? Do you think there are better and worse products to order that way?
5. If you could choose a product to boycott, which would you choose? Why?

## Activity

1. **What's the Best Deal?**

    Direct students to choose a product and, following the three steps under the "Deciding What to Buy" section of the chapter, determine what the best buying decision would be.

# 23. Smart Shopping on the Internet

## Objectives

- buying over the Internet
- using the Internet to comparison shop

## Vocabulary

brick-and-mortar stores      e-commerce      Internet security

## Background

In this chapter, students learn about buying on the Internet and using the Internet to comparison shop.

Students begin by learning about the advantages of shopping online. Convenience, choice, and cost are the main advantages. The disadvantages are preferences for traditional shopping; shipping charges; safety concerns; and concerns about delivery, returns, and other problems. Students may feel that shopping online feels less secure than other ways of shopping. Their credit cards or personal information could be misused, but most sites have security protection.

### Further Resources

Gates, Susan, and Rappeport, Amy, eds. *The Bizrate.Com Guide 2001: The Best of Online Shopping.* Berkeley, CA: Publishers Group West, 2001.

Rothman, Kevin F. *Coping with Dangers on the Internet: A Teen's Guide to Staying Safe Online.* New York: Rosen Publishing Group, 2000.

# For Discussion

## Review
What are the advantages of buying from companies that have both a web site and traditional retail outlets?

## Critical Thinking
How would you feel about paying a shipping charge for an item ordered online? What if you could get it at a local store for the same price without paying shipping?

# Activities

**1. Practice Shopping**

Divide students into teams of two. Ask them to go online; choose a type of online store (clothing, electronics, music, etc.), and try shopping at three stores of that type. Have them compare the three online stores in terms of convenience, ease of use, selection, quality, and price. Compare results in class.

**2. Security Online**

Divide students into teams of two. Ask them to go online and look up the privacy statements of well known, reputable companies and of lesser known companies. Do their statements differ? Does one type of company offer the consumer more security than the other? Is there a standard statement that all web site companies have? Ask students to bring this information to class for a comparison.

**3. Special Sources: Brick-and-Mortar and Web-Site Stores**

Divide students into teams of four. Ask them to go to the library and look up information about two famous brick-and-mortar stores that also are online. How long have the stores been in business? When did they go online? Are sales better in the stores than online? Why? Have students bring their findings to class for a discussion.

# 24. Smart Shopping for Food

## Objective
- how to shop for food

## Background

This chapter helps students to learn a lot about why they eat what they eat, how to shop smart, and how to store and cook their food safely. Students discover that what they eat is influenced greatly by various factors: family and culture, advertising and media, nutritional information, and personal preference. Students probably don't plan a lot of meals at home, but learn that process entails knowing how to shop smart, budgeting their money, considering individual preferences, evaluating food nutritionally, and considering fat and amounts of servings.

Students find helpful shopping strategies in this chapter. Students can look at the choices and learn how to make better decisions in choosing frozen or fresh vegetables and food grown locally. Students learn what affects food prices.

Students become acquainted with how to compare prices, the various stores one can shop in, the needs each family may have, and how these needs may determine where they will shop. They learn about buying brand names over store brands, bulk buying, coupon cutting and weekly specials, using a frequent-shopper card, joining a shopping club, and food co-ops. After reading the chapter, students may look at eating out in a new way. They may consider the reasons they eat out, the nutritional benefits, and the costs as compared with those of making their own food. Students probably have a lot of experience with the fast food industry. Here, they learn that, every day, about 20 million Americans eat in fast food restaurants, and that a great percentage of them are children, which may be contributing to the current epidemic of overweight children.

To supplement this material, you will find a blank grocery list copy master on page T69 of this text.

### Further Resources

Tattersall, Clare. *Understanding Food and Your Family (Teen Eating Disorder Prevention Book).* New York: Rosen Publishing Group, 1999.

# For Discussion

## Review

What are the four strategies smart shoppers use?

## Critical Thinking

1. Do you prefer a wide range of food, or do you keep your menu simple? How is that different from what with which you grew up?

2. What are some ads that have influenced you? Why did they do so?

# Activities

### 1. Plan a Meal

Divide students into pairs. Using a restaurant menu as a guide, ask them to choose a dinner from the menu and note the price. Ask them to make a list of the ingredients they would need to recreate that meal at home (without actually creating the meal), go to the grocery store, price those ingredients, and compare the costs.

### 2. Eating Out or In? The Survey

Divide students into groups of four. Ask them to take a survey around school and from their families about eating out or in. How much do they eat out? What do they enjoy more? If they could, would they do either one more or less? Do they eat better, nutritionally speaking, when they eat out or in? Have teams report their findings to the class.

# 25. Smart Shopping for Clothing

## Objective
- how to shop for clothes

## Vocabulary

department stores
discount stores
drape
durability
fad
International Textile Care Labeling Code
markup
natural fibers
synthetic fibers
texture

## Background

In this chapter, students get information on a subject that probably already interests them: clothing. They learn about listing what they need, adding items, working within a budget, and planning purchases over the year.

They can choose between store-brand and designer clothes at department or discount stores. Students learn positive and negative effects of choosing trendy over classic clothes, and things to look for, before they purchase an item, that will give them clues about the item's longevity and quality. When students choose an outfit to buy, they probably don't look first at the fabric, but they find out that this is an important part of choosing clothing. For example, how fabric "breathes" and drapes are important considerations.

If students have trouble reading some of the care instruction symbols on their clothing, they can use the chapter's chart on the International Textile Care Labeling Code. The information on where to shop and on finding the best deals can aid students in their quest to stay within their budgets.

### Further Resources

Menhard, Francha Roffe. *Teen Consumer Smarts: Shop, Save, and Steer Clean of Scams.* New York: Enslow Publishers, Inc., 2002.

Zollo, Peter. *Wise Up to Teens: Insights into Marketing and Advertising to Teenagers.* New York: New Strategist Publications, 1999.

# For Discussion

## Critical Thinking

1. What is the general difference between natural and synthetic fibers?

2. How carefully do you consider fit when you purchase an item of clothing? What do you look for when determining the fit of your clothes?

3. Of the types of stores listed, from where do you buy most of your clothes?

# Activities

### 1. Where Do You Shop?

Divide students into pairs and ask them to take a survey of at least twenty-five people: their friends and family, and other students around school about where they shop for clothes. Also ask, why they shop there—the price the quality? the brand name?

### 2. Internet: Shopping

Ask students to get online and visit the web sites of their favorite stores from which to buy clothes. Ask them to assess the websites. Do they have a lot of clothes from which to choose? Is there a range of styles? Is it easy to access the information they want? How are the prices for shipping and handling? Was it a good shopping experience?

# 26. Smart Shopping for Health Care

## Objectives

- getting appropriate health care
- paying for health care

## Vocabulary

| | | | |
|---|---|---|---|
| alternative medicine | health insurance | pharmacy | primary care physician (PCP) |
| catastrophic coverage | health maintenance organization (HMO) | point of service (POS) | quackery |
| COBRA | | pre-existing condition | specialist |
| co-pay | holistic medicine | preferred provider organization (PPO) | stress |
| deductible | managed-care plans | | |
| diagnosis | out-of-pocket expenses | premium | |
| generic brands | pharmacist | preventive medicine | |

## Background

In this chapter, students learn about the importance of leading a healthy lifestyle in terms of their long-term physical and mental health, and their abilities to obtain and afford quality health care throughout their lives.

A healthy lifestyle can help students reduce their need for health care over the long term. They will soon have to begin choosing health care providers and become aware of their overall health care options. They learn about traditional, alternative, and holistic approaches to medicine, and how to keep an eye out for quackery. Students also learn smart and responsible ways to research and handle their health care options. In addition, an explanation is provided on how their primary doctors and specialists work together to address their needs, as well as how mental health facilities, hospitals, and dental practices operate.

Finally, students learn about the three main types of insurance plans—HMOs, PPOs, and POSs—and reasons for keeping one's coverage. Also, as students learn tips on how to shop for health insurance, they are given a sense of the kinds of devastating expenses that can pile up if one is among the 42 million people—healthy or not—who are currently uninsured in America.

Alabama Citizenship Workbook

# For Discussion

## Review

1. What are the three main types of health insurance plans?

2. What are five useful tips that young people can follow when shopping around for health insurance?

*Teacher Section*

# Activities

1. **Internet: Finding the Right Health Care Plan**

   Have students search the Internet for information on specific HMO, PPO, and POS plans in their region, to determine which would best serve their needs. Either on paper or in class, have them explain why the particular plan, provider, and level of coverage they chose is right for them.

2. **Special Sources: Being an Informed Consumer**

   Have students research for any favorable or unfavorable information about their family's health care plan, insurance provider, local medical facilities, and primary care provider. When they are finished, have them present their findings and describe to the class the level of satisfaction they feel about their "current health care options."

# 27. Making a Home

## Objectives
- evaluating housing needs
- renting v. buying
- house hunting

## Vocabulary

| | | | |
|---|---|---|---|
| amenities | cooperative | finance | multi-family housing |
| closing | condominium | landlord | notice |
| co-housing | default | liable | single-family housing |

## Background

In this chapter, students find our how to determine their housing needs, the difference between renting and buying, and important tips for house hunting. They need to consider whether they want to live alone or with a roommate, and they examine the advantages and disadvantages of both options. Choosing a roommate can be a tricky process also, and students are advised to be careful, no matter how well they know the person. Living with a spouse is another arrangement that students will have to consider someday, and they'll find that it's different than living with a roommate.

When students reach the point where they need to look at different types of housing, they will see a variety of choices, some of which will not suit their needs. Apartments, condominiums, co-ops, co-houses, houses, and low-income housing are some choices students will have. They may find their first situation is an apartment, the most affordable option. Students discover that buying property involves more responsibility and expenses that they probably won't be prepared to take on in early adulthood. Students also learn about government-subsidized housing and Habitat for Humanity, which builds houses for low-income families.

Students explore all of the differences between renting and buying. They get tips on the most efficient way to search for an apartment and on things they must include in their rental agreements, so they aren't held responsible for anything unexpected later. Students learn about the costs involved in renting, as well as about their rights and those of their landlords. Students also learn the advantages and disadvantages of buying property. They find out how to determine how much they can spend, and how to finance a home.

### Further Resources

Burkett, Larry and Strauss, Ed. *The World's Easiest Pocket Guide to Renting Your First Apartment*. Chicago: Northfield Publishers, 2002.

Smith, Marguerite. *Your Dream Home: A Comprehensive Guide to Buying a House, Condo, or Co-op*. Los Angeles, CA: Warner Books, 1991.

# For Discussion

## Review

1. What are the three suggestions for how you can zero in on places that will fit your monthly housing expense?

2. What are the issues you should consider before you pick a roommate?

3. What are the most common types of housing?

4. What are the three important financial factors you will need to consider when purchasing a home?

## Critical Thinking

1. What would your ideal housing situation be? How would it look? What would it cost?

2. Of the housing choices listed on page 238, which sounds the most desirable to you? Why?

3. Of the pros and cons of renting listed on page 242, do you think the pros outweigh the cons? If you had the choice, would you rather own? Why?

# Activities

1. **Looking at Ads**

   Divide students into teams of two. Ask them to go through a couple of newspapers with ads for apartments. Ask them to choose three neighborhoods nearby. What do apartments cost in those neighborhoods? What are they offering? Is location a big factor? What can you get in one neighborhood that you can't get in another? Ask them to bring their findings back to class for a comparison.

2. **Survey Students: What Are Their Plans?**

   Divide students into teams of two. Ask them to survey other students about their future living arrangements. What are they envisioning their living arrangements will be after leaving home? How would they live while going to college, undergoing another kind of training, or working? Would they plan to live alone or with one or more roommates? How do they plan to pay for this? Compare the results in class.

3. **Internet: Buying a House**

   Divide students into teams of two. Give each pair an "income" to work with. Have students figure out (roughly) what price of house they can afford, based on their income level and other expenses. Have them go online, compare real estate sites that offer houses, and find the best house in the neighborhood they want for the price they think they can afford. Have them compare their findings in class.

4. **Special Sources: Library Research on Low-Income Housing**

   Divide students into teams of four. Have them go to the library and research the history of government-supported, low-income housing in the U.S. How and when did it begin? What are its advantages and disadvantages to the government and to the people who live in it? How are taxpayers affected? Have students bring their findings to class for a discussion.

# 28. Getting Around

## Objectives

- the different types of transportation
- how to choose the right mode of transportation
- how to buy a car

## Vocabulary

depreciate

hybrid electric vehicles (HEVs)

lease

lemon laws

manual transmission

mass transit

odometer

options

rebates

standard equipment

sticker price

## Background

In this chapter, students become more informed and better aware of the wide variety of public and personal transportation options available to them. They are taught practical, needs-based approaches on how to choose transportation for themselves and their budgets. This includes how to research and buy new or used automobiles—the most common form of transportation in the U.S.

The first section begins by having students evaluate their transportation needs, with regard to what they can afford. Students are then prompted to evaluate key factors that will help them determine the most suitable means of transportation for themselves. This includes evaluating where they have to go each day, their lifestyles, safety issues, their personal preferences about comfort and convenience, and, of course, cost. They become more aware of the advantages and disadvantages of their transit options, and what is personally important to them and why they commute the way they do.

Students then move on to learn, in detail, about all the various forms of public and personal transportation that are available. They are given in-depth evaluations of the pros and cons of taking subways, trolleys, light rail, buses, and taxis. They become informed about the costs and merits of various bicycle options, motorcycles and electric bikes, cars, and "alternative" forms of transport. These include innovative, inexpensive, and energy-efficient programs involving "free bikes" and carpools.

In the final section, students come to see that the decision to buy and own a car is big one that needs to handled seriously and with wisdom. This purchasing process involves deciding what kind of car they would like, what it would be used for, how much they can afford, and other related concerns. Students then learn key facts and tips about researching and buying new and used cars, which will better help them to determine which type of car to purchase. They take into account the additional costs of options and operating expenses, and finally learn about the pros and cons of buying and leasing.

### Further Resources

Burkett, Larry. *Buying Your First Car*. Chicago: Moody Press, 2000.

Hammer, Heinz. *Routes: The Lighter Side of Public Transit*. Seattle, WA: Gordon Soules Book Publishers, 1989.

# For Discussion

## Review

1. What are four questions to consider when determining how to get to where you need to go?
2. What are eight different kinds of mass transit?
3. What are four private transportation options?
4. What are the Big 10 of auto maintenance?

## Critical Thinking

1. How many personal, practical, and financial benefits can you think of for using a bicycle as your primary means of transportation?
2. How are taxis different from other forms of public transportation? In what circumstances can they be a poor choice?
3. In general, which of the following options appeals to you more: getting exercise by walking to a destination or enjoying the convenience of taking a car? Why?
4. If you worked for a company that offered a carpool or vanpool program, would you participate in it? Why or why not?
5. In the future, do you think electric-powered vehicles like hybrid electric vehicles (HEVs) will become more commonplace? Why or why not?

# Activities

1. **Comparing Modes, Comparing Options**

   Have students evaluate the pros and cons of all the modes of transportation available to them locally for going to and from a place they visit frequently. Ask them to evaluate each option in terms of lifestyle, safety, comfort and convenience, and cost. Discuss any surprising findings or confirmations of their present choices of transportation.

2. **Interview: Talking with My Insurance Agent**

   Have students talk to their family's insurance agent to learn the cost of insuring their family's car or the kind of car they've always wanted to own. Among other things, they should ask about the different kinds of coverage and what kind of financial situation they would face if they got into a car accident. Have them write a report describing what they learned and how this affected their thoughts about owning and insuring a car.

3. **Internet: Getting Informed about Cars Online**

   Divide the class into pairs. Have each team come up with a specific car they like. Then have them go online to learn as much as they can about the car from useful consumer sites for *Kelly Blue Book*, *Consumer Reports*, *Edmund's*, and others. Then have them search for current deals being offered for the car from dealerships, advertisements, and elsewhere. Have them report their findings and impressions of this critical auto research process.

4. **Special Sources: Cars and the Greenhouse Effect**

   Have students, in groups, research the greenhouse effect and how auto use contributes to its development. Assign a different angle of this ongoing concern to each group: specific environmental damage information, how the government and manufacturers are addressing the growing crisis, what Americans are doing to limit its development, and so on.

# 29. How Insurance Can Protect You

## Objectives
- different types of insurance
- how to choose the best insurance for you
- how to keep coverage once it's in place

## Vocabulary

| | | | |
|---|---|---|---|
| assets | financial responsibility laws | life insurance | real property |
| claim | infrastructure | no-fault auto insurance | renter's insurance |
| dependents | insurance policy | personal property | unemployment compensation |
| disability insurance | liability coverage | policy holder | waiting period |

## Background

In this chapter, students learn about the different types of insurance, how to choose the one that's right for their needs, and how to keep coverage once they have it. They discover how insurance works and how to buy it. Students also learn how to protect their assets, car, personal property, or home. Students find that health and life insurance are necessities, and understand the need for disability coverage and natural disaster coverage. Students find that the government has sometimes aided citizens in rebuilding after major natural disasters.

Since students are either at or approaching driving age, the chapter prepares them with facts about their car insurance needs, costs, and requirements, and how to problem-solve if they are denied coverage. Students probably won't find the need for homeowner's insurance, renter's insurance, or personal property insurance at this point, but the chapter equips them for these future concerns by explaining how to evaluate their needs and what the different types of insurance are. Students also learn about life insurance. Students can protect themselves if they become sick or injured by getting disability coverage. Students also find that they're protected by unemployment compensation if they should lose their income. Finally, they learn some tips for maintaining their coverage after purchasing insurance.

### Further Resources

Baldwin, Ben G. *The Complete Book of Insurance: The Consumer's Guide to Insuring Your Life, Health, Property, and Income.* Chicago: Probus Publishing Co., 1996.

Brenner, Lynn, ed., and Taylor, Barbara J. *How to Get Your Money's Worth in Home and Auto Insurance.* Columbus, OH: McGraw-Hill, 1990.

# For Discussion

## Review

1. What are the three important reasons that you should buy insurance carefully?

2. What are the natural disasters that occur?

3. What are the three things that car insurance covers?

4. What three types of insurance are there for protection of possessions and property?

## Critical Thinking

1. What are some items that you own that you could not replace? Look at the tips on page 303. Can you think of any other tips to protect the items you've named?

2. When, if ever, would you feel the need to buy long-term care insurance? Explain.

3. From personal experience or your knowledge of other cases, in the case of a natural disaster, how much of the damage do you think insurance covers?

4. If you bought car insurance for yourself, would you rather have a higher premium or a higher deductible? Why?

5. Of the two types of life insurance, term and cash-value, which would you prefer to have? What are the differences between them?

# Activities

1. **Different Types of Insurance**

   Divide students into teams of five. Have each team choose a type of insurance—health, auto, homeowner's, disability, or life insurance. Have them call one or more insurance agents to get information and costs. Discuss the results in class.

2. **Student Survey: Your Thoughts about Insurance?**

   As a class, prepare a student survey about what students expect to pay for insurance and what they think is offered. Do they believe insurance is necessary? What kinds of insurance do they think are important? Send students out in teams to get answers, and ask them to bring their findings to class for a comparison and compilation.

3. **Internet: Statistics on Car Accidents**

   Divide students into teams of two. Ask them to get on the Internet and find statistics on car accidents. Ask them to investigate what percentage of these accidents are covered by insurance. What are the age groups most prone to accidents? How does that affect that age group's insurance costs? By what are most of the accidents caused? Have them compile their information and bring it to class for a discussion.

4. **Special Sources: Library Research on Natural Disasters in the U.S.**

   Divide students into teams of four. Ask each of them to choose a type of natural disaster or an incident of a natural disaster that has occurred in the U.S. What states seem to have the most of this type of disaster? What insurance coverage is available for these disasters? What percentage of the damage is typically covered? Ask them to bring their findings back to class for a discussion.

# 30. How to Invest for Your Future

## Objectives

- planning for your financial future
- the power of compound Interest
- investing money

## Vocabulary

| | | | |
|---|---|---|---|
| bonds | Individual Retirement Accounts (IRAs) | mutual fund | stock |
| diversification | invest | securities | |

## Background

In this chapter, students learn about planning for their financial futures, about the importance of compound interest, and about investing their money. They discover that long-term planning is the key to smart investing. Students learn of the need to start saving when they're young. There are basic principles that students gain information about, but they must first figure out their goals. The most common goals that students can start thinking about are college, buying a home, and retirement. Students learn about investment tools to save for these, as well as how to develop a strategy for saving effectively.

In the chapter, students read a lot about stocks. They gain information about buying shares of companies—a good way to invest their money, provided they research the companies in which they are investing. They learn how to go through a newspaper's financial pages or watch the stock market channels to gain more information about stocks. They also learn about the different stock exchanges, where stocks are bought and sold. The chapter also introduces students to bonds, another investment tool. They discover that, when they buy stocks, they are buying a share in a company, and that buying bonds is like making a loan. Students learn what corporate and government bonds are and how they compare. Mutual funds are another investment possibility to which students are introduced. Students may be interested to learn that the primary reason to consider mutual funds is diversification.

Students learn that working with a financial advisor may be a good choice if their money grows enough to warrant it. Some students will want to consider retirement investing from the start, so they become acquainted with options such as Individual Retirement Accounts, KEOGH plans, 401(k)'s, stock ownership, company pension plans, and profit sharing.

### Further Resources

Bateman, Katherine. *The Young Investor: Projects and Activities for Making Your Money Grow.* Chicago: Chicago Review Press, 2001.

Gardner, David, et al. *The Motley Fool Investment Guide for Teens: 8 Steps to Having More Money Than Your Parents Ever Dreamed Of.* New York: Fireside Publishing Co., 2002.

# For Discussion

## Review

1. What are the two tips to follow to reap the greatest benefit from compound interest?
2. What are the basic tools for most investors?
3. What are the two major corporations that help investors in bonds?
4. What are the two special types of IRAs?

## Critical Thinking

1. Give an example each of what you consider a conservative investment and what you consider a risky investment. Explain.
2. What are some long-term goals that you have?
3. If you wanted to start saving for a house and retirement right now, which investment tools would you choose to employ? Why?
4. Under what circumstances might a person want to consult with a financial advisor?
5. Would you feel more comfortable with an employer-sponsored savings plan, or with saving on your own? Why?

# Activities

1. **Saving for College**

   Divide students into teams of three. Ask each one to choose a college that they'd like to attend. Have them research the costs of going to that school, including room and board, tuition, books, food, transportation, laundry, and so on. Ask them to total the approximate costs and consult with their parents about when in their lives they should have started saving to pay for that. Have them compare their information with the others in their group and with the class.

2. **Survey Students on Investment Tools**

   Divide students into teams of two. Ask them to survey students around school to determine what they know about investment tools. Have them ask students what stocks, bonds, and mutual funds are, for example. What do they know about them? Have they thought about using them? Have them bring their information back to class for comparison.

3. **Internet: Stock Exchanges**

   Divide students into four groups. Ask each group to choose one of the major stock exchanges: NYSE, NASDAQ, American Stock Exchange, and regional exchanges. Ask them to go online and to research the exchange and how it works. Ask them to bring their findings back to class to compare with those of the other groups.

4. **Special Sources: Stock Markets around the World**

   Ask each student to choose a foreign country to research its investment practices. Do people there invest as they do in the U.S.? Who advises them and manages their money? For what kinds of things do they save their money? What are their priorities? How does their cost of living compare to ours? Compare the results in class.

# Application for Employment

Pre-employment Questionnaire
Equal Opportunity Employer

## Personal Information

Date

| Name (Last Name First) | | Social Security No. | | | |
|---|---|---|---|---|---|
| Present Address | | City | State | Zip Code | |
| Permanent Address | | City | State | Zip Code | |
| Phone No. ( ) | | Referred By | | | |

## Employment Desired

| Position | Date You Can Start | Salary Desired |
|---|---|---|
| Are You Employed? ☐ Yes ☐ No | If So, May We Inquire of Your Present Employer? ☐ Yes ☐ No | |

## Education History

| Name & Location of School | Years Attended | Did You Graduate? | Subjects Studied |
|---|---|---|---|
| Grammar School | | | |
| High School | | | |
| College, Trade, Business or Correspondence School | | | |

## General Information

| Subjects of Special Study/Research Work or Special Training/Skills | |
|---|---|
| U.S. Military or Naval Service | Rank |

## Former Employers (List Below Last Four Employers, Starting with Last One First)

| Date/Month & Year | Name & Address of Employer | Salary | Position | Reason for Leaving |
|---|---|---|---|---|
| From | | | | |
| To | | | | |
| From | | | | |
| To | | | | |
| From | | | | |
| To | | | | |

## Reference
Give Below the Names of Three Persons Not Related to You, Whom You Have Known at Least One Year

| Name | Address | Business | Years Known |
|---|---|---|---|
| | | | |
| | | | |
| | | | |

Date _____ Signature _____

## Monthly Budget

### Income

| Gross Income: $ | Net Income: $ |

### Expenses

| | |
|---|---|
| Housing | $ |
| Utilities | $ |
| Transportation | $ |
| ∗ Monthly payment | $ |
| ∗ Insurance ($^1/_{12}$ annual cost) | $ |
| ∗ Gas | $ |
| ∗ Maintenance/repairs | $ |
| Food | $ |
| Phone | $ |
| Clothes | $ |
| Debt (student loan, credit cards) | $ |
| Health care (insurance, copays) | $ |
| Savings | $ |
| Emergency fund | $ |
| Household supplies | $ |
| Charitable donations | $ |
| Entertainment | $ |
| Miscellaneous | $ |
| **Total Expenses** | $ |

## Check Front & Back

Alabama Citizenship Workbook

# Check Register

| TRANS. TYPE / CHECK NO. | DATE | DESCRIPTION OF TRANSACTION | PAYMENT / DEBIT(-) | FEES(-) | DEPOSITS / CREDITS(+) | $ BALANCE |
|---|---|---|---|---|---|---|
| | | | | | | |
| | | | | | | |
| | | | | | | |
| | | | | | | |
| | | | | | | |
| | | | | | | |
| | | | | | | |
| | | | | | | |
| | | | | | | |
| | | | | | | |

| TRANS. TYPE / CHECK NO. | DATE | DESCRIPTION OF TRANSACTION | PAYMENT / DEBIT(-) | FEES(-) | DEPOSITS / CREDITS(+) | $ BALANCE |
|---|---|---|---|---|---|---|
| | | | | | | |
| | | | | | | |
| | | | | | | |
| | | | | | | |
| | | | | | | |
| | | | | | | |
| | | | | | | |
| | | | | | | |
| | | | | | | |
| | | | | | | |

# Grocery List

| Category | Item | Cost |
|---|---|---|
| Bread, Rice, Pasta, Noodles, Cereal | | |
| Vegetables | | |
| Fruit | | |
| Milk, Eggs, Cheese | | |
| Meat and Seafood | | |
| Beverages | | |
| Snacks, Desserts, and Other Items | | |

Alabama Citizenship Workbook

Name _____

# 1. American Citizenship

**As you read Chapter 1, write an answer to each question below.**

1. In what sense is citizenship in the United States a contract? Explain.

   _____

   _____

   _____

2. Which form of government would you prefer to live under, a monarchy or a dictatorship? Why?

   _____

   _____

   _____

3. What is the "American Dream"? What does it mean to you and to most citizens of the U.S.?

   _____

   _____

   _____

4. In what respect is America becoming more and more diverse? Which image do you think most accurately captures this diversity, a "melting pot," a "salad bowl," or a "mosaic"? Why?

   _____

   _____

   _____

5. What kinds of duties are individuals expected to fulfill as citizens of the U.S.? What responsibilities are we expected to meet?

   _____

   _____

Alabama Citizenship Workbook 1

Name _____

# 1. American Citizenship

Circle the best answer for each item.

1. What is something that cannot be taken away by people or government, such as natural rights?
   a. negotiable
   b. inalienable
   c. mediate
   d. compromise

2. What is a state of political power resulting from the absence of government?
   a. liberty
   b. anarchy
   c. chivalry
   d. civility

3. What is a group of ordinary citizens chosen to decide the guilt or innocence of the person accused in a trial?
   a. jury
   b. trial
   c. party
   d. society

4. What is the term for a person who owes allegiance to a government and who is entitled to government protection?
   a. steward
   b. officer
   c. immigrant
   d. citizen

5. What is the social science dealing with the rights and duties of citizens?
   a. psychology
   b. philosophy
   c. civics
   d. ethics

6. What is a government in which power is held by the people and exercised either directly or through representation, usually determined by elections?
   a. democracy
   b. dictatorship
   c. monarchy
   d. anarchy

7. What is a government in which the ruler is a hereditary head of state who rules for life?
   a. democracy
   b. dictatorship
   c. monarchy
   d. anarchy

8. What is a sudden, violent overthrow of a government by a small group?
   a. siege
   b. seizure
   c. treaty
   d. coup

9. What is the term to admit or grant citizenship to someone who was born in another country?
   a. transform
   b. incorporate
   c. relinquish
   d. naturalize

10. What is a voluntary association of people bound together by common interests and standards?
    a. society
    b. system
    c. delegate
    d. representative

Name _____

# 1. American Citizenship

**Read each description, and write the letter of the correct term on the line.**

1. The Pledge of Allegiance is _____.
   a. an official oath or statement of loyalty
   b. a spoken contract made by the U.S. government to new immigrants
   c. a promise by the U.S. government to uphold the rights of its citizens
   d. a promise of payment for an overdue debt

2. One of the requirements of the naturalization process is to _____.
   a. be a native-born citizen of the U.S.
   b. be a foreign-born child of a U.S. citizen
   c. establish proof of residency, and active employment of at least five years with the INS
   d. complete an interview and oral exam on the U.S. government and history, as given by the INS

3. The most important job of government is to _____.
   a. protect the people
   b. provide order in society
   c. provide public services
   d. maintain key service institutions

4. Establishing schools, jails, and hospitals is part of the government's responsibility to _____.
   a. protect the people
   b. provide order in society
   c. provide public services
   d. maintain key service institutions

5. The form of government that is usually established after a coup is _____.
   a. a monarchy
   b. a dictatorship
   c. a democracy
   d. an oligarchy

6. From 1820 to 1930, the U.S. received about _____ of the world's immigrants.
   a. 10 percent        c. 60 percent
   b. 30 percent        d. 90 percent

7. The number of _____ in the U.S. rose nearly 13 million, or 53 percent, from 1990 to 2000.
   a. whites            c. Asians
   b. African-Americans d. Hispanics

8. The American government was established and built upon the theory of natural rights, which holds that the natural rights of people _____.
   a. come from themselves as human beings
   b. are given to them by their government
   c. come from nature or God
   d. must be earned through public service

9. Citizens with religious objections are sometimes exempted by the U.S. government from _____.
   a. obeying laws
   b. defending the nation
   c. paying taxes
   d. attending school

10. Each of the following is among the responsibilities of U.S. citizens EXCEPT _____.
    a. voting
    b. protecting each other's rights
    c. giving to charity
    d. helping to make society better

## Essay Question

As compared to the "contract of citizenship," how would you rate or grade yourself as a citizen? Why? In what ways could you improve your contribution to society by becoming a better and more loyal citizen?

Name _____

# Immigration and Urban Distribution

**Alabama Planner**
Citizenship Course of Study
9.c, 6.b

Learning Objectives:
- Interpreting an immigration map
- Analyzing the distribution of urban areas to determine how they are linked together

Circle the best answer for each item.

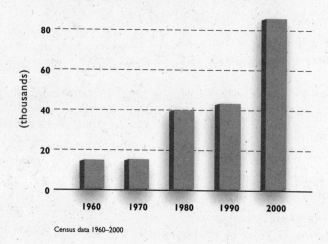

Alabama ranked 13th nationally in the rate of foreign-born change between 1960–2000.

1. According to the graph, which decade indicates the largest increase in Alabama's immigrant population?

   a. 1960–1970
   b. 1970–1980
   c. 1980–1990
   d. 1990–2000

2. What was the immigrant population growth in Alabama by 1980?

   a. 18,000 people
   b. 19,000 people
   c. 40,000 people
   d. 42,000 people

4  Alabama Citizenship Workbook

## Alabama Foreign-Born Population 1960–2000

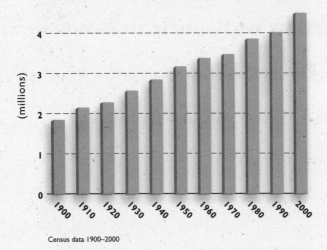

Census data 1900–2000

**Alabama had the 29th highest rate of population increase in the country between 1960–2000.**

3. Alabama's highest rate of population increase was between which of the following years?

   a. Between 1900 to 1920
   b. Between 1920 to 1940
   c. Between 1940 to 1960
   d. Between 1960 to 2000

Use the Census 2000 pie graph on page 9 of your *Civics in America* book to answer questions 4 and 5.

4. What is the main idea of this graph?

   a. America consists of only one race.
   b. The people of the United States are a "melting pot" of many nations and cultures.
   c. Diversity weakens America as a nation.
   c. Immigrants must give up their own cultures to be a part of American culture.

5. What is the largest racial group in United States?

   a. American Indian and Alaska Native
   b. Asian
   c. White
   d. Native Hawaiian

Name _____

# 2. The Foundations of American Government

**As you read Chapter 2, write an answer to each question below.**

1. What is the difference between a direct democracy and a republic?

   _____

   _____

   _____

2. What are some of the advantages of a republic? Explain.

   _____

   _____

   _____

3. How did the Mayflower Compact and the House of Burgesses influence the founders in writing the U.S. Constitution?

   _____

   _____

   _____

4. In what ways did the colonist react to the passing of unfair British laws like the Stamp Act?

   _____

   _____

   _____

5. What were the three main parts of the Declaration of Independence?

   _____

   _____

   _____

Name _____

## 2. The Foundations of American Government

Find the best answer for each item. Then circle that answer.

1. What is the term for the authority granted to an organization, such as a colony, to operate?
   a. legislature
   b. republic
   c. chapter
   d. charter

2. What is a form of government run by elected representatives that does not have a king or queen?
   a. monarchy
   b. republic
   c. dictatorship
   d. direct democracy

3. What is the term for the power of a government to make decisions for itself within its own territory or jurisdiction with freedom from foreign control?
   a. sovereignty
   b. unicameral
   c. due process
   d. habeas corpus

4. What is an alliance or loose union of independent states?
   a. association
   b. confederation
   c. organization
   d. affiliation

5. Which term describes the right of an arrested person to be brought before a judge who determines whether his or her imprisonment is legal?
   a. libel
   b. due process
   c. ex post facto
   d. habeas corpus

6. What is the branch of U.S. government that makes laws?
   a. executive
   b. legislature
   c. judicial
   d. parliament

7. What is a written or published statement that damages another person's reputation?
   a. bail
   b. treaty
   c. libel
   d. summons

8. What was the name for the plan for governing the Pilgrim colony, also considered America's "first written constitution"?
   a. Mayflower Compact
   b. Articles of Confederation
   c. Intolerable Acts
   d. Stamp Act

9. What is the right or power to prevent a bill that has passed the legislature from becoming law?
   a. libel
   b. verdict
   c. repeal
   d. veto

10. What is the act of a governing body to withdraw or cancel an existing law?
    a. confirm
    b. impeach
    c. repeal
    d. veto

Alabama Citizenship Workbook

Name _____

## 2. The Foundations of American Government

**Read each description, and write the letter of the correct term on the line.**

1. The first people to develop a democracy were the
   a. ancient Greeks
   b. ancient Romans
   c. British
   d. Americans

2. A _____ is a system of government where citizens have the ability to run for election and become law-making representatives.
   a. monarchy
   b. dictatorship
   c. republic
   d. direct democracy

3. The _____ established due process of law in England, or the right of an accused person to a trial.
   a. Magna Carta of 1215
   b. English Bill or Rights in 1689
   c. unwritten constitution
   d. use of common law

4. The English Bill of Rights of 1689 _____.
   a. gave the king more power to rule the country
   b. gave members or Parliament the right to speak and debate freely without punishment
   c. gave citizens the right to elect a ruler
   d. established the Habeas Corpus Act

5. At the time of the Revolution, the colonies had each of these elements of government EXCEPT a _____.
   a. charter that established the colony
   b. Bill of Rights for the citizenry
   c. legislature to make laws
   d. governor to represent the king

6. Roger Williams was driven out of _____ by the Puritans for fighting for religious freedom.
   a. Massachusetts
   b. Rhode Island
   c. New York
   d. Virginia

7. The Intolerable Acts were imposed on the colonies after _____.
   a. protests broke out in the colonies over the Stamp Act in 1765
   b. the Boston Tea Party dumped English tea in Boston Harbor in 1773
   c. the Second Continental Congress gathered in 1775
   d. Thomas Paine published *Common Sense* calling for colonial rebellion against British rule

8. The delegate chosen to write the Declaration of Independence was _____.
   a. John Adams
   b. Thomas Paine
   c. Richard Lee
   d. Thomas Jefferson

9. _____ was an Enlightenment philosopher who asserted that people have certain "natural rights."
   a. Thomas Hobbes
   b. John Locke
   c. Daniel Shay
   d. Thomas Jefferson

10. The main problem with the Articles of Confederation was that it created a _____.
    a. strong central government
    b. weak central government
    c. strong national currency
    d. weak national military

**Essay Question**

If you were a colonist fighting for America's independence, what ideas, values, or principles do you want your new government to be founded on? Why?

Name _____

# The Influence of John Locke

**Alabama Planner**
Citizenship Course of Study
1.b

Learning Objectives:
- Describing the influence of John Locke

AHSGE: II.1

The most important influence on ideas of the Founding Fathers of United States government came from the writings of political philosophers such as John Locke (1632–1704). Locke saw society as a collection of individuals. He believed each person has the basic right to pursue interests in order to improve his or her life. Locke said all people are born with the following individual rights:

**Life.** People want to live freely without threats to their security or possessions.

**Liberty.** People want to make their own decisions and live as they please.

**Property.** People want to work and be free to own land, things, and money.

Locke felt that these ideas of natural rights were unalienable, that is, they are a part of human nature and cannot be taken away or given up. Today in the United States these are considered natural rights and any citizen has the right to defend them if anyone threatens to take them away. Locke's ideas were so important that Thomas Jefferson included them in the Declaration of Independence.

## Short Answer Question:

How did the ideas of John Locke influence the Founding Fathers in planning the United States government?

_____
_____
_____
_____
_____

Name _____

# 3. The Constitution

**As you read Chapter 3, write an answer to each question below.**

1. In what ways were the Virginia Plan and New Jersey Plan of the Constitutional Convention different?
   _____
   _____
   _____

2. What were the key measures that made up the Great Compromise?
   _____
   _____
   _____

3. How did the basic government principles of the Constitution help to empower the people and prevent any group in government from becoming too powerful?
   _____
   _____
   _____

4. In general terms, what are the seven Articles of the U.S. Constitution?
   _____
   _____
   _____

5. What are the two ways a Constitutional amendment can be proposed? What are the two ways that states can ratify amendments?
   _____
   _____
   _____

Name _____

# 3. The Constitution

**Find the best answer for each item. Then circle that answer.**

1. What is the term for an official representative of some larger group or body, like a state assembly?
   a. loyalist
   b. delegate
   c. nationalist
   d. confederationist

2. What is the system of government in which power is shared between the central government and the state governments?
   a. federalism
   b. nationalism
   c. representation
   d. sovereignty

3. What is a formal meeting of a group for a particular purpose?
   a. constitution
   b. ratification
   c. legislation
   d. convention

4. Which part of the U.S. government interprets the laws through its decisions in legal cases?
   a. executive
   b. legislative
   c. judicial
   d. parliament

5. Which of the following terms means to officially approve?
   a. ratify
   b. clarify
   c. repeal
   d. amend

6. What is the name of the introductory part of the Constitution?
   a. Preface
   b. Preamble
   c. Prologue
   d. Preview

7. What is a change or addition to a document or plan, such as the Constitution?
   a. stipend
   b. amendment
   c. annulment
   d. arraignment

8. What is the term to describe the consent of the governed or the power to govern that comes from the people?
   a. due process
   b. checks and balances
   c. popular sovereignty
   d. proportional representation

9. Which of the following plans was presented by Edmond Randolph at the Constitutional Convention and provided a basis for the Constitution?
   a. Preamble
   b. Bill of Rights
   c. New Jersey Plan
   d. Virginia Plan

10. Who were opponents of the central government, as defined in the Constitution?
    a. delegates
    b. nationalists
    c. Federalists
    d. Anti-Federalists

Alabama Citizenship Workbook

Name _____

# 3. The Constitution

**Read each description, and write the letter of the correct term on the line.**

1. The Founding Fathers were those who _____.
   a. formed the first Continental Congress
   b. wrote the Declaration of Independence
   c. wrote the Articles of Confederation
   d. wrote the U.S. Constitution

2. _____ was elected to lead the Constitutional Convention of 1787.
   a. George Washington
   b. Thomas Jefferson
   c. James Madison
   d. Benjamin Franklin

3. James Madison earned the title of "Father of the Constitution" for writing the _____.
   a. Preamble
   b. Bill of Rights
   c. Virginia Plan
   d. New Jersey Plan

4. _____ proposed the Great Compromise that enabled the Constitution to be ratified.
   a. James Wilson
   b. Roger Sherman
   c. John Marshall
   d. Alexander Hamilton

5. As part of the convention's compromise over commerce, it was agreed that _____.
   a. Congress could only regulate foreign trade
   b. states could only regulate their foreign trade
   c. only states could regulate their own commerce
   d. Congress had the power to regulate commerce for all states

6. According to the Constitution, _____ would elect the president of the United States.
   a. Congress
   b. the voting public
   c. the Supreme Court
   d. the Electoral College

7. The *Federalist Papers* sought to _____.
   a. uphold the Articles of Confederation
   b. base the Constitution on the New Jersey Plan
   c. persuade Anti-Federalists to ratify the Constitution
   d. persuade Federalists to ratify the Constitution

8. Under the Constitution, both national and state governments had the power to _____.
   a. collect taxes
   b. coin and print money
   c. conduct elections
   d. establish a postal system

9. Under the federal government's system of checks and balances, the legislative branch is able to _____.
   a. appoint federal judges to the judicial branch
   b. declare executive actions unconstitutional
   c. impeach or remove the president
   d. grant pardons to federal offenders

10. _____ of the Constitution allows for the Constitution to take on future amendments or changes.
    a. Article I
    b. Article III
    c. Article V
    d. Article VII

**Essay Question**

How successful do you think the Founding Fathers were in creating the U.S. Constitution, as a plan of government, in 1787? Why? What aspects of the document stand out to you? Explain.

Name _____

# 4. Bill of Rights

**As you read Chapter 4, write an answer to each question below.**

1. What kinds of basic of rights and freedoms were ensured under the Virginia Declaration of Rights of 1776?
   _____
   _____
   _____

2. In what sense does the success of our democracy depend on the Bill of Rights?
   _____
   _____
   _____

3. What are some of the limits of the First Amendment right to free speech, as determined by the Supreme Court?
   _____
   _____
   _____

4. Under the Fourth Amendment, or the "Privacy Amendment," authorities are prohibited from taking what actions?
   _____
   _____
   _____

5. What is the Ninth Amendment, and what kinds of rights are people guaranteed under it?
   _____
   _____

# 4. Bill of Rights

Find the best answer for each item. Then circle that answer.

1. What is the right of the government to take private property for public use?
   a. due process
   b. probable cause
   c. double jeopardy
   d. eminent domain

2. What is the condition of being tried a second time for the same crime?
   a. due process
   b. probable cause
   c. double jeopardy
   d. eminent domain

3. Which term means to make a person appear guilty of a crime?
   a. incriminate
   b. indictment
   c. intimidate
   d. incarcerate

4. What is a formal laying of charges leading to a trial?
   a. incriminate
   b. indictment
   c. intimidate
   d. incarcerate

5. What is it to make a formal request of an authority?
   a. petition
   b. plea
   c. refute
   d. attain

6. What is the act of telling lies to damage someone's reputation?
   a. treason
   b. slander
   c. fraud
   d. extortion

7. What is the crime of endangering the country by giving information to or helping the enemy?
   a. extortion
   b. slander
   c. fraud
   d. treason

8. What is a legal document issued by a judge authorizing actions such as search, seizure, or arrest?
   a. contract
   b. invoice
   c. warrant
   d. petition

9. Which of the following terms describes the grounds for a reasonable person to believe that a crime may have been committed?
   a. double jeopardy
   b. impartial jury
   c. eminent domain
   d. probable cause

10. Which term describes an army of citizens who are not professional soldiers and who may be called for service in times of emergency?
    a. committee
    b. convention
    c. cartel
    d. militia

Name _____

# 4. Bill of Rights

**Read each description, and write the letter of the correct term on the line.**

1. Some American leaders in the 18th century agreed to ratify the Constitution only if _____.
   a. the Constitution was revised
   b. a "bill of rights" was added
   c. the British acknowledged past civil rights abuses
   d. America first defeated Britain in the Revolution

2. To address the concerns of most people about the Constitution, the First Congress of the U.S. ratified _____ amendments, known as the Bill of Rights.
   a. 10     c. 12
   b. 11     d. 13

3. In the First Amendment, the right to express one's ideas without fear of punishment is _____.
   a. freedom of speech     c. freedom of petition
   b. freedom of the press  d. freedom of assembly

4. Under the First Amendment, the government is allowed to _____.
   a. establish a state religion
   b. ban peaceful public protests
   c. decide the time and location of protests
   d. ban offensive books and other materials

5. All Americans who seek to improve public laws have the right to petition the government _____.
   a. through their employers
   b. through their representatives
   c. through the President
   d. through the Supreme Court

6. The Second Amendment's right to bear arms was originally established to _____.
   a. secure people's rights to hunt
   b. secure people's rights to protect themselves
   c. legally arm police and the military
   d. support militias that protected America during the Revolution

7. Under the Fourth Amendment, law officers are allowed to perform search and seizures _____.
   a. whenever they desire
   b. only when the person gives permission
   c. when there is probable cause
   d. when they request a search or arrest warrant

8. Under the Fifth Amendment, a person accused of a crime can _____.
   a. have property taken away without due process of law
   b. be forced to testify against himself
   c. be put on trial with little or no evidence
   d. not be put on trial again if found not guilty

9. The Sixth Amendment _____.
   a. guarantees an accused person the right to a speedy trial by an impartial jury
   b. guarantees citizens the right to a trial by jury in civil cases
   c. declares that people have rights beyond those mentioned in the Constitution
   d. stops the U.S. government from taking more power than the Constitution gives it

10. The _____ protects accused persons against excessive bail and cruel and unusual punishment.
    a. First Amendment     c. Eighth Amendment
    b. Fifth Amendment     d. Tenth Amendment

**Essay Question**

What does the Bill of Rights mean to you? Support your answer.

Alabama Citizenship Workbook

Name _____

## 5. The Living Constitution

**As you read Chapter 5, write an answer to each question below.**

1. What are five important changes or amendments the Constitution has needed since its passing in 1787?
   _____
   _____
   _____

2. How did the Northwest Ordinance, Missouri Compromise, and Dred Scott decision affect the state of slavery in America in the late 18th and early 19th centuries?
   _____
   _____
   _____

3. What impact did the Thirteenth, Fourteenth, and Fifteenth Amendments to the Constitution have in changing slavery in America?
   _____
   _____
   _____

4. To what extent did women have to go to gain the right to vote in America? Support your answer.
   _____
   _____
   _____

5. What were some of the significant events of the civil rights movement?
   _____
   _____
   _____

Name _____

# 5. The Living Constitution

**Find the best answer for each item. Then circle that answer.**

1. Who were the people that worked for women's right to vote?
   a. suffragists
   b. abolitionists
   c. nationalists
   d. confederationists

2. Who were the people who worked to end slavery?
   a. suffragists
   b. abolitionists
   c. Federalists
   d. Anti-federalists

3. What is the policy that forces the separation of one group of people from another, based on race, sex, religion, or other similar characteristic?
   a. prohibition
   b. suffrage
   c. abstinence
   d. segregation

4. Which term describes the formal withdrawal from a group or organization, such as the Confederate states' withdrawal from the Union in 1861?
   a. deride
   b. expel
   c. secede
   d. recede

5. Which of the following is defined as a regulation or law?
   a. ordinance
   b. proposition
   c. exposition
   d. ratification

6. What is a fee paid in order to vote?
   a. tip
   b. toll
   c. poll tax
   d. excise tax

7. What is the term for the policies and efforts made to improve opportunities for minority groups?
   a. segregation
   b. affirmative action
   c. reverse discrimination
   d. racial profiling

8. What is the act or process of treating people of one group differently because of race, religion, or any factor not based on individual merit?
   a. mediation
   b. indoctrination
   c. discrimination
   d. emancipation

9. What term is used to describe the making of generalizations based on skin color or ethnicity in policing or security work?
   a. surveillance
   b. interrogation
   c. criminal profiling
   d. racial profiling

10. What are rules about the number or proportion of people admitted to an organization, school, company, or country?
    a. equity
    b. shares
    c. quota
    d. inventory

Alabama Citizenship Workbook

Name _____

# 5. The Living Constitution

**Read each description, and write the letter of the correct term on the line.**

1. The founders made the Constitution a living document when they _____.
   a. issued it as the law of the land
   b. revoked the Articles of Confederation
   c. created the Bill of Rights
   d. created Article V

2. Each of the following is among the amendments that have been added to the Bill of Rights, EXCEPT _____.
   a. right to bear arms
   b. abolition of slavery
   c. women's right to vote
   d. two-term limits for presidents

3. The founders did not address the issue of slavery in the Constitution or Bill of Rights because _____.
   a. they felt the issue of slavery should be ignored
   b. they felt slavery was critical to the nation's growing economy
   c. they strongly supported slavery
   d. they wanted Southern states to join the Union

4. _____ proposed the Missouri Compromise in 1820.
   a. Abraham Lincoln
   b. Henry Clay
   c. Thomas Paine
   d. Frederick Douglass

5. Abraham Lincoln issued the Emancipation Proclamation _____.
   a. after the Supreme Court's Dred Scott decision
   b. before the Civil War
   c. during the Civil War
   d. after the Civil War

6. The _____ allowed for the direct election of senators by the people.
   a. 17th Amendment     c. 21st Amendment
   b. 19th Amendment     d. 23rd Amendment

7. The Seneca Falls Declaration of 1848 _____.
   a. condemned slavery and sought its abolition
   b. cited how many states ignored new laws that helped former slaves
   c. fought for the elimination of poll taxes
   d. sought women's voting rights and equality between men and women

8. The Twenty-fourth Amendment eliminating poll taxes was credited to the work of the _____.
   a. suffragist movement
   b. Civil Rights movement
   c. Prohibition movement
   d. abolitionist movement

9. Baby Boomers and soldiers in Vietnam helped in passing the Twenty-sixth Amendment, which lowered the _____.
   a. drinking age to 21     c. voting age to 21
   b. drinking age to 18     d. voting age to 18

10. Some white people feel they have suffered from _____ when overlooked by public or private affirmative action policies.
    a. reverse discrimination     c. emancipation
    b. racial profiling           d. segregation

**Essay Question**

As with America's abolitionists, suffragists, and civil rights protesters, why do you think it takes many years of hard work and considerable sacrifices to get new constitutional amendments passed?

18  Alabama Citizenship Workbook

Name _____

# 6. The Legislative Branch

**As you read Chapter 6, write an answer to each question below.**

1. What are some basic differences between the House of Representatives and Senate with respect to the duties, terms, and qualifications?

   _____
   _____
   _____

2. Do the House of Representatives and Senate operate in the same way? Why or why not? Explain.

   _____
   _____
   _____

3. Describe the basic leadership structure of the House of Representatives and Senate.

   _____
   _____
   _____

4. What is the difference between the expressed and implied legislative powers of Congress? Support your answer.

   _____
   _____
   _____

5. Describe the kind of sequence a bill would need to go through in order to become a law.

   _____
   _____

Name _____

# 6. The Legislative Branch

**Find the best answer for each item. Then circle that answer.**

1. Which term describes that which is composed of two legislative chambers?
   a. unicameral
   b. bicameral
   c. trilateral
   d. quadrilateral

2. What is a proposed law presented for approval to a legislative body?
   a. subpoena
   b. plea
   c. bill
   d. veto

3. What is a legislative act making a person guilty of a crime without trial?
   a. ex post facto law
   b. bill of attainder
   c. writ of habeas corpus
   d. Elastic Clause

4. What is a law that affects an act done in the past, effectively allowing the government to punish a person for committing an act before the act is illegal?
   a. ex post facto law
   b. bill of attainder
   c. writ of habeas corpus
   d. Elastic Clause

5. What is a group of House and Senate members who investigate issues related to legislation but have no power to draft legislation?
   a. standing committee
   b. joint committee
   c. select committee
   d. conference committee

6. What is a group of House or Senate members who work to reconcile different versions of the same bill passed by the House and Senate?
   a. standing committee
   b. joint committee
   c. select committee
   d. conference committee

7. Who is the member of the majority party elected to lead the U.S. House of Representatives?
   a. Speaker of the House
   b. president pro tempore
   c. floor leader
   d. whip

8. What is the title for a senator who presides over the U.S. Senate in the absence of the vice president?
   a. Speaker of the House
   b. president pro tempore
   c. floor leader
   d. whip

9. What is the term for a member of a legislative body who helps the party leader by encouraging party members' loyalty and support?
   a. floor leader      c. lobbyist
   b. whip              d. staff

10. What is the part of Article I, Section 8, of the Constitution that gives Congress the power to make laws necessary to carry out its duties?
    a. ex post facto law
    b. bill of attainder
    c. writ of habeas corpus
    d. Elastic Clause

Name _____

# 6. The Legislative Branch

**Read each description, and write the letter of the correct term on the line.**

1. Under the Constitution, Congress derives its power from _____.
   a. God
   b. the people
   c. the president
   d. the Supreme Court

2. The Congress is divided into two chambers that share power and provide a system _____.
   a. to protect the people from foreign invasion
   b. of lawmaking that empowers the president
   c. of checks and balances against abuses of power
   d. of control between federal and state legislatures

3. Each of the following is among the five delegates to the House of Representatives, EXCEPT a _____.
   a. representative from the District of Columbia
   b. representative from Alaska
   c. commissioner from Puerto Rico
   d. representative from American Samoa

4. The founders gave Senators longer terms in office in order to _____.
   a. limit the number of federal elections to be held
   b. better secure the legislative branch of the nation
   c. ensure they stay in active contact with the people they represent
   d. provide senators with more independence and stability

5. The majority party in the House of Representatives _____.
   a. usually has more power to pass laws and set priorities
   b. can pass laws without the consent of the minority party
   c. automatically assumes the power of the members of the minority party
   d. represents the second greatest number of members in the House

6. The _____ is the leader of the Senate.
   a. Speaker of the House
   b. president pro tempore
   c. president
   d. vice president

7. If the president or vice president is unable to serve because of death or sickness, the _____ takes over until new elections are held.
   a. Speaker of the House
   b. president pro tempore
   c. majority leader of the Senate
   d. majority leader of the House

8. Congress forms a _____ when both houses pass different versions of the same bill.
   a. standing committee
   b. joint committee
   c. select committee
   d. conference committee

9. The Constitution empowers _____ to impeach government officials in cases of wrongdoing.
   a. the Senate
   b. the Supreme Court
   c. the House of Representatives
   d. both the Senate and House of Representatives

10. Committees that receive and study bills can do each of the following, EXCEPT _____.
    a. rewrite the bill
    b. request presidential approval for the bill
    c. ignore or "kill" the bill
    d. make not changes to the bill

**Essay Question**

If you could introduce a bill to Congress through your representative, what would it be? How do you think it would perform in Congress's system for considering bills and making them into laws? Why?

Alabama Citizenship Workbook

# 7. The Executive Branch

As you read Chapter 7, write an answer to each question below.

1. What are the characteristics of a bureaucracy?

2. What are the four different presidential powers?

3. In the past, what are some situations that caused a president to claim executive privilege? Under what circumstances would it not apply?

4. Which are listed as among the most important executive agencies?

5. What are the different responsibilities of the Department of the Treasury?

Name _____

# 7. The Executive Branch

**Find the best answer for each item. Then circle that answer.**

1. What is the name of the group of top advisors to the president? It includes the heads of the executive departments and other officers the president may choose.
   a. bureaucrats
   b. civil service employees
   c. Cabinet
   d. diplomats

2. What is the term for all of the people working within the bureaucracy of the government?
   a. diplomats
   b. civil service
   c. Cabinet
   d. ambassadors

3. What is the name of a person who works with leaders of other nations to carry out U.S. foreign policy?
   a. diplomat
   b. Cabinet member
   c. bureaucrat
   d. civil service employee

4. What is the name for taxes on goods entering the country?
   a. regulator
   b. commission
   c. duties
   d. pension

5. Who are a group of people chosen from each state and the District of Columbia to elect the president and vice president?
   a. Electoral College
   b. Cabinet
   c. civil service
   d. diplomats

6. What is the term for the right of a president to keep information secret from Congress in order to protect the nation's security?
   a. presidential succession
   b. pardon
   c. regulator
   d. executive privilege

7. What is the plan for how the United States will deal with foreign countries?
   a. foreign policy
   b. ambassador policy
   c. diplomat policy
   d. amnesty

8. What is the plan for what happens if the president dies or can't perform the duties of the office?
   a. executive privilege
   b. presidential succession
   c. amnesty
   d. president's privilege policy

9. What is the term for the business world outside the government?
   a. bureaucracy
   b. civil service
   c. private sector
   d. civil sector

10. What is the term that describes a pardon issued to a group of people who have broken the law?
    a. diplomat
    b. regulator
    c. licensing
    d. amnesty

Alabama Citizenship Workbook 23

Name _____

# 7. The Executive Branch

**Read each description, and write the letter of the correct term on the line.**

1. The _____ appoints the top-level managers in bureaucracies.
   a. president
   b. House of Representatives
   c. Senate
   d. vice president

2. In January 2001, Congress voted to raise the salary of the president from _____ to _____ per year.
   a. $50,000/$100,000
   b. $200,000/$400,000
   c. $125,000/$225,000
   d. $175,000/$375,000

3. The term of the presidency is _____.
   a. three years
   b. two years
   c. five years
   d. four years

4. _____ can stop the office of the president from becoming too powerful.
   a. The Secret Service
   b. Congress or the Supreme Court
   c. The vice president
   d. The secretary of state

5. The _____ must approve the heads of the Cabinet departments.
   a. Supreme Court
   b. Speaker of the House
   c. Senate
   d. vice president

6. The Supreme Court has agreed that power over foreign policy belongs to _____.
   a. the president only
   b. Congress only
   c. the president and Congress
   d. the secretary of state

7. The _____ has the power to approve treaties.
   a. vice president
   b. House of Representatives
   c. secretary of state
   d. Senate

8. The president heads a branch of the government with more than _____ employees.
   a. 3 million
   b. 9 million
   c. 8 million
   d. 10 million

9. The _____ advises on domestic, foreign, and military policies that affect the nation's security.
   a. Office of Management and Budget
   b. Department of Defense
   c. National Security Council
   d. Department of Justice

10. The _____ do the major work of running the government.
    a. Senate and the House of Representatives
    b. 14 executive departments
    c. Secretary of Defense and the Senate
    d. Supreme Court and Congress

**Essay Question**

Considering all of the roles and responsibilities of the president, why do you think the government is set up to have only one person in charge? What would be the negative and positive aspects of having more people in charge?

Name _____

# 8. The Judicial Branch

**As you read Chapter 8, write an answer to each question below.**

1. What is the difference between the roles that Congress, the president, the executive branch, and the federal courts have in relation to the law?

   _____
   _____
   _____

2. What is the process by which the judiciary is checked by the executive and legislative branches?

   _____
   _____
   _____

3. How does the appeals process work?

   _____
   _____
   _____

4. What is the "Rule of Four"?

   _____
   _____
   _____

5. What are the two opposite interpretations of a justice's role in the Supreme Court?

   _____
   _____

# 8. The Judicial Branch

**Find the best answer for each item. Then circle that answer.**

1. What is the term for the authority of a court to review the judgment of a lower court?
   a. concurring opinion
   b. concurrent jurisdiction
   c. appellate jurisdiction
   d. original jurisdiction

2. What are the federal courts that conduct trials of cases that have not previously been heard?
   a. district courts
   b. appeals courts
   c. appellate courts
   d. local appeals courts

3. What is a formal charge of an official of a crime or corruption?
   a. exclusive jurisdiction
   b. rule of four
   c. jurisdiction
   d. impeachment

4. What is the manner in which a judge applies the law based on the belief that the court can create new policy?
   a. judicial restraint
   b. judicial activism
   c. Rule of Four
   d. original jurisdiction

5. What is the constitutional provision for courts to decide if acts of the government are constitutional?
   a. judicial restraint
   b. exclusive jurisdiction
   c. judicial review
   d. dissenting opinion

6. What is the term that means system of courts of law or judicial branch of government?
   a. judiciary
   b. magistrate
   c. original jurisdiction
   d. jurisdiction

7. What is the area of power or authority of a court to hear a particular case or type of case?
   a. judiciary
   b. special court
   c. judicial review
   d. jurisdiction

8. What is the term for an officer of a district court who handles many of the duties of the district court's judge?
   a. magistrate
   b. judiciary assistant
   c. bailiff
   d. marshal

9. What are the specific punishments required for certain crimes?
   a. nonmandatory consequences
   b. mandatory sentences
   c. impeachments
   d. dissenting jurisdiction

10. Who is the government's legal representative who brings charges in a case?
    a. magistrate
    b. prosecuting attorney
    c. chief justice
    d. defense attorney

# 8. The Judicial Branch

**Read each description, and write the letter of the correct term on the line.**

1. The federal court system consists of more than _____ courts across the country.
   a. 50
   b. 100
   c. 300
   d. 1,000

2. The federal court system follows some specific rules set up by _____ and _____.
   a. the House of Representatives and the Senate
   b. the president and the Senate
   c. the president and the vice president
   d. Congress and the Constitution

3. The federal judges that are appointed by the president and confirmed by the senate are appointed for_____.
   a. a term of four years
   b. a term of two years
   c. life
   d. a term of five years

4. Congress created ____ district courts in 1789, and today we have ____ federal district courts.
   a. 10/100
   b. 13/94
   c. 16/104
   d. 3/75

5. United States district courts are _____, or courts that hear criminal and civil cases.
   a. trial courts
   b. courts of appeals
   c. special courts
   d. appellate courts

6. Most legal cases are settled in the _____ court system.
   a. appeals       c. local
   b. district      d. state

7. The U.S. Attorney works with a staff of attorneys _____ for the federal government.
   a. to submit amicus curiae briefs
   b. to keep order in the court
   c. to prosecute and defend cases
   d. to issue warrants

8. Courts of appeal have no _____, which means they never hear a case from the beginning (or origin) with all the evidence presented.
   a. dissenting opinion
   b. original jurisdiction
   c. original judicial review
   d. amicus curiae

9. If the court decides that a law is unconstitutional, the section of the law in dispute is considered_____.
   a. optional         c. null and void
   b. a mistake        d. amicus curiae

10. Every year, nearly _____ cases are appealed to the Supreme Court.
    a. 7,000
    b. 10,000
    c. 600
    d. 800

**Essay Question**

How do you feel about how the court system works in this country?

Name _____

# 9. State Governments

**As you read Chapter 9, write an answer to each question below.**

1. What are the concurrent powers that both the state and national government have?
   _____
   _____
   _____

2. What is the difference between standing committees and interim committees?
   _____
   _____
   _____
   _____

3. What are the governor's duties as chief of state?
   _____
   _____
   _____
   _____

4. Describe the job of lieutenant governor and the job of secretary of state.
   _____
   _____
   _____
   _____

5. How are the state courts organized?
   _____
   _____
   _____
   _____

Name _____

# 9. State Governments

**Find the best answer for each item. Then circle that answer.**

1. What is the term that means the guarantee of a person's qualifications for a job?

    a. proposition
    b. extradition
    c. certification
    d. delegation

2. What is the term that means to reduce a sentence imposed by the court?

    a. commute
    b. extradite
    c. veto
    d. impeach

3. What are the lawmaking areas shared by the states and the federal government?

    a. exclusive powers
    b. concurrent powers
    c. reserved powers
    d. parliamentary procedure

4. What is the term that means to assign?

    a. extradite
    b. censure
    c. initiate
    d. delegate

5. What is the term that means powers assigned only to the national government?

    a. concurrent powers
    b. reserved powers
    c. exclusive powers
    d. private powers

6. What is the process of returning a fugitive to the state where a crime was committed?

    a. felony process
    b. extradition
    c. initiation
    d. interstate commerce

7. What is the power of most governors to veto only parts, or items, in a longer bill sent from the state legislature?

    a. single veto
    b. line item veto
    c. legislative veto
    d. impeachment

8. What are the rules under which legislatures hold meetings?

    a. parliamentary procedures
    b. referendum
    c. supremacy clause
    d. censured

9. What is a proposition taken directly to the voters?

    a. delegation
    b. appropriations
    c. initiative proposition
    d. referendum

10. What is the article in the U.S. Constitution making federal laws the highest laws of the land?

    a. parliamentary procedure
    b. appropriations article
    c. supremacy clause
    d. proposition

Alabama Citizenship Workbook 29

Name _____

## 9. State Governments

**Read each description, and write the letter of the correct term on the line.**

1. The founders of the nation set up a system based on _____, in which power is divided and balanced between the national and state governments.
   a. legislation
   b. federalism
   c. extradition
   d. democracy

2. Every state's _____ must guarantee that voters can elect their state leaders.
   a. motto
   b. attorney general
   c. constitution
   d. preamble

3. Holding elections, providing education, and regulating businesses are examples of _____.
   a. services provided by the state's attorney's office
   b. services provided by states
   c. services provided by the auditor's office
   d. services provided by the secretary of state

4. Except for Nebraska, every state legislature has two houses; the larger is usually called the _____ and the smaller is usually called the _____.
   a. House of Representatives/Senate
   b. General Senate/House of Representatives
   c. State House/ General Assembly
   d. General Court/ State House

5. The legislatures in many states meet each year for between _____.
   a. one week and three months
   b. three and ten days
   c. six and eight weeks
   d. one and six months

6. In most states, the minimum age is _____ for state senators and _____ for state representatives.
   a. 30/35
   b. 32/36
   c. 25/21
   d. 35/40

7. When state governors appoint certain officials, they must get approval from _____.
   a. the secretary of state
   b. one or both houses of the state legislature
   c. the attorney general
   d. the lieutenant governor

8. In any state, a candidate for governor must have been a resident of the state for _____.
   a. a year and a half
   b. a number of years
   c. one month
   d. nine months

9. A state's constitution and laws are interpreted by _____.
   a. the governor
   b. the secretary of state
   c. state courts
   d. state auditors

10. The state supreme court hears appeals from _____.
    a. appeals courts or general trial courts
    b. the magistrate's courts
    c. municipal courts
    d. justice courts

### Essay Question

If you were governor of your state, what changes would you want to make in terms of the services, the court system, and the laws?

Name _____

# State and Local Governments: How Does it Work in Alabama?

**Alabama Planner**

Citizenship Course of Study
3.b, 3.c

Learning Objectives:
- Identifying major offices and office-holders of state and local governments
- Explaining the historical background of the 1901 Constitution of Alabama and its impact on state and local governments

AHSGE: II.2

Article IV of the Constitution defines the role of state governments. The structure of the state government is similar to the federal government with the governor holding executive authority, including the power to veto bills.

The legislative branch, which makes the laws, is made up of two departments (a bicameral legislature) in all states except Nebraska.[1] To interpret the laws, all states have their own court system, which includes a state supreme court and trial courts.

Each state has its own constitution and a system of checks and balances in place among the three branches, resembling the structure of the federal government. The Constitution of the United States serves as the official guide for state constitutions, and states should not contradict the laws within it.

If the provisions of the constitution of Alabama and the federal constitution conflict, a case may be brought before the Supreme Court of the United States. This court decides on proper interpretation of the national constitution and would determine if the Alabama constitution is contrary to the law as described in the Constitution. The state of Alabama would lose in such a case. The Constitution always wins in court because it is the law of the whole country and what the Supreme Court uses as a basis for its decisions.

Article III of the Constitution of Alabama of 1901 divides the powers of its state government into three distinct departments or branches. Each department is defined as a separate body. These branches are called the executive, legislative and judicial branches of government.[1] The Constitution states that no branch should ever "exercise" any powers of the other branches. To prevent any one branch from imposing its will on the others, the Constitution allows for certain actions by one branch to restrain the activities of another. For example, when the legislative branch creates a law, the judicial branch has the authority to declare it unconstitutional, or against federal law.

The legislative branch of government is made up of no more than 35 Senators and 105 representatives.[2] All state senators and representatives are elected officials who represent residents in districts or counties of the state. Each official serves a four-year term with a possibility of being reelected.

# An Organizational Chart for Alabama Government[3]

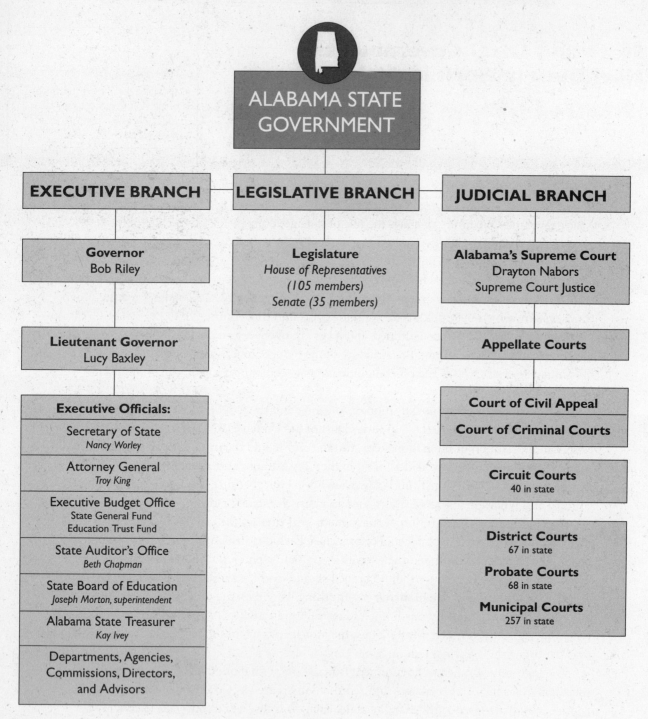

Sources:
1 http://www.judicial.state.al.us/chart_judicial.cfm
  http://www.unicam.state.ne.us/learning/history.htm
2 United States Constitution and Alabama Constitution of 1901. Office of the Secretary of State Glen Browder (Secretary of State). The Michie Company, Charlottesville VA, 1987.
3 http://www.governor.state.al.us/cabinet/cabinet_members.htm

# A Short History of Alabama's Constitution of 1901

A state constitution is very different in form and purpose from the federal constitution. Since all powers not specifically defined in the federal constitution are reserved to the states, the writers of a state constitution have a great deal of freedom when they decide what to include in the state law, as long as it doesn't contradict the law of the nation.

After the Civil War a coalition of native Republicans, migrant northerners, and freed African-American slaves took control of Alabama state government and wrote the Constitution of 1865 which conferred suffrage on African-American former slaves. Only three years later a new Constitution was created. The Constitution of 1868 presented a different view of Civil War Reconstruction than the previous constitution.

The Democrats revolted and overturned the Republican government when their party came into power in the election of 1874. They called Alabama Whites that supported the Republican Party "scalawags" and northerners who settled in the south "carpetbaggers." Democrats, known as "redeemers" or "Bourbons" wrote yet another new constitution. A constitutional convention met in 1875 and a new constitution was ratified the same year. These laws kept taxes low and government services to a minimum. It didn't allow the state to engage in internal improvements and limited power to white property owners and industrialists.

A group called the Farmers' Alliance, better known as the Populist Party, threatened the power that the Bourbons had on the state of Alabama. Citizens of this political party were tired of Bourbon control in Alabama. In response, the Bourbons called for a new state constitution to firm up their position. As a result, the Alabama Constitution of 1901 was drawn up to keep taxes low and governmental services to a minimum. The result of the new Alabama constitution took voting privelages away from poor Whites and Blacks and kept the power in White landowners' hands.

**Use what you learned about Alabama on pages 31–33 to help you answer the following questions. Short Answer Questions**

1. Name the three branches of the Alabama State government.

_____

_____

_____

2. According to "A Short History of the Alabama Constitution of 1901" on page 33, why was a new Alabama constitution written in 1901?

_____

_____

_____

**Read each description, and write the letter of the correct term on the line.**

1. Where are laws defined for the Alabama state government?
   a. Legislative Branch
   b. Judicial Branch
   c. Executive Branch
   d. Alabama state constitution

2. Which of the following governmental leaders is not part of the executive branch?
   a. Alabama Supreme Court Justice, Drayton Nabors
   b. Secretary of State, Nancy Worley
   c. Attorney General, Troy King
   d. Lieutenant Governor, Lucy Baxley

3. If the people in Pell City, Alabama want to support a bill that is about to be voted upon in the state legislature, whom should they call or write to encourage him/her to vote for the bill to be passed?
   a. Alabama State Treasurer
   b. State representative and senator
   c. Attorney General
   d. Lieutenant Governor

4. If Alabama's state law conflicts with federal law, to which court will this federal complaint be submitted and possibly tried?
   a. Alabama Supreme Court
   b. Alabama appellate court
   c. United States Supreme Court
   d. Municipal court

5. An escaped convict broke out of prison in Alabama and fled to South Carolina. The fugitive was caught after a policeman stopped his car for a traffic violation. Where will the convict be tried in court?
   a. North Carolina
   b. Alabama
   c. U.S. Supreme Court
   d. a neighboring state

6. Which one of the following is not considered a way in which states regulate business?
   a. Saint Vincent's Hospital is inspected routinely.
   b. Plumbers obtain a certified state license to practice.
   c. Homeowners must obtain permission from the court to own a home.
   d. Teachers must be certified to teach in the state of Alabama.

7. If a state experiences extreme losses as a result of a hurricane or tornado, from which government should that state request assistance?
   a. a neighboring state
   b. a regional state
   c. local government
   d. federal government

8. What was another name for the Democratic Party around the time the Constitution of 1901 was written?
   a. Populist party
   b. Bourbons
   c. Farmers Alliance Party
   d. Scalawags

34  Alabama Citizenship Workbook

Name _____

# 10. Local Government

**As you read Chapter 10, write an answer to each question below.**

1. What are some of the different levels on which local governments operate?

   _____
   _____
   _____

2. What are the two methods that state governments use to grant local governments home rule powers? Does this mean that the local government has absolute authority?

   _____
   _____
   _____

3. Who established the county form of government in America?

   _____
   _____
   _____

4. What is the most common kind of local government in the United States and how does it function?

   _____
   _____
   _____

5. What are the approaches that governments can take when they are faced with sharing authority?

   _____
   _____
   _____

Alabama Citizenship Workbook

Name _____

## 10. Local Government

**Find the best answer for each item. Then circle that answer.**

1. Who is a city council member or legislator in a local government?
   a. trustee
   b. clerk
   c. treasurer
   d. alderman

2. Which is defined as a group of people authorized or elected to perform certain duties?
   a. alderman
   b. municipality
   c. commission
   d. member

3. Which is defined as a group of people elected or appointed to serve as legislators or administrators?
   a. council
   b. board of trustees
   c. board members
   d. auditors

4. What is the largest division for local government within a state?
   a. township
   b. county
   c. municipality
   d. village

5. What is the term for money given for a specific purpose?
   a. zoning
   b. charter
   c. grant
   d. commission

6. What is the power of a local government to direct its own affairs with some degree of independence from the state?
   a. Dillon's Rule
   b. strong-mayor plan
   c. charter
   d. home rule

7. What is the term that means a city and its suburbs?
   a. municipality
   b. metropolitan area
   c. zoning
   d. county

8. What is a local government unit—often called a board, authority, or corporation—created to provide a specific service?
   a. special district
   b. county
   c. township
   d. zoning district

9. What is the form of local government in which an elected mayor has executive powers?
   a. weak-mayor plan
   b. mayor-administrator plan
   c. strong-mayor plan
   d. home rule

10. Who are the people elected or appointed to direct the funds and policy of a government body?
    a. commissioners
    b. trustees
    c. administrators
    d. aldermen

Name _____

# 10. Local Government

**Read each description, and write the letter of the correct term on the line.**

1. Property taxes provide more than ____ of local government money.
   a. 20 percent
   b. 10 percent
   c. 30 percent
   d. 50 percent

2. Local governments spend the most money on ____.
   a. public safety
   b. education
   c. health and welfare
   d. environment and housing

3. The ____ is the most widely used city government plan.
   a. council-manager plan
   b. commission plan
   c. board of trustees plan
   d. mayor-council plan

4. States are divided into areas, usually called ____.
   a. counties
   b. townships
   c. towns
   d. neighborhoods

5. The type of county government that usually consists of a board, or small group of supervisors or commissioners, is called ____.
   a. commission-administrator
   b. commission
   c. council
   d. council-executive

6. A ____ is established when the state gives power to the local government.
   a. parish
   b. borough
   c. town or village
   d. county

7. ____ provide many of the services the county would otherwise provide.
   a. Townships
   b. Towns
   c. Villages
   d. Neighborhoods

8. Some ____ are called boards, authorities, or corporations.
   a. municipalities
   b. commissions
   c. special districts
   d. council-executives

9. Many special districts are governed by ____.
   a. a municipality
   b. an elected board of directors
   c. a trustee
   d. an administrator

10. In 1978 in California, ____ reduced taxes back to 1976 levels and limited how much the government could raise them in the future.
    a. Proposition 13
    b. the Fourteenth Amendment
    c. Article 10
    d. Proposition 16

## Essay Question

What other services would you want your local government to provide to you as citizen? Would you be willing to pay more taxes for those services?

Name _____

# 11. How Our Political System Works: Parties, Politics, and Participation

**As you read Chapter 11, write an answer to each question below.**

1. What do members of the same political party decide as a group?

   _____
   _____
   _____

2. How have third-party political groups shaped politics in America?

   _____
   _____
   _____

3. What are the ways in which a person can become a candidate for political office?

   _____
   _____
   _____

4. What is the difference between a closed primary and an open primary?

   _____
   _____
   _____

5. What are the criteria a person must meet in order to vote in the United States?

   _____
   _____
   _____

38  Alabama Citizenship Workbook

# 11. How Our Political System Works: Parties, Politics, and Participation

**Find the best answer for each item. Then circle that answer.**

1. What is a meeting of party members for the purpose of choosing a candidate or setting policy?
   a. debate
   b. runoff
   c. nonpartisan meeting
   d. caucus

2. What is an orderly discussion of issues between two parties?
   a. caucus
   b. debate
   c. primary speech
   d. proposal

3. What is the term that means not associated with a political party?
   a. nonpartisan
   b. GOP
   c. FEC
   d. caucus

4. What is a group of citizens organized to promote and support specific ideas for government and candidates for public office?
   a. policy group
   b. policy conventioneers
   c. political party
   d. pollsters

5. What is a formal declaration of the principles and policies of a political party?
   a. caucus
   b. political platform
   c. public policy
   d. primary election

6. What is the term that means, for election purposes, a division of a county, town, or city?
   a. precinct
   b. caucus
   c. political platform
   d. polling place

7. What is the election in which voters decide which of the candidates within a party will represent the party in the general election?
   a. political platform
   b. political caucus
   c. polling caucus
   d. primary election

8. What are the principles that form the basis for our laws?
   a. polling principles
   b. political platform
   c. public policy
   d. proposal

9. What is a new election held to decide a close outcome in the first round of voting?
   a. recount
   b. split ticket
   c. political convention
   d. runoff election

10. What is the ballot cast by a person who votes for candidates from more than one party?
    a. absentee ballot
    b. split ticket
    c. recount ticket
    d. partisan ballot

# 11. How Our Political System Works: Parties, Politics, and Participation

**Read each description, and write the letter of the correct term on the line.**

1. ____ had hoped to build a strong, unified nation in which there would be no need for political parties.
   a. Thomas Jefferson
   b. Franklin D. Roosevelt
   c. George Washington
   d. Abe Lincoln

2. The ____ emerged during the 1850s as an anti-slavery party.
   a. Democratic Party
   b. Republican Party
   c. Progressive Party
   d. Independent Party

3. The Green Party, led by Ralph Nader, focused on ____ in the 2000 presidential election.
   a. tax issues
   b. budget deficit issues
   c. environmental and consumer issues
   d. education issues

4. "Independent" voters increased from less than 20 percent in the 1940s to ____ percent in the 1990s.
   a. more than 40
   b. less than 10
   c. less than 5
   d. more than 30

5. In a political campaign, the ____ directs and coordinates the campaign.
   a. finance manager
   b. campaign manager
   c. press secretary
   d. pollster

6. ____ determine the strategy for their candidate's television, radio, and print advertisements.
   a. Press secretaries
   b. Pollsters
   c. Volunteers
   d. Media consultants

7. The Dole and Clinton presidential campaigns spent a combined total of ____ in the 1996 presidential election.
   a. $232 million
   b. $850,000
   c. $1 million
   d. $150 million

8. Citizens can give ____ from their income taxes to a presidential campaign fund.
   a. $10
   b. $40
   c. $50
   d. $3

9. In the United States, ____ of all eligible voters actually vote in a presidential election.
   a. slightly more than half
   b. slightly more than two-thirds
   c. slightly less than one-fourth
   d. three-fourths

10. People convicted of felonies and people being treated for mental disabilities _____.
    a. are allowed to vote via absentee ballot
    b. can only vote in a runoff election
    c. are not allowed to vote
    d. can only vote after proving capable

## Essay Question

If you could choose one political party to be affiliated with, which one would you choose and why? Explain.

Name _____

# 12. Public Opinion and Interest Groups

**As you read Chapter 12, write an answer to each question below.**

1. How is spin used with the media?

   _____
   _____
   _____

2. During the 2000 presidential election campaign, in what types of divisions did polls by groups like CNN and Gallup measure public opinion?

   _____
   _____
   _____

3. What is the difference between special interest groups and lobbyists?

   _____
   _____
   _____

4. When special interest groups launch grassroots campaigns, how do they gain support for their issues?

   _____
   _____
   _____

5. What do critics fear about large interest groups?

   _____
   _____

Name _____

## 12. Public Opinion and Interest Groups

Find the best answer for each item. Then circle that answer.

1. What is the term for huge corporations composed of several smaller companies?
   a. factions
   b. conglomerates
   c. grassroots
   d. lobbyists

2. What are words or terms used to make something sound less unpleasant?
   a. euphemisms
   b. generalities
   c. muckraking
   d. testimonials

3. What are groups of citizens divided by different interests?
   a. conglomerates
   b. factions
   c. lobbyists
   d. PACs

4. What is public popularity or endorsement of a candidate by large numbers of voters at the local level?
   a. testimonials
   b. transfers
   c. grassroots support
   d. lobbyists

5. Who are professionals who represent an organization's interests by influencing individual legislators?
   a. factions
   b. grassroots support
   c. testimonials
   d. lobbyists

6. What is the term that means digging up dirt or uncovering unflattering facts about a candidate or issue?
   a. transfer
   b. name-calling
   c. muckraking
   d. propaganda

7. What are organized groups that raise money to support candidates and issues?
   a. special interest groups
   b. political action committees (PACs)
   c. factions
   d. conglomerates

8. What is the communication of information to spread certain ideas, beliefs, or practices and to shape public opinion?
   a. propaganda
   b. proliferation
   c. projection
   d. enculturation

9. What are feelings, thoughts, and positions that people have on political or social issues?
   a. approval rating
   b. euphemisms
   c. public opinion
   d. muckraking

10. What are the political donations that are given to political parties rather than to individual candidates?
    a. hard money
    b. transfers
    c. propaganda
    d. soft money

Name _____

# 12. Public Opinion and Interest Groups

**Read each description, and write the letter of the correct term on the line.**

1. _____ range from small informal groups that protest local political decisions at a town meeting to large organized associations.
   a. Special interest groups
   b. Factions
   c. Lobbyists
   d. Mass media

2. Candidates and politicians hire _____ to discover how well the public accepts them.
   a. conglomerates
   b. lobbyists
   c. polls
   d. PACs

3. In some elections, only _____ percent of eligible voters actually vote.
   a. 10
   b. 30–40
   c. 20–30
   d. 5–15

4. The _____ secured the rights of citizens to assemble, to speak freely, to publish their ideas, and to petition the government.
   a. Fourteenth Amendment
   b. First Amendment
   c. Fifth Amendment
   d. Sixth Amendment

5. The League of Women Voters is an example of _____ type of interest group.
   a. an economic
   b. a professional
   c. a governmental
   d. a political or ideological

6. Lobbying efforts are mainly directed at _____.
   a. state and federal decision makers
   b. first-time voters
   c. older voters
   d. the general public

7. In 1996, Congress passed the Communications Decency Act (CDA) to protect young people from inappropriate material _____.
   a. on the radio
   b. on television
   c. on the Internet
   d. in newspapers

8. _____ donations are direct donations to individual politicians' election campaigns.
   a. Soft money
   b. Transfer
   c. Clear money
   d. Hard money

9. The courts have ruled that limits on lobbying are _____.
   a. unconstitutional
   b. constitutional
   c. unnecessary
   d. necessary

10. Congress has restricted the _____ that lobbyists can give governmental officials.
    a. value of gifts
    b. amount of written material
    c. amount of biased material
    d. number of suggestions

## Essay Question

In what area(s) do you feel the process of influencing public and government opinion needs improvement? What, specifically, needs to be done?

Name _____

# 13. Law and Our Legal System

As you read Chapter 13, write an answer to each question below.

1. What are the three types of protected property? Provide an example of each.

   _____
   _____
   _____

2. What are the rights of someone who owns a copyright?

   _____
   _____
   _____

3. When two people commit the same criminal offense, why might a minor receive a different—often less severe—punishment? What are the pros and cons and your view of this policy?

   _____
   _____
   _____

4. Look at the offenses and punishments in the Code of Hammurabi. What is your view of this system of law?

   _____
   _____
   _____

5. Discuss the ways in which you are a responsible citizen and an irresponsible citizen. With that in mind, how do you see yourself in terms of contributing to society?

   _____
   _____
   _____

44   Alabama Citizenship Workbook

Name _____

# 13. Law and Our Legal System

**Find the best answer for each item. Then circle that one.**

1. What is the term for something done or said in a previous court case that serves as an example for a future court decision?
   a. pristine
   b. precedent
   c. precursor
   d. pinnacle

2. What is the act of a court that commands a person to stop doing something or to keep doing something?
   a. infusion
   b. injunction
   c. esteem
   d. estuary

3. What is the word for the right to own and copy intellectual or artistic property?
   a. copyright
   b. administrative right
   c. ownership right
   d. cursory right

4. What is the term for something owned or possessed, and also the right to use that thing?
   a. personal
   b. precedent
   c. prescription
   d. property

5. What word describes the system of rules for conduct and action made and enforced by an authority, such as the government?
   a. civil           c. code
   b. law             d. administration

6. Which word means to force someone to obey?
   a. enforce
   b. enjoin
   c. entreat
   d. eschew

7. What is the term for someone younger than 18 years of age who does not have the legal rights of an adult?
   a. misanthrope
   b. miscreant
   c. minor
   d. matriarch

8. What is the term that means relating to the good of the community at large?
   a. common decency
   b. sweeping generalization
   c. good graces
   d. common good

9. What is the name for a person who refuses to serve in the military, based on a moral or religious belief that war is wrong?
   a. conformist observer
   b. contemptuous objector
   c. conscientious observer
   d. conscientious objector

10. What is the term for the act of breaking the law to express disagreement with the law?
    a. civil disobedience
    b. civil objector
    c. civil pretext
    d. civil strife

Alabama Citizenship Workbook

# 13. Law and Our Legal System

**Read each description, and write the letter of the correct term on the line.**

1. Citizens influence the laws of society by _____.
   a. developing the laws that govern them
   b. electing and communicating with lawmakers
   c. hiring lawyers to speak for them
   d. boycotting the election process

2. According to housing laws, a landlord _____.
   a. can evict someone anytime he or she wants
   b. must live in the building he or she owns
   c. must keep a rented apartment in good working order
   d. is responsible for keeping the neighborhood safe and clean

3. Copyright law is violated when _____.
   a. someone takes someone else's newspaper
   b. a student borrows a friend's school book
   c. a speech-giver quotes from a noted source
   d. students swap music files on the Internet

4. Laws should to be fair, but sometimes they _____.
   a. are unfair
   b. treat offenders differently for the same offence
   c. are too hard to understand
   d. all of the above

5. A law that suggests that dog owners always keep their dogs indoors is _____.
   a. unenforceable
   b. not understandable
   c. unreasonable
   d. fair because most people don't own dogs

6. Forbidding gang members from hanging around for "no apparent purpose" is _____.
   a. a street-gang curfew law
   b. a bad law
   c. an understandable law
   d. one's right to join any group

7. Criminal law is designed to _____.
   a. protect society as a whole
   b. give the government rights to enforce laws
   c. seriously punish the guilty
   d. all of the above

8. Constitutional law makes sure that power is properly balanced and divided, and that _____.
   a. individual rights are protected
   b. property rights are protected
   c. business-related laws are fair
   d. church and state are divided

9. The Securities and Exchange Commission (SEC) is an agency that _____.
   a. secures the right of people to exchange
   b. is elected by the people
   c. makes and enforces laws
   d. makes money exchanging secure items

10. _____ is NOT an example of an ancient source for American laws.
    a. The Code of Hammurabi
    b. The Justinian Code
    c. Dutch provisionary law
    d. English law

## Essay Question

British philosopher John Locke said, "The end [purpose] of law is not to abolish or restrain, but to preserve and enlarge freedom . . . where there is no law, there is no freedom." What do you think Locke means by that statement?

Name _____

# What is "Rule of Law"?

**Alabama Planner**
Citizenship Course of Study
3.b, 3.c

Learning Objective:
- Explaining what is meant by the term "rule of law."

AHSGE: II.2

**Rule of law** is the general principle that government and the governed alike are subject to law, as regularly adopted and applied.[1] In other words, the people should be governed by laws they can know and follow rather than by the decisions of kings, presidents or bureaucrats.[2]

## Multiple-Choice Question

At school we assume that principals, teachers, parents and public officials have the right to make rules and laws to govern our schools. Rules can be hard to make, especially for students with various backgrounds and nationalities. Which one of the following is NOT a characteristic of a good law.

　　a.　Laws must include the information people need to understand to know exactly what they must or must not do.
　　b.　Laws must be reasonable and makes sense.
　　c.　People are to be treated fairly.
　　d.　Laws should not be enforceable.

## Essay Question

A school located in a suburb of Birmingham, Alabama initiated a school law: "students are not to bring pagers, telephones, or other communication devices to school. If this rule is broken, the device in question will be taken and parents will have to come to school to pick it up." Do you think this rule possess the characteristics of a good law. Identify the components of this school's law.

_____

_____

_____

1 *Encyclopedia of the American Constitution, 2nd edition.* Macmillan Reference, 2000.
2 Encyclopedia Britannica Online

Alabama Citizenship Workbook

Name _____

## 14. The American Justice System

**As you read Chapter 14, write an answer to each question below.**

1. Explain the three main stages of a civil trial procedure. How is the basis for decision different from that of a criminal trial?

   _____
   _____
   _____

2. In civil law, why do people often settle before trial? What alternatives do they use?

   _____
   _____
   _____

3. Describe what happens in each of the four main stages of a trial.

   _____
   _____
   _____

4. What are the three main factors that courts try to balance when dealing with juvenile offenders?

   _____
   _____
   _____

5. Consider the arguments listed for and against trying juveniles as adults. With which side of the argument do you most agree? Explain.

   _____
   _____
   _____

48  Alabama Citizenship Workbook

Name _____

## 14. The American Justice System

**Find the best answer for each item. Then circle that one.**

1. What is the term for a formal accusation that leads to a trial?
   a. inducement
   b. indictment
   c. subpoena
   d. incident

2. What is the judicial ruling that a person has failed to do what the law requires (the alternative to a ruling of guilty in juvenile court)?
   a. delinquent
   b. distain
   c. detained
   d. disturbed

3. What is the word for a pre-trial court appearance during which an accused person answers formal charges against him or her with a plea of guilty or not guilty?
   a. arrangement
   b. adjustment
   c. assuagement
   d. arraignment

4. What is the name for a person who files a legal action or claim?
   a. juvenile
   b. plaintiff
   c. proprietor
   d. defendant

5. Which of the following describes making up in some way for the harm caused by an accused person?
   a. decommission
   b. restoration
   c. restitution
   d. reformation

6. Which word describes the damage, injury, or wrongful act caused to one person, other than breaking a contract, for which a civil lawsuit can be filed?
   a. turf
   b. treatise
   c. trite
   d. tort

7. What is the word for being paid back for a loss?
   a. compensated
   b. castigated
   c. consigned
   d. crestfallen

8. Which term means justice under the law that is influenced by fairness?
   a. equine
   b. eschew
   c. equity
   d. epiphany

9. Which of the following words means to restore to a useful life, usually through treatment and education?
   a. rehabilitate
   b. reinvigorate
   c. restrain
   d. respire

10. What term means to make an agreement in which a defendant pleads guilty to a lesser charge and the prosecutor, in return, drops more serious charges?
    a. plea deal
    b. sidebar
    c. side motion
    d. plea bargain

Alabama Citizenship Workbook

Name _____

# 14. The American Justice System

**Read each description, and write the letter of the correct term on the line.**

1. When a judge orders a person to stop making noise that disturbs a neighbor, it is an example of _____.
   a. equity
   b. tort
   c. contract
   d. Grand Jury

2. Most torts result from _____.
   a. intentional harm
   b. broken contracts
   c. carelessness
   d. none of the above

3. If a storeowner cheats you, civil law has provisions for _____.
   a. false promises
   b. consumer conviction
   c. consumer protection
   d. business protection

4. Domestic-relations law deals with _____.
   a. divorce
   b. adoption
   c. child custody
   d. all of the above

5. Unlike murder, manslaughter means that a person kills another _____.
   a. without intending to do so
   b. intending to do so
   c. reluctantly
   d. in self defense

6. Battery is _____.
   a. harming someone without touching them
   b. implying that you will harm someone
   c. harming someone else's property
   d. touching and harming someone

7. When someone appears in court for the first time, the judge _____.
   a. advises them of their rights
   b. advises them of the charges against them
   c. considers setting bail
   d. all of the above

8. Since the mid 1980s, prison populations have _____.
   a. doubled
   b. tripled
   c. quadrupled
   d. steadily decreased

9. In the "In re Gault" case, the Supreme Court decided that _____.
   a. juveniles and adults have the same rights
   b. adults, like juveniles, deserve compassionate treatment
   c. juvenile law should be more strict
   d. the court has no jurisdiction over juveniles

10. _____ could cause juvenile crime.
    a. Child abuse
    b. Poor parenting
    c. Drugs
    d. All of the above

## Essay Question

Prisons are often overcrowded, dangerous places filled with many repeat offenders. In your view, is the system working? How would you change it?

Name _____

# 15. Economics and the American Economy

**As you read Chapter 15, write an answer to each question below.**

1. Explain the main differences between capitalism, communism, and socialism.

   _____
   _____
   _____

2. What is free about a free market? Why are many Americans against laissez-faire?

   _____
   _____
   _____

3. Describe the concept of supply and demand. How does it control prices?

   _____
   _____
   _____

4. What is the barter system? Have you ever used it? Explain.

   _____
   _____
   _____

5. Consider the arguments made for and against privatizing Amtrak. Are you for or against privatization? Explain your view.

   _____
   _____

Alabama Citizenship Workbook  51

# 15. Economics and the American Economy

**Find the best answer for each item. Then circle that answer.**

1. Which of the following is another word for the factors of production that include natural resources, human resources (labor), and capital?

   a. resources
   b. profits
   c. supply
   d. market

2. What is the term for money paid for the use of money?

   a. profit
   b. economy
   c. interest
   d. stocks

3. What is the word for the amount of a particular good or service that producers are willing (and able) to provide at a given price?

   a. labor
   b. laissez-faire
   c. production
   d. supply

4. What is the name for the exclusive control (or right to control) sales of a product or service in a market?

   a. free enterprise
   b. monopoly
   c. scarcity
   d. liability

5. Which of the following describes the use of resources to create goods and services?

   a. production
   b. free market
   c. profit
   d. partnership

6. What word describes the legal obligation to pay debts or damages?

   a. scarcity
   b. liability
   c. interest
   d. supply

7. What is the term that describes natural resources as factors of production such as oil, acreage, or timber?

   a. stocks
   b. land
   c. labor
   d. free market

8. Which of the following describes the situation in which there are not enough resources available to satisfy existing needs or wants?

   a. supply
   b. liability
   c. monopoly
   d. scarcity

9. Which of the following words means shares of ownership in a company?

   a. stocks
   b. resources
   c. interest
   d. profit

10. What term means the amount of money remaining after all of a business's operating expenses have been paid?

    a. resources
    b. economy
    c. profit
    d. supply

Name _____

## 15. Economics and the American Economy

**Read each description, and write the letter of the correct term on the line.**

1. The free enterprise system balances _____.
   a. freedom and protection
   b. communism and socialism
   c. market and mixed economies
   d. economic and social issues

2. The freedom to compete helps _____.
   a. sellers
   b. buyers
   c. both sellers and buyers
   d. neither sellers nor buyers

3. *Hunt v. Washington Apple* determined that _____.
   a. a government can control the economy
   b. a state cannot economically discriminate against other states
   c. state taxes are legal in all states
   d. businesses should be protected

4. The freedom to compete allows a business to _____.
   a. sell to anyone
   b. sell to the same customers as competitors
   c. compete with others for new clients
   d. do all of the above

5. If you obey business laws in a free market economy, the government _____.
   a. can only interfere by collecting taxes
   b. can correct improper marketing plans
   c. can do nothing to interfere
   d. can still do anything it wants

6. _____ is an example of intellectual property.
   a. A car
   b. An original song
   c. A dream
   d. A process

7. The "technology gap" means that _____.
   a. America is falling behind in technology
   b. technological advances are few and far between
   c. people who have no technological skills will not get higher-paying jobs
   d. the gap between the real world and technology is growing

8. A corporation _____.
   a. exists outside of the employees or owners
   b. sometimes sells stock to raise money
   c. protects its owners from personal liability
   d. does all of these things

9. Unlike the other ways of organizing a business, a not-for-profit _____.
   a. is not really a business
   b. only tries to make enough money to complete its goals
   c. tries to work not for profit, but for personal gain
   d. earns more money for the owners than the others

10. _____ is/are a basic area(s) of economic decision making.
    a. Production
    b. Distribution
    c. Consumption
    d. All of these options

### Essay Question

Sir Winston Churchill said: "The inherent vice [the weakness] of capitalism is the unequal sharing of blessings; the inherent virtue [the strong point] of socialism is the equal sharing of miseries." What do you think he meant by that?

Alabama Citizenship Workbook  53

# Name

## Supply and Demand

**Alabama Planner**

Citizenship Course of Study
7.b, 7.c

Learning Objective:
- Analyzing distribution and production maps to determine patterns of supply and demand
- Describing the effects of government policies on the free market

Between the years of 2000 to 2002 Alabama was home to more new manufacturing projects than any other state in the region (AL, KY, MS, TN) and was second when compared to all southeastern states. Alabama has made great strides in new business investments. It has made history in successfully recruiting Mercedes-Benz to the state. Since then, Honda, Toyota and Hyundai, Boeing and International Diesel have also built manufacturing plants in Alabama. As a result of these new corporations making their home in Alabama, the manufacturing sector now accounts for almost 20 percent of the goods and services produced in the state. Today there are over 350 automotive related businesses in Alabama. Manufacturing is credited for 16 percent of the state's nonagricultural jobs. Along with the economic growth, the economy has been characterized by great diversity.

Economic Development Partnership of Alabama, An Alabama Industry Profile. www.edpa.org

### Use the Paragraphs above to help you answer the following questions.
### Multiple-Choice Questions

1. Based on what you know about supply and demand, why did other automotive manufacturers come to Alabama to build manufacturing plants?

   a. The demand for manufacturing businesses has increased in Alabama

   b. Automobile corporations do not pay taxes to the state.

   c. New businesses do not have to obey business laws in Alabama.

   d. The new companies can get free labor in Alabama.

2. Since the supply of vehicles are on the increase in Alabama and in other Southeastern states, prices for these products are expected to:

   a. increase

   b. remain the same

   c. decrease

   d. force manufacturers out of the state

54 Alabama Citizenship Workbook

# Current Vehicle Production Capacity (as of 2002) & 2005 Vehicle Capacity Projection for Southern States

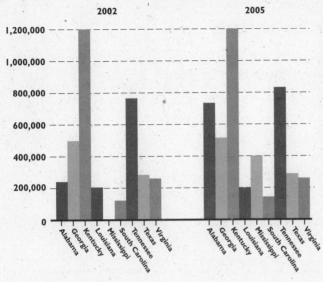

| 2002 Vehicle Production Capacity and Share of Region's Capacity ||||| 
| Southern State | Vehicle Production Capacity 2002 | Vehicle Production Projected 2005 | Share of Region's Capacity | Projected Share of Region's Capacity 2005 |
| --- | --- | --- | --- | --- |
| Kentucky | 1,200,000 | 1,200,000 | 34.52% | 26.48% |
| Tennessee | 770,000 | 820,000 | 34.52% | 18.10% |
| Georgia | 502,673 | 511,104 | 34.52% | 16.77% |
| Texas | 250,000 | 250,000 | 34.52% | 11.28% |
| Virginia | 240,000 | 240,000 | 34.52% | 8.83% |
| Alabama | 230,000 | 760,000 | 34.52% | 5.52% |
| Mississippi | | 400,000 | 8.83% | 5.30% |
| Louisiana | 200,000 | 200,000 | 34.52% | 4.41% |
| South Carolina | 120,000 | 150,000 | 34.52% | 3.31% |

Source: Economic Development Partnership of Alabama, An Alabama Industry Profile.

**Use the chart and bar graph above to help you answer the following questions.**

## Short Answer

3. According to the chart, which state will have the greatest increase in production of vehicles between 2002 and 2005? What is the amount of the increase?

_____

_____

## Multiple Choice Questions

4. Using what you know about supply and demand and the charts above, what do the numbers say about the projected production of vehicles in 2005 in Texas?

   a. There will be a greater increase in production.
   b. Texas' productivity of vehicles will remain the same.
   c. The production for Texas will surpass Virginia's production numbers.
   d. There is only one state that will produce less than Texas' production.

5. In 2005, the Automobile industry is expected to account for 760,000 vehicles manufactured in the Southeastern states annually. How will this affect the supply and demand for automobile skilled workers?

   a. People need to be trained to meet the demands of new technical jobs related to the automobile industry.
   b. Jobs for automobile skilled workers will be available in Alabama.
   c. More vehicles will be available to meet consumer demands.
   d. All of the above

Alabama Citizenship Workbook

# 16. Government's Role in the Economy

**As you read Chapter 16, write an answer to each question below.**

1. Explain the two most important tools the government uses to improve the economy.

   _____
   _____
   _____

2. What are the three federal agencies that protect consumers? What is their main focus?

   _____
   _____
   _____
   _____

3. What is the EPA and what does it do?

   _____
   _____
   _____
   _____

4. What are the methods that unions use to protect workers? Why might these pose a problem for the American economy?

   _____
   _____
   _____
   _____

5. What is your view on the national debt? Should the government always have a balanced budget or borrow money to meet its needs? Explain your view.

   _____
   _____
   _____
   _____

Name _____

# 16. Government's Role in the Economy

**Find the best answer for each item. Then circle that answer.**

1. Which of the following describes a period of at least six months of no growth in the economy?

   a. reserve requirement   c. trust
   b. recession   d. labor

2. What is the term for an alliance of firms formed by legal agreement to gain a competitive advantage?

   a. deficit
   b. antitrust laws
   c. trust
   d. collective bargaining

3. What is the word for a period characterized by an increase in the overall level of prices for goods and services?

   a. budget surplus
   b. budget deficit
   c. inflation
   d. deflation

4. What is the name for the period in the economic cycle characterized by a decrease in the overall level of prices for goods and services and in the value of assets?

   a. deflation
   b. discount rate
   c. picket
   d. strike

5. Which of the following describes the laws developed to restrict monopolies and trusts and to ensure fair competition among companies?

   a. collective bargaining
   b. government securities
   c. reserve requirement
   d. antitrust laws

6. What word describes a severe recession that lasts significantly longer than six months, prolonged period of low economic activity and employment?

   a. depression   c. peak
   b. business cycle   d. inflation

7. What is the term that describes a peaceful protest or demonstration?

   a. expansion
   b. trust
   c. picket
   d. labor union

8. Which term describes the signs of the economy's performance, such as the value of goods produced or changes in the prices of certain products?

   a. Gross Domestic Product
   b. reserve requirement
   c. national debt
   d. economic indicators

9. Which of the following words means the excess of spending over income?

   a. budget deficit
   b. peak
   c. expansion
   d. inflation

10. What term describes the periods of growth and shrinkage of business activity?

    a. collective bargaining
    b. business cycles
    c. inflation
    d. expansion

Alabama Citizenship Workbook 57

Name _____

# 16. Government's Role in the Economy

Read each description, and write the letter of the correct term on the line.

1. According to the Constitution, _____.
   a. no state can discriminate against another state
   b. the budget must be balanced
   c. states must have national government approval to raise taxes
   d. states must provide for national defense

2. Business enterprises _____.
   a. must pay taxes to federal, state, and local governments
   b. cannot compete unfairly with others
   c. cannot harm consumers
   d. are required to do a, b, and c

3. If the economy is weak or slow, the government may _____ to help it expand.
   a. lower taxes
   b. increase taxes
   c. raise export taxes
   d. raise interest rates

4. In an expansion period, _____.
   a. people are more careful with their spending
   b. businesses hire fewer workers
   c. demand for goods and services grows
   d. demand for goods and services declines

5. In a peak period, _____.
   a. businesses wish to borrow more money
   b. demand for loans lowers interest rates
   c. businesses have too many workers
   d. neither a, b, nor c is true

6. In a recession, _____.
   a. companies tend to hire more workers
   b. businesses make more money by firing workers
   c. momentum gathers in a downward direction
   d. momentum gathers in an upward direction

7. A depression is _____.
   a. a light recession
   b. a period of expansion
   c. a recession that lasts longer than six months
   d. an expansion that lasts more than six months

8. During the Great Depression, people lost their homes because _____.
   a. inflation increased the value of their assets
   b. deflation decreased the value of their assets
   c. unemployment rates went down and new workers bought out poorer owners
   d. of a, b, and c

9. The Fed influences the economy by _____.
   a. changing the reserve requirement
   b. adjusting the discount rate
   c. buying and selling securities
   d. doing a, b, and c

10. Trusts are busted because _____.
    a. they create too much competition
    b. they create an unfair alliance that hurts other businesses
    c. they use their power to avoid paying fair wages
    d. they hurt demand for products and services

**Essay Question**

Consider the arguments for and against the Endangered Species Act. What is your personal view? Explain your answer.

58 Alabama Citizenship Workbook

Name _____

# Government policies on the free market

**Alabama Planner**
Citizenship Course of Study
7.b, 7.c

Learning Objective:
- Describing the effects of government policies on the free market

AHSGE: II.2

Use pages 248, 249, 253–255, 259–274 of chapters 15 and 16 in the *Civics in America* book to help you answer questions 1–17.

**Short Answer**

1. Give an example of a business in which the U. S. Government had to set restrictions to keep the company from becoming a monopoly on sales of a particular product or products in the U. S. economy. Justify your reasons.

_____

_____

_____

2. Which one of the following organizations is not a not-for-profit organization?
   a. Alabama A. & M. University
   b. The Food World Stores
   c. A. G. Gaston Boys Club
   d. Cahaba Girls Scout Council

3. The advantages or disadvantages on the left are given to describe a command economy, a market economy, and mixed economy. In column B, write the type of system that describes the particular market. In column C, Identify who makes the decisions for that economy. The first one is completed for you.

| Column A | Column B | Column C |
|---|---|---|
| Advantage or Disadvantage | Name the System of Economy | Who makes the decisions |
| 1. Prices are determined by supply and demand only. | Market Economy | Natural market forces |
| 2. Government does not interfere with economy | | |
| 3. Wealth is rewarded | | |
| 4. People are not rewarded for working hard, so production drops | | |
| 5. Profit alone determines economic activities | | |

Alabama Citizenship Workbook 59

4. In Chapter 16 you have learned that it is the government's job to steer the economy through ups and downs. Choose one way which government can help to boost the economy during slow or weak times.

   a. Raise taxes
   b. Provide assistance to farmers
   c. Increase oil prices
   d. Encourage consumers to spend less

5. Identify one way that government can hurt an economy:

   a. unwise spending
   b. enforcing laws
   c. providing security
   d. Encourage consumers not to work

6. Which one of the following is not part of the business cycle that identifies the four stages of economic change in the economy?

   a. Depression
   b. Peak
   c. Expansion
   d. Welfare

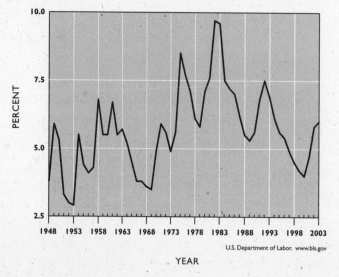

**Unemployment Civilian Work Force**
(Estimated Rates)

Directions: Use the graph to answer Questions 7 and 8.

7. Which year range indicates the largest estimated increased percentage of unemployment?

   a. 1948–1953
   b. 1988–1993
   c. 1978–1983
   d. 1983–1988

8. How is the unemployment rate calculated?

   a. the total of all unemployed people
   b. number of people looking for work divided by civilian workforce
   c. divide the number people working by unemployed.
   d. add the number of people employed to the unemployed.

60  Alabama Citizenship Workbook

**Short Answer Questions:**

9. Using the primary source document on page 260 of *Civics in America* as your reference, give an example of the U. S. government's role in the economy.

_____

_____

_____

10. Give one example of how the following groups can help to improve the economy during an inflation period: U.S. government, citizens, businesses.

_____

_____

_____

Identify the following as a corporation, sole proprietorship, partnership or not-for-profit organization: (*Civics in America:* pp. 251–253)

_____ 11. Sells stock or shares to investors to raise money.

_____ 12. Two or more persons share ownership of the company.

_____ 13. Only operates on needed funds.

_____ 14. Owners are not liable for debts or losses of the company.

_____ 15. All net profit belongs to the owner.

_____ 16. The business is kept separate from its owners or employees.

17. According to the diagram of "The Business Cycle" on page 261 of *Civics in America*, which of the following conclusions is not true about a recession?

   a. If a recession lasts long enough, it will lead into a depression.
   b. People have less money to spend
   c. Workers are laid off
   d. Interest rates and prices reaches an all time high

Name _____

# 17. United States Foreign Policy

**As you read Chapter 17, write an answer to each question below.**

1. What are the four main ways that the U.S. provides humanitarian assistance?

   _____
   _____
   _____

2. What domestic groups influence foreign policy? What do they want?

   _____
   _____
   _____

3. When did the U.S. end its isolationism? What did it do after this change in foreign policy?

   _____
   _____
   _____

4. What are the four non-UN international organizations?

   _____
   _____
   _____

5. In your view, what is the most challenging obstacle to overall world peace? Explain your answer.

   _____
   _____
   _____

# 17. United States Foreign Policy

Find the best answer for each item. Then circle that answer.

1. Which of the following describes the former U.S. policy of avoiding alliances or involvements with other nations?

   a. estrangement
   b. isolationism
   c. boycotting
   d. containment

2. What is the term for something that is opposite of foreign or international, that is, related to internal issues?

   a. domestic
   b. foreign
   c. treaty
   d. diplomacy

3. What term describes a trade, or a military or other formal agreement between nations?

   a. containment
   b. asylum
   c. treaty
   d. sanctions

4. What is the name for the nonviolent penalties imposed on a nation or group by others; that is, punishments aimed to force the offender to act according to a prior agreement?

   a. sanctions
   b. political asylum
   c. containment
   d. alliance

5. Which term means acting together to refuse to use, deal with, or buy as an expression of protest?

   a. collective bargaining
   b. boycotting
   c. isolationism
   d. diplomacy

6. What word describes a special agreement among nations for military or trade purposes?

   a. alliance
   b. intelligence
   c. Cold War
   d. political asylum

7. What is the term that describes the U.S. Cold War policy of preventing the spread of communism?

   a. sanctions
   b. isolationism
   c. boycotting
   d. containment

8. Which term describes the process of handling international relations through negotiation?

   a. embassy
   b. diplomacy
   c. foreign policy
   d. alliance

9. Which of the following words means information, especially about political or military matters?

   a. intelligence
   b. containment
   c. sanctions
   d. entrapment

10. What term describes the shelter granted by a country to refugees from a foreign country who are escaping persecution by their government?

    a. alliance
    b. domestic
    c. political asylum
    d. isolationism

Alabama Citizenship Workbook 63

Name _____

# 17. United States Foreign Policy

**Read each description, and write the letter of the correct term on the line.**

1. Foreign policy for national security includes _____.
   a. directing the armed forces
   b. developing new weapons
   c. providing health insurance
   d. a and b

2. The National Security Council _____.
   a. provides security at national events
   b. spies on other countries
   c. coordinates sources of information for national security
   d. draws on one main source of information for national security

3. Foreign countries lobby the United States to _____.
   a. change public opinion
   b. get favorable tariff and trade terms
   c. protest U.S. foreign policy
   d. achieve a, b, and c

4. Foreign aid to other countries can be in the form of _____.
   a. money
   b. arms
   c. goods
   d. a, b, and c

5. After the Constitution was in place, _____ shaped America's goals in foreign policy.
   a. Washington's farewell address
   b. the Monroe Doctrine
   c. fear of foreigners
   d. options a, b, and c

6. The Monroe Doctrine said that _____.
   a. foreign countries could not colonize
   b. European powers could not trade with countries in the Western Hemisphere
   c. foreign countries could not interfere in the Western Hemisphere
   d. foreign countries had to ask the U.S. to trade with the U.S.

7. The General Assembly is _____.
   a. an assembly of foreign policy experts who vote on U.S. policy
   b. the UN's forum for all its member nations
   c. the National Security Council's team for collecting information
   d. an international court of justice

8. _____ is/are a major concern(s) for America's European foreign policy.
   a. NATO
   b. The EU
   c. The economic transition of Eastern Europe
   d. Options a, b, and c

9. A major Middle East issue is _____.
   a. the lack of drinking water
   b. the Jordan-Egypt conflict
   c. the Arab-Israeli conflict
   d. Bosnia

10. The United States would like to do business in China, but _____.
    a. the Chinese prefer their own products
    b. want government to respect human rights
    c. it's too expensive to ship goods there
    d. is deterred by options a, b, and c

## Essay Question

Consider the arguments for and against keeping Elian Gonzalez in the U.S. What is your view?

64  Alabama Citizenship Workbook

Name _____

## 18. Global Issues

As you read Chapter 18, write an answer to each question below.

1. What are the main advantages of living in an industrialized nation versus in a poorer, developing nation?

   _____

   _____

   _____

2. What are the three main values of a consumerist culture? How do these values contrast with beliefs in developing nations?

   _____

   _____

   _____

3. What are the three separate problems that contribute to world hunger? Explain each.

   _____

   _____

   _____

4. Explain the four main problems caused by drug abuse.

   _____

   _____

   _____

5. Some people say that law enforcement is not effective in cutting down the use of illegal drugs, and therefore suggest that some drugs be legalized. What do you think should be done about this problem?

   _____

   _____

   _____

Alabama Citizenship Workbook

# 18. Global Issues

Find the best answer for each item. Then circle that answer.

1. Which of the following describes people who flee into another country for safety, often in times of conflict or persecution?
   a. refugees
   b. terrorists
   c. the resistance
   d. transnational workers

2. What is the term for the support framework of a society that allows further development?
   a. closed market
   b. renewable resources
   c. infrastructure
   d. nonrenewable resources

3. What term describes the percentage of population over age 15 that can read and write?
   a. child labor rates
   b. literacy rates
   c. industrial rates
   d. sanction rates

4. What is the name for the fuels formed from decaying organic matter, such as oil and natural gas?
   a. renewable resources
   b. infrastructure
   c. hydro fuels
   d. fossil fuels

5. Which is the term for those who unlawfully use of fear or violence, frequently against civilians, to achieve a goal?
   a. refugees
   b. expatriates
   c. isolationists
   d. terrorists

6. What word describes an environmental issue that deals with the increase in the average temperature of the earth's climate?
   a. developing countries
   b. global warming
   c. global climate
   d. political asylum

7. What is the term that describes how natural resources can be regrown, replaced, or restored?
   a. renewable resources
   b. nonrenewable resources
   c. fossil fuels
   d. infrastructure

8. Which is the term for poor countries without much modern industry or infrastructure?
   a. closed markets
   b. transnational countries
   c. developing countries
   d. industrialized countries

9. Which of the following refers to an organization which operates in more than one country?
   a. transnational company
   b. transglobal market
   c. global company
   d. nonprofit organization

10. What term describes the natural resources that cannot be restored after they are used, such as oil?
    a. renewable resources
    b. nonrenewable resources
    c. fossil fuels
    d. global resources

# 18. Global Issues

Read each description, and write the letter of the correct term on the line.

1. Poorer, developing countries have _____.
   a. higher birth rates
   b. lower literacy rates
   c. lower GDPs
   d. all of the above

2. By attracting transnational businesses, developing countries _____.
   a. quickly become fully industrialized nations
   b. earn business taxes and create jobs
   c. hope to improve the lives of their people
   d. do both b and c

3. Japanese corporations were successful because they _____.
   a. demanded that workers obey
   b. paid high wages
   c. adapted Japanese culture to business practices
   d. introduced consumerism to motivate workers

4. A tariff _____.
   a. makes competition unfair for domestic workers
   b. is a tax that favors domestic workers
   c. is an export tax
   d. is a closed-market practice

5. The NAFTA agreement _____.
   a. is designed to protect the U.S. market from Canadian and Mexican exports
   b. joins the U.S., Canada, and Mexico to create a large free trade zone
   c. creates an unfair trading zone for the U.S. and its neighbors
   d. does neither a, b, nor c

6. Free global trade should create _____.
   a. new markets for U.S.-produced goods
   b. American jobs
   c. prosperity for U.S. citizens
   d. all of the above

7. Air pollution is caused by _____.
   a. mostly natural processes
   b. the burning of fossil fuels
   c. industrial pollutants and leftover waste
   d. b and c

8. Some experts warn that air pollution and the global warming it causes could _____.
   a. cause disasters around the globe
   b. naturally ebb and flow like tides, leading to alternating years of good and bad weather
   c. not threaten the earth anytime soon
   d. be a hoax that shouldn't worry people

9. _____ greatly threaten(s) world health.
   a. HIV
   b. Hepatitis C
   c. Cholera
   d. Diseases a, b, and c

10. If a woman is not granted full citizenship, it is _____.
    a. considered a violation of human rights
    b. fair if the culture says so
    c. clear that women do not want citizenship
    d. something that should be accepted by others

## Essay Question

The choice to modernize or become self-sustaining can be difficult for developing countries. Considering options A or B on page 299, which would you choose if you were a leader? Explain.

CHAPTER 19

# Making a Budget

**In this chapter, you will learn about:**

- developing a budget
- keeping records
- paying taxes

When Jamal first left home to live on his own, he was excited but also nervous. One of the things that worried him was money. At home, his mother had always paid the bills. Now he would have to pay the bills himself. He knew he'd be okay in the beginning because he had some savings and he had just started a new job. But how would he know if he had enough money to make it each month? What would happen if he came up short? Knowing that he needed some help figuring these things out, he asked his mother how she organized the monthly bills. Jamal's mother told him the key was making a budget. One evening, Jamal and his mother sat at the dining room table with all her monthly bills spread out before them, and she showed him how to make a budget. Now, not only does he pay his bills on time every month, but he has even managed to put a little something aside for a rainy day.

### Setting Priorities

If you're like most young people, you probably have more goals than time or resources to accomplish them. If so, you need to set priorities, or select the most important things on your list. What are the five most important things on your list? Rewrite your list with these at the top.

Many of your goals will require money. That's where budgeting comes in. Budgeting will help you manage your money so you can meet daily living expenses *and* plan for longer-term goals.

## Developing a Budget

Budgeting is a plan for making the amount of money you earn match the amount of money you spend and save. Understanding how to budget is the first step toward accomplishing your goals.

For many people, *budget* is not a favorite word. When you hear it, you might groan and say something like, "I really should have one, but it's too much trouble." Maybe you have a budget but, like a diet, you can't seem to stick to it. Either way, a budget probably seems like something that restricts your freedom.

Actually, a good budget can do just the opposite. A budget can increase your freedom by giving you control over your finances. Without it, too often your finances control you.

A **budget** is a plan for keeping track of **income** (the money that comes in) and **expenses** (the money that is spent). In a good budget, expenses are less than or equal to income. This allows you to live within your means, or within the amount of money you earn.

### Keeping Track of Expenses

To prepare a budget, you have to know **two** things:

1. Your income.
2. Your expenses.

Your income usually comes in chunks in the form of a paycheck, an allowance, presents, or money you receive for providing such services as yard work or baby-sitting. This income is relatively easy to track. Sometimes you might receive chunks of income from one or more sources each month.

Expenses are harder to track. Most people have daily expenses and also regular monthly expenses. They can lose track of what they are spending.

### Regular Expenses

Everyone needs to eat, wear clothes, get around, and have a place to live. The expenses to take care of these needs are made very regularly—daily, weekly, or monthly. When you live on your own, you cannot avoid these expenses:

* Housing (rent or mortgage).
* Insurance (car, health).
* Transportation (gas, bus fare).
* Food.
* Clothing.
* Phone.
* Utilities (electricity, water, gas).
* Taxes.

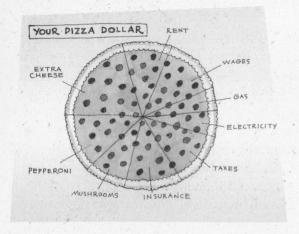

Some of your regular expenses are the same every month, such as your rent or your car payment. Because these costs don't change, they are **fixed expenses**.

Other regular costs *can* change, depending on your behavior.

**EXAMPLES:** You ride a bike to save on transportation. You follow energy-saving tips to reduce your utility bill. You change some eating habits to save on groceries.

These kinds of regular expenses are called **flexible expenses**. You have to spend money on them every month, but you can influence the amount you spend.

## Discretionary Expenses

**Discretionary expenses** are made for things you can do without. Suppose you want a new CD. What effect will it have on your life if you don't buy it?

Not much. However, if you don't pay your phone bill, what will happen? Your phone service will be canceled. Your **credit rating**—reputation with lenders—may go down.

Hobbies, recreational activities, snacks, and movies make life fun and interesting. Your budget should include money for these. However, your plan must take care of regular expenses first. In emergencies, discretionary expenses can be cut back.

## Longer-Term Expenses

In addition to weekly and monthly expenses, you will have planned expenses that come less often. Car insurance may be one. Others, like the need to make repairs to a car or other property, may be unexpected. But you should know you will have them. Money to pay these kinds of bills needs to be set aside so it's there when you need it.

## Dividing Up Your Paycheck

Now that you understand the basic categories of expenses, you need to think about how to divide up your paycheck to meet fixed and discretionary expenses.

No one is "average." However, it is helpful to know about how much of their income people spend in these **five** areas:

1. **Housing** takes about 32 percent of an average American's paycheck. If you live in a popular urban area, such as New York, Seattle, or San

### Get Smart

### Pay Yourself First

Many financial planning books use the phrase: *Pay yourself first*. It doesn't mean give yourself money before meeting your fixed expenses. It means budget for savings as if it were a fixed amount. Plan to save a certain amount each month, and pay that "bill" first. Deposit it in your savings account. If you don't do this, you'll find out what most people learn the hard way. The $50 or $100 you can squeeze out for savings will disappear before it makes it into your savings account.

Savings are important to help you with:

* Longer-term expenses.
* Long- and short-term savings goals.
* Emergencies.

Francisco, or have a low-paying job, this percentage might be higher.

2. **Food** usually takes about 13 percent of an average paycheck. This includes eating out.
3. **Clothing** usually takes about five percent of an average paycheck. This percentage can vary depending on your clothing needs for work, your personal style, and your willingness to shop for secondhand clothes or make your own.
4. **Health-care** usually takes about five percent of an average paycheck. This percentage will be affected by the type of health-care insurance you have and whether or not your employer provides health-care benefits.
5. **Entertainment.** On average, American households in 2000 spent a little less than five percent of their income on entertainment.

In addition to fixed expenses, there are others that will vary depending on your lifestyle:

* *Transportation.* If you purchase and insure a new car, and drive it frequently, you could spend up to 20 percent of your paycheck on this category. A used car, public transportation, a bike, or walking will reduce the amount you need to spend on transportation.
* *Utilities.* Depending on the energy efficiency of your home, and your use of phone and Internet services, this expense can vary greatly.
* *Savings.* A seven percent savings rate is considered good in this country. However, to meet one of your goals, you might have to save more.

    **EXAMPLE:** If you're saving for a big purchase, you might find that seven percent will not cover general savings needs and still allow you to put something aside for it.

After meeting your fixed expenses, remaining money can be used for discretionary expenses such as entertainment, vacations, and recreational activities, or it can be used as additional savings.

## Living with a Budget

Most people start by planning a monthly budget. This is because most expenses, such as rent and utilities, are paid monthly. You might need to add or remove categories, depending on your circumstances.

### By the Numbers

#### Slicing Up the Paycheck Pie

Suzy has just landed her first job after high school. She is still living at home but wants to move out. She has started looking at apartments to rent and is planning to buy a new car.

Her take-home pay is $1,150 a month. The only apartment she has found that she likes rents for $475 a month. The payment and insurance for the car she wants come to $300 a month. These are the only fixed expenses for which she has definite amounts right now.

Do you think Suzy will be able to afford the apartment she wants, a car, and her other fixed and discretionary expenses? To find out, calculate the percentage of her income she will be spending on:

* Housing.
* Transportation.

Do her anticipated expenses fall within the typical American household budget? If not, what advice would you give Suzy so she can afford to live on her own?

Alabama Citizenship Workbook 71

For expenses that are not paid monthly, a monthly amount needs to be calculated. For example, some bills, such as car insurance, can be paid annually (once a year), semi-annually (every six months), or quarterly (every three months). Annual bills should be divided by 12 to come up with a monthly amount. Quarterly bills should be divided by three to get the monthly amount.

A monthly budget will help you understand and control your finances. However, an annual budget is also important. It allows you to compare your annual income with your annual expenses. This can be helpful for many reasons. It allows you to:

* Organize long- and short-term savings plans.
* Adjust your expenses and savings if you have a change in income.
* Adjust flexible and discretionary expenses over a number of months in case of emergencies that require more than your savings plan allows.

Living within a budget is as much psychology as planning. Often, it is the little things that lead us astray. A cup of coffee every day, an extra CD, or a cab ride when you could take the subway may not amount to much by themselves. Add up the expenses, though, and your emergency savings fund can be gone before it's saved.

**EXAMPLE:** A $2.50 soda 20 days a month adds up to $50 a month!

## Sticking to a Budget

Small behaviors can throw your plan off track quickly. To stick to a budget, try these ideas:

* Continue to keep an expense notebook. It will focus your attention on your spending.
* If you go over one month, reduce discretionary spending the next.
* Post your long- and short-term goals in a prominent spot in your home. It will help you focus on the important things you want from life.

* Don't carry around a lot of cash. That makes it easy to overspend.
* Don't buy on the spur of the moment—often called "impulse buying"—no matter how inexpensive the item. The food, shirt, shoes, or CD will likely still be there tomorrow, after you've had time to think about it.
* Plan major purchases in advance. If you're tempted to buy something you haven't planned for, wait a day. During that day, review your budget to see how it will affect you. If you still want to buy the item, revise your budget to come up with the money.

### Making it REAL

**Budget 911 Needed**

Barbara just changed jobs. Her new job will pay her $300 more per month, but her transportation costs are going up. Before, she was able to take the train to work, which cost her $84 a month. Now, she must drive to work, and she needs a reliable car to get to her new job.

She traded in her old car for a newer used car. To pay for the car, she will make monthly payments of $390.94 for two years. In addition, because she will be driving more to get to work, her insurance premiums have increased by $210 per year.

Barbara has been told that she can expect her salary to increase after she has been in her new job for a year. Her concern is affording her higher transportation costs for the next 12 months.

Think about ways Barbara could cut back on expenses to handle this increased cost. What would you do if you were Barbara?

| Barbara's Monthly Budget | | | |
|---|---|---|---|
| Income | Gross Income | Net Income | Expenses |
| | $ 1,700.00 | $1,445.00* | |
| Expenses | | | |
| Housing | | | $375.00 |
| Utilities | | | $60.00 |
| Transportation | | | |
|    ✲ Monthly payment | | | $390.94 |
|    ✲ Insurance ($1/12$ annual cost) | | | $86.00 |
|    ✲ Gas | | | $35.00 |
|    ✲ Maintenance/repairs | | | $20.00 |
| Food | | | $149.00 |
| Phone | | | $25.00 |
| Clothes | | | $30.00 |
| Debt (student loan, credit cards) | | | $50.00 |
| Health care (insurance, copays) | | | $100.00 |
| Savings | | | $25.00 |
| Emergency fund | | | $20.00 |
| Household supplies | | | $15.00 |
| Charitable donations | | | $14.00 |
| Entertainment | | | $30.00 |
| Miscellaneous | | | $20.00 |
| Total | | | $1,444.94 |

* Barbara makes $10.63 an hour and works 160 hours a month. With 15 percent taken out for taxes, her monthly net income is $1,445. She has a roommate, and they split the rent and utilities.

## Get Smart

### The Electronic Budget

Personal finance software can make budgeting faster and easier than doing everything by hand. Its biggest advantage is that it lets you try out different expense amounts easily.
**EXAMPLE:** If you are looking at two apartments, you can quickly see how the monthly rental cost affects how much you will have available for other expenses—all without having to redo your calculations by hand.

Imagine being able to do this for every item in your budget, from savings and food expenses to entertainment and transportation costs.

Here are some guidelines to follow when looking for budgeting and personal finance software:

* Look for software that has the features you need. Avoid programs with lots of expensive additional features you probably won't use.
* Make sure the software is compatible with your computer and operating system.
* Pick something that doesn't require that you already know a lot about budgeting.
* If you bank online, select software that will allow you to download your account information.
* Select a program that allows you to easily view the information as charts and graphs. This can be very helpful in getting a picture of how you are spending your money.

## Get Smart

### Get Frugal!

Here's a word you might want to get to know: *frugal*. A person who is frugal is efficient, sparing, or conservative in his or her use of things, not wasteful. It doesn't mean being deprived or being a cheapskate. Being smart about being frugal can mean having a rich, fun life without spending more than you earn. Here are some tips to get you started:

* Walk or bike to work or school instead of taking public transportation or driving.
* Make your lunch instead of buying it.
* Buy snacks in bulk, pack them in plastic bags, and take them with you instead of buying individual snacks.
* Organize a potluck dinner or picnic with friends instead of going out for a meal.
* Buy generic brands instead of brand names at the grocery store.
* Research new services or products before buying.
* Find inexpensive or free forms of recreation and entertainment. Hikes, bike rides, street fairs, and free concerts in the park are just a few of the many fun activities that are often available. Also, don't forget early showings of movies. They are often half-price or less.

Can you think of other areas where you can reduce expenses without reducing your quality of life?

### Revising a Budget

Even the most carefully planned budgets sometimes need to be revised if circumstances change—for example, if you lose a job. Generally, people need to revise a budget because:

* They are overspending and cannot meet all their expenses.
* Their income has gone down.
* Their expenses have gone up.
* Their income has increased.

The easiest way to reduce your expenses is to start with nonessentials, or discretionary expenses. If that doesn't reduce your expenses enough, you will need to reevaluate your fixed expenses.

Here's a **three**-step plan for getting your expenses to match your income:

1. Reduce discretionary expenses.
2. Reduce flexible expenses.
3. Reduce fixed expenses. For example, get a roommate or move to a cheaper home.

At some point, you may find yourself in the lucky position of needing to revise your budget because your expenses have gone down or your income has gone up.

**EXAMPLES:** Your expenses might decrease if you're moving and your rent is lower. Your income might go up if you get a raise at work or you take a new job that pays more.

When your financial situation changes, you should complete an annual budget. (Remember: Multiply each monthly income and expense by 12.) This will allow you to compare your new annual income to your changed circumstances.

If you are going to have more income than your current budget is based on, you can enjoy deciding what to do with it. Should you add more to savings, plan a vacation, move to a better apartment, or make other changes in your lifestyle and goals? Is your first inclination to add all the extra income to discretionary expenses or to increase some fixed expenses—like housing or clothes—that are acceptable at their current level? In the long run, you will probably be more satisfied if you put some of the excess toward savings and other long-term financial goals.

## Handling Unexpected Expenses

Everyone has emergency expenses from time to time. For example, you might have car repairs. You might have higher-than-expected medical bills, or you might need to travel to help an ill parent or attend an important family event, such as a funeral. If you budget for emergencies, you will be able to handle these unexpected events.

## Record-Keeping

Keeping track of expenses and income, planning for emergencies, and being prepared to file your taxes all require keeping track of financial information. These tasks would be very difficult without good paperwork. To control your financial life, get organized right from the start.

### Getting and Staying Organized

There are many ways to get organized. Pick a system that fits your style, and then modify it to suit your needs. Here are **three** tried-and-true methods for organizing financial information:

1. **Large envelopes** labeled by category.
2. **File folders** labeled by category in a file drawer or box.
3. **An accordion folder** and labels for identifying each pocket.

### Sorting Receipts

To plan a budget that works, you have to know what you're doing with your money. Since you will want—or need—to revise your budget periodically, keeping track of expenses is important.

A set of envelopes or file folders or an accordion file where you store receipts by category will make this task easy. Write your budget categories on the envelopes or file folders. Many office supply stores carry special accordion file folders that come labeled with household expense categories. When you buy something, file the receipt in the appropriate folder.

Add up your receipts regularly. Note the amounts in your budgeting notebook or software. This is an important way to stay on top of how much you're spending on food, transportation, entertainment, and other regular expenses.

### Personal Records

Keeping and sorting receipts is important, but it's not enough. You also need to organize important documents. Here are some important categories for keeping your personal records in order. Include the ones that match your needs, and add new ones if necessary.

* Automobile (insurance, maintenance, title, registration and license plates, loan information).

### By the Numbers

#### Make Your Own Budget

What are your fixed expenses each month? Which ones are flexible? How about your discretionary expenses? Do you have short-term and long-term goals for which you need to save money?

Think about how you spend and save money now and how you would like to spend and save money in the future. Create a budget for yourself. Start with a monthly one and then calculate your annual budget. Be realistic and create a budget you can stick to!

* Checking account statements.
* Credit card statements.
* Charitable contributions.
* Contracts.
* Health insurance.
* Investments.
* Medical costs.
* Paycheck stubs.
* Pet records.
* Retirement contributions.
* Savings account statements.
* Social Security statements.
* Tax returns from previous years.
* W-2 forms (forms supplied by your employer in January of each year that show your earnings and deductions for the previous year).
* Warranties (for TV sets and other appliances).

Sort and file these documents in labeled file folders or an accordion file folder as you do your receipts.

## Understanding Your Paycheck

Getting your first paycheck can be a thrill. It's money you earned yourself! But it can also be a shock. At first, it might seem like the check is too small.

**EXAMPLE:** Let's see: 40 hours a week at $8 an hour. That comes to $320. Why is the check for only $272? What happened to the missing $48? The answer is: It was deducted to pay your taxes.

### Taxes

Taxes are your contribution to running the government. In return for this payment, you receive services and benefits.

**EXAMPLE:** When you retire you will receive a monthly payment to help with living expenses from Social Security.

Your taxes are also used to support public needs, such as schools and roads.

### Get Smart

#### Money Management Tips

Brenda W. and Scott T. are both out of high school and living on their own in a small college town in Oregon. Brenda is finished with college and is already thinking about marriage and her future. Scott just finished high school and is going to attend a community college for two years while he saves money to complete his degree.

Here are some practical suggestions they think will help you get off to a good start when you go out on your own:

* Pay the important things first.
* Group bills and pay them once or twice a month instead of when each one is due.
* Over-estimate expenses. It's better to have a little left over than not enough.
* Buy used! Used clothes, cars, and appliances are especially good deals.
* Out of sight, out of mind is the best rule for savings and emergency money. Put your savings in an account every month—or have it deposited into your savings account directly from your paycheck—and then forget about it until you need it.

Alabama Citizenship Workbook 77

## Your Paycheck Stub

Each time you receive a paycheck from your employer, you also receive a **paycheck stub**. This stub shows exactly what taxes were deducted from your paycheck and what the deductions are for.

A typical paycheck stub shows:

* Gross wages.
* Net wages.
* Payroll taxes (including Social Security).

### Gross Wages

**Gross wages** are the total amount you earn in a given time period. But you don't get to take home all of it. Some of it is taken out to cover taxes and other required payments. These amounts are called **deductions** because they are deducted from, or taken out of, your wages before you get your paycheck.

### Net Wages

The amount left after deductions are taken out is called **net wages**. This is the amount you will have available to spend for your daily, monthly, and annual living expenses. Net wages can be quite a bit less than gross wages. Subtract the current deductions from $640 to discover the take-home pay in the Anatomy of a Paycheck Stub example on page 44.

The amount of tax taken out of your paycheck is affected by **two** factors:

1. **Your filing status.** This is the number of dependents you claim. For tax purposes, dependents are people in your household, including yourself, whom you support.

### Students Get Involved

Members of Students in Free Enterprise (SIFE) are out to change the world. With the help of their business professors, students from more than 700 U.S. colleges work to:

* Educate young people about financial issues and responsibility.
* Improve the lives of people in low-income communities by teaching them about business ownership.

In Chico, California, SIFE students set up and ran the Youth Entrepre-neurship Camp for children aged 10 to 12 years old. Participants learned about business ownership and got hands-on experience applying math, computer, and writing skills to business-ownership questions.

SIFE students from La Sierra University went to Karandi village in India to help villagers set up The Cow Bank. Instead of lending money, The Cow Bank lends a cow! Families can drink some of the milk themselves and sell the extra milk. Instead of repaying the loan with money, it is repaid with the first female calf produced by the cow.

2. **The amount you earn.** Up to a certain high income, the more you earn, the higher the percentage deducted.

## Payroll Taxes

Payroll taxes are the different types of taxes deducted from your paycheck. The federal government taxes your income, as does your state government.

## Other Deductions

In addition to payroll taxes, there may be additional required or voluntary deductions. For example:

* *Required local taxes.*
* *Contribution toward health insurance.* If your employer provides health insurance benefits, you may be required to pay a portion.
* *Retirement plan contribution.* If your employer provides a retirement benefit, you can have money automatically deposited in your retirement account.
* *Charitable contribution.* Some employers match employee donations and send the total directly to the charity.
* *Union dues.* If you belong to a union, your membership dues will be deducted automatically from your paycheck.
* *Savings.* Some companies will deposit a part of employees' paychecks into a savings account.

### Anatomy of a Paycheck Stub

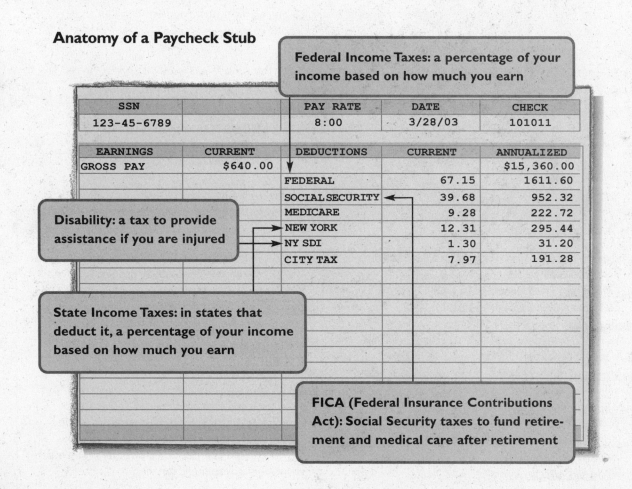

| Payroll Taxes | |
| --- | --- |
| Type of Deduction | Purpose |
| Federal taxes | Deductions used to support the federal government's services and programs. |
| FICA (Federal Insurance Contribution Act) | Deductions to support retirement programs such as Social Security and Medicare. |
| Workers' compensation or disability programs | Deductions to provide support if you're injured or unable to work. |
| State taxes | Deductions used to support state government services and programs. |

## Chapter 19 Wrap-up
### MAKING A BUDGET

A good budget can pave the way to financial well-being. Tracking your income and expenses puts you in control of your money and helps you achieve your short and long-term financial goals. Getting and staying organized, keeping records, and sorting receipts are important habits to develop. They will help you stick to your budget.

You will need to revise your budget, if you lose a job or get a raise. If you move into a more or less expensive home, your expenses will change. Revising monthly and annual budgets will help you cope with changes in your circumstances.

One set of expenses you cannot avoid is taxes. When calculating your income, keep your net wages in mind. That's what you get to take home.

**budget**—spending plan designed to balance income and expenses.
**credit rating**—evaluation made by lenders based on ability to pay and bill-paying history.
**deductions**—required and voluntary amounts removed from your paycheck to cover taxes and optional benefits.
**discretionary expenses**—costs for items or services that are not essential.
**expenses**—money spent to purchase goods and services.
**fixed expenses**—costs of living that are the same amount every month.
**flexible expenses**—costs of living that vary.
**gross wages**—amount you earn before deductions

**income**—money received for labor or services (your work), for the sale of goods or property, or from financial investments.
**net wages**—amount you earn after deductions; your take-home pay.
**paycheck stub**—slip that shows your pay and gives you an accounting of all amounts deducted from your paycheck.
**Social Security**—federally funded government program designed to provide partial retirement benefits for older Americans; program is funded with worker payroll taxes.
**taxes**—required contribution all workers must make to support government services.

Name _____

# 19. Making a Budget

**After you read the chapter, write an answer to each question below.**

1. What are five key expense areas that people spend their paychecks on and what are the average percentages?

   _____
   _____
   _____

2. Why would doing an annual budget be helpful to you?

   _____
   _____
   _____

3. What is the three-step plan to get expenses to match your income?

   _____
   _____
   _____

4. What are three "tried and true" methods for organizing financial information?

   _____
   _____
   _____

5. What are the four different types of deductions that fall under payroll taxes?

   _____
   _____
   _____

Name _____

## 19. Making a Budget

**Circle the best answer for each item.**

1. What is the term for a spending plan designed to balance income and expenses?
   a. spreadsheet
   b. balance sheet
   c. budget
   d. monetary outline

2. What are referred to as the required and voluntary amounts removed from your paycheck to cover taxes and optional benefits?
   a. deductions
   b. net wages
   c. fixed allowance
   d. flexible taxes

3. What is the term for the amount you earn before deductions?
   a. interim wages
   b. flexible wages
   c. net wages
   d. gross wages

4. What is the money received for labor or services (your work), for the sale of goods or property, or from financial investments?
   a. income
   b. taxes
   c. fixed income
   d. budget

5. What is the required contribution all workers must make to support government services?
   a. fixed fee
   b. allowance
   c. register
   d. taxes

Name _____

## 19. Making a Budget

**Read each description, and write the letter of the correct term on the line.**

1. In a good budget, expenses are less than or equal to _____.
   - a. one paycheck
   - b. last year's salary
   - c. three months' salary
   - d. income

2. Hobbies, recreational activities, snacks, and movies are examples of _____.
   - a. flexible expenses
   - b. planned expenses
   - c. discretionary expenses
   - d. fixed expenses

3. Many financial planning books say: _____.
   - a. pay yourself first
   - b. pay yourself last
   - c. pay your bills last
   - d. save first

4. A _____ percent savings rate is considered good in this country.
   - a. three
   - b. five
   - c. seven
   - d. six

5. "Don't buy on the spur of the moment" and "Plan major expenses in advance" are examples of _____.
   - a. how to revise your budget
   - b. how to be frugal
   - c. how to stick to a budget
   - d. how to organize your finances

6. Deductions to provide support if you're injured or unable to work are called _____.
   - a. union dues
   - b. health insurance benefits
   - c. worker's compensation
   - d. worker's reward

CHAPTER 20

# Handling Your Money

**In this chapter, you will learn about:**

- developing a budget
- keeping records
- paying taxes

Picture this: It's a beautiful sunny day. You're relaxing on a park bench, soaking up the rays. After a few moments, you're joined by a man with a small metal box. You greet each other warmly, and then you hand him all the money you made for the last week. He writes you a receipt for the money, puts it in the metal box, and promises to safeguard it until you need it. On another day, you might meet on the bench again, but not to give him more money.

On this day, you might request a loan and then linger on the bench to work out the details of how you'll pay him back.

Sound improbable? Well, if you had lived in Italy in the 15th century, that is probably how you would have handled your money. Most people did, which is why our word "bank" comes from the Italian *banca*, which means bench—the location where many banking activities took place.

# How Banks Work

Banks and other financial institutions provide an important service to society. When most people say the word *bank*, they are referring to several different financial institutions, including commercial banks—what most of us call a *bank*—savings and loans, savings banks, and others. There are differences between the institutions, but for most ordinary purposes, these differences are slight. Whatever you call them, banks allow people to:

* Protect their money from theft.
* Borrow money.
* Smoothly carry out transactions—deposits, withdrawals, and payments in checks you write to pay your bills.
* Earn money by receiving interest, or a percentage of the amount in the account that is paid to you in return for keeping your money with the bank.

Banks are businesses. To stay in business, they need to make money, or a profit, just like any other business does. The **two** main ways they make money are by:

1. **Providing loans** (lending money to their customers).
2. **Charging for financial services,** such as loans and checking accounts.

## Banks and the Government

In the United States, banking is a regulated industry. This means financial institutions that take your money have to follow certain laws. For example, to protect customers' money, banks are allowed to lend only a percentage of the amount they take from depositors. Depositors are people, like you, who deposit money in a bank. The amount of money they put in each time is called a deposit.

With the billions of dollars circulating in the United States, you might wonder how all that money is regulated. It's done by a national agency called the Federal Reserve. Often called "The Fed" for short, the Federal Reserve:

* Manages the federal government's money.
* Controls the flow of money in this country.

To handle both these activities, the Federal Reserve functions as a regulatory agency and as a bank. (It has one main bank in Washington, D.C., and 12 regional banks around the country.)

## Banks and the Community

Banks keep money moving through a community, which helps the economy. For example, banks loan money so consumers can buy houses and cars. Since most people do not have enough cash on hand to purchase such expensive items, a bank loan makes it possible. These kinds of purchases stimulate, or spur, the economy. In the same way, bank loans to businesses also benefit the local economy.

## Understanding Fees and Interest Rates

Banks are businesses that make money by charging for services and by lending money. The costs for their services are called fees.

Banks don't only charge fees. They also pay depositors interest. You might wonder how they can afford to do that. The answer is simple. They lend money at a higher interest rate (percentage paid on a loan or deposit) than they pay out. This difference between the interest they pay depositors and the interest they receive from loan payments is an important source of income for banks.

# Other Financial Institutions

Each type of institution offers advantages and disadvantages, primarily involving differences in fees and services. In some cases, the main advantage is that a particular institution offers all the services you need. For example, commercial banks and credit unions, whose members are affiliated in some way (work for the same organization or graduated from the same college), offer the widest range of services and products. This includes checking and savings accounts, loans, and investment tools. While fees can be higher at commercial banks than some other institutions, the convenience of one-stop banking can make them a practical choice. Credit union services and products compare well with those offered by commercial

| What Banking Institutions Do | |
| --- | --- |
| Type of Institution | Services Offered |
| Savings and loans | First set up to promote home ownership, they offer home mortgages, and car loans, savings, and checking accounts. |
| Credit unions | Nonprofit cooperatives whose members are affiliated in some way. They offer full banking services at lower costs. |
| Commercial banks | Referred to as full-service banks because they offer complete lending, checking, and saving services. |
| Savings banks | Services limited to savings accounts, loans, and safe-deposit boxes. |
| Virtual banks | Full-service banks without branches; all transactions are conducted electronically. |
| Loan companies | Primary function is consumer loans. |

banks. In addition, fees can be lower because credit unions are **cooperatives** (groups owned and managed by members). If you are eligible for membership in a credit union, this can be a good choice.

Other institutions offer specialized products. As a result, they can offer more choices in their area of specialization. For example, a loan company may be able to find a loan for you that better meets your needs than one from a commercial bank. Even if you use a commercial bank or credit union for your banking needs, it can pay to research fees and choices with more specialized institutions, such as loan companies, savings banks, and savings and loans.

## Checking Accounts

Writing someone a check is like giving them cash. It's just a more convenient and safer substitute. It's hard to function in our society without a checking account. Since you'll probably stick with the bank you choose for a number of years, spend some time researching account options. Compare:

* Fees.
* Interest rates.
* Check costs.
* Check-writing restrictions, if any.
* Overdraft policies.
* Minimum requirements for your balance (the amount of money you have in the account).

### Opening an Account

To open an account:

* Select the bank and type of account that meet your needs.
* Gather personal information to complete an application.
* Take your personal information to the bank to meet with a customer service representative (or, complete your online application for a virtual bank).
* Complete a signature card so the bank knows what your signature looks like.
* Make a deposit.

Don't forget to bring the following when opening a checking account:

* Photo identification.
* Money for an initial deposit.
* Address and phone number.
* Name and address of a relative or reference.

## Anatomy of a Check

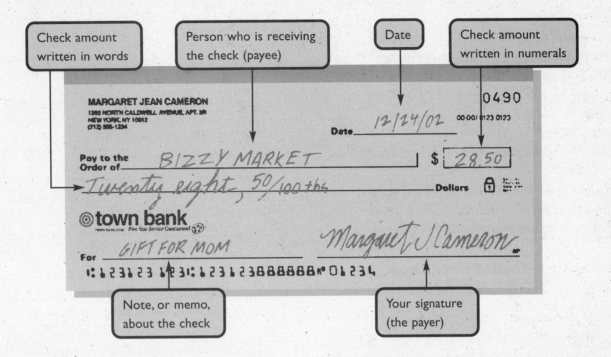

## Using Checks

When you write checks, you should always follow these **three** steps:

1. **Fill in all the information.** This will include the name of the payee (the person or company to whom you wrote the check), date, amount of the check in numerals, amount spelled out in words, and your signature. Otherwise, the check may not be accepted. Then you'll have to spend time straightening out the mess that results.

   "Memo" is optional. You can use it to write a note reminding yourself what the check is for, such as "electricity bill," or to provide information for the payee, such as the account number of your cell phone if you're paying your cell phone bill.

2. **Complete the check register.** Write the amount of the check, the date, the check number, and the payee in the check register (the booklet where you record checks and track your bank balance).

3. **Figure your balance.** Subtract the amount of your check from the balance, which is the amount you had in your account before you wrote the check. This will give you a new balance.

When you make a deposit or put money in the account, record that in your check register, too. Each time you deposit money, you need to fill out a slip telling the bank the amount of the deposit. Your checkbook will have deposit slips in the back. Make sure you also record ATM or debit withdrawals.

## How to Read a Bank Statement

Every month, you will receive a bank statement. This monthly statement shows all the checks you wrote during the month. It also shows all your deposits, withdrawals, and other important information.

A bank statement includes the following information with which you need to be familiar. At a minimum, a bank statement includes these **six** pieces of information:

1. **Statement Period** The period of time covered by that statement and the transactions that occurred during that period. The statement period is usually one month, most often from the first day of the month to the last.

2. **Ending Balance** The amount of money in the account on the last day of the statement period.

Alabama Citizenship Workbook  **87**

3. **Checks Deducted** A list of each check and debit card transaction for which money was taken out of the account.
4. **Deposits Credited** A list of all money put into the account during the statement period.
5. **Fees or Charges Deducted** A list of deductions made against your account during the statement period. These deductions can include a charge for checks, or a fee for dropping below the minimum balance or writing a bad check (a check that bounced).
6. **Interest Earned** The amount of money the bank paid you on the amount of money in your account during the statement period.

## Balancing Your Checkbook

Balancing a checkbook involves making sure:

* The amount you have in your checkbook balance matches the amount the bank says you have.
* You have enough money in the account to cover checks you write.

When you receive your statement, it will come with an account-balance reconciliation form, which you use to make sure your records match the bank's records. *Reconciling* your account means balancing your account based on the information in the bank statement. If your account is balanced, it means you and the bank agree on the amount of money in your account.

Balancing your checking account involves these **five** steps:

1. **Check the current balance.** Determine what your account balance was on the last day of the statement period by looking on the monthly statement (ending balance).
2. **Check deposits and checks written.** Compare the deductions and deposits in your check register to those on the bank statement.
3. **Include new deposits.** Add up all the deposits made after the ending date on your monthly statement, and add them to the ending balance.
4. **Include new deductions.** Add up all your deductions—checks you've written, ATM fees, and the like—after the end of the statement period, and deduct them from the balance you got when you added your deposits to the ending balance.
5. **Balance the totals.** The amount in step 4 is the amount you have now in your checking account because it includes transactions you've made since the statement was prepared.

### Anatomy of a Check Register

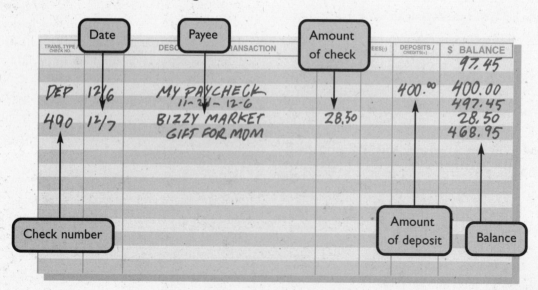

Here are some tips to help you keep track of items when you're balancing your checkbook so you don't add or subtract the same item more than once. As you compare the statement to your check register:

* Put a check mark next to each withdrawal (check, ATM, or debit card) that is in your check register and on the statement.
* Put a check mark next to each deposit that is in your check register and on the statement.
* If some checks or deposits don't have checks next to them, determine why.
  **EXAMPLES:** was a deposit you made not recorded by the bank? Are there checks, debit card transactions, or deposits on the statement that you forgot to add to your register?

Can you think of other items that might not match? Why?

## Endorsing Checks

Sometimes you will not be the one to write a check. You will be the one to receive a check from someone. When this happens, you can do one of two things with it:

* Cash it.
* Deposit it into an account.

No matter which option you choose, you have to **endorse** the check. When you endorse a check, you write your name on the back. This signature indicates that you accept the transfer of someone else's money to you.

In addition to a signature, you might want to include other information on the back, depending on whether you plan to cash or deposit the check. If you plan to cash the check, write only your signature on the back. However, wait until you are at the bank. If someone finds or steals an endorsed check, it is as good as money. It can be cashed at a bank.

If you plan to deposit the check, add the following information above or below your signature:

* "For deposit only."
* The account number to which you want the check deposited.

This information will tell the bank that the check is meant to be deposited only to the account with the number written on the back. If someone tries to cash the check or deposit it to another account, the bank will not accept it.

### Anatomy of an Endorsed Check

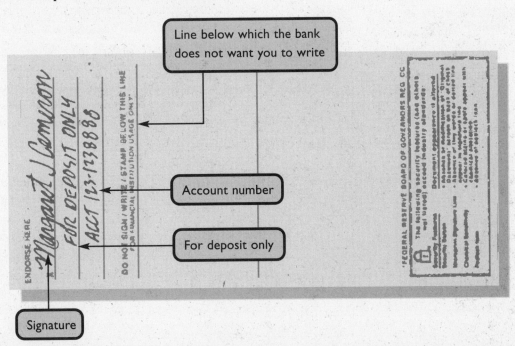

## Handling Mistakes

Even if you keep track of every check you write and balance your checkbook every month, the day will probably come when there will be a mistake with your account. Here are some common mistakes that everyone experiences now and then:

* Your balance doesn't match the bank's. (If this occurs, balance your account again. If it still doesn't balance, contact the bank. If a mistake is due to bank error, check your next statement carefully. You should not be charged bank fees for any problems that might result.)
* A check written quite some time ago has not cleared. (Contact the payee to see if the check was cashed.)
* Your checkbook is lost or stolen. (Report it to your bank immediately.)
* You believe someone has forged one of your checks. (Contact the bank immediately. You should not be responsible for the amount of the check. If the bank cashed the check without verifying the signature, it will have to reimburse, or pay back, your account.)

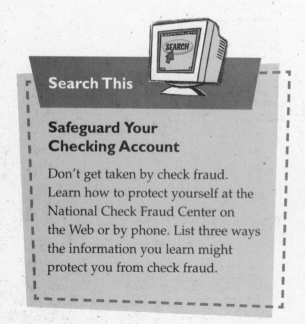

**Search This**

**Safeguard Your Checking Account**

Don't get taken by check fraud. Learn how to protect yourself at the National Check Fraud Center on the Web or by phone. List three ways the information you learn might protect you from check fraud.

## Savings Accounts

What should you do with the money you have earmarked for savings and an emergency fund? Avoid keeping this money in your checking account for **two** main reasons:

1. **The money is too easy to reach.** It should take extra effort to get to money saved so you don't use it for the wrong purpose.
2. **Savings accounts earn more.** Generally, checking accounts don't pay interest or pay less than what you'll receive on a savings account.

### Shopping for the Best Interest Rate

Remember that interest is a percentage of your deposit. This percentage is called the interest rate. The higher the interest rate, the more money your deposit will earn. When researching where to put your savings, consider these **three** types of savings vehicles:

1. **Standard savings accounts** (usually the lowest interest rate of the three listed here). A standard savings account is the place to keep enough money to handle an emergency, but it is not a good place for the largest share of your savings. The advantage is, you can get your money whenever you want it.
2. **Money market accounts** (usually a higher interest rate than a standard account). A <u>money market account</u> allows you to write checks, but only up to a certain number each month. Usually, you must keep a minimum balance in a money market account, whereas a regular savings account has no minimum balance requirements (or a much lower minimum).
3. **Certificates of deposit,** called CDs (higher interest rate than other options). The money placed in a <u>certificate of deposit</u> cannot be touched for a certain amount of time, usually at least six months, without paying penalties. It's a good way to increase your earnings on savings, as long as you know you will not need the money for any other purpose.

## What Banks Charge

| Fee | Description |
| --- | --- |
| Monthly service charge | A fixed amount deducted from your account each month. |
| Check costs | Charges for printing new checks. |
| Minimum balance charge | A charge if the balance falls below a certain dollar amount. |
| Returned check or overdraft charge | A charge for checks that were written when there wasn't enough money in the account to pay for them. |
| Overdraft protection | A service in which banks will move money from a savings account to a checking account when you don't have enough money in the account to cover the check. |
| Teller usage fees | A charge for speaking with a teller if you select an account in which you carry out all your transactions online or with an Automated Teller Machine. |

## Anatomy of a Bank Statement

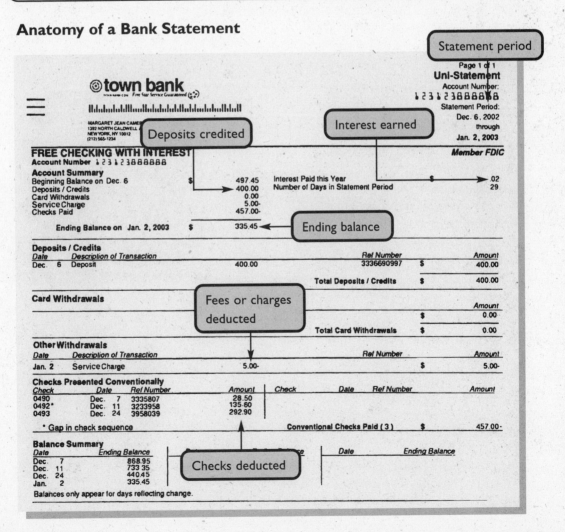

Alabama Citizenship Workbook

## By the Numbers

### Compare the Savings

Let's say you've been following your savings plan every month. Some of your savings are still sitting in your checking account. You've saved up enough money now that you can begin to divide it into funds for emergencies, short-term savings, and long-term savings.

Research interest rates for a savings account, a money market account, and a certificate of deposit.

Now, imagine you are going to put $100 in each account for six months. You will not withdraw money from or deposit money into the account during that time. Calculate how much you'll have in each account in six months:

* First, multiply $100 by the interest rate of each account. (For example, if the interest rate is 2.5%, multiply $100 by .025 to get $2.50 in interest.)
* Next, determine your earnings. Since the interest just calculated is for one year, divide it in half to get the interest for six months (2 into $2.50 = $1.25).

Where will you go in your area to get the best interest rate?

## Getting the Right Kind of Account

Your reasons for saving influence the kinds of accounts you use. For example, emergency funds need to be "liquid," or easy to reach. For these funds, standard savings accounts and money market accounts are appropriate. Look for accounts with:

* The highest interest rate.
* The lowest fees.
* The minimum penalty if your balance falls below a certain amount.

While you need easy access to emergency funds, that is not necessarily true for non-emergency savings. The account you select depends on the purpose for which you are saving. For example, short-term savings needed in less than six months can be placed in a regular savings or money market account.

If you use a money market account, find out how many checks you can write on the account in a given

### Tracking Savings

Write down the amount you save each time you spend less on something than you used to. There are many reasons you might spend less. Perhaps you've waited to buy until a needed item came on sale. Maybe you've decided to start buying generic items instead of brand-name products, or skip the expensive popcorn and soda at movies, or take your lunch to school or work everyday. Whatever the reason, make a note of the amount saved and the reason you were able to save.

Also, keep a record of times you decide not to spend money at all when you might have in the past. At the end of the month, add up your savings. How did you do for the month?

time period. Most money market accounts restrict the number of checks you can write. This has advantages and disadvantages:

* *It can help you stick to a savings plan* because you can't make unlimited withdrawals.
* *It can be difficult to withdraw money* if you've already reached the allowed number of withdrawals.

For savings that won't be touched for at least six months, consider CDs. You'll get a higher interest rate than in a savings or money market account. You'll also get the benefit of forced savings, since you can't get the money out easily.

### Protecting Your Savings—From Yourself

No matter how well you stick to a savings plan, you always run the risk of undoing all your hard work. All it takes is one withdrawal for the wrong reason. That's why it's a good idea to have a plan for protecting your savings from yourself.

Here are **four** guidelines to help you avoid jeopardizing your savings:

1. **Don't mix savings** funds with funds for paying daily and monthly expenses.
2. **Transfer money regularly** from your checking to savings accounts.
3. **Make it hard to get to your savings.** For example, put money in CDs. You can't remove it early without paying a penalty.
4. **Save automatically.** Ask your bank to set up automatic monthly deposits into savings vehicles through the automatic deposit of your paycheck or through banks and other financial institutions.

### Your Highest Returns

Vincelle L. is a high school junior. He has a job and a savings account that he has had since he was a small child. He needs to pay for car insurance, but he doesn't have other monthly bills.

Because he will not need his savings for at least another year, he put three-quarters of his savings in a 12-month certificate of deposit. The CD earns 4.9 percent interest.

To pay his car insurance premiums, he put most of his remaining savings in a money market account, so he can write checks while he earns 3.2 percent. In his savings account, he keeps monthly amounts that are being saved toward less regular payments (like his car insurance) and for planned repairs. It pays only 2.9 percent, but he can get the money out whenever he needs it.

**bank**—business that receives, safeguards, and lends money, and offers related financial and monetary services.

**certificate of deposit**—savings tool in which you loan money to the bank for a fixed term (a specific amount of time). In return, you receive a higher interest rate than a traditional savings account, but you must wait to make withdrawals.

**check register**—small booklet used to keep track of each check written and your bank balance.

**cooperative**—group in which members band together to form a business or association that's owned and operated by the members themselves. Members share the profits.

**credit union**—cooperative savings and lending institution in which members are affiliated in some way, such as working for the same organization or attending the same college.

**deposit**—amount of money placed in an account, such as a checking or savings account.

**depositor**—person who puts money in an account.

**endorse**—to sign one's name on the back of a check, indicating approval of the transfer of money from one party to another.

**interest**—amount of money received as a benefit of keeping funds in a bank or other financial institution, or the amount paid to borrow money from a financial institution.

**interest rate**—percentage paid on a loan or deposit.

**money market account**—specialized savings account that has limited check-writing options and offers a higher interest rate than a regular savings account.

**payee**—person or company being paid.

**profit**—amount of money returned after all of a business's operating expenses have been paid.

**transactions**—bank activities, such as deposits and withdrawals, conducted as part of doing business with the bank.

Name _____

# 20. Handling Your Money

**Circle the best answer for each item.**

1. What is a cooperative savings and lending institution in which members are affiliated in some way, such as by working for the same organization or attending the same college?

   a. credit union
   b. check-cashing center
   c. pawnshop
   d. lending shop

2. What is the term for a person who puts money into an account?

   a. payee
   b. endorser
   c. depositor
   d. loanee

3. What is the term for the amount of money received as a benefit of keeping funds in a bank or other financial institution, or the amount paid to borrow money from a financial institution?

   a. interest
   b. cooperative
   c. depositor
   d. transactions

4. What is the percentage paid on a loan or deposit?

   a. bank fee
   b. profit
   c. application fee
   d. interest rate

5. What is a term for the person or company being paid?

   a. depositor
   b. payee
   c. loan officer
   d. cooperative

6. The costs for bank services are called _____.

   a. interest
   b. principal
   c. fees
   d. assessments

7. Credit unions are _____, which are groups owned and managed by members.

   a. corporations
   b. cooperatives
   c. not-for-profit organizations
   d. constituents

8. _____ your account means balancing your account based on your bank statement.

   a. Reinvesting
   b. Reconnecting
   c. Reconciling
   d. Interpreting

9. "Put a check mark next to each withdrawal and deposit," is _____.

   a. an example of how to stick to a budget
   b. a tip to help you balance your checkbook
   c. directions on how to endorse a check
   d. a tip for making more money

10. For savings that won't be touched for at least six months, consider a _____.

    a. standard savings account
    b. certificate of deposit
    c. money market account
    d. checking account

Alabama Citizenship Workbook

Name _____

## 20. Handling Your Money

**After you read the chapter, write an answer to the question below.**

If you want to deposit a check, what three things do you need to write on the back of the check?
_____
_____
_____

CHAPTER 21

# Using Credit Wisely

**In this chapter, you will learn about:**

- understanding credit
- keeping a good credit rating
- avoiding getting into debt

Alex and Shauna each got a credit card. Both were tempted to get the things they wanted by charging the purchases. Alex caved in to his temptations. He wanted a new stereo system for his apartment, so he put it on his credit card. He also used credit to buy a car, and he opened charge accounts at several stores so he could buy the latest trendy clothes. Soon, Alex was deeply in debt. Most of his income went to making his credit card and loan payments, leaving him with no money to have fun.

Shauna, on the other hand, used credit only when it was really necessary and when she knew that she would be able to pay it off right away. Her clothing and her car were not always the coolest among her friends, but, after a year or two, Shauna had money left from her paycheck to buy new clothing and even to take a trip. She also had no debt.

Alabama Citizenship Workbook

# Understanding Credit

Omnika wanted a cool set of speakers that cost $500, and she had only a few dollars in her checking account. The salesperson suggested she buy the speakers on **credit**. "Buy now, pay later!" he encouraged Omnika.

Getting what you want on credit seems easy, but what the ads fail to tell you is that credit often causes many financial problems and heartaches. If Omnika gets several cash loans and if she charges many purchases, she may find herself so heavily in debt that she cannot enjoy life because she is always worried about paying her bills. However, Omnika can avoid sleepless nights, having her car taken away, and being harassed by people to whom she owes money. She can make credit work for her rather than against her. So can you. The way to make credit work for you is to understand how it works and when to use it.

## What Is Credit?

Credit goes by many different names, such as borrowing, charging, and getting a loan. Credit is really using someone else's money. Credit may be borrowing cash, or it may be buying something now and paying for it in the future. In either case, not only must the amount borrowed or charged be paid back, but also a fee will be charged that is some percentage of the amount borrowed. The amount charged or borrowed is called the **principal**, and the fee that is paid for the use of the money is called the interest.

## Immediate Versus Delayed Gratification

Let's say you really want a new CD. If you go out and buy it right away, you're getting something called **immediate gratification**. Using credit is a way of getting immediate gratification. However, if you wait a few weeks to save up the money to buy the CD, you have **delayed gratification**.

Buying on credit helps you get immediate gratification, but there are disadvantages. You may not have money you need at some later date because you have committed your future income to pay for things you get now. Some of your earnings also must go to pay credit fees rather than to purchasing things you might need or want.

## Commercial and Personal Credit

Like individuals, businesses and even governments often borrow money. When a business wants to expand or increase its inventory, it gets a loan, called **commercial credit**, to cover the costs. There are times when a government spends more than it raises in taxes. When this happens, it also has to borrow money.

Credit used by individuals is called **personal credit**. Personal credit also affects the economy. Having credit available makes it easy to purchase more goods. When people buy more, jobs are created for those who make and sell those products. What happens to the economy if consumers use too much credit? If people buy on credit and save little, a time may come when they have to pay off their debts and cannot buy anymore. When this happens, there are fewer people to purchase goods and fewer jobs for people who make and sell the products.

## Uses of Credit

Credit is neither good nor bad in itself. It is *what* you use it for and *how* you use it that make it good or bad. When is it to your advantage to use credit? When should you pay cash or give up the purchase? These are often not easy questions to answer. Here are some guidelines to help you make these decisions.

### Advantages of Using Credit

Credit is necessary for almost everyone. For example, very few people could buy a house without credit. Here are **three** examples of the advantages of using credit:

1. **If you don't have ready cash,** buying something on credit makes it possible to use the product while you are paying for it, rather than waiting until you save enough to buy it. If you buy a DVD player on a one-year credit plan, you can use it immediately. If you saved for it first, the satisfaction of having it will be delayed for a year. Buying now and using the product while you pay for it is most appropriate for major purchases, such as homes and automobiles, since it's difficult to save in advance for the full purchase price.

## My Notebook

### Buying Now or Later?

Describe a time when you waited to save up the money to buy something you wanted. What happened? Did you still want the item by the time you saved up the money for it? What can you learn from this experience?

Now describe a time when you purchased something big without waiting. What, if anything, did you give up to buy the item? If you had to do it again, would you purchase the item in the same way, or at all? Why or why not? What did you learn to help you in the future?

2. **Using credit may help you save money.** Suppose you see inline skates that you've been wanting. They are on sale for a limited time for $20 off. If you don't have the money but have a credit card, you can take advantage of this sale.

3. **Credit comes in handy** for short-term needs and emergencies. Suppose your car breaks down and you have no ready cash for repairs. If you had no other way to get to work, you might lose your job without using credit to make the needed repairs.

## Disadvantages of Using Credit

Along with the advantages that credit offers, though, there are risks when you use credit to make your purchases. Here are **three** examples:

1. **Credit makes it easier to overspend** and to make impulse purchases. It's so easy to buy things today thinking you'll pay for them "in the future." But the future is uncertain. Suppose you use too much credit? What if you're laid off from your job or have unexpected medical expenses?

2. **Very little in this world comes free.** Not only do you have to pay back the money you borrow, but credit requires you to pay for the use of the money in interest.

3. **When you buy many things on credit, payments sometimes pile up** so much that you may have little money left to do anything beyond the essentials. Even taking care of basic needs may be at risk. You may have your property taken away, have part of your wages taken by creditors, or even be forced into bankruptcy.

## Rates and Fees

Have you ever heard the saying, "Knowledge is power"? If you know how credit works and the meaning of terms used in credit advertising and contracts, you will have the power to get the best rates on loans and protect yourself from being cheated. Remember, the better the interest rate on the loan (the lower it is), the more money you will have to spend on other things.

When comparing different kinds of credit, the most important piece of information is the <u>annual percentage rate</u> (or APR). The APR is a number stated as a percentage, such as 20 percent, which means that each year you have the loan, you will be paying the lender a fee that equals 20 percent of the amount you owe.

In most cases, the calculation of the interest charges is quite complicated and too difficult for the average consumer to calculate. However, because there are laws that tell lenders exactly how they must do the interest calculations, you don't have to do the calculations on your own. (If you want to calculate the APR and other elements of a loan, there are web sites that will help you.)

What you really want to know is the APR number the lender quotes for the loan, because the lower the APR, the less costly the loan is to you. Because all lenders are required to state an APR, it is the best comparison point to use when shopping for the cheapest loan.

Another important credit term is the **finance charge**. This term tells you in dollar amounts what the total cost of the loan will be to you. By knowing this dollar amount, you can understand your immediate cost of borrowing and be able to budget for the repayment of the loan. Although it is important to know the finance charge, the APR is a better way to compare loans when other terms of loans are different.

## The Three Cs of Credit

Most people qualify for some type of credit. There are many forms of credit to choose from. Some cost much more than others. The challenge is to do everything possible to qualify for credit with the most favorable terms (the lowest APR).

Lenders look at three indicators of a borrower's ability to repay a loan: character, capacity, and capital. These are called the "**three** Cs of credit:"

1. Your **character** is measured by your past record of paying bills on time. Creditors don't like to lend money to people who make late payments or fail to make payments altogether.
2. Your **capacity** is determined by whether you have steady employment with enough income to make payments on the loan.
3. Your **capital** includes money you may have saved, any investments, and any property you own, such as a car or house. Lenders know that if the loan isn't repaid, they can get what is owed by taking your capital.

## Loans

Loans come in many forms and amounts. Although many purchases may be made with credit cards, some of your largest credit transactions will be installment purchases for big-ticket items, such as televisions, washing machines, cars, and homes. Before financing a major purchase, do some research in order to get a loan with the best rates.

* **Banks:** These privately owned businesses have been lending large and small amounts of money in the form of secured and unsecured loans for decades.
* **Credit Unions and Savings and Loan Companies:** These offer similar credit services as do the banks, except they are owned by the people they serve. This means they may give better service and offer lower loan rates.
* **Retailers:** Many retailers offer their own credit on the products they sell. The goods you buy often serve as collateral (security) for the loans.
* **Sales Finance Companies:** Many retailers may offer you credit for products that you buy, but *they* are not giving you the credit. Rather, they arrange for you to get credit from some other lender, called a sales finance company. A sales finance company usually does not lend money directly to the borrower, but only makes consumer loans through the retailer selling the product.

## Types of Loans

Many different kinds of loans are offered to businesses and consumers by financial institutions. For individuals, the most common loans are used for very expensive purchases: cars, an education, and a home.

### Car Loans

Max is considering buying that hot red convertible he always wanted. He wants to get the best deal he can so he will have money left over to buy accessories, insurance, gasoline, and all the other things that go with automobile ownership.

As part of his shopping, he looks at ads that say, "best credit term in town;" "we finance anyone;" "a few dollars down and drive the car home;" and "0.0% financing."

What do these ads really promise? In most cases, the messages in advertising for automobile financing are meaningless at best and fraudulent at worst.

Max could finance his car purchase in several different ways. The first option he should try is to apply for a car loan at his bank or credit union. The loan officer will not only check his **credit history**—his record of borrowing and repaying debts—with a **credit bureau** (a company that gathers credit information), but also look up the loan value of the car. Based on this information, the loan officer will decide if Max qualifies for a loan and how much the lender is willing to lend him to buy that particular car.

Many dealers advertise that they will finance the cars they sell. If Max has not already gotten a loan in advance, the dealer will try to convince him to finance it with the dealer. When the dealer says it will finance, this usually means the dealer will make the financial arrangements along with doing all the other paperwork involved in the purchase. In most cases, the dealer is not giving the loan but is arranging the loan through a sales finance company.

Although dealer-arranged financing is usually quicker and more convenient, it is often a more expensive way to finance than if Max had applied for a bank or credit union loan on his own, because the dealer makes a profit on loans it arranges. Here are some of the tricks a less-than-honest auto dealer may pull on Max:

* Quote a low APR in conversation and then sneak a higher APR into the written contract.
* Say he must buy a service contract or extended warranty in order to get financing.
* Say he must buy all kinds of insurance from the dealer.

### Student Loans

Are you planning on going to college? Because of rapidly rising tuition and other college-related costs, many students can't afford to go. Fortunately, there are relatively low-cost loans to help with college expenses. Depending on which school you attend, you may borrow from the federal government, from your state government, or from a private lender.

If you can prove financial need based upon your and your parents' finances, you may qualify for a subsidized loan. With a subsidized loan, the government pays off part of the amount borrowed, so you won't have to pay back the full amount of the loan.

Student loans can add up fast, and the amount can be staggering. Make sure that you understand the amount you will be required to pay back, when you will need to start making payments, and that you are able to assume this debt.

### Mortgages

The loan you obtain to buy a home is called a **mortgage**. It's much like other installment loans, in which your monthly payment includes both part of the principal (the amount of money borrowed) and interest. Since homes are expensive, mortgage loan terms are generally from 15 to 30 years. The home is collateral. If you don't make your mortgage payments, the lending institution can take your house.

When you buy a home, in most cases you will need to invest savings in addition to the money you borrow. This is called a **down payment**. As you make your mortgage payments, part of the payment is for principal, and part is for interest. The combination of your down payment, the principal you have paid, and any increase in the home's value in the years since you took out the mortgage loan is the **equity** you have in the home. Your equity is the difference between what your home would sell for and what you owe on the mortgage.

If you already have a mortgage and need to borrow a large amount for another purchase, such as home improvements or college, you can apply for an additional mortgage called a **home equity loan**. This type of loan usually has a lower APR and a longer repayment period than other types of loans. But, if you can't make the payments, you could lose your home.

### Student Loan

Mary F. knew she wanted to go to a private college, and that it would be expensive. To save up money for school, she started working at a toy store when she was 15 years old. While she was in high school, she worked at the store every day after school and all day on Saturdays. She also baby-sat for neighbors' kids a couple of evenings per week.

During college, she worked at a financial-aid job serving food. During winter and summer vacations, she worked at the toy store or as a waitress in restaurants.

Even though she worked part-time, her parents paid half her tuition, and she got a small scholarship from her college, it still wasn't enough. So she took out a loan from the state of Illinois, her home state. Over the course of four years, she borrowed $10,000 at an interest rate of nine percent, which she was originally supposed to pay back within 10 years.

When she graduated from college, she had a year grace period before she had to start paying back the loan. Once she started making the payments, it was very difficult to come up with the $125 loan payment every month. Twice, she couldn't make the payments and had to renegotiate the loan. Once, she lost her job, and another time, she got behind on her bills.

Finally, when she was 35 years old, she paid off the loan! It took her 20 years to pay for her education. Was it worth it? "Absolutely," says Mary.

### Troublesome Loans

Have you seen billboards or heard radio ads for "Instant Cash!" "Easy Loans!" "No Credit Checks!" "Friendly Credit!" and other such claims?

Think of a situation where you might need cash quickly and don't have an established credit history or have a bad credit record. Under such circumstances, you may be lured into getting one of these loans. Lenders who do this type of advertising usually give you cash on the spot with no credit check and few questions asked.

Remember, if it's that easy, there must be a catch. There is one *big* one—you will pay interest charges many times greater than for other types of loans.

## Credit Cards

Do you already have a credit card, or are you thinking about getting one? Do you seem to be on every credit card company's "most wanted" list? More than a half billion cards have been issued, and the average American credit card debt is around $8,000. Credit card issuers know that teenagers are big spenders. They want to profit from them. Many people just out of high school find themselves with huge credit card problems—and debt—fast. You don't want to be one of them.

Surviving in our economy without a credit card is very difficult, although some people challenge themselves to do just that. Still, it is almost impossible to buy something over the phone or on the Internet, or to rent a car or buy a plane ticket, without a credit card. Knowing how credit cards work will help you make good choices about how and when to use them.

### How Credit Cards Work

Having a credit card is like having a pre-approved line of credit—that is, you can borrow or charge up to a certain amount agreed to by you and the lender. For credit cards, the pre-approved line of credit is called your **credit limit**. You may make charges at any time during the payment period as long as you don't exceed your limit.

102 Alabama Citizenship Workbook

There are ways to use a credit card without paying interest charges. In most cases, if you pay the full balance on time, you don't pay any interest or other fees. However, if you pay less than the full balance owed, you will be charged interest. When you pay less than the minimum due or if you pay late or go over your credit limit, you may be required to pay additional fees.

## Advantages of Credit Cards

Carrying a credit card is usually safer than carrying cash. If your credit card is lost or stolen, and you report it immediately, you lose nothing. If cash is lost or stolen from you, it is usually gone for good.

Reviewing the charges on your credit card statement is a good way to keep track of spending and may even help you with budgeting.

One of the biggest advantages of credit cards is the **charge back** feature. Suppose you purchase a DVD player on your credit card and find it defective. When you return it, the seller refuses to credit your account. If the product cost more than $50 and was purchased within your home state or within 100 miles from home, you can withhold payment for the purchase until the problem is resolved.

## Disadvantages of Credit Cards

Because you are buying something and won't pay for it for a month or more, it's easy to overspend. Many people in financial trouble are there because of credit card spending sprees. They end up able only to pay the minimum balance each month. The amount they owe continues to rise, along with the interest they must pay. It is very difficult to pay down a credit card once you get to this stage.

One of the biggest disadvantages of credit cards is their cost. In recent years, most credit card companies have added many new fees, increased existing fees, and raised the APR.

## Choosing the Right Card

Choosing the right card is not easy, because interest rates, terms, and fees vary greatly from one card to the next, even though they may look alike. Although your credit card may say "Visa" or "MasterCard," the actual credit comes from a bank, credit union, or other lender. Some may be good choices, while others should be avoided.

Most credit cards are **revolving credit** accounts. Visa and MasterCard accounts use revolving credit. These types of cards permit you to make charges to your account at any time without paying the full balance each month. A **charge card** is similar to a credit card, but you must pay your balance in full each month. However, there may be high annual fees. American Express and Diner's Club are examples of charge cards.

Retailers offer credit and charge cards. They are similar to most other types of cards, except they may be used only at the store or chain that offers them.

## Cost of Credit Cards

The biggest factor in choosing a credit card is the cost. For all the convenience credit cards provide, there are costs to you that are not obvious at first glance.

* *Annual fees.* Some credit card companies charge annual membership fees that can be as high as $60. The amount is automatically added to your account balance. If you don't read your statement carefully, you won't even notice it.
* *Interest charges.* Almost all credit cards charge interest, but you may not have to pay it. In most cases, if you pay the full balance on time at the end of each payment period, you are not charged interest.
* *Grace period.* The number of days between the billing date and the payment due date is called the **grace period**. You are charged a stiff fee if the credit card issuer does not receive payment before the end of the grace period.
* *Fees, fees, and more fees.* You might think you are a savvy consumer because you shopped around and found the lowest APR available. However, you may have missed the most important part of the contract—the fine-print information about fees charged. Charging fees is a very lucrative way for credit card companies to increase profits. New fees are often added to the contract and old fees are frequently increased.

## Credit Card Fees

Often the most costly part of having a credit card are the fees and penalty interest rates that go along with it. These include:

* *Late fee:* fee charged when the payment is received after the due date.
* *Over-the-limit fee:* fee charged when your balance goes over the specified credit limit.
* *Penalty or punitive interest rates:* big increase in your APR if you have paid late or exceeded your credit limit.

## Cash Advances

If you need cash quickly, your credit card company makes it easy for you to get a <u>cash advance</u>, which is really a loan from your credit card company. You simply insert your credit card in an ATM machine, key in your personal identification number, and out comes the money. You may get a momentary rush seeing those bills come out of the machine, but is this really a good way to get cash? Only if you don't mind paying ATM fees, cash-advance fees, and an APR for the advance that is a few percentage points higher than for a credit purchase.

## Credit Card or Debit Card?

When you purchase that computer game, should you use a debit or a credit card? Because debit cards are heavily advertised as a convenient alternative to credit cards, they have become very popular. Although they may look like credit cards, they are very different.

### Search This

#### Comparing Credit Costs

Use the Internet and other sources to research different types of loans. Investigate the ones listed here in terms of typical length and APR. What is the cost of each type of loan per $100 for one year?

* Mortgage loans.
* Automobile loans.
* Credit card loans.
* Pawnshop loans.
* Payday loans.

On the basis of your research, which types of loans would you recommend, and why? Which loans cost consumers the most? Are there any you would definitely avoid? Why?

With a credit card, you are increasing your debt each time you use it, but when you use your debit card, you are immediately withdrawing money from your checking account without having the inconvenience of writing a check. Not only are debit cards more convenient, but for some people, it helps them control their spending. A person can only use the debit card when there is money in his or her checking account.

A smarter strategy is to use a credit card *and pay the full balance each month to avoid credit charges*. Why use a credit card instead of a debit card? You have greater responsibility for loss with a debit card. If you lose your debit card, you may have to cover unauthorized charges up to $500, while your liability limit for a credit card is only $50.

Another advantage is that it is much easier to correct improper charges to a credit card account than to a debit card account.

## By the Numbers

### ATM Costs

Jack plans to borrow $100 for his weekend date using a credit card cash advance from an ATM machine.

How much will this cash advance cost him?

* Fee for the use of the ATM machine: $4.
* Fee from Jack's bank for not using its machine: $2.
* Fee for getting a cash advance from a credit card account: $5.
* Interest paid on the cash advance: $2.
* Total cost for getting the $100: $13.

What if Jack gets a cash advance every week for a whole year? How much will that cost him?

## Avoiding Trouble

More trouble comes from using credit cards than with most other types of credit, yet with careful planning, it's possible to handle credit cards responsibly.

### Living Within Your Means

Unless you keep track of each charge purchase, the balance owed can quickly become much higher than you plan. Reality sets in when you get your statement, and you find you can only make the minimum payment. If you only make minimum payments, the balance owed decreases only slightly. If you continue to make purchases, the balance will rise. You may reach your credit limit, apply for more cards, and head toward your credit limit on these cards by making only minimum payments. Soon, you are trapped! You can do little to enjoy life because most of your income goes to pay credit card bills.

Live within your means! Here are some guidelines to help you:

* Look carefully at your monthly budget. Decide whether it can handle a new expense. If not, create some options for yourself.

## Get Smart

### My Wallet Is Missing!

You reach for your wallet and suddenly, anxiety runs though your body. It's not there! What do you do now? Follow these **three** steps:

1. **Notify authorities or law enforcement.**
   If you are in a store, restaurant, or other public place, notify the management.
   If you are in a foreign country, contact the American Embassy.
2. **Notify your bank and credit card companies *immediately*.** Only by promptly notifying the bank and credit card companies of your loss can you limit your responsibility for charges that may be made on your card and checks written on your account. Then you will be billed only for charges made on your account *before* the notification, with a maximum charge of $50 to you.
3. **Keep a copy of all relevant credit card information in a safe place.** Your list should include each credit or debit card number and the toll-free number of each institution. For an annual fee, some banks and credit unions will register all your credit cards with one company. This lets you make just one call to cancel all your cards. Update your list every year to keep it current.

* Make sure your paycheck isn't all going to paying off credit card debt.
* Save some emergency money for car repairs or other unexpected expenses.
* If you decide to charge a new item, set a schedule for paying off the new debt. Each month, pay on time and keep to your schedule.

## Credit Card Fraud

Not only can excessive use of credit cause you to exceed your budget, credit card fraud can create additional problems for you. There are **three** types of credit card fraud, all of which can cost you money and damage your reputation:

1. **Fraud by credit card companies.**
2. **Fraud by sellers.**
3. **Fraud by other people.**

## Fraud by Credit Card Companies

Do you think that all credit card companies are ethical and operate within the law? Not so. Some companies send you credit cards without your asking. Some charge high rates and fees. Others advertise competitive interest rates and low fees and then quickly raise them soon after you get the card—a form of bait and switch. Many say you will have a credit limit "up to" some amount, but after you request the card, you're given a credit limit of only a few hundred dollars.

## Fraud by Sellers

Do you check all charges on your credit card statements? Because of a practice called **cramming**, you should check to see if all the listed charges are made by you. Cramming is where businesses involved in fraudulent practices obtain your credit card number and then charge you for purchases you didn't make or bill you more than once for purchases you did make.

Check your statement as soon as you receive it and immediately notify the credit card company of any suspicious charges. Usually, they will help you eliminate any fraudulent charges.

## Fraud by Other People

Many dishonest individuals are ready to fraudulently use your credit card. This happens in a variety of ways:

* A person may snoop in your wallet to get your credit card number.
* A restaurant server or store clerk may discreetly copy your credit card information.
* Someone may steal your wallet.

Once people have the information on your card, they can start making purchases and other transactions for which you will be charged.

## Making it REAL

### Evaluating Credit Card Offers

How do you know which credit card is best for you? Gather several credit card offers that either you or your parents receive in the mail. Evaluate each card to see which one has the:

* Lowest APR. Be careful of introductory teaser rates that go much higher after a short time.
* Longest grace period.
* Highest credit limit.
* Lowest (or no) fees for: annual membership, going over credit limit, late payments, paying with bad check.
* Lowest penalty APR for: exceeding the credit limit, paying late.

What language or terms in the credit contract don't you understand? How can you find out the answers to your questions?

### Your Life

**Making Minimum Payments**

Why do credit card companies require you to pay only a small part of the balance due each month and sometimes even give you the opportunity to skip a payment? They prefer that you don't pay your balance in full or even a large part of it. Why? Because the larger your credit balance, the more profit they can make from you.

For example, if you made only the minimum payment of $40 on a $2,000 balance with an APR of 21 percent, how would you answer the questions given below:

1. How many years would it take to pay off the balance without making additional charges?
2. What is the total amount of interest that you would pay (not including payment to principle)?
3. What is the total amount, including principle and interest, that you would pay?

You won't be able to do the math yourself, but there are web sites that will let you plug in the figures and give you the results. Use the keywords "credit card calculators" to find a number of sites that will help you. Is it really to your advantage to make only the minimum payment when you can afford more? Look at the numbers. You might be shocked.

### Get Smart

**Watch Your Card!**

* Don't leave the restaurant copy of a credit card receipt on the table. Hand it to the waiter.
* Tear up carbons of credit card slips.
* Make sure you were given back your own card.

Sometimes friends may ask for your account number to make a purchase, saying they'll "pay you back" when you get your statement. This is like giving them free access to cash. You have no control over when and where they use your account. If you have freely given your account number to someone, the credit card company may not be sympathetic to your request to have charges removed.

<u>Identity theft</u> is the worst thing that can happen. In identity theft, a person not only gets your credit card numbers, but your Social Security number and other personal data. The thief becomes you on paper. She can make all kinds of transactions, including using your credit card and opening new credit card accounts in your name. To prevent identity theft, always check your credit card statements, and periodically check your credit bureau files.

## Rating Your Credit

Have you ever wondered how a lender decides whether to give you credit and what rates to charge? To apply for credit, you must typically complete a lengthy application form that asks questions that establish your three Cs of credit worthiness. Credit bureaus collect credit-related information on consumers and sell this information to businesses.

### Your Credit Score

The information credit bureaus sell to lenders is in

the form of a **credit report**, which may contain a **credit score**. This score is a number based on many pieces of information found in your credit record. The higher the score, the more likely you are to get a better loan rate.

Your credit score comes from information related to **four** areas:

1. **Employment and income.** Consumers get a higher score when they have a history of having a steady job and enough income to pay the bills.
2. **Housing.** Do you rent or own your home? Creditors believe that people who own homes are more financially stable.
3. **Assets.** What do you own of value, such as investments and savings accounts? The higher the value of your assets, the higher your score.
4. **Credit history.** How many loans and credit cards do you have? What balances do you maintain? How prompt have you been in paying your debts? This tells how well you will likely meet future credit obligations.

## Getting Your Credit Report

By law, consumers have access to their files. If there are mistakes, the consumer can demand they be corrected. If there is a dispute between the consumer and the creditor, the consumer has the right to have his or her side of the story in the file.

Most consumer credit experts suggest checking your credit file with at least one bureau once a year or six months before making a large credit purchase, such as taking out a mortgage to buy a home. Here are some tips:

* Although you can request a copy of your file by telephone or U.S. mail, the simplest way is through the Internet. Search for national credit bureaus and follow the instructions. Each will charge about $10, but if you were denied credit because of a negative report, there is no charge.
* Be careful of Internet sites that offer "free" credit reports. They typically require personal information and credit card numbers, and there is always risk when you divulge this information on the Internet. What's more, you only get the "free" report when you subscribe to a credit service that costs much more than simply paying for the report in the first place.
* Always avoid firms that promise to repair your credit rating or remove all bad credit information from your file. They can't do it, and if they try, not only are they violating the law, but you are, also.

## Keeping a Good Credit Rating

A good credit rating is important. How do you keep it that way? First, continually track how much you are borrowing or charging. Before applying for any more credit, ask yourself the following:

* Am I able to pay my current bills without any trouble?
* Do I have enough income to make an extra credit payment?
* Will I be able to make my payments if there is an unexpected emergency?
* Will I be able to make my payments if I lose my job or my income decreases?

## If You Become Overextended

What do you do if you find you're **overextended**, meaning you have more bills than you can pay? This can occur if you're careless in using credit, incur an expensive emergency, or lose your job. When this happens, not only will your credit rating be damaged, but you may create other serious financial problems as well.

* *Your property may be repossessed.* To get out of financial trouble, it may be tempting to just let the creditor take back your car or some other property, especially if the amount owed is not much more or even less than the value of the item.
* *Your wages may be garnished.* One way creditors collect money owed is to put a claim, called a garnishment, on your wages. This means that a creditor will take money out of your paycheck before you even see it.
* *You may be forced into bankruptcy.* If you are heavily in debt with little or no prospect of ever paying off your bills, you may be forced to file for bankruptcy.

## By the Numbers

### Paying Off Debt From Several Credit Cards

What would you do if you found you had large balances from several credit cards? You might consider getting a consolidation loan. Study the chart below and then answer the questions that follow.

1. How much money could you save each month by taking out a loan to pay off the balance owed on all four cards?
2. What might be the danger in doing that?
3. If a consolidation loan weren't possible, what would be your second-choice strategy, and why?

| Card Company | Monthly Balance | APR | Monthly Interest |
|---|---|---|---|
| Card #1 | $1,000 | 15% | $12.50 |
| Card #2 | $2,000 | 24% | $40.00 |
| Card #3 | $500 | 18% | $7.50 |
| Card #4 | $4,000 | 21% | $70.00 |
| Consolidation loan: | $7,500 | 12% | $76.30 |

## Bankruptcy

There are two types of **bankruptcy**. In one type, if you can pay at least a part of your debts, the bankruptcy court will create a plan for you to pay a portion of what you owe over a set period of time. If the court doesn't believe you have enough money to pay any part of your debts, it will cancel all your debts except for taxes and child support. If this happens, you must give up much of the property that you own.

Having a bankruptcy in your credit file may prevent you from getting the job you want, make it hard to insure your automobile, and make it difficult to get credit for a long time. If and when you do, you will pay much higher rates.

## Help for Credit Problems

Once you find that you have serious problems with credit, is there a way out other than bankruptcy? In most cases, there is. Some people are able to solve the credit problems on their own, while some may need professional help.

### Self-help

To solve your own credit problems will take a lot of discipline. Here are some steps to take:

* You must cut up your credit cards (but do not cancel them until they are paid off, as companies often raise rates if you cancel the card). Do not apply for any new credit.
* You may have to go without things you want in order to pay for what you bought in the past.
* Most important of all, you will have to budget your finances not only to get out of your current debt problems, but to avoid getting back into them in the future.

There is one immediate step you can take to help resolve your problems. Sometimes you can get your creditors to help you. Because creditors frown on people who just stop making payments without any explanation, you should contact your creditors and

### Your Life

**Signs of Financial Difficulty**

Financial problems don't just happen all at once. Usually, they creep up on you. Here are indications that you might be overextended:

* More than a quarter of your take-home pay, other than car and mortgage payments, goes to pay off debt.
* You are able to make only the minimum payments on your credit card balances.
* You make payments after the due date because you don't have the cash.
* You open new credit card accounts because the old ones are maxed out.
* You are harassed by creditors to pay your bills.
* You worry about paying bills and avoid answering the phone.
* You experience strains in your family and close relationships because of increasing stress and credit anxiety.

If you are overextended, seek professional help—from a consumer credit counselor and perhaps also from a therapist.

---

explain your situation. They may work with you by lowering the monthly payments, letting you skip a payment, or lowering the interest rate. Seldom will they forgive the loan, but they may be more patient with you in making the payments.

### Professional Help

Sometimes it is beyond your own resources to get out of financial trouble. When this happens, you should seek outside help. Nonprofit credit counseling agencies are a major source of help. Counselors at these agencies may help you in two ways. They may contact your creditors and, because of their experience, may be more successful than you are in reducing the payments and possibly even reducing the interest charges. In most cases, the agencies force discipline on you by handling your bills. You pay them a specific amount of money each month, and they will pay your bills out of that. These counselors will also advise you in how to budget your finances to put you back on the road to financial health. A small fee is usually charged for such services.

### Staying Free of Credit Problems

If you have credit problems, not only will resolving them require a lot of effort, but staying out of trouble in the future will take discipline. Here are some strategies you can practice now to avoid credit problems later:

* Pay off the full balance each month to avoid any interest charges.
* Maintain only one credit card and use it sparingly. Once you pay off a card, cut it up and notify the company to close the account.
* Charge purchases only if you can afford to pay for them now.
* Don't apply for other loans unless absolutely necessary.
* Realize you don't have to buy everything that you want. In other words, don't buy on impulse.
* Realistically budget your finances.
* If you have saved money, take money from that account rather than using credit, and start putting money back in savings as soon as possible.

Another way to avoid credit problems is to continually make yourself aware of the disadvantages of credit. Before you get a loan or buy something with the credit card, ask yourself: *What will I be giving up by buying this item on credit?* Not making the purchase at all may be the best way to avoid the costs and problems that often come with credit.

# Chapter 21 Wrap-up
## USING CREDIT WISELY

*You are very likely to use credit in some form sometime in the future, whether it is in the form of a credit card, mortgage, car loan, or some other type of loan. Most of the time, using credit can be a help if you use it only when necessary and then use it wisely.*

*Far too many people have abused credit either because they wanted everything right away or they did not have the skills to get the best credit terms available. They often suffer from anxiety, strains in family relations, unwelcome calls and mail from creditors, repossessions, and even bankruptcy. However, those who limit their use of credit and employ their skills to get the best credit deals will have a more carefree life.*

**WORDS TO KNOW**

**annual percentage rate (APR)**—interest rate stated as the percentage charged on the unpaid balance of the debt for the period of one year.

**bankruptcy**—legal arrangement to deal with the affairs of individuals unable to pay their debts.

**capacity**—borrower's ability to earn enough to make debt payments.

**capital**—wealth in the form of money or property.

**cash advance**—cash that may be borrowed against a credit card account.

**character**—borrower's history of making debt payments on time.

**charge back**—option of withholding payment on a credit card for a disputed purchase.

**charge card**—type of credit card where the entire balance must be paid each month.

**commercial credit**—loan extended to a business.

**cramming**—fraudulent practice in which charges are billed when no purchases were made.

**credit**—system of buying goods and services with payment at a later time.

**credit bureau**—company that gathers credit information on consumers and sells it to other businesses.

**credit history**—record of borrowing and repaying debts, either loans or credit card purchases.

**credit limit**—highest balance permitted on your credit account.

**credit report**—statement by a credit bureau that gives the credit history of a consumer.

**credit score**—number calculated by a credit bureau that indicates the creditworthiness of a consumer. Also known as a credit rating.

**delayed gratification**—satisfaction postponed, usually because the person is willing to wait for something wanted.

**down payment**—amount of money you must pay up front in order to obtain a loan. Home mortgages and car loans usually require a down payment.

**equity**—value of a business or property after debts and mortgages are subtracted.

**finance charge**—total cost of a loan expressed in dollars.

**grace period**—number of days between a billing date and the due date.

**home equity loan**—loan secured by the owner's equity in the home. It is in addition to the mortgage and is usually at a higher rate of interest than the mortgage, but lower than most other forms of loans.

**identity theft**—unauthorized use of another person's Social Security number, birth date, driver's license number, or other identifying information to obtain credit cards, car loans, phone plans, or other services in the victim's name.

**immediate gratification**—satisfaction of getting something as soon as you want it.

**mortgage**—consumer loan for the purchase of a home or other building where the building is collateral.

**overextended**—state in which a borrower has more debt than can be paid.

**personal credit**—loan extended to an individual.

**principal**—amount of money borrowed from a lender.

**revolving credit**—type of account in which the consumer is not required to pay off the balance before making new purchases.

**sales finance companies**—lenders that finance purchases for the consumer through retailers.

Alabama Citizenship Workbook   111

Name _____

# 21. Using Credit Wisely

**After you've read the chapter, write an answer to each question below.**

1. What is the difference between the principal and the interest on a credit card?

   _____
   _____
   _____

2. What is the difference between commercial credit and personal credit?

   _____
   _____
   _____

3. If you were financing a car from a car dealership, what kinds of tricks could a less-than-honest auto dealer pull on you as a customer?

   _____
   _____
   _____

4. What are the current options available for students to get loans for college?

   _____
   _____
   _____

5. What are some of the ways an individual can fraudulently use your credit card?

   _____
   _____
   _____

Name _____

# 21. Using Credit Wisely

**Circle the best answer for each item.**

1. What is a legal arrangement to deal with the affairs of individuals unable to pay their debts?
   a. charge back
   b. credit limit
   c. cramming
   d. bankruptcy

2. What is the amount of property a borrower owns?
   a. capital
   b. capacity
   c. equity
   d. personal credit

3. What is the term for the record of borrowing and repaying debts, either with loans or credit card purchases?
   a. credit history
   b. credit limit
   c. credit score
   d. personal credit

4. What is the value of a business or property after debts and mortgages are subtracted?
   a. finance charge
   b. grace period
   c. principal
   d. equity

5. Which term describes the theft of another person's name, credit card numbers, Social Security number, and other personal data that allows the thief to pretend to be someone else?
   a. fraud
   b. cramming
   c. identity theft
   d. slamming

6. When comparing different kinds of credit, the most important piece of information is the ____.
   a. annual percentage rate
   b. credit limit
   c. application fee
   d. annual fee

7. In your mortgage payments, part of the payment is for ____, and part is for ____.
   a. fees, equity
   b. insurance, fees
   c. principal, interest
   d. savings, collateral

8. If you only make minimum payments on your credit card, the balance owed ____.
   a. decreases only slightly
   b. stays the same
   c. increases over time
   d. decreases a lot

9. To get out of financial trouble, you may need outside help from ____.
   a. any financial institutions
   b. credit bureaus
   c. finance companies
   d. nonprofit credit counseling agencies

10. One way to avoid credit problems later is to ____.
    a. pay off the full balance each month to avoid any interest charges
    b. not use credit cards at all
    c. keep your credit cards at home
    d. use your credit cards only once a month

Alabama Citizenship Workbook   113

CHAPTER 22

# Becoming a Wise Consumer

In this chapter, you will learn about:

- what influences your buying decisions
- how to be a smart shopper

For Maria's 16th birthday, her Aunt Rita gave her a generous present: a check for $100. Maria decided to spend it on a new jacket. The seasons were changing, and her old jacket didn't fit anymore. She went to the mall with some of her friends.

On her way to the coat department of her favorite department store, one of her friends stopped to look at all the pretty blouses hanging on the racks. A sign said, "Bargain Blouses: 2 for $99." Maria thought the blouses were beautiful, and they came in her favorite colors: blue and purple. Her friend grabbed a bunch of blouses and whisked her into a dressing room. Maria tried on a couple of blouses, and they looked great on her. "Maria, you should get two of these," her friend said. "After all, you've got that check from your aunt to spend!" Maria was very tempted.

However, then she remembered that she really did need a new jacket. She took another look in the mirror, and thought, "The blouses do look very pretty, but I've got a lot of blouses in my closet already. I can do without these." She went to the jacket department and found a jacket she liked very much. Walking home wearing her new jacket, she felt good. She knew she had made the right decision.

# Understanding Your Buying Behavior

Think of all the things you'll buy this week. Maybe you'll buy your lunches or other meals. Maybe you'll buy transportation to and from school or work. You might spend money on some entertainment, such as a movie. Maybe you'll buy newspapers or books. Perhaps you'll buy someone a present. We buy things all the time for many different kinds of reasons.

You might be asking, "What's the big deal? We buy stuff because we need it or want it. It's not rocket science!" It's true that buying isn't rocket science, but it can be complicated.

Why we buy what we buy is the result of a mixture of influences:

* Psychological (our emotions, personal values, beliefs, and self-image).
* Sociological (how our culture and society influence us).
* Economic (how much money we have, our attitudes toward money, how we choose to spend it).

## Needs and Wants

Our shopping behavior is affected by what we want and need. What is the difference, though, between a need and a want? A <u>need</u> is something necessary to survival, such as food and shelter. A <u>want</u> is something you desire, but is not necessary for survival. It can be difficult to separate needs and wants.

**EXAMPLE:** Both food and clothes are necessary—they both fulfill needs. But when do they become wants? When are they luxury items?

## Evaluating Our Needs

We are bombarded every day with advertising that tells us we "need" the latest, greatest gadget. This can make it hard to differentiate, or tell the difference between, needs and wants.

Psychologist Abraham Maslow developed a theory about human needs. He called it the <u>hierarchy</u> of needs. (A hierarchy organizes things according to importance. The most basic is at the bottom. The most advanced is at the top.) Understanding Maslow's hierarchy will help you differentiate needs from wants.

Maslow's hierarchy has five levels. Before the needs of one level can be fulfilled, the needs of the level below it must be met. For example, it is difficult to be a creative artist or scientist when you are hungry.

**Maslow's Hierarchy of Needs**

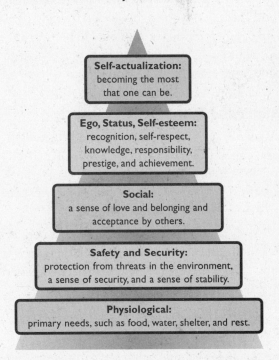

| Needs and Wants | | |
|---|---|---|
| Item | Definition | Examples |
| Need | Something required for survival. | Basic food, shelter, clothes, safety. |
| Want | Something desired but not required for survival. | Special clothes, candy, CDs, jewelry. |

Alabama Citizenship Workbook

Maslow's hierarchy shows that physical or physiological needs are our most primary or basic human needs.

In general, it is hard to meet higher needs when basic needs have not been met. Keep this in mind as you become an independent adult. Develop spending habits that allow you to meet basic needs responsibly. This will ensure opportunities to fulfill higher-level needs that provide satisfaction in life.

## Higher-Level Needs

As self-aware, social beings, we have a drive to fulfill more than primary survival needs. The top three levels in Maslow's hierarchy describe these higher-level needs. Higher-level needs affect our spending habits.

**EXAMPLE:** With increased self-understanding, you might realize you want to go into an unusual line of work. This could require specialized training or experience. Saving for that education will become an important goal that will affect how you choose to spend your money.

## Evaluating Our Wants

It is not always easy to tell when a need is really a want. One clue is cost. Fulfilling wants often costs more than fulfilling needs.

**EXAMPLE:** A luxury condominium is more expensive than a modest home or apartment.

There's nothing wrong with fulfilling a need with a want, in most cases. A luxury condominium is fine if you can afford it. But when basic needs are sacrificed, that is a problem.

## Psychological Aspects

Our psychological make-up affects our wants. Owning certain items—and even the process of buying—can provide psychological satisfaction.

**EXAMPLE:** Wearing certain clothing might make some people feel attractive and accepted. A fancy car might serve the same purpose for someone else. A cozy couch might provide a sense of comfort or security. Tools or recreational gear might help some people feel competent, effective, and alive.

> **My Notebook**
>
> ### Needs or Wants?
>
> Make a chart with four headings: "Item," "Need," "Want," and "Need or Want?" Under "Item," write the names of three things you are considering buying. In the "Need" column, write down all the reasons you need the item. In the "Want" column, write down all the reasons you want the item.
>
> Review your reasons carefully. Consider Maslow's hierarchy and how advertising works. After thinking through all the issues, indicate in the last column if the item is a need or a want.

There is nothing wrong with getting psychological satisfaction from purchases. It is important, though, to make sure the satisfaction doesn't encourage overspending. When this happens, your financial goals can be jeopardized. Also, it is important to find satisfaction in other areas of life.

## Advertising

Basic human needs influence many of your purchases. Your individual psychology and values play a role. In addition, your environment exerts a strong influence.

Advertising, your peers, special offers, and affordability are some of the most common things in the environment that affect your buying decisions.

### Market Research

American companies spend more than $200 billion annually on **advertising**. The purpose of every one of these ad dollars is to try to get you to buy goods or services. In addition to money spent on ads, companies also spend over $5 billion on market research. **Market research** is the study of people in order to understand their buying behavior.

Let's say a company wants to sell more jeans to young people. It will conduct market research to discover the characteristics of the group being studied—teens your age. Such a company might create a survey with the following questions:

* How old are you?
* Are you a boy or a girl?
* What is your family income?
* How do you spend your own money?
* What are your favorite colors?
* Name two of your most important values.
* Name two public figures you admire.

Answers to these kinds of questions will help the company create ads that appeal to the needs and wants of people like you.

## How Ads Influence People

It's no surprise that ads are carefully designed to influence you. To be successful, an ad has to:

* Get your attention.
* Make you want the product.
* Persuade you to buy the product.
* Tell you where you can get it.

Advertising accomplishes this by creating psychological, intellectual, or social desires.

It should be clear by now that ads:

* Are designed to get you to buy.
* Use a variety of techniques to accomplish that goal.

Knowing that, can you make wise buying decisions with the help of advertising? Ads can be useful for letting you know:

* Where you can purchase products.
* When products are on sale.

However, ads should not be the only source of information you use when considering an important purchase. While some ads do include factual information, none will tell you about problems with the product. You need to find that information on your own.

## Truth in Advertising

Advertisers cannot say anything they want to about their products or services in an ad. They cannot lie. In fact, if they make false claims, it is considered to be **fraud**. Fraud, which deceives or tricks people with lies to get them to spend their money, is illegal. However, advertising can be misleading without being illegal. Misleading ads are deceptive but do not lie.

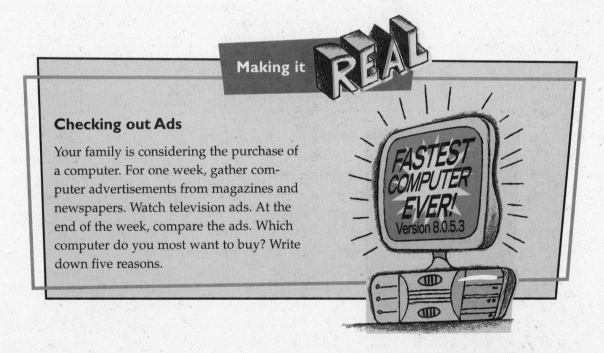

### Checking out Ads

Your family is considering the purchase of a computer. For one week, gather computer advertisements from magazines and newspapers. Watch television ads. At the end of the week, compare the ads. Which computer do you most want to buy? Write down five reasons.

## Types of Advertisements

| Type of Ad | Description | Example | Appeal |
|---|---|---|---|
| **Informational** | Describes features to convince you to buy the product. | *Get your new WOW computer now. Its 900-megahertz processor is the fastest on the market. The 50-gigabyte hard drive can't be beat, and the price is lower than any other new model.* | Appeals primarily to the intellect: It looks like a great deal for the amount of money. |
| **Persuasive** | Tries to create desire by giving you the impression you will feel fulfilled, satisfied, or happy if only you have this product. | *Tummy Tucker slacks make every woman look great. With our new special design, you'll look and feel like a new woman. On sale now in stores across the country.* | Appeals primarily to our emotions, since little factual information is provided. |
| **Image-Enhancing** | Tries to make you feel like you will belong to a special group if you buy the service or product. | *It's no accident that superstars Josie Jose and Tanya Tonya love their new Phoenix sports cars. The Phoenix is the best and made for the best. That's why you'll love yours, too.* | Appeals to emotions and social needs. |
| **Brand** | Reassures you that you can count on the quality because the product is coming from a well known, reputable manufacturer. | *Now, from the people who brought you the wildly popular ChocoCrunch snack bar, comes the PeesaPizza meal in a pocket for busy teens who want taste and nutrition.* | Appeals to emotions. Relies solely on success by association. |

Avoid being taken in. Analyze ads carefully. Do your own research before you buy.

## Peer Influences

Most people want to feel they belong to a group. For this reason, people are influenced by their peers, the people most like them with whom they spend time. This desire to belong is a natural and healthy human desire. Much of the time, this desire is constructive.

**EXAMPLE:** Belonging to a service or church group encourages people to help those who are less fortunate.

In some cases, though, the desire to belong influences you inappropriately. Sometimes this can affect your spending habits.

**EXAMPLE:** Imagine you are working to save for an important goal. Should you buy the brand-name shoes your friends have? Would it be better to buy less expensive shoes and put some money in your savings account? If you want to meet your goal, the answer is probably "buy less expensive shoes."

### My Notebook

#### Which Ads Work?

Learn what pushes your buttons. Make notes for a week about at least five ads that catch your attention and make you want to buy. Analyze how they make their point with you. Do they appeal to your image of how you would like to be? Do they connect with someone or something you admire? Do they offer to solve a problem for you?

How could understanding the appeal of those ads help you make smart purchasing decisions?

### Your Life

#### Shop-aholic Syndrome

Do you shop to lift your spirits? Do you spend more than you can afford? Do you buy things you never use? Are you in debt from excessive shopping? If you answered yes to these questions, you might suffer from a compulsive shopping disorder. This disorder can lead to difficult financial and emotional problems. Nip it in the bud by getting help from a mental health professional.

Resisting peer influence can be a challenge. It is made harder by advertisements that appeal to your desire to belong. Here are some tips to help you resist peer influences and advertising:

* Stay focused on *your* goals.
* Learn to tell the difference between your needs and wants.
* Analyze ads.
* Remember that ads tell only one side of the story.
* Base your purchases on independent research.

## Special Offers

A special offer tries to induce, or encourage, you to buy a product or service offered by the advertiser. Common special offers include:

* Two-for-one sales.
* Coupons.
* Contests.
* Rebates (you get money back later from the manufacturer).

Special offers can be valuable if:

* You buy something you had intended to buy anyway.
* You get something you were going to buy anyway, but at a better price.

The problem with special offers is that they often encourage you to buy something you don't need or want, or that you wouldn't have purchased at the time.

## Affordability

Sometimes, you will find that the forces conspiring to get you to buy something will assure you that it is **affordable**. That means that you can pay for it. How would they know? How do you know when something is truly affordable? Answer these **four** questions:

1. Did you plan to buy it?
2. Does it cost the amount that you had budgeted?
3. Is there another planned purchase you can give up or postpone?
4. Did you earn extra money or receive a gift that your budget didn't plan on? Is this the thing you would most want to spend that extra money on?

You need to be especially honest and careful with yourself in answering question 3. Can you really get along without the item you would give up?

Also, beware of spending money before you have it. Many people think they can afford something because they are expecting to earn extra money or are sure they are going to get a raise. Then, guess what happens? It's only affordable if you can pay for it now.

## Becoming a Smart Shopper

By now, you understand many of the factors that influence your buying decisions. The next step is to understand how to make buying decisions that:

* Will meet your requirements.
* You won't regret later.

### Deciding What to Buy

The information about differentiating needs and wants, peer influence, and values can help you decide whether to make a purchase or not. But once you've decided to make a purchase, how can you be sure you'll be pleased with your final choice?

| Deceptive Techniques | | |
|---|---|---|
| Technique | Description | Problem |
| Exaggeration | Claims are puffed up with words like *fabulous, the best*, and *super-strength*. | Something starts to sound awfully good, even though there is no information to back up the claim. |
| Testimonials | A celebrity or someone who has used the product is quoted as saying the product is great. | What authority or experience does the person have? Has he or she ever used a similar product? If not, how would he or she know which is best? |
| Offer a Gift | When you make a purchase, you get something along with the purchase for which you don't pay any more money. | Gifts are free. If you have to buy something before you get the "gift," it isn't free. |

The best way to accomplish this is to use a rational, or logical and reasonable, approach. This requires:

* *Gathering information* (product research).
* *Evaluating alternatives* (price-value comparison, comparison shopping, brand loyalty).
* *Evaluating your satisfaction* after the purchase.

## Researching Products

Advertising and peer influence do give you information about products or services, but they have their pitfalls. To buy with confidence, it's important to:

* Follow a systematic approach to gathering and organizing information.
* Use several different sources of information.

This process may not be necessary for small purchases, such as a CD—if it's in your budget—but it's important for more expensive items, such as a CD player, that you expect to use and own for a long time.

## Gathering and Organizing Information

Creating a grid that compares products can be a useful way to help you gather and organize information. A grid will help you:

* Compare the same features, or characteristics, of different models.
* Keep track of the information you gather.
* Compare choices once you've gathered all the information you need.

To set up your own grid, do a little preliminary research to determine how many features you want to compare.

**EXAMPLE:** If you're buying a CD player, you might compare these **five** features:

1. **The number of CDs it will play.**
2. **Recording capability.**
3. **Cord and battery operation.**
4. **Sound quality.**
5. **Repair and durability record.**

### Get Smart

### But the Survey Said...

You've seen the ads that use numbers to persuade you to buy. They usually go something like this: "Four out of five doctors recommend . . ." or "100 percent of teens chose . . ." If advertisers can't lie, it must be true. Right?

Well, yes and no. For example, a clothing manufacturer hired a market research company to identify the top clothes items high school students would pick from a pre-selected group of clothes. However, there was only one pair of jeans included—the manufacturer's.

When the company reported the survey results in an ad, it said 90 percent of high school students preferred their jeans. What the ad didn't tell you was that the company's jeans were the only ones the survey participants could choose.

Did the ad lie? No. Did the numbers really mean anything? No. Be skeptical. It's your best defense.

Alabama Citizenship Workbook

In your grid, set up a column for each of the five features. You'll always want a price column. A column to indicate where different models are available is also helpful. Keep in mind that you will often have more than one price and availability location for one model. For this reason, you should make the spaces large enough for all your notes. Try to compare at least four to six models, but no fewer than three.

## Sources of Information

Since the purpose of advertising is to sell you something, the information in an ad is likely influenced by the advertiser's motive to sell. When you make important purchases, you want objective, or unbiased, information.

Where can you get unbiased information? There are a number of sources:

* ***Consumers Union.*** Consumers Union is an independent product-testing laboratory. Its magazine, *Consumer Reports*, publishes the results of the lab's tests. Almost all public libraries subscribe to this magazine. Look up the product you want to purchase in the index. From shoes and ice cream to cars, CD players, and nearly everything in between, you'll find test results.
* ***Specialized magazine reviews.*** For example, if you want to buy a computer, research product reviews in computer magazines.
* ***Certifications or seals of approval.*** To obtain these, a manufacturer has to meet certain standards.
* ***Salespeople and manufacturers*** can provide some information about features, but do not rely on them alone.
* ***Friends, family, and coworkers*** can provide useful information about their purchases and degree of satisfaction after the purchase.

## Price-Value Comparison

A price-value comparison analyzes the cost as compared with what you get, or the value.
**EXAMPLE:** In researching CD players, you might find you definitely want to be able to play five CDs. A CD player that only plays three might cost less, but it won't meet your needs. In this case, the results of the price-value comparison indicate you will have to pay a little more to get the value you want.

## Comparison Shopping

Now you're ready to find out who has the best deal on exactly what you want. In this case, you want a five-disc CD player, model 123 or XYZ. Both models got the highest ratings in your independent research.

### By the Numbers

### Evaluating Price and Value

Does the least expensive model always give you the best value? Here's one way to find out:

1. Select a product you want to buy.
2. Research it in magazines.
3. Select at least one model that has a high repair rate.
4. Call repair shops and ask the price of each repair.
5. Add up the cost of the possible repairs. Add them to the price of the less reliable models.
6. Compare that cost with the cost of more expensive but more reliable models.

Which product really costs less? Which product gives you the best value for the price?

Now you need to get online or use the phone to do some **comparison shopping**, which means looking for the best product at the lowest price you can find.

Price is the most common reason people comparison shop, but there may be other reasons as well.
**EXAMPLE:** You might want to buy from a company that is environmentally or socially responsible. If so, you'll compare manufacturers' records in these areas.

### Brand Loyalty

Sometimes you already own a certain brand of product. You like it, and it has held up well. You are inclined to buy that brand again, even if it costs a little more. You feel you can't go wrong. Sometimes brand loyalty makes good sense.

## Deciding Where to Buy

Once you have decided on the product you want to buy, you'll need to figure out where to buy it.

### Warranties and Contracts

Warranties and service contracts are agreements about how problems with products will be handled. A **warranty** covers problems that occur because the product was not made properly, including defective materials or workmanship. It comes at no extra cost when you buy a product and guarantees that a defective product will be repaired or replaced for free.

Service and repair contracts are designed to cover the costs of some kinds of repairs that might be needed after you have used the product for a while. However, most service and repair contracts are not worth the additional cost.

Most products do not require special servicing or repairs during their useful lives. Besides, by setting aside a small amount each month, you can save up enough to cover repairs yourself if it becomes necessary. If you never need to make the repair, you can use the money for something else. If you've paid the money out on a service contract, though, the money is gone even if repairs are never needed.

**Search This**

### Comparison Shopping

Shop for an item valued at approximately $100 in a department store and online. Create a comparison grid to decide what features to research and how to organize your information. When your grid is complete, compare costs and availability between the two shopping methods. Don't forget to include shipping and handling charges. Which gives you a better deal on this item, stores or web sites?

### After the Purchase

Once you've made a significant purchase, it's important to keep track of how the product:

* Holds up.
* Meets your needs.

This information will tell you if your purchasing process was effective.

### Take Care of Your Things

Treating your purchases properly is the best protection against the cost of repairs. Remember, warranties won't pay for repair costs if *you've* damaged or misused the product. If you cause the damage, you'll be stuck with the cost even if the product is still under warranty.

Here are some tips to help you take care of your things:

* Follow the manufacturer's instructions for care and maintenance.
* Use the product only for the purpose intended.
* Treat the product in a reasonable manner.

## Different Kinds of Stores

| Retailer | Description | Advantage/Disadvantage |
| --- | --- | --- |
| **Department Stores** | Offer items in clearly defined departments, such as shoes, apparel, kitchenware, and others. | * They offer a wide variety of merchandise.<br>* They offer some specialty merchandise.<br>* Prices can be higher than other retail outlets. |
| **Specialty Stores** | Offer items in a specific category, such as shoes, books, office supplies, and others. | * Many choices are offered in that specialty category.<br>* Salespeople tend to be more knowledgeable about what they're selling.<br>* Prices may be higher than in other stores. |
| **Discount Stores** | Offer lots of merchandise in many categories at lower prices. | * The physical setting may be plain, like a warehouse.<br>* It may be hard to find a salesperson or get your questions answered.<br>* Salespeople may be less knowledgeable than in specialty or department stores. |
| **Online Stores and Catalogs** | Offer ordering and product selection from an Internet site or by phone or mail. | * They offer convenient shopping from home.<br>* Merchandise that is not available locally can be found.<br>* You cannot try on or look at the product before buying.<br>* They can pose security issues.<br>* You need to verify return policies and contact information before ordering in case there is a problem with the order.<br>* You often must pay shipping fees. |

## Avoid Problems

They say the best defense is a good offense. Translated to the realm of consumer economics, this means:

* Don't get taken.
* But if you do, fight back.

Your best protection against fraud is to recognize and avoid it.

## Don't Get Taken

The Federal Trade Commission (FTC) helps consumers avoid fraud. Visit the FTC web site to learn how to avoid everything from identity theft, diet, health, and fitness scams to abusive lending practices, and much more.

## Resolving Problems

No matter how wise a consumer you become, you still may encounter problems. When you try to resolve a problem with a company, be sure to:

* Document every contact you have with the company.
* Keep a log of all visits or phone calls to the company, including date, person you spoke with, and a summary of the conversation.
* Keep copies of all correspondence (regular mail and e-mail).

### Dealing with Defective Products

The first step in trying to deal with a defective product should be a visit in person or on the Web or a phone call to the company where you bought it. If you go in person:

* Take the product and your receipt and log book.
* Explain in detail the problem you are having and show your receipt.
* If the salesperson says he or she cannot do anything, ask to speak to the manager.
* If the manager will not help, explain that you are going to contact the manufacturer directly, and also consumer advocacy groups.

If phone calls or visits don't get any results, write a letter. The letter needs to include these **seven** pieces of information:

1. **The make and model** of the item purchased.
2. **The date and location** of the purchase.
3. **The problems** you are experiencing with the item.
4. **The date of your visit(s)** and/or phone call(s).
5. **The name(s) of the person(s)** you spoke with.
6. **A summary** of your conversation(s).
7. **A statement** of what you want (a replacement product or your money back).

Stick to the facts. Do not threaten or accuse. After a week from the date you sent the letter, contact the company if it has not contacted you. If you are not going to get a refund or replacement product, seek assistance. If you have made phone calls and written letters and have gotten nowhere, it's time to contact a professional organization or consumer advocacy group.

## Consumer Rights and Responsibilities

Even if you research thoroughly before making a major purchase and you avoid deceptive and fraudulent selling practices, the time may still come when you will have a problem that needs to be resolved. That's when it becomes important to know your rights, responsibilities, and power as a consumer. You have more power as a consumer than you probably know.

# Chapter 22 Wrap-up
## BECOMING A WISE CONSUMER

*Being a wise consumer takes work and practice. Once you've decided what you need and what you want, you can decide what, where, and from whom to purchase an item at the best price.*

*Businesses rely on different kinds of advertising to get customers. Learn how to spot deceptive techniques before you buy. Check into the product's warranty, and know where to go for help if you have problems in dealing with a store or manufacturer.*

*The choices you make as a consumer are very important to businesses, which rely on your "voting" dollars to keep them in business. Sometimes, you may decide to vote by boycotting a particular product or business, or you may choose to be part of a consumer cooperative.*

*As a consumer, the more you know the better decisions you'll make.*

**advertising**—business act of attracting attention to products or services with information designed to stimulate consumer buying.

**affordable**—able to be paid for. *Affordable* doesn't mean "cheap;" it means the item is at a price you can pay.

**comparison shopping**—process of gathering pieces of information about products (price, features, ratings) and sources and comparing them to make a wise purchasing decision.

**fraud**—deliberate deception by one party to get an unfair or unlawful gain from another party.

**hierarchy**—list of things in order of importance.

**market research**—collection and interpretation of data about a specific group (or groups) of consumers.

**need**—something required for survival.

**peers**—people who have similar characteristics, such as age, gender, income, or hobbies.

**want**—something desired but not required for survival.

**warranty**—guarantee by a manufacturer or service provider.

Name

## 22. Becoming a Wise Consumer

**After you read the chapter, write an answer to each question below.**

1. What is the difference between market research and advertisement? How are they connected?

_____

_____

_____

2. What are the differences among the four types of advertisements?

_____

_____

_____

3. What kinds of items do you think would be best to find at each of the four kinds of stores listed? Why?

_____

_____

_____

4. Why is giving feedback to a company about their product important?

_____

_____

_____

# 22. Becoming a Wise Consumer

**Circle the best answer for each item.**

1. What is the business act of attracting attention to products or services with information designed to stimulate consumer buying?
   a. hierarchy
   b. market research
   c. fraud
   d. advertising

2. What is the term that means able to be paid for, or at a price you can pay?
   a. comparison shopping
   b. affordable
   c. persuasive
   d. testimonials

3. What is the process of gathering information about products (price, features, ratings) and comparing them in order to make a wise purchasing decision?
   a. market research
   b. market evaluation
   c. comparison shopping
   d. shop-smart comparison

4. What is the deliberate deception by one party to get an unfair or unlawful gain from another party?
   a. fraud             c. ethics
   b. advertising       d. exaggeration

5. What is the term that means a guarantee for service by a manufacturer or service provider?
   a. promise
   b. guarantee of quality
   c. contract
   d. warranty

6. Every ad dollar used is to get you to _____.
   a. become a wise consumer
   b. join a co-op
   c. buy goods or services
   d. not be deceived

7. In advertising, when claims are puffed up with words, this is called _____.
   a. exaggeration       c. a testimonial
   b. false advertising  d. image enhancing

8. Stay focused on your goals, and learn to tell the difference between your needs and wants. These are examples of tips on how to _____.
   a. avoid being scammed
   b. know whether something is affordable
   c. help you resist peer influence and advertising
   d. decide where to buy

9. A _____ analyzes the cost compared with what you get, or the value.
   a. price check
   b. consumer cost comparison
   c. price evaluation
   d. price-value comparison

10. When the sale item is "out of stock," or "sold out," and the salesperson suggests you look at other, more expensive models, this is a _____.
    a. pyramid scheme    c. loss leader
    b. sweepstakes       d. bait and switch

CHAPTER 23

# Smart Shopping on the Internet

In this chapter, you will learn about:

- buying over the Internet
- using the Internet to comparison shop

Brandon wanted to send a birthday present to his older brother Josh, who was attending a college in a different state. Josh was taking a French class, and Brandon thought he might like some books about France. "Why not use the Internet?" asked a friend, who pointed out that it would be fast and convenient to order some books online and have them shipped directly to Josh at school. Brandon went online to a bookstore recommended by his friend. The site was easy to use, and Brandon quickly selected two books about France for his older brother.

Josh received the books on his birthday, and he was delighted with them. Brandon was very pleased with his Internet purchase ... until a few days later, when unexpected e-mail messages began to appear on the family's home computer. One message sold expensive apartments in Paris. Another promoted companies that rented cars in France. Brandon was annoyed by the unwanted e-mail messages. He didn't know that when he bought the books for his brother, he should have checked off the box saying, "Please don't reuse or resell my personal information." Internet shopping is great, but as with any other kind of shopping, you need to know how to go about it.

Alabama Citizenship Workbook 129

# Why Shop Online?

How would you like to get locked in a room for a week with nothing but a credit card (with no credit limit) and a computer connected to the Internet? If your experience turned out to be anything like that of people who have really done that as an experiment, you wouldn't have any trouble getting everything you needed to survive and then some. You could order a phone in a matter of hours, and you'd probably have clothes and bedding the next day. By the end of the week you'd be living it up, surrounded by every imaginable product.

Despite its rapid growth, shopping online remains only a very small part of the $3 trillion annual retail market in the United States. Of this huge amount of money, less than two percent is spent online. Electronic commerce, or **e-commerce**, in which business transactions occur online, has become a significant way of selling some types of products. By 2000, almost one-fifth of all computer hardware and software was sold via e-commerce, and one out of ten books sold was purchased via the Internet.

## Advantages of Online Shopping

The advantages of shopping online include:

* Convenience.
* Choice.
* Cost.

## Convenience

In contrast to traditional **"brick-and-mortar" stores** that have physical locations, such as your local department store or discount store, Internet sites are open 24 hours a day, 7 days a week, 365 days per year. You can shop at an Internet site while wearing your pajamas or listening to your favorite music. When you order a gift for someone via the Internet, you don't have to wrap it or stand in line at the post office to mail it. The web site handles those services for you.

Mail order and catalogue merchants offer many of the conveniences of Internet shopping, but not all its advantages. On the Internet, you can shop at sites located around the world and be notified within seconds when a sale occurs.

Physical safety is also part of the convenience of online shopping. You don't have to drive your car on slippery or crowded roads. You don't have to walk through dimly lit parking lots. Nor do you have to worry about pickpockets or other criminals you might encounter in brick-and-mortar stores—although there are online criminals to watch out for.

## Choice

In addition to convenience, the Internet greatly expands your choices. The whole world becomes your shopping mall when you search for items on the Internet. The expanded number of "stores" provided by the Internet is especially helpful to people living in small communities with a limited number of retailers.

Even if you live in a big city with lots of different stores, what if you are looking for a CD by an obscure group or a clothing item in an unusual style, color, or size? The stores in your city may not carry the precise item you want, but the Internet likely will.

The Internet is particularly useful for people who like to collect rare items. Imagine that you collect old comic books. At some point, you may have bought all the comic books in your neighborhood. On the Internet, you could get in touch with collectors located around the world.

## Cost

Shopping on the Internet can also save you money. Fierce competition on the Web often results in low prices.

There are web sites that help you locate the best deals among Internet stores, among online auctions, and even among some of the stores in your neighborhood. You can print discount coupons from web sites. Often, you can avoid paying sales tax on an Internet purchase. When buying an expensive item, this can be a big savings.

Last-minute sales are perhaps one of the most impressive ways to save money on the Internet. **EXAMPLE:** Consumers can take advantage of last-minute sales of airline seats, hotel rooms, rental cars, or any other item that must be sold by a given date.

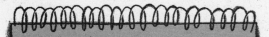

## My Notebook

### What Kind of Internet Shopper?

Some people love shopping on the Internet. They can't get over the ease, speed, and convenience of it. Other people are petrified of shopping online. They fear that their credit card number will be stolen, their privacy invaded, or their money taken by a company that doesn't really exist.

If you have tried Internet shopping, what are your feelings about it?

* Were the benefits as great as you expected?
* What about the dangers?
* Were any of your fears justified?

If you haven't done any shopping on the Internet, give it a try. You don't have to actually buy anything. Just pretend. At each step of the process, jot down your reactions or questions.

The travel industry is full of products that aren't sold out, such as seats on planes that aren't full. Airlines, railroads, and resorts sell such products on the Web at a discount. Thus, travel companies can sell something that otherwise wouldn't have sold at all, and consumers get great bargains.

To get the best travel bargains on the Web, you need to be flexible. If you're willing to be flexible about when you travel, your exact destination, and the hotel you'll stay at, the Internet can offer inexpensive travel options.

You don't have to buy a product on the Internet to get the advantages of using the Internet. You can simply use it as a tool in the buying process.

**EXAMPLES:** You can find out the amount an automobile dealer pays for a particular car and use this information when you are in the showroom negotiating a price.

Also, you can search for the least expensive or most convenient flight between two cities and then buy the ticket via the phone or at a travel agency.

Or, you can use the Internet to find out which television, camera, or computer is best for your needs and then buy it at a local store.

### Disadvantages of Online Shopping

With all the potential benefits of buying online, why doesn't everyone with a computer and a credit card do it? Most of the reasons why people choose not to shop online have to do with:

* Preferences for the traditional, offline shopping experience.
* Resistance to paying shipping charges.
* Uncertainty about the safety of sending credit card information over the Internet.
* Concerns about delivery, returns, and how to handle problems if they occur.

### Preferences

If one advantage of e-commerce is being able to shop while wearing your pajamas, a disadvantage is that when buying a pair of pajamas, you can't examine the softness, color, and workmanship of the garment! Some kinds of information can't be adequately conveyed through a photograph on a web site.

This is no different from shopping through a mail-order catalogue. If you prefer to be able to touch and examine a product before you buy it, shopping online may not appeal to you.

Many people enjoy the traditional offline shopping experience. The sights, sounds, smells, and personal service can be sources of pleasure.

### Shipping Charges

Another disadvantage of buying online is shipping charges. Although the cost of shipping is often balanced by the savings of not having to pay sales tax, many consumers still object to the idea that they are paying something for an online item that they don't pay in the offline world. In general, consumers dislike shipping charges, even though they typically have to spend money on gas when they buy from a brick-and-mortar store.

When considering an online purchase, don't forget to include the shipping costs in your calculation. If you want the item delivered within a few days, you'll pay even more for shipping than if you can wait the standard seven to ten business days.

## Security

When it's time to pay for an item purchased online, many consumers are concerned about the security of their credit card information. Fortunately, this concern is generally misplaced. Most online sellers have taken steps to insure the security of data transmission. As a result, there have been few documented cases in which credit card numbers have been stolen in communication between buyers and sellers.

Still, the fear of having a credit card number stolen and misused prevents many people from buying online. These same people are unconcerned when they hand their credit card to a waiter in a restaurant or to a clerk in a brick-and-mortar retail store. In general, the risk of using your credit cards online is no greater than in those situations.

## Delivery, Returns, and Other Problems

If customers have worries about placing an order online (and many do), they are also concerned about what happens after the order is placed. Consider

### Making it REAL

### What Kinds of Products?

The Internet seems well suited to the sale of some products but not others. So far, the products most frequently purchased online are:

* Books and CDs.
* Computers and software.
* Clothing.
* Airline tickets.

Think about the items listed above, and then answer these questions about online shopping:

* What is it about these types of products that makes them attractive to buy via the Internet?
* In the next few years, what additional types of products do you predict will become popular to buy online? Why?
* What types of products do you think will never be well suited for sale online? Why?

delivery time. Can you wait seven to ten business days for the merchandise to arrive? If you can't wait that long, are you prepared to pay an extra fee to get the item overnight?

Another drawback of online buying involves returning goods that are defective or unsatisfactory. You can't just jump into your car, drive to a store, explain your problem, and get a replacement, refund, or store credit. Some online companies have brick-and-mortar stores to which goods can be returned, but in most cases you have to mail goods that need to be returned—sometimes at your own expense. If you want to exchange an item, you have to wait for the item to be shipped in two directions.

Finally, if you have a problem with an online purchase that cannot be readily resolved with the company involved, it may be difficult for you to assert any consumer rights or bring legal action. This is especially true if the seller is based in another country.

## Is Shopping Online Safe?

All methods of payment carry some risk. Cash can be lost or stolen. A check sent through the mail can be intercepted or misdirected. A credit card number can be copied by a dishonest waiter or sales clerk. But because online shopping is comparatively new, people are very concerned about **Internet security**—the level of protection given to data collected online and sent over the Internet.

Buying by credit card over the Internet entails the same risks that exist when you use your credit card anywhere else, but it remains a convenient and secure method of payment. In addition, consumers enjoy certain protections with credit card purchases that they do not have with other payment methods.

## Buying by Credit Card

The vast majority of Internet purchases are made with credit cards. You are typically asked to enter the type of credit card, your credit card number, and its date of expiration. Sellers generally ask for your address as well and check that it is the same address to which the credit card statement is sent.

Some consumers who are worried about the misuse of their credit card number use a clever strategy. They get an additional credit card and dedicate it solely to Internet purchases. This allows them to notice any unexpected or suspicious charges more easily.

If you are uncomfortable sending your credit card information via the Internet, many online merchants allow you to fax, phone, or mail your credit card details to them. Other merchants will accept a check or money order sent by regular mail. Both methods slow delivery, because sellers will wait to receive payment before sending out your merchandise.

## Security Policy Statements

Most web-based companies make great efforts to ensure that transmission of your payment information via the Internet will be secure. These companies explain their efforts through privacy statements, privacy seals of approval, or both. Many sellers explain their use of special systems that encrypt, or code, any data you submit. They may also guarantee that if your credit card information is somehow used fraudulently, the seller will cover your share of any loss ($50 for a credit card).

Some companies provide logos, such as a picture of a key, to assure customers that high levels of security are being employed. In addition to increasing consumer confidence in a site's security policies, the logos allow site visitors to verify a site's identity.

Note that there are **two** potential threats to the security of any information you provide online:

1. Data transmitted via the Internet might be intercepted.
2. Someone might gain unauthorized access to your personal data after it has safely reached its intended destination.

The second threat may be the greater one. For example, criminals are more likely to "hack" into a company's records, gaining access to thousands of credit card numbers, than they are to intercept one transmission over the Internet. Careful consumers look for companies that explain what they do to minimize both types of security threats.

## Consumer Recourse

Consumers can take advantage of special protections when they use a credit card online. According to the Fair Credit Billing Act, you are protected by **two** safeguards:

1. **You can challenge charges** that you believe you did not make.
2. **You will only be held responsible for $50** when a lost or stolen credit card or credit card number is used by someone else.

## Chapter 23 Wrap-up
### SMART SHOPPING ON THE INTERNET

The advantages of Internet shopping include the convenience of not having to leave your home, a wide variety of choices, and many opportunities to compare prices. However, you can't see, pick up, hold, and feel the merchandise the way you can in a brick-and-mortar store. You will have to pay shipping charges to send or receive goods.

Shopping online is just as safe as traditional shopping, maybe more so. You can't be responsible for more than $50 if a thief should use your card, and many sellers will not charge you this. Privacy is another issue for many consumers. Internet stores do track their customers to personalize their promotions, and many customers find they like it. However, you can insist that information about you not be sold or given to anyone else.

The Internet makes it easy to participate in auctions. Learn what's involved before you do. And finally, gift registries online offer many aids to givers and receivers.

**brick-and-mortar stores**—traditional retail stores that have one or more fixed physical locations.

**e-commerce**—buying and selling of goods on the Internet.

**e-tailer**—company whose sales are made entirely or in part via the Internet.

**Internet security**—level of protection given to data collected online when it is transmitted on the Internet and stored upon receipt.

Name _____

## 23. Smart Shopping on the Internet

**After you read the chapter, write an answer to each question below.**

1. What is your best Internet shopping experience so far? Why?

   _____
   _____
   _____

2. What is the difference between what someone needs to have in order to shop in a store and what they need to have to shop online?

   _____
   _____
   _____

**Circle the best answer for each item.**

3. What is the term that means traditional retail stores that have one or more fixed physical locations?

   a. e-commerce stores
   b. shopping bots
   c. brick-and-mortar stores
   d. e-tailer

4. What is the term for the buying and selling of goods on the Internet?

   a. e-commerce
   b. e-tailer
   c. shopping bot
   d. cookies

Alabama Citizenship Workbook    135

CHAPTER 24

# Smart Shopping for Food

In this chapter, you will learn about:

- how to shop for food

Win Jing wanted to have a special dinner party for her friend Lee on his birthday. Her first idea was to take him to dinner at his favorite Italian restaurant. Then she worried it would cost more money than she could afford. She wondered if there was a less expensive way to give Lee a special Italian dinner. Perhaps she could cook it!

She knew Lee liked linguini with clam sauce. Win Jing went to Lee's favorite Italian restaurant, Luigi's, and looked at the menu. At Luigi's, linguini with clam sauce cost $14. Dinner for 6 would cost $84, plus tax and tip.

Win Jing went to the grocery store and priced the ingredients needed to make linguini with clam sauce at home. She discovered that for only $13, she could make the pasta dish for six people and also buy ingredients for a tossed salad and garlic bread to go with it! Lee loved the dinner, and he was very impressed that Win Jing went to the extra effort to cook it herself.

136  Alabama Citizenship Workbook

## Budgeting/Affordability

What food you buy depends a lot on how much you can afford to spend on food. Do you know how much your family spends on food each week? Do you know how much you spend personally? Average Americans spend about 16 percent of their weekly income on food. People with more money spend a lower percentage, while those with less money spend up to 30 percent or more of their income. It's a mistake to assume that you need to spend a lot of money to eat tasty, nutritious meals.

Knowing how to plan menus that give you good nutrition and fit your budget is a valuable skill. The least expensive way to eat is to buy basic ingredients and prepare meals from scratch. Many people feel they don't have time to cook that way, so they pay more to buy processed, packaged food. When you do that, you're paying extra for the time and energy the manufacturer spent to process the food.

**EXAMPLE:** You could make mashed potatoes by cooking potatoes and mashing them, or you could buy processed mashed-potato flakes in a box. Five pounds of potatoes may cost $1.79, whereas one 13 oz. box of brand-name mashed potatoes may cost $3.49. That's nearly 12 times as much! Cooking with fresh ingredients clearly saves a lot, and the food usually tastes better and may be more healthful.

## Food Preferences

What is your favorite food? Do you like fatty, salty foods like potato chips and bacon? Or do you prefer sweet, creamy items like banana splits and milk shakes? Perhaps you love your fresh fruit and veggies. Your tastes and preferences for different foods greatly influence what you choose to eat. Be aware, however, that your preferences are continually being influenced by cultural forces, such as advertising, that aren't concerned with your health.

## Nutrition

The slogan "You are what you eat" sounds funny, but it states an obvious fact that we seldom think about. We are physically composed of what we consume. The food we eat builds our bones, muscles, and organs. If you don't eat right, you can damage your body. A lack of certain nutrients often shows up first in the condition of your skin, hair, and nails.

**EXAMPLE:** A steady diet of junk food, such as pizza, hamburgers, chips, and fries, will give you a bad complexion and oily hair.

Nutrition should be a major factor in determining how you select the foods you eat. Although you don't want to discount the importance of good taste and you should certainly make a point of eating food you enjoy, you definitely want to eat food that will contribute to your good health.

## Anatomy of a Nutrition Label

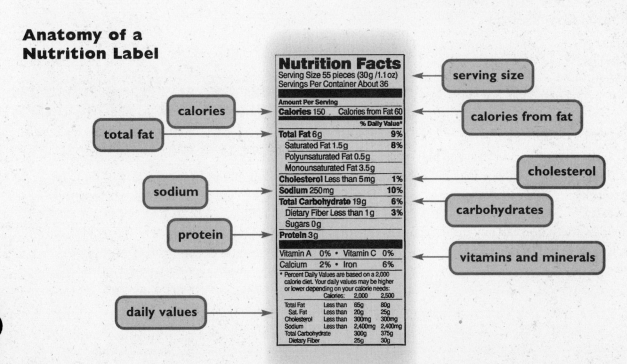

# Shopping Strategies

To get the most for your food dollar, you'll need to learn how to be a smart grocery shopper. These are strategies smart shoppers use:

* *Always shop from a list.* Plan your meals ahead of time. Make a list of what you'll need and what basic items you need to replace. Then stick to it.
* *Shop on a full stomach.* When you're hungry, it's hard to resist all the enticing sights and smells you encounter in a grocery store. Eat before you go shopping.
* *Compare prices.* Within a store, compare the costs of one brand against another. Compare prices from one store to another. Keep a list of the prices you pay for given amounts of items you buy frequently. It's the only way to know if a "sale" is really a bargain.
* *Buy what you like to eat.* Don't go overboard on price and nutrition. Tofu is cheap and nutritious, but if you don't like it, it will just go green and fuzzy in your fridge. Then it's a waste.

## Fresh vs. Packaged

When you shop, you'll face choices between buying the ingredients for a dish or buying the dish already prepared. How will you decide?

### Food Made from Scratch:
* Tastes better.
* Costs less.
* Takes time.
* Is limited by your skill and know-how.

### Prepared Foods:
* Are convenient. You don't have to buy quantities of different ingredients you may not use.
* Are quick.
* Are easy.
* Provide variety. You can buy dishes you don't know how to prepare.
* Are expensive.

## Food Grown Close to Home

Another set of choices you face as you shop involves where the food comes from. There are good arguments to be made for choosing food grown in your local area:

* Locally grown food is fresher.
* Locally grown food often tastes better.

Fruit that is transported long distances is picked before it is ripe. It may look ripe, but it doesn't have the full fragrance and taste of ripe food. You will need to experiment to discover which out-of-season food is worth buying.

## Food Prices

Food prices are influenced by many of the same factors that affect other commodities:

* *Supply.* An early frost in Florida may kill much of the orange crop, making oranges more expensive nation-wide.
* *Demand.* A surge in the popularity of a certain kind of food will mean suppliers can, and will, charge more for it.
* *Transportation costs.* Imported foods generally cost more.

**Get Smart**

### Take Your Own Bags

Some stores offer up to a nickel or a dime off of your purchase price when you bring your own shopping bag. This may not sound like a lot, but it adds up over time. Taking a cloth or plastic bag with you when you shop also helps the environment because it conserves resources and produces less garbage.

### Get Smart

## Using Labels

Almost all packaged foods in stores today have labels that describe what they contain. It is important to learn how to read these labels and choose foods that contain lower amounts of fat, sugar, and sodium.

### The Nutrition Label

* *Serving size.* Be sure to note the serving size indicated and adjust the information to the amount you actually eat.
* *Calories.* Calories are all about energy. A calorie is a unit of measurement that expresses the heat-producing or energy-producing value of food when it is oxidized in the body. How many calories you need depends on your age, your size, and how active you are. An average-sized active woman needs about 2,200 calories a day, while an average-sized active man needs about 2,900 calories a day.
* *Calories from fat.* Fat is essential, but don't overdo it. Try to keep fat calories down to below 30 percent of total calories for a day.
* *Total fat.* Recommended fat intake for a diet of 2,000 calories a day is 65 grams with no more than 20 percent as saturated fat.
* *Cholesterol.* Try to keep your intake below 300 mg a day.
* *Sodium.* Sodium may be in the form of regular table salt (sodium chloride) or other additives such as monosodium glutamate. Aim for fewer than 2,400 mg a day.
* *Total carbohydrates.* Carbohydrates provide energy. Most of your carbohydrate intake should come from complex carbohydrates, such as whole grains, bread, fruit, and vegetables. Avoid simple carbohydrates like sugar.
* *Fiber.* Try to maximize your fiber intake. You should get about 11.5 grams of fiber per 1,000 calories.
* *Protein.* Protein helps build your bones and muscles. Most Americans get plenty of protein in their diet without even trying.
* *Vitamins and minerals.* These are the essential micronutrients. Labels will indicate which of these nutrients are in the food and the percentage of the RDA.
* *Daily values.* The RDA's values are based on a 2,000-calorie daily diet. These percentages indicate important nutritional information. Use them to tell how nutritious the food is. Look for high percentages for total carbohydrates, dietary fiber, vitamins, and minerals. Look for low percentages of fat, saturated fat, cholesterol, sodium, and sugar.

## Comparing Prices

One way to be a smart food shopper is to shop around. Of course, most people shop at stores that are located in their neighborhood. You probably don't want to go too far away to buy groceries on a regular basis, because then any cost advantage of a particular store will be cancelled out by the transportation cost of getting there. However, if you're stocking up on a lot of items, it might pay to travel occasionally to a store that has significantly lower prices.

## Convenience Stores vs. Grocery Stores

Convenience stores are those small stores, often located at gas stations, that keep late hours and carry a few basic food items, such as milk and bread, along with lots of snack items and newspapers. Such stores are relatively expensive to operate. The rent they pay, the people they pay, and the prices they pay are all higher than other, larger stores. So their prices to you are higher than the price of these same items in standard grocery stores.

## Brand Names vs. Store Brands

Many supermarkets have their own brand versions of certain basic items, and these brands usually cost less. Depending on what kind of food you're looking for, store brands may be just as tasty and nutritious as more expensive national brands. It is certainly worth it to try store-brand versions of items that you usually buy. If you find that you prefer the brand name, you can always go back to buying it.

## Bulk Buying

Bulk buying means that you buy items in large quantities, which generally means that you pay a lower price per unit. Bulk buying can save money, but it doesn't make sense unless you have a lot of storage space and a large enough family to eat the food before it gets too old and goes bad.

## Coupons and Weekly Specials

Newspapers, store circulars, and Sunday paper inserts advertise weekly specials and provide coupons that give discounts on specific items. In fact, the average American household receives about 3,000 coupons every year.

If you're very organized and willing to make the extra effort, checking for weekly specials and clipping coupons can help you save money on groceries. The smart use of coupons can cut about 15 percent off of your food bill. Be careful, however, to clip coupons only for items that you would buy anyway. Don't buy the particular brand you have a coupon for if another brand is cheaper.

Also, be aware that specials and coupons are designed to get you into the store where you'll be tempted to buy more. Pay attention to your shopping list and don't give in to the temptation to buy items you don't need.

## Frequent-Shopper Cards

Many supermarkets offer "frequent-shopper" or "preferred-shopper" cards, which provide automatic discounts at the check-out counter on specific items. Discounted items are identified on the shelf, but you don't need a coupon to get the discount. Instead, you need a card, which you get by filling out an application at the store.

The card has a bar code that identifies you and thus provides the store with information about what you buy and how often. This trend in the supermarket industry is made possible by computer technology. The supermarket hopes that these cards will increase customer loyalty and keep you coming back for added savings.

## Shopping "Clubs"

Shopping clubs are large, industrial-sized stores that tend to sell items in large-quantity packages. Sometimes, these stores cover an entire city block. You pay an annual fee to belong to the "club." Items are stacked in huge, open warehouses. These places can be fun to shop in, and sometimes you can find some pretty good deals. As with bulk buying in general, however, shopping at these clubs may save you some money if you choose wisely, but it doesn't really pay unless you have enough storage space. Still, you might want to shop with two or three friends in your neighborhood and divide up the bulk items in order to take advantage of the cost savings and still take home a reasonable amount of food.

## Food Co-ops

If farmers can avoid wholesalers, they can sell at a price that includes only their price and a fair profit. This helps keep prices relatively low. Many early cooperatives in the U.S. were farm co-ops. Co-op food growers may collect, process, sell, and ship their products out of member-owned facilities.

### Honeysuckle Farm

Food cooperatives can be as creative as the people involved. Honeysuckle Farm offers a whole farm "experience" for its members. Co-op members pay in advance for a bundle of fresh produce from the farm. The produce is preselected depending on availability. Members pay a flat fee for twelve months. Orders are delivered to each house once a month.

As part of the co-op arrangement, families help plant, pick, and weed. They also bring their children out to experience "a day on a farm" by gathering eggs, grooming or riding animals, picking fruits and vegetables, braiding lavender, or making apple cider or fruit leather.

## Eating Out

Eating out is a major form of entertainment, and it is often more convenient than eating at home. Think of the last time you ate out at a restaurant. Was it a special occasion with your family or just stopping for a burger with friends after a game? Americans eat out more now than they ever have before. The pace of modern life and the availability of good, interesting restaurants contribute to this trend.

## Reasons

There are several reasons that eating out is so popular. In many families, both parents work, and it is easier to go out to eat than to come home after a long day and fix dinner. When you eat out, you don't have to spend time preparing food yourself and cleaning up afterwards. Eating out saves you time and labor. However, it costs more than making your own meals.

Alabama Citizenship Workbook 141

## Nutrition

Nutrition may be one of the first areas to suffer when you eat out. Restaurants don't supply a nutritional content label when they serve you your plate, so you don't know the nutritional content of the food prepared in restaurants. Because really good restaurants make a point of buying the freshest, highest-quality food they can, the nutritional value of their food can be quite high. On the other hand, many restaurants will try to spend as little as possible on ingredients so they can increase their profits.

## Cost

The cost of eating out can vary dramatically. Generally, whenever you pay for food, you want to look for the highest-quality food at the lowest price. Sometimes, of course, you just want to have a really great time and, if you have the money, you may be willing to splurge so you can enjoy a special occasion without the effort of cooking the food yourself.

## Fast Food

The fast-food industry has a lot of clout in our economy. Americans spend $103 billion a year on fast food. Every day, about 20 percent of Americans eat in fast-food restaurants. Approximately half of all the money spent eating out in America is spent in fast-food restaurants.

Four out of five times when children eat out, they eat fast food. This fact goes far in explaining why there is currently an epidemic of overweight children—double the number in 1980. Fast food tends to be high in calories, fat, cholesterol, sodium, and sugar, all of which contribute to heart disease, high blood pressure, cancer, and obesity.

Fast-food companies have a lot of buying clout. Because they purchase food in such large quantities, they're in a position to exert a lot of influence over the suppliers they deal with and get low prices.

### By the Numbers

### Eating In vs. Eating Out

When you go to your favorite restaurant, what do you order? How much does it cost? Don't forget to include tax and tip!

Now, consider that meal. What ingredients are in it? Make a shopping list and take it with you to the grocery store. How much would it cost to cook that meal?

How much would you save on that meal if you made it yourself instead of eating it at your favorite restaurant?

Name _____

## 24. Smart Shopping for Food

**As you read Chapter 8, write an answer to each question below.**

1. What methods are used for growing fresh, frozen, and canned vegetables? What do farmers feed most of the animals that produce meat and dairy products?

   _____

   _____

   _____

2. What influences food prices?

   _____

   _____

   _____

3. What is bulk buying and how does it differ from other types of shopping?

   _____

   _____

   _____

Name _____

## 24. Smart Shopping for Food

**Read each description, and write the letter of the correct term on the line.**

1. There are good arguments to be made for choosing food grown in your local area, it _____.

    a. is fresher and tastes better
    b. costs less
    c. takes less time to get
    d. provides more variety

2. _____ may collect, process, sell, and ship their products out of member-owned facilities.

    a. Grocery-store owners
    b. Co-op food growers
    c. Shopping-club owners
    d. Bulk-store operators

3. Many restaurants will try to spend as little as possible on ingredients so they can _____.

    a. increase their profits
    b. offer more food choices
    c. buy more equipment for the kitchen
    d. decrease their labor

CHAPTER 23

# Smart Shopping for Clothing

In this chapter, you will learn about:

- how to shop for clothes

Al-Malik looked in his closet, which was full of clothes. "I have nothing to wear!" he thought. His favorite shirt was dirty, and most of his clothes didn't fit him anymore. Besides, he just didn't feel like wearing most of them.

He took a bright red jacket out of the closet. "When I bought this jacket," he recalled, "I thought it was so cool. Now, I feel embarrassed when I wear it. I wish I had picked something else."

Although the jacket was in style when Al-Malik bought it, it was out of style now. The jacket turned out to be a fad, a style that is really popular for a short time but quickly becomes dated. Having a few trendy items in your wardrobe is fine, but Al-Malik's problem was that most of his clothes were so trendy when he bought them that they went out of date very quickly.

When building a wardrobe, it's wise to buy classics.

# Shopping for Clothes

You don't have to buy something every time you go shopping. Smart shoppers look around a lot before they buy. Why? Because then when they decide to make their purchase, they know these **two** important things:

1. Where to find the item in a style they like.
2. How much they'll have to pay for it.

Smart shoppers don't stop the first time they discover where they can buy the clothes they like. They keep looking. Another store may have the same or a similar item for much less, or the same store may reduce the price on this item later in the season.

Also, by looking at lots of choices, you may find that your idea of how to meet the particular wardrobe need you're addressing has changed. **EXAMPLE:** You think you can get one more outfit for knocking around on Saturdays by buying a pair of shorts. You look and look for the shorts you have in mind. The more you look, the more you see these jogging pants. They grow on you. You think it over, and decide you can meet this need for a casual outfit with the jogging pants instead of the shorts.

## Fashion Considerations

How fashionable you want to be is up to you. If you want to follow fashion closely, there are a couple of things you should be aware of.

## Store Brands vs. Designer Clothing

Many large <u>department stores</u> have their own special brand names. Clothing with their labels is sold only in their own stores. It is usually of a decent quality, because the store would not want to put its name on an inferior product. However, such stores also sell some "designer" labels alongside their own brands.

Designer clothes are created by well known fashion designers. Designer clothes almost always cost more than department store brands. Sometimes, it's because the clothes use high-quality fabrics and have a superior cut. Often, however, it's because the manufacturers spend a lot of money on marketing and merchandising.

If you like the look of designer clothes, look for them in special <u>discount stores</u>. Some shopping malls specialize entirely in discounted merchandise. You need to shop carefully in them, though, or you could get ripped off.

Here's where your smart shopping comes in. If you've done your shopping well, you know how much you'd have to pay for a certain style in a department store. So you'll know if the markdown indicated on the price tag is a real bargain or not.

## Fad vs. Classic

Fads can be fun, but classic clothes are always in style. A **fad** is a fashion sensation that lasts for only a relatively short period of time—perhaps only a single season or a couple of years at most.

**EXAMPLE:** Low-rise jeans. It may seem daring to walk around in clothes that show off your bare skin. But in another year, these may look ridiculous and no one will be caught dead in them.

Classic clothes, on the other hand, are clothes that may still look good and feel right many years into the future.

Here are some clothes considered classic, or timeless:

* Black slacks.
* Skirts no shorter than just above the knee.
* White dress shirts and blouses.
* Navy blue blazers.
* Trench coats.
* Black lace-up shoes for men and pumps for women.

These items will be in style for a long time, and you can make them look up-to-date by changing the shirt or blouse you wear with them, or adding funky accessories.

## Practical Considerations

Visual appearance isn't the only consideration when choosing clothes. There are practical considerations, too.

## Durability and Longevity

Well made clothes that use good fabrics will last longer and provide better service than poorly constructed clothes made with cheap fabrics. **Durability** is determined by how well clothes are constructed, or sewn, and by the kind and quality of fabric used. Here are some tips for learning to recognize durability:

* Look at the labels in clothes you own that have lasted well. What are they made of?
* Look at the hems. You should not be able to see the threads of a hem on the outside of a garment. Also, if the hem is beginning to unravel while the item is still on the store rack, you know it will pull out about the second time you wear it.
* Check the buttons. Are they sewn on tightly, or are they already loose?
* Is the jacket, skirt, or pants lined? A lining makes a garment last a lot longer.
* Is the sweater starting to "pill" just from the wear of other people trying it on? Look carefully.
* Learn about fabrics and what to expect from them. Some are much more durable than others.

### Get Smart

#### Look Before You Buy

Closely examine any item of clothing you're considering purchasing.

Before you buy clothes, follow this process:

* *Always check the seams* to make sure that the stitching is thorough and strong.
* *Check the fabric in seams* to be sure it is symmetrical and evenly matched.
* *Check threads at the ends of seams* to see that they are neatly clipped.
* *Pay special attention to high-wear areas* such as collars and underarms in shirts and jackets.
* *Check the crotch of pants* to look for complete and reinforced stitching.

*Alabama Citizenship Workbook*

## Safety Issues

It's very important to choose clothes and shoes that are comfortable and safe. Pay attention to the following safety issues when you choose clothes:

* Children's pajamas should be made from fabrics that will not catch fire easily.
* Clothes that are too tight can impair circulation.
* Cotton is absorbent and can help draw moisture away from skin. It can help prevent infections and is a good choice for socks and underwear.
* If you've discovered that some dyes, perfumes, and materials cause you to have allergic reactions such as rashes, avoid them.

## Fabric Selection

Fabric is fundamental. Good fabric is essential to good clothes. Fabric gives clothing its texture and its drape. *Texture* is how the fabric feels. It may be:

* **Soft.** Flannel is soft.
* **Rough.** Some wools are rough.
* **Smooth.** Satin and polished fabrics are smooth.
* **Nubby.** Some weaves have a bumpy texture.

*Drape* refers to how the fabric hangs on your body. The fabric can be:

* **Lightweight** and moves as you move.
* **Heavy.** It holds its shape well.

## Natural Fibers

Natural fibers come from plant and animal sources. Many people prefer fabrics made with natural fibers because they allow your body to "breathe," and they feel good to the touch. The fabric's ability to breathe, or let air circulate around your body, helps to disperse moisture and provides greater comfort in both hot and cold weather than synthetic fibers do.

Natural fibers can require special care. Cotton shrinks in heat. If you wash cotton clothes in hot water or dry them with a high heat, you may not be able to wear them. For this reason, cotton is often mixed with another fabric. Cotton clothes may also need to be ironed more often than some synthetics that can be dried and worn without ironing. Most

wool clothes can be washed, but very carefully. They need cool water (because wool also shrinks) and gentle soaps. They need to be laid out flat to dry and gently pulled into their original shape. Silk is another natural fiber with wonderful qualities, but often it cannot even be hand washed. Many silks have to be dry-cleaned.

## Synthetic Fibers

People who like synthetic fibers, or man-made fabrics, are often attracted by their ease of care and their lower cost. Many synthetics can be machine-washed and dried and can be ready to wear without any ironing. Usually, however, these fabrics don't "breathe" as well as natural fibers.

## Natural and Synthetic Blends

Lots of clothes are made from blends of natural and synthetic fibers that aim to provide the best traits of both. These blends can reduce cost and compensate for some trait of the natural fiber.

**EXAMPLE:** Polyester blended with cotton makes the cotton more wrinkle resistant.

| Natural Fibers | | |
|---|---|---|
| **Fabric** | **Source** | **Characteristics** |
| **Cotton** | Seed pod of cotton plant. | Soft, absorbent, versatile, easy to wash. |
| **Wool** | Sheep hair. | Durable, warm, variety of textures. |
| **Silk** | Created by silk worms. | Soft, smooth, lightweight, warm, fluid drape. |
| **Linen** | Flax plant. | Crisp, nubby texture, cool in warm weather, absorbent, dries quickly, wrinkles easily. |
| **Leather** | Animal skins. | Smooth, protective, rugged, wind-resistant. |

| Synthetic Fibers | |
|---|---|
| **Fiber** | **Characteristics** |
| **Acetate** | Soft, silky, drapes well, wrinkle-resistant. |
| **Acrylic** | Similar to wool, not itchy, shiny, blends well with other fibers. |
| **Nylon** | Strong, silky, slippery, stretchable when knitted. |
| **Polyester** | Shiny, silky, wrinkle-resistant, warm. |
| **Rayon** | Silky, fluid texture, nice drape, versatile. |

Generally, synthetic blends are more comfortable than 100 percent synthetics. Look for fabrics with a higher ratio of natural fibers—for example, 70 percent cotton to 30 percent polyester.

## Color

Along with good construction and quality fabric, color is a major factor to consider when buying clothes. Obviously, everyone looks better in some colors than others. Your own personal coloring determines what colors work best for you.

**EXAMPLE:** People with darker skin and hair often look much better in bright colors than people with light skin and hair. Bright, vibrant colors may overwhelm and fade the lighter person. A darker person may look a bit dull in pastels, which would look good on someone with blond hair and blue eyes.

Experiment with colors. Ask your friends which colors they think look best on you.

Neutral colors such as black, gray, and navy provide a good foundation for your wardrobe. You can then use accessories in brighter and trendier colors to provide variety and style. Remember that some colors, such as bright ones like fuchsia, go in and out of style.

## Fit

So, now you've found an item that's well made with good quality fabric. The color works well for you, too, but when you try it on, something isn't quite right. Clothes that don't fit properly look bad and are often uncomfortable.

Look for the following elements when judging the fit of clothes:

* Make sure jackets can be buttoned and still look and feel comfortable.
* Check that jackets have enough room in the shoulders. Having a tailor adjust the shoulders is expensive and very difficult—often impossible.
* Avoid jackets, sweaters, and shirts if the sleeves are too short. Conversely, long sleeves can be hemmed easily.
* When buying shirts, jackets, and coats, cross your arms in front of your chest to make sure there's enough fabric to prevent the garment from binding across your back.
* Make sure pants are long enough. You can hem pants if they're too long, but you can't fix pants that are too short.

* Look for pants that can be buttoned or zipped up comfortably.
* Remember to sit down when you try on pants or skirts, to make sure they aren't too tight or too short.

## Cleaning and Care

The care required by different types of fabric is an important consideration when purchasing clothes. Clothes that can be washed and dried with minimal effort can be worn more regularly and still look good. Clothes that must be dry-cleaned continue to cost more money even after you have paid the initial purchase price. You may find that you won't often wear clothes that have to be hand-washed, because you aren't willing to put forth the extra time and effort to wash them by hand.

These days, most items of clothing come with a label that explains the best care for the garment. Often, care instructions are written in English and say things like "Wash in warm water. Tumble dry—low." However, because of international commerce, visual symbols have been developed to explain fabric care to people who speak many different languages. Five basic symbols make up the **International Textile Care Labeling Code**.

It's important to follow the care instructions on your garments. Treat your clothes well, and they'll last longer.

## Where to Shop

If you want to get the most for your clothing dollar, you'll need to learn where to shop and how to recognize the best values when you find them. Where you shop for clothes makes a big difference in what kind of clothes you'll have to choose from.

Most communities in America today offer a wide range of possible places to shop for clothes. You need to know the territory. Survey the shopping places in your community. You'll be able to tell rather quickly which places appeal to you and which ones you never want to visit again.

### International Textile Care Labeling Codes

| Symbol | Variations | Meaning |
|---|---|---|
| **Wash tub** | With the number 40 inside. | Washing instructions—Wash in lukewarm water. |
| | With X through it. | Do not wash. |
| **Triangle** | With CL inside. | Bleaching instructions—Use chlorine bleach. |
| | With X through it. | Do not bleach. |
| **Square** | With three vertical lines inside. | Drying instructions—Drip dry. |
| | With circle inside. | Tumble dry. |
| **Circle** | With A inside. | Dry-cleaning instructions—Use any solvent. |
| | With X through it. | Do not dry clean. |
| **Flat iron** | With one dot inside. | Ironing instructions—Use cool iron (225° F). |
| | With two dots. | Use warm iron (300° F). |
| | With three dots. | Use hot iron (400° F). |

### Get Smart

### Clothing Care Tips

"Wash with similar colors" is one of the most important instructions you'll ever read. If you've ever washed all your white clothes with a new, red T-shirt and ended up with an all-pink wardrobe, you know why. Here are some other laundry tips:

* Separate light and dark clothes and wash them in different loads.
* Delicate clothing, silk, and wool should be hand-washed using a gentle soap.
* Bright colors should be washed in cold water to prevent fading.
* Fabric softeners help prevent clothes from clinging due to static electricity.
* If you have sensitive skin, use laundry products without dyes or perfumes.

You can buy clothes at the following places:

* Department stores.
* Discount stores.
* Specialty stores.
* Catalogs and online stores.
* Factory outlet stores.
* Used clothing stores.

The **markup** on clothes varies greatly, depending on where you shop. Markup refers to the additional cost that wholesalers and retailers tack onto what it cost to manufacture the clothes.

What if you find a great winter coat at a department store? If the coat costs $100, that probably means that the store paid about $40 for it. The store's

### Types of Stores

| Type of Store | Advantages | Disadvantages |
| --- | --- | --- |
| Department stores | * Wide variety of items available.<br>* Wide variety of brands and styles available. | Big markup on clothes, up to 60 percent. |
| Discount stores | Lower prices than department stores. | Often lower quality. |
| Specialty stores | Carry a wide variety of a specific type of item. | Don't offer especially good prices. |
| Catalog and online stores | Shopping from home. | * Can't touch or try on the clothes before buying.<br>* Shipping time and cost. |
| Factory outlet stores | Prices often low because the manufacturer is selling its own clothes. | Products may have defects or didn't sell well in retail stores. |
| Used clothing stores | * Frequent shoppers may find great deals.<br>* Proceeds often benefit charities. | * Clothing may be in poor condition.<br>* Selection varies greatly from day to day. |

markup on that coat is $60, or in this case, 60 percent. The manufacturer took about $20 in profit over what it cost to make the coat. The fabric may have cost only $5, and labor was $15. Now, you may feel that you don't want to pay $60 over wholesale to buy that coat.

What are your options? Let's consider the advantages and disadvantages of the different places to shop.

### Get Smart

**Vintage Clothes**

Used, or "vintage," clothing shops, like thrift stores and consignment shops, can be great resources if you're trying to stretch your clothing budget. Look here for items such as:

* business suits
* winter coats and jackets
* formalwear
* purses, scarves, and hats
* designer clothing

### Search This

**The Price of Jeans**

How much can you pay for a pair of jeans? Jeans have become very prestigious items in some quarters during the past 20 to 30 years.

American jeans are very popular in Europe and some other parts of the world. Interestingly, European-made jeans fetch pretty high prices in the United States.

Go online and see if you can find out how much you can pay for a pair of jeans. What's the most you can pay? What is the least you can pay?

# Chapter 25 Wrap-up
## SMART SHOPPING FOR CLOTHING

Your clothes tell the rest of the world about you. Your family, your friends, and other social factors affect your clothing choices. So too do advertising, affordability, and your personal style. When making clothing decisions, consider your wardrobe as a whole. Take an inventory of your clothes, evaluate what you have, and figure out what you need. Work within your budget.

Shop before you buy. Consider fashion, but remember that some clothing fashions come and go. Choose classic clothes that will stay in style for years. Consider also such practical things as durability and longevity.

Clothing involves many choices. Learn about fabrics and how they wear. Understand what colors suit you best. Consider how you will have to take care of an item before you buy it. Shop where you'll get the most for your money.

Finally, grooming aids and cosmetics have a place in your budget. Investigate ingredients and know what you're paying for.

**department stores**—stores that sell merchandise in different departments according to type, such as sportswear, shoes, or ties.

**discount stores**—stores that offer merchandise at reduced prices.

**drape**—manner in which a fabric hangs on your body.

**durability**—ability to withstand wear and tear; sturdiness.

**fad**—style of clothing that comes and goes very quickly.

**International Textile Care Labeling Code**—code of visual symbols that explains how to care for clothes.

**markup**—amount added to the cost of an item to figure its selling price.

**natural fibers**—threads made from plants or animal hair.

**synthetic fibers**—man-made fibers. Most are made from petroleum-based chemicals, or petrochemicals.

**texture**—appearance and feel of a surface.

Name _____

## 25. Smart Shopping for Clothing

**After you read the chapter, write an answer to each question below.**

1. What is the difference between designer clothes and department store brand clothes?
   _____
   _____
   _____

2. What are some ways to determine clothing's durability?
   _____
   _____
   _____

3. Why is it necessary to have the International Textile Care Labeling Code?
   _____
   _____
   _____

Name _____

# 25. Smart Shopping for Clothing

**Circle the best answer for each item.**

1. What is a style of clothing that comes and goes very quickly?
   a. accessories
   b. drape
   c. fad
   d. classic

2. What are the visual symbols that explain how to care for clothes?
   a. International Textile Care Labeling Code
   b. International Clothing Code
   c. Care and Symbols Code
   d. International Use and Care Code

3. What is the term that means the amount added to the cost of an item to figure its selling price?
   a. inventory
   b. markdown
   c. wholesale
   d. markup

4. What are the threads made from plants or animal hair?
   a. synthetic fibers
   b. natural fibers
   c. man-made fibers
   d. coarse fibers

5. What is the term that means man-made fibers?
   a. coarse fibers
   b. natural fibers
   c. synthetic fibers
   d. petrol fibers

6. Fads last _____.
   a. many years
   b. a single season or a couple of years
   c. weeks
   d. overnight

7. If you choose a shirt that has blended fabrics, look for fabrics with a higher ratio of _____.
   a. synthetic fibers
   b. natural fibers
   c. silk
   d. nylon

8. When trying on pants or skirts, remember to _____.
   a. sit down in them to make sure they aren't too tight
   b. jog in them to make sure they aren't too tight
   c. bring shirts along to try to match them
   d. hold them up to the light to make sure they're not of poor quality

**Essay Question**

How can you be sure you shopped smart and got the best deal? What are the steps you have to take to ensure this?

Alabama Citizenship Workbook

CHAPTER 26

# Smart Shopping for Health Care

**In this chapter, you will learn about:**

- getting appropriate health care
- paying for healthcare

Last week, Greta and her family moved her grandfather to a nursing home because his health was very poor. He was overweight and had trouble breathing, in part because he had smoked cigarettes his entire adult life. The doctors were very worried about his blood pressure. It just wasn't safe for him to live on his own anymore.

Greta knows that a lot of health problems run in families, and she's scared that she will end up like her grandfather when she's old. Her friend Miguel says the problem is that her grandfather never took good care of himself. Now his body has worn out after all those years of neglect. Miguel says the human body is like a machine. Just like a car, the body needs to be taken care of properly. Miguel certainly knows a lot about cars. He has restored several beat-up old cars that run beautifully now, and they look good too!

## Obtaining Health Care

Good health and dental care are important components of living a full, healthy life. If you are fit, manage your weight well, avoid too much **stress**, and avoid substance abuse, you can reduce your need for health care. Still, you will want to get regular check-ups and have access to health care when you become ill or injured.

As you become an independent adult, you will be choosing health-care providers.

### Health-Care Options

There are many types of health care to choose from. There are many more medications, treatments, and procedures available. On the one hand, the range of choices and treatments means many diseases and conditions can be treated effectively. On the other hand, it means that you, as a health-care consumer, must take responsibility for being informed.

### Standard Medicine

Standard medicine in the United States focuses on diseases or abnormal conditions and treats those conditions specifically. Medication and surgery are common treatments. Physicians specialize in a particular field, such as orthopedics (the treatment of the skeletal system) or neurology (the treatment of the nervous system).

Standard medicine offers many effective options for **diagnosis**—the identification of an illness through tests and examination, or in other words, figuring out what is wrong—and treatment of all kinds of medical conditions. Technologies such as laser surgery improve the quality of millions of lives a year. Medications such as antibiotics and vaccines have made many deadly diseases a thing of the past.

In addition, traditional medicine's focus on research and scientific data helps prevent many diseases. **Preventive medicine** saves lives by stopping diseases from developing in the first place.
**EXAMPLE:** Many doctors prescribe a baby aspirin a day to help prevent their older patients from having heart attacks.

### Alternative Medicine

While standard medicine offers many health-care benefits, some consumers and health-care practitioners look to **alternative medicine** to meet their health-care needs. Alternative medicine includes:

* Chiropractic treatment.
* Acupuncture.
* Relaxation treatment.
* Vitamin treatment.
* Herbal treatment.

About one-third of all Americans use some form of alternative medicine. Many standard medical practitioners see value in some alternative practices and incorporate them into their practice.

### Holistic Medicine

**Holistic medicine** is the practice of looking at all aspects of a person's life in treating disease. In holistic medicine, a person's diet, stress level, exercise habits, and attitudes are all considered as factors in treating disease and maintaining health. This approach is based on the belief that the mind and body affect each other, and that a person's health can be improved by taking this into account. Examples of this approach in action include:

* The use of relaxation techniques for people in chronic pain.
* Diet and exercise programs for people with heart disease.

## Avoiding Quackery

Medical **quackery** is the use of an ineffective or unproven treatment by people who are not trained medical professionals. Unfortunately, people who suffer from a disease or debilitating condition are vulnerable to untruthful claims. They may have received standard medical treatment without improvement and are desperate for a cure or improvement in their condition.

The Food and Drug Administration defines medical quackery or fraud as the promotion, for profit, of a medical remedy known to be false or unproven. However, sometimes a person who promotes a false cure believes it really works. Is this person a quack? To complicate matters more, not all unproven treatments are quackery.

**EXAMPLE:** Legitimate medical researchers conduct studies with unproven treatments to determine if they are effective.

If quackery is not clearly defined, how can you protect against it? Here are some things to look for:

* You're told the cure is secret but very effective.
* The person you deal with has credentials that you've never seen or heard of before.
* The treatment claims to cure many conditions or diseases.
* Anecdotes and testimonials—not scientific facts—are used to support the claims of success.

If you have questions or are considering trying some kind of treatment, check it out:

* Ask your doctor if he or she recommends it.
* Check with the Department of Health in your state government.
* Click on http://www.hhs.gov/ to see what the U.S. Department of Health and Human Services suggests.

## Exercising Your Options

When you make choices among the various health-care options, you will want to:

* Research thoroughly. Use the library and the Internet. Read widely about the health issue you face.
* Get recommendations from trustworthy individuals.
* Use only licensed health-care practitioners.
* Ask for references.

## Health Care Providers

Most health care falls under one of the following **two** categories:

1. **Routine Care:** visits to family or general practitioners for regular check-ups and minor ailments or injuries such as colds and sprains.
2. **Specialized Care:** visits to specialists such as internists, gynecologists, neurologists, surgeons, physical therapists, mental-health therapists, and those who perform diagnostic tests.

## Primary Care Physicians

A **primary care physician**, often called a PCP, is a general or family physician who serves as your main doctor and coordinates all of your care. He or she provides all your routine care and some specialized care. If you develop a serious illness or have a serious injury, your PCP will refer you to a specialist.

Since this is the doctor you will turn to first, it is important to select the right one. Ask friends, family members, and coworkers if they can recommend someone. Your local medical society can also give you the names of doctors.

158 Alabama Citizenship Workbook

| Medical Specialties | | |
|---|---|---|
| Area of Specialty | Specialist | What The Specialist Does |
| Cardiology | Cardiologist | Treats heart and blood vessel symptoms and diseases. |
| Dermatology | Dermatologist | Treats skin diseases and conditions. |
| Family Practice | Family Practitioner | Treats routine and some specialized conditions of children and adults. |
| Gynecology | Gynecologist | Treats female reproductive system disorders. |
| Immunology | Immunologist | Treats disorders of the immune system (including allergies and asthma). |
| Internal Medicine | Internist | Treats chronic, complicated diseases. |
| Neurology | Neurologist | Treats disorders of the nervous system, including the brain and spinal cord. |
| Obstetrics | Obstetrician | Supervises the care of pregnant women and delivers babies. |
| Oncology | Oncologist | Treats cancer. |
| Orthopedics | Orthopedist | Treats injuries or disorders of the skeletal system. |
| Pediatrics | Pediatrician | Monitors the healthy development of infants and children and treats childhood diseases. |
| Radiology | Radiologist | Uses specialized equipment—x-rays, sonar, magnetic imaging—to help diagnose diseases, treats some diseases with radiation therapy. |
| Surgery | Surgeon | Treats injury, deformity, or disease by physical manipulation or adjustment of the affected area, often involving the cutting and reattachment of body tissues. Most surgeons further specialize in an area, such as bones and joints (orthopedics). |

### In the Doctor's Office

Before a visit with a doctor, write down on a piece of paper any questions you have and take it with you. It's easy to forget everything you wanted to ask once you're in the doctor's office.

### Choosing Your Doctors

Here are some questions to ask about any physicians you're considering using:

* Are they board certified?
* Will care be covered by your insurance plan?
* How long will you have to wait to get in to see them?
* Are they affiliated with area hospitals? Which ones?

Once you've seen someone, make sure you feel that:

* You can communicate easily with him or her.
* You were treated respectfully.
* Staff were helpful and courteous.

Keep in mind also that you need to take responsibility for your health care. Always communicate clearly to your doctor, ask questions about anything you don't understand, and follow your physician's advice for treatment.

## Specialists

Most of the time, your PCP will be able to handle your health-care needs. But when you are seriously ill or injured, it is necessary to see a medical **specialist**. Specialists have received additional training beyond that required to become a medical doctor. When you have a serious condition, it is a good idea to see two specialists. This allows you to get a second opinion to compare what two highly trained physicians say about your condition.

## Mental Health

Mental health and drug- and alcohol-abuse treatments play an important role in our society's health care. Modern life is complex and stressful. As a result, many people turn to therapists for help in dealing with difficult life circumstances and daily stresses. This is not something to be ashamed of. Seeking help can often make the difference between leading a full, happy life and experiencing depression or anxiety.

Seeking treatment for drug and alcohol abuse is also not something to be ashamed of. It takes courage to admit that a problem exists. In addition, current treatments provide a great deal of hope for people with addictions.

Treatment can be either of **two** kinds:

* Outpatient.
* Residential.

In outpatient care, you see a therapist, or attend group sessions, on a daily or weekly basis. During that time, you continue to live on your own and carry on with your regular life.

In residential treatment, you live in a hospital or other care facility for a certain amount of time. During that time, you are involved in an intensive daily treatment program. After residential treatment, you usually continue treatment in an outpatient program on a weekly or daily basis for a period of time.

## Hospitals

In some situations, you may be required to go to a hospital or specialized medical facility for treatment or diagnostic tests. Hospitals are the most common facilities. They offer both in-patient care (when you stay in the hospital overnight) and outpatient care. For example, in a hospital, you might:

* Go for several hours to get a diagnostic test, such as an x-ray.
* Spend a day in outpatient or short-stay surgery.
* Be required to spend several days or longer for major surgery.
* Go to the emergency room for a critical or life-threatening injury or condition.

Hospitals should be accredited with the Joint Commission on Accreditation of Healthcare Organizations. In addition, the more experience the hospital you choose has with your procedure or treatment, the better.

If you are seeking unusual care, try to find a facility with much experience in that area. Research shows that the more experience a medical facility has in a particular area, the higher the success rate. Some magazines publish reports that rate hospitals. Check them out.

Outpatient facilities include such things as urgent-care centers, physical therapy clinics, and pain treatment centers. As with all other health-care facilities, it is important to verify that the facility is accredited and the people who practice there are licensed or certified.

## Dental Care

Preventive dental care plays an important role in a good personal health-care plan. A dentist who practices general dentistry can provide preventive care, fill cavities, and do restorative work, like crowns. (Crowns are permanent gold or porcelain caps placed over the tooth to prevent cracked teeth from breaking apart.)

Preventive care includes check-ups and regular cleanings. Brushing and flossing daily, and getting your teeth cleaned twice a year can help you avoid more costly dental care.

### Time for the Emergency Room?

Dr. Gary Young, medical director of an emergency room in a mid-sized Oregon college town, sees many young people who come into the emergency room when they shouldn't. Emergency rooms are not set up for routine medical problems. You should see your primary care physician for those. But if it's the middle of the night and all of a sudden you have chest pains, what should you do?

Dr. Young says deciding whether to use the emergency room or not depends on the situation. What kind of problem are you having, and what is your age and medical condition?

Dr. Young recommends first contacting your primary care physician. If it is not during regular hours, an on-call doctor will be available. If you don't have a primary care physician, he recommends getting one.

In addition, many cities now have urgent-care centers that are open 24 hours a day and are much less expensive than emergency rooms. Some communities and health insurance programs have a 24-hour line you can call to get advice from nurses about your symptoms.

Even though many people use the emergency room when they shouldn't, there *are* times when it is appropriate. In fact, there is a law in every state that says people with one of the following conditions must be treated if they come to an emergency room:

* Severe bleeding.
* Severe pain.
* Life-threatening symptoms.
* Labor.

Knowing this, what would you do if:

* You broke your arm, the bone is sticking out, and you're bleeding? *If you said go to the emergency room, you're right.*
* You tripped and now your ankle is very swollen? The pain is pretty bad. *If you said go to an urgent-care facility, good answer!*
* You felt nauseated all day, and now you're vomiting? If you're vomiting continuously, you could become dangerously dehydrated quickly. *Go to an urgent-care facility immediately, or an emergency room if an urgent-care facility is not available.* If you are vomiting occasionally, *contact your primary care physician or go to an urgent-care facility.*
* Your friend fell off a ladder and now acts confused and says his head feels as if it is going to blow up? *If you said go to an emergency room, good answer!* Your friend could be in shock, or have a hemorrhage, both of which can be life-threatening.

**EXAMPLE:** If you don't clean your teeth properly, you can develop gum, or periodontal, disease. This is an infection of the gum that requires treatment by a gum specialist, called a periodontist.

Just as there are specialists in the practice of medicine, there are also dental specialists. These include:

* Periodontists (specialize in diseases of the gums).
* Orthodontists (specialize in straightening teeth).
* Oral surgeons (specialize in removing teeth and other mouth surgery).

As with all health-care providers, it is important that you receive your dental care from licensed or certified practitioners.

## Paying for Health Care

For decades now, the cost of health care has risen faster than any other essential living expense.

### The Spiraling Cost of Care

Americans spend more than $1.2 trillion a year on health care. In the early 1990s, the figure was a little over $900 million. This trend of increasing health-care costs will undoubtedly continue. Why? First, people are living longer and receiving more health care during their lifetimes. In addition, diagnosis and treatment options are increasing and becoming more technologically sophisticated.

### Insurance Coverage

With rising health-care costs, many people find it difficult or impossible to pay for the health-care services they need. This is especially true if you face a major illness, such as cancer. That's where **health insurance** comes in.

As with all insurance, you exchange a fixed payment for protection against the heavy costs of uncertain events. Insurance comes from the word *insure*, which means "to make safe or secure." With health insurance, you pay a certain amount, the insurance **premium**, in exchange for a guarantee of payment for health-care services described in the plan. Your health-care needs are secured.

Here's how it works. Many people pay premiums into one big pot, out of which the insurance company pays the costs it has agreed to pick up. Some people need very little health care. Others need more. As a result, the amount in the pot is enough to cover everyone's expenses. The insurance company makes its profit in **two** ways:

1. Premiums are a bit higher than the company's actual expenses.
2. Money taken in is invested and earns a return before it is paid out for medical expenses.

The second way is by far the largest source of insurance-company income.

Within this health-care insurance system, there are **three** main types of health insurance plans.

### ❶ HMO Plans

Within a **health maintenance organization (HMO)** are all the services you are expected to need, both to maintain good health and to receive treatment for illnesses and injuries. HMOs are **managed-care plans**. They manage, or control, your use of health-care services. Your doctor—your PCP—coordinates your access to services.

**EXAMPLE:** If you need a specialist, you must see your doctor and get a referral to one in the organization. If you go to a doctor without a referral, the HMO will not cover any of the cost of your care.

## Your Life

### Rates for Individual Health Policies

The idea behind insurance coverage is that risks are spread across a diverse group of people. Some people have no or very few claims and some have a lot. It's all supposed to average out, and rates should stay low.

Unfortunately, insurance companies have a practice for individual health policies (not group policies) that prevents this from happening. Their premiums become more disproportionately high for people the longer they stay in the plan. What are insurance companies doing to cause this?

1. People are placed in a group when they first sign up, and the group is fixed. It never gets any new members.
2. As group members get older and have more claims, the premiums for that group go up.
3. Younger and healthier people in the group drop out, looking for lower premiums.
4. The sicker people remain in the group, and their premiums go up even more because there are more claims.

The result is that people who need insurance the most can afford it the least because the premiums are so high. Ultimately, they can't afford it at all.

---

This approach allows the insurance company to control costs in **three** ways:

1. **One doctor is responsible for all your care.** He or she becomes familiar with you and can work with you to prevent and manage illness.
2. **Expensive procedures are not performed unnecessarily.** Plan doctors are discouraged from ordering expensive tests without good reasons.
3. **The insurance company must approve any nonroutine care** that your doctor orders.

In an HMO, you pay only a small fixed amount for visits, your **co-pay**, not a percentage of overall costs. So families with young children, who make frequent visits to the doctor, often choose HMOs.

### ❷ PPO Plans

PPO stands for **preferred provider organization**. A PPO is a network of health-care providers approved by the insurance company. A PPO network includes primary care physicians, specialists, hospitals, and other facilities.

Generally, a PPO includes many more doctors and hospitals than an HMO. You have more choices. When you use providers in the network, you get the maximum amount of insurance coverage under your plan. Often, unlike in an HMO, you can see providers who are not in the plan and still get some insurance coverage.

In most PPO plans, there is an amount, called your **deductible**, that you must pay each year before the insurance company begins to pay. After that, you will continue to pay a percentage of the costs (often 20 percent) up to a maximum. It could be $1,000. After that, the insurance company will pay all insured costs. For people seeking protection from the costs of catastrophic illness, such as cancer, a PPO is a likely choice.

*Alabama Citizenship Workbook*

### Get Smart

**Shopping for Health Insurance**

Dan Beltran has been an insurance agent for 15 years. He specializes in health insurance, and he has **five** useful tips for young adults looking for health insurance:

1. **Consider a short-term policy.** If you're just out of high school or college and you anticipate getting a job with health coverage, a short-term policy may be advisable. The premiums for short-term coverage are lower than regular policies, so you'll be covered but won't have to pay as much.

2. **Evaluate your health status.** Are you healthy? Do you rarely go to the doctor? Can you build up a good health-care savings account? Then a policy with a higher deductible and lower premium might be a good choice for you.

3. **Evaluate how often you visit a doctor.** Do you make frequent visits for routine care from a family or general practitioner? Do you have young children—or do you plan to start a family in the near future? If so, an HMO with co-pays and no deductible might be the right choice for you.

4. **Comparison shop for good premium prices.** Talk with an insurance agent. Get premium quotes on the Web. Be sure to carefully compare the coverage offered for each premium. If one premium looks much lower than others, check it out carefully. That policy might not cover as much as the other policies do.

5. **Check on the rating of the insurance company.** Before signing up, review Standard & Poor's and A.M. Best publications. Your public librarian can help you find these publications.

### ❸ POS Plans

POS stands for **point of service**. This means your costs are determined by who provides the service. It is a plan that combines the way HMO and PPO plans work.

* Each time your care is coordinated by your doctor, the insurance company will pay the maximum amount.
* You can see someone who is on the preferred provider list without a referral from your PCP, but you will get a smaller amount of coverage.
* If you choose to see someone who is not on the preferred provider list, you will get an even smaller amount of coverage, perhaps nothing.

This approach gives you flexibility, but you pay more when you take advantage of it.

### Maintaining Coverage

Once you get coverage, it is important to keep it because:

* Insurance companies usually refuse to cover conditions you had before you became insured with them. This is called a **pre-existing condition** exclusion. Asthma, diabetes, heart disease—all can be excluded from coverage when you get a new insurance provider.
* If you have a serious illness or injury, it can be difficult or impossible to find an insurance company who will sell you health insurance.

Many people can afford health insurance only when it is provided as part of a job. More than 42 million people have no health-insurance coverage at all. Some of them feel they are healthy and don't

One way to save money on prescriptions is always to ask for **generic brands**. These are non brand-name medications that have the same ingredients and properties as brand-name medications, but they cost less. It is also important to purchase all your prescriptions at the same **pharmacy**.

A **pharmacist** is specially trained to understand how drugs work before he or she dispenses prescription medications based on a physician's prescription order. When you have all of your prescriptions filled by the same pharmacy, the pharmacist can keep track of any medications you take to make sure they are not dangerous when taken with each other. When getting a new prescription from a doctor, be sure to mention any other medications you are already taking.

need it, but most of these people are uninsured because they don't belong to a group—like a work group—that provides insurance. They can't afford to purchase individual health insurance. This is a serious issue facing our country.

There are some federal laws that help:

* **COBRA**. This law guarantees anyone who leaves a job the right to continue the health-insurance plan for 18 months. However, now you must pay the whole premium—the part you've been paying plus the part your employer has paid.
* *Insurance portability.* If you don't have gaps in your health-insurance coverage, a new company can't exclude pre-existing conditions. When you end insurance coverage with one company, ask for a "certificate of creditable coverage" to show your new insurance company.

## Prescription Drug Coverage

Coverage for prescription drugs is often included in a standard health-insurance plan. Depending on the type of plan (HMO, PPO, or POS), you will pay a fixed amount, such as $15, or a percentage of the bill.

If you don't have health coverage through an employer, you can save money on premiums by using a plan that does not cover medications. However, if you need prescription drugs, you will pay 100 percent of the cost. You need to evaluate your individual situation to decide what is appropriate.

## Catastrophic Coverage

**Catastrophic coverage** is coverage that pays for a medical situation that is very serious and expensive. This catastrophe might be a terrible car accident or cancer.

There are **two** kinds of catastrophic coverage:

1. Coverage that pays for costs at the point your regular plan runs out. This is usually a high number, $750,000 or $1 million. However, if you have a serious accident or get a disease like cancer, medical costs could go this high.
2. Coverage that takes over after you've paid a certain, fairly high amount of money.

If you don't have regular health insurance, consider a catastrophic plan. The premiums are low, and you have protection against the very worst situations.

## Out-of-Pocket Expenses

As you can see, there are many ways that individuals are helped with the high cost of medical care. However, if you use health-care services, you will always have some expenses to pay yourself. These expenses are called **out-of-pocket expenses**. Your out-of-pocket expenses are all amounts you pay toward your own health care in addition to the premium you pay for health-care insurance. Such expenses include a deductible and co-pay amounts.

## Government Health Insurance Programs

| Program | Sponsored by | Description | Issues |
|---|---|---|---|
| **Medicare** | Federal government. | A basic medical insurance program, paid for with payroll tax deductions, that covers:<br>* People 65 or over.<br>* Older adults who have certain qualifying disabilities but may not be 65. | * Coverage is very basic, so many older people purchase additional insurance called "medigap" insurance.<br>* You may need to deal with Medicare when you are still young to help an aging parent receive appropriate benefits. |
| **Medicaid** | Federal and state governments. | A program that provides medical care for people who are:<br>* Low-income.<br>* Disabled. | * Helps people who cannot afford health insurance.<br>* Offers a safety net if you fall on difficult times. |
| **Workers' Compensation** | State governments. | A program, paid for by employers, that helps cover the cost of on-the-job injuries. It covers:<br>* All medical expenses.<br>* Partial salary until you can work again.<br>* Cash benefits for survivors in the case of a death. | A potentially work-related illness or injury must be reported immediately. If it is not, you may not be able to prove it was work-related. As a result, you may not be eligible for benefits. |

## Noncovered Expenses

Health insurance never covers all medical expenses. It doesn't cover nonprescription medications. It may not cover eyeglasses. It probably won't cover "elective" surgery, such as cosmetic surgery, that you want to have. You should read your plan carefully, to see what kinds of treatment are excluded. For noncovered expenses you must pay 100 percent of the cost yourself.

## Limited Coverage

Many kinds of health-care coverage are limited. There may be a cap on how much a plan will contribute to the cost of certain kinds of medical care. Often, psychiatric treatments are limited to only a certain number of visits within a fixed time, and then payment is provided at a lower percentage than for other services.

## Self-Insurance

Self-insurance means that you choose not to carry health insurance. In this case, you take on all the risk of paying 100 percent of all your medical bills. Very wealthy people who have enough money to cover their own medical bills are probably the only people who can afford to be self-insured.

## By the Numbers

### The Cost of Medical Care

There are many different kinds of health-care costs, from routine care and specialized treatments, to diagnostic tests, prescription drugs, and insurance premiums and co-pays. How much can you really expect to pay once you're out on your own or starting your own family?

To find out, interview a family about their health-care costs over a period of several months. Don't forget to ask about insurance premiums, co-pays, deductibles, and over-the counter medications in addition to direct expenses for health care.

From that information, find an average monthly amount. Next, develop a monthly health-care budget that would allow you to meet those expenses.

## Chapter 26 Wrap-up
### SMART SHOPPING FOR HEALTH CARE

*Leading a healthy lifestyle pays off. It reduces your medical expenses and protects you from chronic illness and pain as you age. Research shows maintaining a healthy lifestyle is not complicated. In fact, it can be as easy as getting adequate exercise (as little as 30 minutes a day!), managing your weight and stress levels, eating and sleeping regularly, and avoiding tobacco, drugs, and excessive alcohol.*

*Even though a healthy lifestyle can protect you from medical problems, it is still necessary to receive good preventive medical care, like medical check-ups and dental cleanings. It is also necessary to have a way to pay for these expenses, and expenses for illnesses or injuries.*

*Medical insurance is the most common way to receive help in covering health-care costs. There are many options and issues to consider when purchasing insurance. For this reason, it is important to know about different types of insurance. It is also important to understand how to utilize the benefits properly, once you have chosen a plan.*

**alternative medicine**—nonstandard medical practices, including chiropractic and acupuncture treatments.

**catastrophic coverage**—health-insurance coverage that pays for expenses incurred when a serious and expensive medical situation occurs.

**COBRA**—federal law guaranteeing employees the right to continue with employer-sponsored health coverage for up to 18 months after leaving a job.

**co-pay**—in some insurance plans, amount paid every time you receive care.

**deductible**—annual amount you must pay before the insurance company pays anything.

**diagnosis**—identification of an illness through tests and examinations.

**generic brands**—non brand-name medications that have the same ingredients and properties as brand-name medications but are less expensive.

**health insurance**—program that guarantees payment for certain health-care costs to individuals or group members.

**health maintenance organization (HMO)**—type of insurance plan that manages all of your health care in exchange for a fixed amount of money.

**holistic medicine**—medical practice of looking at all aspects of a person's life in treating disease.

**managed-care plans**—health-care plans that use a primary care physician to coordinate, or manage, individuals' care.

**out-of-pocket expenses**—amounts an individual pays toward his or her own health-care expenses in addition to the premium. These include co-pays and deductibles.

**peer pressure**—compelling influence of others like yourself.

**pharmacist**—specialist who dispenses prescription medications based on a physician's prescription order.

**pharmacy**—store where prescriptions are filled; drugstore.

**point of service (POS)**—medical plan in which costs are determined by who provides the service.

**pre-existing condition**—health condition you had before seeking coverage from or becoming insured with an insurance company.

**preferred provider organization (PPO)**—group of health-care providers who are approved by an insurance company to provide health care to people insured by the company.

**premium**—amount paid for insurance.

**preventive medicine**—medical care designed to prevent illness from occurring.

**primary care physician (PCP)**—general or family physician who serves as your main doctor and coordinates all your care.

**quackery**—ineffective, unproven, or fraudulent medical treatment provided by people who have not been trained to give medical advice.

**specialist**—physician who has received training in a particular branch of medicine beyond that required to become a medical doctor.

**stress**—pressure or strain. Humans seem to need some stress, but extreme pressure or difficulty causes our systems to fail.

Name _____

## 26. Smart Shopping for Health Care

**After you read the chapter, write an answer to each question below.**

1. How does traditional medicine differ from alternative medicine in the United States?

   _____

   _____

   _____

2. What are some important measures to take when searching for a physician or choosing among various health care options?

   _____

   _____

   _____

3. What are the three ways that HMOs are able to control costs?

   _____

   _____

   _____

# 26. Smart Shopping for Health Care

**Circle the best answer for each item.**

1. What is the amount, in some insurance plans, that you pay every time you receive care?
   a. rebate
   b. co-pay
   c. stipend
   d. voucher

2. What is the annual payment you must pay toward your medical care before the insurance company pays anything?
   a. rebate
   b. gratuity
   c. deductible
   d. tariff

3. Which of the following is the medical plan in which costs are determined by the service provider?
   a. health maintenance organization (HMO)
   b. point of service (POS)
   c. preferred provider network (PPO)
   d. primary care physician (PCP)

4. What is a health condition a person has before seeking coverage from or becoming insured with an insurance company?
   a. addiction
   b. carcinogen
   c. periodontal disease
   d. pre-existing condition

5. What is the word for ineffective, fraudulent medical treatment provided by people who have not been trained to give medical advice?
   a. felony
   b. larceny
   c. quackery
   d. alimony

6. When a person has a serious medical condition, it is important that he or she sees _____.
   a. one primary care physician (PCP)
   b. two primary care physicians (PCP)
   c. one specialist
   d. two specialists

7. With outpatient facilities like urgent care centers, physical therapy clinics, or mental health centers, it is important to verify that they _____.
   a. are accredited
   b. offer accreditation
   c. take credit
   d. offer credit

8. From the premiums they collect, insurance companies are able to cover the costs of providing health care to those they insure because _____.
   a. all people need only a little health care
   b. all people need a lot of health care
   c. some people need only a little health care, while others need more
   d. the government provides funding to help insurance companies remain profitable

9. Once you have insurance coverage, it is important to keep it because _____.
   a. insurance costs rise quickly
   b. insurance companies only take long-term clients
   c. insurance policies cover fewer and fewer costly conditions as time goes on
   d. insurance companies can refuse to cover you if you have a pre-existing condition or serious illness

10. _____ represent some out-of-pocket expenses that people have to pay for medical care.
    a. Premiums and co-pays
    b. Co-pays and deductibles
    c. Deductibles and premiums
    d. Premiums, co-pays, and deductibles

CHAPTER 27

# Making a Home

**In this chapter, you will learn about:**

- evaluating housing needs
- renting vs. buying
- house hunting

Imagine you live tens of thousands of years ago in Europe. You're returning home after a day out hunting and gathering berries and fruit. Flames are flickering ahead. "Ah, home at last," you think. Home for you is a hillside cave.

Now fast forward to your home today. You probably think it's quite different from a hillside cave, but is it?

The basic purpose of housing is to provide shelter and protection from the elements. However, even caves used by early humans provided more than shelter. We know that early humans decorated their cave walls with paintings. They also used their caves to conduct religious rituals, prepare food, and make craft items for everyday use.

Alabama Citizenship Workbook 171

## Housing Needs

While our houses might be much more comfortable than caves, we use many of the same criteria to evaluate our housing needs as cave dwellers did:

* Is the size appropriate?
* Is it located near things I need or want?

In addition, we are concerned about cost.

### Space Needs

Most young people starting out on their own will probably not be able to afford a large place. This is because when you rent a house or apartment, you pay the owners for use of their space. Since it costs them money to maintain and manage the property, they want to make a reasonable profit from renting it. If you are buying, you'll find that large homes may also be out of your price range. Most young people can only afford small homes, often called starter homes. For this reason, you'll need to be realistic about the amount of space you will be able to afford.

**EXAMPLE:** If you're going to live alone, a studio apartment might be most realistic. Studio apartments have one main living space with a kitchen and bath, but no bedroom, and limited storage. In a studio, you'll need to be creative about how to use the space efficiently.

If you can afford it, or plan to have a roommate, you can look into larger apartments, townhouses, and even small houses. All of these living arrangements have bedrooms that are separate from the main living space. They may also have extra storage, utility rooms, small patios, balconies or yards, and garages.

The cost of an apartment or house will also be affected by its location. Rents will generally be higher in more desirable areas. The same rule applies when buying a home.

### Location

Real estate professionals love to ask, "What are the three most important things to look for in a new home?" "Location, location, and location," they answer. It's an old joke, but it has a kernel of truth. Where your home is located is very important.

Even though you might not be able to afford to live in a fancy neighborhood, where you live can affect your happiness and quality of life. Are the neighborhoods you're considering safe? Will you be able to meet your daily needs for things like shopping and transportation conveniently? How close to your place of employment—and your friends and family—is the home you're considering?

### Safety

Fulfilling the desire to feel safe is a basic human need. Safety might be less tangible than the number of square feet you'll have, but it is just as important. Don't sacrifice safety by renting in an unsafe area because you can't afford a larger apartment in a safer location.

### Making it REAL

#### Your First Place

Where we live and how our living quarters are arranged can have a dramatic effect on our satisfaction in life. Some people like the hustle and bustle of an urban setting and would be happy living in a studio apartment downtown. Other people prefer living in a quiet area surrounded by nature rather than cars.

What do you prefer? Think about these issues and others that will influence where you choose to live. For example, do you want a yard or patio? Extra space for hobbies? Lots of storage space?

## Neighborhood

In most towns and cities, there are always some neighborhoods that are more or less safe than others.

Here are some ways to evaluate a neighborhood's safety:

* Walk through it. How do you feel? Be sure to visit the area at night as well as during the day.
* Call the chamber of commerce to ask about the neighborhood.
* Discuss the neighborhood with property managers who are helping you find an apartment.
* Contact the police department for crime statistics.
* Ask coworkers, friends, and family members what they know about the area.
* Contact the student housing office if you are attending school.

## Environment

In addition to safety issues, consider other aspects of the neighborhood that will affect your quality of life. Here are some questions to ask:

* Do you like the feel of the neighborhood? Does it feel like your kind of place?
* What is the noise level? Is it quiet?
* Is the neighborhood attractive? Are the buildings well maintained? Are there trees and shrubs?
* What is the traffic level?
* If you're looking at apartment complexes, are there desirable **amenities**, such as an elevator or parking spaces.

## Schools

Access to schools for yourself or children, if you have them, is an important thing to consider—especially if you're considering a home you plan to live in for many years, such as a house. If you have children, it might make it hard to get to school or work on time yourself if their schools are not within easy walking or driving distance.

If you plan to attend school, your life will be less hectic if you can walk or bike to campus. Of course, rents might be higher closer to campus where the student population increases demand. If this is the case, you will need to balance the cost of rent against increased transportation costs and time spent traveling to and from school.

### My Notebook

### Location, Location, Location

Can you think of a neighborhood you would like to live in? Describe why you like it. Is it near your family and friends, or places of interest or entertainment? Is it a bustling, busy, noisy street with a lot of action, or a quiet block with lots of trees? Can you imagine living there?

## Convenience

Imagine you've found the perfect place. It has just the right amount of space. It's new and well maintained. There is a lot of light inside, and a great little deck where you can grow a few herbs and read a book on a sunny day. There's only one problem. Well, several, actually.

You don't have a car, and the closest bus stop is almost seven blocks away. The neighborhood shops where you can pick up groceries and other odds and ends are only four blocks away, but they're on the opposite side of your apartment from the bus stop. That means a 16-block trek on your way home from work or school to run errands. Not only that, your two best friends have decided to rent apartments much closer to campus. They've decided to do that because a bus route goes right by their apartment building, and one block over is a small shopping center.

If you rent the apartment you love, you might be happy when you're actually inside. The many inconvenient aspects of its location, though, could mean a tiring, frustrating, and even lonely daily life. When looking at housing, whether to rent or buy, it's important to find a place you like. It's just as important, though, to make sure the resources you need for daily life are available.

Alabama Citizenship Workbook 173

When thinking about a new home, ask yourself if these quality-of-life facilities are available in the neighborhoods you're looking at?

* Parks.
* Community centers.
* Libraries.
* Places of worship.
* Museums.
* Movie theaters.
* Restaurants.
* Shops.

## Cost

Housing costs are influenced by size and location. This is true whether you plan to rent or buy. By the time you begin looking for housing, you should have a budget that includes a monthly housing expense.

With that information, how can you zero in on places that will fit your monthly housing expense? Here are **three** suggestions:

1. **Study newspaper ads** to get a sense of neighborhoods with housing options within your budget.
2. **Narrow down neighborhoods.** For example, if your research shows that in safe neighborhoods you can only afford studio apartments, look first at the ads grouped under "studios" or "efficiency apartments."
3. **Visit apartments for rent** that might interest you by contacting the landlord and attending open houses. When considering buying, start by going to open houses.

These activities will help you get to know the housing market in your community so you can get the most "home" for your housing expense.

Do you want to live alone or with a spouse or roommate? Does a single-family house with a yard appeal to you, or do you like high-rise buildings? These are just a few options you'll need to consider when you start living on your own.

## Out on Your Own

The prospect of living on your own for the first time can be both exciting and terrifying. On the one hand, you have more freedom to live as you want. On the other hand, you have more responsibility. Bills need to be paid. Groceries need to be purchased and meals prepared. Laundry has to be done.

Do you want to share these responsibilities with others, or manage them on your own? Each approach has advantages and disadvantages.

## Living With Roommates

Sharing your living arrangements, or having roommates, offers the advantages of companionship, shared expenses, and shared responsibility for tasks like shopping, cooking, and cleaning up.

### The Chore Wheel

During her senior year in college, Emily H. lived with four other seniors in a town house owned by the college. All five women were friends, with varying degrees of closeness. Each had made the choice to live in the town house because she had grown tired of life in a dormitory and craved an atmosphere more like home.

At the beginning of the school year, Emily and her housemates held a house meeting. In it, they talked over ways to share the household chores.

First, they agreed they wanted to eat a home-cooked meal together five nights a week (Sunday through Thursday, leaving the weekends free). Fortunately, there were five of them so each could cook one night of the week.

Next, they decided to divvy up the chores. They agreed on four important chores that needed to be taken care of each week: grocery shopping, cleaning the living room, cleaning the two bathrooms, and cleaning the kitchen. Since there were five of them, one person would get a "chore-free" week. To keep track of whose turn it was to do which task, one of them made a paper wheel with the name of each housemate and the name of each chore. Each week, they would rotate the chore wheel to know who should do what.

Because Emily and her friends talked about their expectations and found they shared the common goal of wanting to live more like a family, their system worked very well for them.

Not everybody wants to be so formal and structured. Do you?

---

No matter how well you know someone, it's best to have a written agreement. If you're the only person on the rent or lease agreement, and the roommate is renting from you, this is especially important. In this case, you are the one who will be held **liable** (responsible) if the apartment is damaged or rent is not paid on time.

## Picking a Roommate

Many a friendship has turned sour once the friend becomes a roommate. Before you pick a roommate, consider these issues:

* *Compatibility*. Do you and your potential roommate have similar lifestyles? Remember the movie and TV show, "The Odd Couple?" You want more harmony than Oscar and Felix had. Is your would-be roommate a neat freak like Felix, while you're a slob like Oscar? Are you the out-going party animal, while your roommate is the quiet studious type? In a good roommate setup, personalities match—or at least mesh.
* *Reliability.* Can you count on your roommate to pay bills on time? Will your roommate wash dishes and dust bookshelves?
* *Willingness to communicate.* If problems arise, will you be able to talk them through and come up with solutions?

Before you live together, talk honestly about what you each expect from the other. Do you want to share groceries and some meal preparation, or would you rather be on your own for dinner? If one of you plans to come home late, should you call the other? How will household chores, such as cleaning the bathroom, get handled? How will you share expenses, such as the phone bill?

## Living Alone

Living alone offers the advantages of being able to set up your living quarters as you like, spend your time as you like without worrying about disturbing a roommate, and arranging activities and chores to fit your lifestyle.

Of course, living alone also means that only one person's income is contributing toward housing, food, and utility costs. This might mean you'll have to live in a smaller place and budget more wisely in general.

Do you think you're the live-on-your-own or the roommate type? Why?

## Living With a Spouse

Living with a spouse is another arrangement that takes special considerations. It is similar to and different from living with a roommate. Living with a roommate is generally seen as a temporary arrangement. Day-to-day and monthly planning and coordination are required, but long-term planning is usually not in the picture. In addition, while many expenses are shared, roommates manage their finances separately.

In contrast, setting up a household with a spouse involves long-term planning, including:

* Sharing chores and household responsibilities fairly.
* Arranging shared living space together.
* Sharing income and expenses beyond those used to manage the household.

# Types of Housing

There are several different types of housing. The most common are:

* Apartments.
* Condominiums, co-ops, and co-houses.
* Houses.
* Low-income housing.

## Apartments

For many young people, apartments will be the first place they live because they are economical. This is because more people can live on the same amount of land than when there is only one house. When many families live in one building, even though they live in separate living spaces, it's called **multi-family housing**.

An apartment can be a small studio or much larger with a number of bedrooms. An apartment building can be small or a large complex with many amenities like common rooms and recreational facilities. Shared laundry facilities are often found in apartment buildings.

When looking at apartments, consider:

* General up-keep of the grounds and building.
* Security.
* Availability of parking for yourself and guests.
* Laundry facilities.
* Extra storage options.
* Services, such as a doorman or superintendent.
* Recreational facilities.

## Condominiums, Co-Ops, and Co-Houses

**Condominiums** are a form of multi-family housing. They often look like apartment complexes but differ in one important way. They are not rented. Instead, they are owned by an individual who is responsible for the interior of the individual unit. Upkeep of the grounds, shared facilities, and buildings are paid by each owner. Condominiums, often called "condos," have the advantage of home ownership without all the responsibilities of home maintenance.

When you buy a home or condo, you actually own the property. **Co-housing** and **cooperatives**, known as co-ops, are twists on the traditional approach to home ownership.

When you buy a co-op, you're actually buying shares in a corporation that owns the property. In a co-housing community, you own your own house and share ownership of common areas—grounds, recreational facilities—with other people.

176  Alabama Citizenship Workbook

### Co-Ops, Condos, & Co-Housing

| Type | Description | How It Works | Value |
|---|---|---|---|
| Condo | Owner purchases a living unit and is responsible for the upkeep of the interior. Exterior upkeep is paid for by association dues. | Owners are members of a homeowners' association and vote on issues of concern to all owners. | Owners have many benefits of home ownership, but not the personal responsibility of maintaining the building and the grounds. |
| Co-op | Owner purchases shares in a corporation and is given a living unit to use in exchange. A board of directors holds the mortgage, not individuals. | Shareholders vote on issues that affect the property and other shareholders. The board is responsible for paying the mortgage, managing the property, making repairs, and handling similar issues. | Shareholders have exclusive rights to their unit, offering them many advantages of home ownership without all the responsibilities. |
| Co-housing | A combination of private home ownership and cooperative:<br>1. People own individual residences.<br>2. Common areas, such as recreation facilities, are owned jointly by all. | Individuals are responsible for their residences but vote on issues related to management of common areas and community issues. | The purpose and physical design of co-housing are to:<br>* Bring people together.<br>* Involve people in the process of managing the community.<br>* Create small, friendly neighborhoods where people know and help each other. |

## Houses

In contrast to apartments, individual homes are called **single-family housing** because there is only one living unit on the property. An individual, a family, or a number of unrelated individuals can live in the house and share the same living space. Compared with most multi-family housing, individual houses often have the advantages of a private yard and more space, privacy, and storage.

In addition to traditional houses, other kinds of single-family units, like mobile homes, offer many of the same advantages of traditional houses at less expense.

## Low-Income Housing

Government and private programs help low-income families rent and purchase homes.

## Government-Subsidized Housing

The federal government offers programs to make housing more affordable for both renters and buyers. The U.S. Department of Housing and Urban Development (HUD), the main agency responsible for this assistance, offers:

* Rental assistance in which a portion of the rent is paid by HUD for qualifying renters.
* Loan guarantees for home buyers who would not otherwise qualify for conventional loans.

In addition to federal assistance, many states and local communities also have programs to help low-income families with housing costs.

## Habitat for Humanity

If you wanted to own your own home but couldn't afford to buy one, would you be willing to help build one and apply the value of your labor to the cost of the home? Since 1976, over 30,000 Americans have had just that opportunity, thanks to the non-profit organization, Habitat for Humanity.

With volunteer labor and donations, houses are refurbished or constructed. The prospective homeowner who helped build the house then buys the house through a no-interest loan. No profit is made on the house by Habitat for Humanity.

Across the country, Habitat for Humanity and similar local programs are putting home ownership within reach of low-income Americans. Potential homeowners are selected by a committee based on their need, their willingness to participate in the building project, and their ability to repay the no-interest loan.

Former President Jimmy Carter has been an enthusiastic supporter of Habitat for Humanity since 1984. In his first project that year, he helped renovate a six-story building in New York City with 19 families. Now, he and his wife work for one week a year on a Habitat for Humanity project.

## To Rent or To Buy?

For many people, owning a home is the American dream. But home ownership does not suit everyone's needs and lifestyle.

### Renting

Most young adults' first steps toward independence involve living in rented housing. Some people do so for a short period of time before buying, and others rent for many years or indefinitely.

It's likely your first place will be an apartment, because apartments offer the most affordable housing options. However, information on apartment renting also applies to renting other units like houses or mobile homes.

### Rebuilding Lives and Communities

In 43 states across the country, 16- to 24-year-olds are building affordable housing for their communities, while rebuilding their own lives. It all started in 1978 in New York City when a group of teenagers asked the director of the Youth Action Program at East Harlem Block Schools to help them figure out how to renovate abandoned buildings in their neighborhood. The success of their first renovated building led to a national program that helps unemployed young adults complete their education and acquire job and leadership skills—all while making their communities more livable.

From this first success in New York, there are now 145 programs across the country. More than 2,000 low-income housing units have been built or renovated, many with housing rehabilitation grants from HUD.

| Pros and Cons of Renting | | |
|---|---|---|
| Topic | Advantages | Disadvantages |
| **Responsibilities** | The landlord is responsible for maintenance and repairs. | You will not be able to make changes, such as painting or other modifications, without the landlord's permission. |
| **Amenities** | You might have access to some amenities, such as recreational facilities and parking, at no extra cost. Some utilities, such as water, might also be covered in the rent. | Your rent includes the cost of amenities, so unless you use them they are an expense with no benefit. |
| **Freedom** | As a renter, you have the freedom to move easily if you desire or if it's necessary. | You do not own the property and cannot benefit if it gains value. |
| **Property Taxes** | You don't have to make a separate tax payment. | Property tax amounts are included in your rent payment. |
| **Equity (share in the monetary value of the property)** | None. | Your rent payments are not going toward ownership, or equity, in the property. |

## Search Strategies

Imagine that you know in which part of town you want to live. How can you find the right apartment in that neighborhood? There are lots of good techniques:

* Look for "For Rent" signs in windows.
* Check the classified rental ads every day for your desired part of town.
* Let coworkers, friends, and family members know you're looking for something.
* Visit or call the property managers of apartment complexes or buildings in which you would like to live.
* Attend open houses.
* Contact property management firms.

Finding an apartment you like will take legwork and organization. Keep track of all your calls and appointments in a small notebook. If an apartment interests you, write down the address and a brief description, and request an application.

In large cities where competition is stiff, additional methods are available for finding apartments.

## Paperwork

Applying to rent an apartment is a little like applying for a job. The **landlord** (the person who owns the property) or property manager wants to know you are a good prospect. This means he or she wants to know that you are responsible, will pay your rent on time, will treat the property well, and will abide by the rules. For this reason it is important to provide all information requested on the application. In addition, you should line up three people as references. These should not be relatives. An employer, a teacher, or a supervisor for volunteer work you do are all good choices.

If your application is accepted, ask to walk through the apartment again before signing a rental agreement. Evaluate its condition carefully and make sure it will meet your needs and standards. Keep a checklist of problems. If the apartment will meet your needs, you're ready to sign on the dotted line.

Before you do, though, review the agreement carefully. Ask questions if there is anything you don't understand. Ask that your checklist of problems be attached to the agreement. This way, you will not be responsible for paying for those problems when you move out because you will have proof you didn't cause them. Your rental agreement, or *lease*, should spell out the:

* Monthly rental amount.
* Rent due date.
* Penalties or consequences for late rent payment.
* Security and cleaning deposit amounts.
* Term of the agreement (month-to-month or annual).
* Utility payment responsibilities. (Are any included as part of the rent?)
* Tenant responsibilities.
* Landlord responsibilities.
* Occupancy restrictions. (Can you sublease? Can you get a roommate?)
* **Notice**. (How many days in advance do you need to notify the landlord that you're moving out? How much notice will the landlord give you if he or she wants you to leave or won't renew the lease?)

## Costs

It takes more than one month's rent to get into an apartment. Typically, you will pay some combination of the following:

* First month's rent.
* Last month's rent. (This is applied to your last month's rent when you give notice.)
* Cleaning fee.
* Security deposit. (This fee covers out-of-the-ordinary repairs. The total amount or remainder after repairs will be refunded when you move out. If you treat the property well, you should get the entire amount back.)
* Key deposit. (This will be refunded when you move out and return the keys.)

## Tenant Rights and Responsibilities

When you rent an apartment, you are paying for the right to use the landlord's property. Both parties in this agreement—you and the landlord—have rights and responsibilities.

There are state laws governing tenant-landlord rights. If a disagreement develops between you and the landlord, these laws will be used to resolve the situation. Public mediation services and legal assistance are available in many communities to help resolve these kinds of disputes.

### Rights and Responsibilities

| | Rights | Responsibilities |
|---|---|---|
| **Landlord** | The right to:<br>* Receive timely rent payments.<br>* Have property treated well.<br>* Have tenant rules followed. | Responsible for:<br>* Ensuring property meets legally required standards.<br>* Providing other items identified in the rental agreement.<br>* Getting permission from the tenant before entering the residence. |
| **Tenant** | The right to:<br>* Use the property as specified in the rental agreement.<br>* Privacy. | Responsible for:<br>* Paying rent on time.<br>* Observing tenant rules.<br>* Notifying landlord of needed repairs.<br>* Giving appropriate notice as specified in the rental agreement. |

## Your Life

### Rental Discrimination Is Illegal

A federal law, The Fair Housing Act, prohibits discrimination in the sale, rental, and financing of housing, based on race, color, religion, sex, national origin, family status, or disability. If you think you might have been discriminated against, contact your state HUD office or local legal assistance office.

## Buying

Just as renting housing works well for some people at certain times in their life cycle, so can owning a home. Do you share the American dream of home ownership?

### Advantages and Disadvantages

Owning your own home can be fun and satisfying. It offers many advantages over renting, but has disadvantages, too. Owning your home is a much bigger responsibility than renting it.

**EXAMPLE:** What happens if something goes wrong, like the roof starts to leak? If you rent an apartment, you call the landlord or super, and he or she solves the problem one way or another. If you own a home and the roof starts to leak, you've got to figure out how to fix it and pay the cost of fixing it.

### Finding a Home to Buy

Throughout your life, your housing needs will change. At different phases of your life, the importance of different factors might shift.

**EXAMPLE:** If you have children or plan to start a family soon, nearness to good schools, playgrounds, and parks will probably be more important to you than when you were single and wanted to be near good restaurants and movie theaters.

To find a home you'll be happy with, you need to evaluate your needs for space, location, and amenities. Then you can use those priorities to help focus your hunt for a house.

### How Much Should You Spend?

While the general rule for how much you can afford to pay for a home is two-and-a-half times your gross annual income, this can vary. If you are getting a conventional loan, the banker or mortgage broker will want your monthly payment, including the loan payment, taxes, and insurance, to come to no more than 28 percent of your monthly income. Interest rates and the amount of your down payment can influence this percentage. This in turn can affect whether or not you qualify to buy certain homes.

In areas where homes are very expensive, you may qualify for special programs that allow people to buy homes when their payment takes up more than 28 percent of their income.

### Financing a Home

Most people **finance** a home, or get loans to buy it. This is because homes are expensive, and most people don't have enough money of their own to pay for a home all at once. Buying a home is usually the biggest purchase a person makes. It is also often an excellent investment because home values grow over time.

There are **three** important financial factors you will need to consider when purchasing a home:

1. **Your down payment.**
2. **A mortgage.**
3. **Points, fees, and other charges.**

A *down payment* is a lump sum of money that you contribute toward the cost of the home. Generally, the buyer needs to make a 10 percent down payment to qualify for a conventional loan.

**EXAMPLE:** If you want to buy a house that costs $90,000, you will need to have $9,000 for your down payment.

### Pros and Cons of Owning

| Topic | Advantages | Disadvantages |
|---|---|---|
| Responsibilities and Costs | You can choose how repairs and maintenance are done. You can make repairs yourself. | You have to save money for upkeep that a landlord would provide if you were renting. |
| Freedom | You can change and fix up the property according to your personal taste. | It might be more complicated to get away or move to another city if, for example, you change jobs. |
| Property Taxes | They are deductible from federal tax returns. | This is an expense that must be budgeted for in addition to payments. |
| Equity Issues | With each mortgage payment, you are buying the home from the mortgage holder. Over time, you gain equity, adding to your net worth. | If property values decrease, your home might be worth less than when you purchased it. |

To meet other requirements, such as a co-op board's house rule, you may have to put 20 percent down. Some banks will require you to take out mortgage insurance if you put down less than 20 percent.

A mortgage is a loan for the purchase price of a home, minus your down payment.

**EXAMPLE:** If you put down $9,000 on a $90,000 house, your mortgage would be $81,000.

When you buy a home with a mortgage loan, you do not own the property until the loan is paid off. You are buying the property from the mortgage holder and securing the loan with the property. This means the mortgage holder can take the property if you <u>default</u>, or don't make your payments.

The **two** most common kinds of mortgages are:

1. **Fixed Rate.** The interest rate, and thus your payment, remain the same for the term of the loan, usually 20 or 30 years. Having the same payment every month allows you to budget well. If interest rates drop, it can be worthwhile to refinance, or get a new loan. When interest rates are low, fixed-rate mortgages are popular.
2. **Variable Rate.** The interest rate goes up and down, depending on market interest rates. This means your monthly payment can change. This is an advantage if interest rates drop and a disadvantage if interest rates go up. When interests are high, variable-rate mortgages are more popular.

In addition to these kinds of loans, there are also low-down-payment and low-interest loans available through government programs for prospective homebuyers who qualify.

When you borrow money to buy a house, you will be charged points and other fees. In addition to the interest you pay on the loan, there are bank fees and other up-front costs to obtain a loan. The most common ones include:

* **Application fee.** A typical application fee is a few hundred dollars.
* **Points.** A point is one percent of the value of the loan. So, if you are charged two points by the lender on a $81,000 mortgage, you will owe $1,620.
* **Title insurance.** This requirement and its cost protect you from a lien, or claim, against the property that creditors of previous owners may have made.
* **Credit report.** Banks make you pay the cost of researching your payment habits.
* **Miscellaneous fees.** These pay recording, survey, notary, and other fees.

## By the Numbers

### How Much Down?

You've been saving toward a down payment for five years. You've finally got enough to begin looking at houses seriously. How much will you need to have saved for the following homes, assuming a 10 percent down payment? How much, assuming a 20 percent down payment?

$73,500
$85,000
$92,500
$103,500

What will the mortgage be on each after deducting the down payment?

---

These fees and charges may be included in the loan amount, so you don't need to pay them out-of-pocket. The application fee is usually due at the beginning of the process, but most of these other charges come at the **closing**, when buyer and seller and/or their representatives come together to transfer the home ownership and "close" the deal.

### Buying on Contract

Most property owners want buyers to get a loan. This is because the seller will get paid in full for the value of his or her property at the time of the sale. In some cases, though, an owner will offer what is called owner financing. This means you purchase the home directly from the owner over time. When this occurs, a legal document, or contract, needs to be written up. This is why this type of home sale is called "buying on contract."

There are two main reasons owners sell on contract:

* A seller wants to collect interest and make more money from the sale of the property.
* The property is not in good enough shape to qualify for a conventional loan.

## Search This

### Mortgage Calculators

The Internet is full of online calculators that can help home buyers figure out the costs of a mortgage. Find a mortgage calculator online. Pretend you're buying a $125,000 home with a 10 percent down payment. Type in the amount of your 30-year mortgage. How much will your monthly payment be if the interest rate is 6.5, 7, and 9 percent?

# Chapter 27 Wrap-up
## MAKING A HOME

Choosing a new home is a complicated process. There are many points to consider.

Location may well be the first. Many real estate professionals say it is the most important feature. Observe the neighborhood you're thinking of living in carefully—and at different times of day and night. Is it safe? Does it fit your personal style? Will you be near stores, parks, and schools?

The people you'll live with will make a big difference, too. Do you want to live alone or with roommates? Or perhaps you're newly married, getting your first home with your spouse.

You'll need to decide which type of home is best for you at this stage of life: apartment, house, co-op, condo, or co-housing arrangement? Are you planning to rent or buy your new home?

Getting a new home can be exciting and satisfying—especially if you take the time to think through all the decisions carefully before you fall in love with a home.

**amenities**—things that increase pleasure. In housing, these might include parking places, plants, even recreational facilities.

**closing**—the final step in the home-purchasing process when all the papers are signed and you become the owner of the property.

**co-housing**—community of single-family housing in which you own your own house or living unit yourself, and co-own common areas (park, meeting hall) with other co-housing owners.

**cooperative**—(co-op) multi-family housing in which each owner holds the purchase of shares in a corporation that owns the property. Your shares give you an exclusive right to your living unit.

**condominium**—(condo) multi-family housing in which the units are owned by individuals who are responsible for their individual units and a share of the building.

**default**—fail to fulfill an obligation, such as making a loan payment.

**finance**—take out a contract or mortgage to purchase property.

**landlord**—owner of rental property.

**liable**—legally responsible for something, such as the damage to an apartment that occurred while you lived there.

**multi-family housing**—living facilities where several families or individuals have separate living units.

**notice**—written statement to a landlord stating the last day on which you intend to live in property.

**single-family housing**—living facilities where one family or group of individuals use the one living unit on a property.

Name _____

# 27. Making a Home

**After you read the chapter, write an answer to each question below.**

1. How are houses built by Habitat for Humanity, and how are potential homeowners selected?

_____
_____
_____

2. What are some good techniques to find the right apartment in the neighborhood in which you want to live?

_____
_____
_____

3. When you buy a home with a mortgage loan, what is the arrangement in terms of ownership of the home?

_____
_____
_____

# 27. Making a Home

**Circle the best answer for each item.**

1. What is the final step in the home-purchasing process, when all the papers are signed and you become the owner of the property?
   a. mortgage release
   b. notice
   c. title meeting
   d. closing

2. What is the term for a community of single-family housing in which you own your house or living unit and co-own common areas with other owners?
   a. cooperative
   b. co-housing
   c. shared houses
   d. condominium (condo)

3. What is a name for multi-family housing in which each owner holds shares in a corporation that owns the property? The owner's shares give him or her an exclusive right to the living unit.
   a. cooperative
   b. condominium (condo)
   c. co-housing
   d. shared houses

4. Who is the owner of a rental property?
   a. manager
   b. buyer
   c. landlord
   d. mortgager

5. What are living facilities where one family or group of individuals uses the one living unit on a property?
   a. shared housing
   b. single-family housing
   c. co-housing
   d. cooperative

6. Real estate professionals say the three most important things to look for in a new home are _____.
   a. location, location, location
   b. price, price, price
   c. price, style, location
   d. size, price, location

7. Housing costs are influenced by _____.
   a. the people in the neighborhood
   b. only the buildings on either side
   c. size and location
   d. décor

8. In a conventional mortgage, the loan company will want your monthly payment to be no more than _____ of your monthly income.
   a. 32 percent
   b. 25 percent
   c. 28 percent
   d. 16 percent

9. Generally, the buyer of a home needs to make a _____ down payment to qualify for a conventional loan.
   a. 15 percent
   b. 10 percent
   c. 23 percent
   d. 30 percent

10. A mortgage is a loan for the purchase price of a home minus your _____.
    a. application fee
    b. points
    c. down payment
    d. other fees

186 Alabama Citizenship Workbook

CHAPTER 28

# Getting Around

In this chapter, you will learn about:

- the different types of transportation
- how to choose the right mode of transportation
- how to buy a car

In 1913, Henry Ford forever changed the way cars are made. Before Ford, they were pieced together by hand. Ford came up with the idea of using a moving assembly line to make cars. That made it possible to make many more cars than before—and to make them less expensively.

Suddenly, cars were cheaper than ever before. Within a few years, cars went from being a luxury only wealthy people could afford to something within reach of many American families. Today, owning a car—like owning a house—is built into the American dream.

But a car is just one type of transportation available to people today. Buses, trains, bicycles, and motorcycles make it possible for millions of Americans to get around every day.

# Evaluating Your Needs

What you spend on transportation must be carefully considered in light of your overall budget. What do you need? What can you afford? One thing is for certain: It is a major financial decision. Unlike other purchases, if you make the wrong choice, you can end up paying much more than you ever expected.

When considering a means of transportation, take some time to think about where you must go each day, your lifestyle, safety, personal preferences, comfort and convenience, and cost.

## Getting to Work or School

The primary purpose of transportation for many people is getting to school or work every day. This daily trek from home to school or work and back again is called a commute. Since most commuting takes place five days a week, it's worth thinking about the most efficient and economical transportation options.

When determining how to get where you need to go, consider these questions:

* How far away do you live from school or work?
* What convenient and reliable transportation options are there?
* How long does it take to get there by each option you listed above?
* What are the advantages and disadvantages of each one?

Of course, cost is a major factor in which transportation option you finally choose.

## Lifestyle Considerations

Knowing your lifestyle will help you determine the best type of transportation for you.

Lifestyle considerations may not be important now, but in a few years, these and other questions may become relevant:

* Do you regularly drive two, three, or more friends to school or work? Do children or older people count on your car?
* Will clients, or potential clients, often ride in your car?
* Do you need to haul dirt, plants, animals, artwork, or tools?
* How important is it to conserve energy?
* Do you love to feel the wind blowing through your hair?
* Do you prefer to get your daily exercise in going to and from school or work?

How do you think the answers to these questions will affect your transportation decisions?

### My Notebook

**Exploring My Options**

Think about every possible means of getting to school or work: car, bus, subway, riding a bike, or walking. How much time will it take to travel to and from school or work by each mode of transportation you listed? What are the advantages and disadvantages of each?

Write it all down. You may want to make a chart to see the comparison more easily. Which mode of transportation best meets your needs?

## Safety

Safety is at the top of the list when choosing any mode of transportation. Picture yourself going to and from school or work using all of your transportation alternatives. Here are some examples of safety-oriented questions:

* Is this mode of transportation safe in all kinds of weather conditions? If not, do you have an alternate plan available?
* Can this mode of transportation safely carry the number of people you need to transport?
* Is available parking safe and would your car, bike, or other vehicle be secure?
* If you're considering public transportation, will it be safe for you to use it when you need it? If you get off work at midnight, the bus may not be the best option.
* Has your vehicle been carefully checked for safety?
* Does the walk from the subway to your school or workplace require you to walk through an unsafe area?

Talk to people who may know more than you about the pros and cons of different transportation modes from your school or workplace. Then pay attention to the information you have when making a final decision. The price of using an unsafe mode of transportation can be more than anyone would want to pay.

## Personal Preferences

You've considered some of the basics: need, lifestyle, and safety. Now it's time to think about comfort and convenience.

* Are you tall? Do you need extra leg room?
* Will there be a baby or young child you need to get into and out of a car seat?
* Would you prefer to let someone else drive you to and from work in bad weather?
* Do you hate paying for the privilege of parking eight blocks away from school?
* Do you regularly have several stops to make on the way home from work?
* Does waiting in the rain on a busy street for the bus bother you?
* Do you like parking your mode of transportation indoors?
* Are you sure you could not walk home faster than the time it takes you to drive?

How would the answers to these questions affect your choice of transportation?

## Cost

Cost is where the rubber hits the road, as the saying goes. You may have big transportation dreams with a very small budget. Check your monthly income. What can you afford for transportation?

---

### By the Numbers

#### Car Costs

Say you just purchased a car. Your expenses are far from over. In fact, they've just begun.

Call around in your area. What might you need to budget for each of these categories?

* License and registration.
* Car insurance.
* Gas and oil.
* Routine maintenance and repairs.
* Unexpected repairs.
* Parking fees.

Some budget items are paid just once a year, others twice a year, and others as needed. Convert each amount to a monthly figure. For example, if your car insurance costs $800 per year, the monthly cost is about $67.

What's the monthly cost of owning a car?

---

Alabama Citizenship Workbook

# Transportation Options

There are usually many ways to get to another location. Take a moment to think of all the public and private transportation options available in your area.

## Public Transportation

Public transportation in the form of **mass transit** is available in cities. Mass transit delivers many people to set destinations in many parts of the city and the suburbs. Mass transit may be in the form of:

* Subways.
* Trolleys.
* Buses.
* Light rail.
* Streetcars.
* Trains.
* Ferries.
* Taxis.

All public transportation systems have advantages and disadvantages.

## Subways

Subways are like small trains. Some systems, like San Francisco's Bay Area Rapid Transit system (BART), run under and above ground and even underwater. In fact, they're called subways because they often travel below, or sub, ground. In Chicago, the subway is called the "El" because it runs on an elevated track above the street as well as underground.

Subways deliver people to set stops. You get off at the stop nearest your destination. You may need to connect with a bus line to get closer to your destination. You can buy tokens or transit cards in advance, which saves time standing in line to purchase a ticket. Subways run frequently, so you usually don't have to wait long for the train you want. However, during commuting hours in large cities like New York City, subways can be packed, with no room to sit or stand.

| Pros and Cons of Mass Transit | |
| --- | --- |
| Advantages | Disadvantages |
| Inexpensive, compared with the cost of driving a car. You don't need a license or insurance and don't have costs of parking, repairs, maintenance, or parking tickets. | You must get to the station and walk from the station to your destination, which may be several blocks. If you drive to the station, you may have to pay for parking there. |
| Cuts down on the number of individual cars on the road, decreasing air pollution and saving energy. | Seating may be hard to find during busy times of day. |
| Takes you to and from the main areas in a large city conveniently and, often, more quickly than driving a car. | You must work around the bus or subway schedule, meaning you have less flexibility. |
| You leave the driving to someone else. No hunting for a parking place. | Traveling to and from certain areas can be unsafe during late-night hours. |

### Trolleys

Some parts of Portland, Oregon, and San Francisco, California, use trolleys. Electrically powered cars that run on tracks, trolleys remind people of the old days, and many people like to ride them for that reason.

Sometimes trolleys have a circular route that transports people between several popular areas, such as a college campus, a shopping mall, an area with popular nightspots, and nearby neighborhoods. Sometimes they even operate as free shuttles!

### Light Rail

Light rail trains are a newer source of public transportation. They are very quiet trains that run on small tracks down city streets. They help congestion by moving people quickly and quietly to different places within the city. Light rail trains are efficient, nonpolluting, quiet, and fast. Salt Lake City, Utah, San Jose, California, and Portland, Oregon, have light rail systems.

### Buses

Buses are another form of public transportation. You wait at the bus stop for the correct bus. You ride until the stop nearest your destination and then get off. In big cities such as New York City, the bus is much slower than the subway. But some people prefer the bus because it travels above ground, just like a car, and you get a better view!

Some buses and trains have special commuter schedules. They make fewer stops at certain times of day to speed up the time needed to move people from one end of town to another. Buses are flexible. New routes or scheduled stops can be added to accommodate changing patterns in a city's growth and riders' changing needs.

### Taxis

Taxis are probably the most expensive means of transportation. This is because a car with a driver picks you up and delivers you right to the door of your destination. In addition to paying the fee on the taxi's meter, you are also expected to tip the driver.

You can save money by sharing a taxi with other people going to the same destination. (The driver may charge you a flat rate of one or two dollars for each extra person, but only one fare will be charged, so it's usually cost-effective to share.)

Besides the cost, there are other drawbacks to relying on taxis as a primary mode of transportation. It's hard to get a taxi in bad weather (everyone wants one), during busy parts of the day (traffic is slow and use is high), and in some parts of town (taxi drivers don't like to go into unsafe areas at night)—in other words, when you need or want one the most! Still, taxis are useful:

* In an emergency.
* If the weather is bad and you don't want to drive or walk.
* When you are in a hurry to reach your destination.
* If you are sick or have a disability that limits your ability to walk, drive, or use a public transportation system.
* If you are new to an area or unfamiliar with the public transportation system.
* If your destination is not easily reached by public transportation.

## Private Transportation

Private transportation options are ones you own, lease, or rent for your personal use. They include bicycles, scooters, motorcycles, electric bikes, and, of course, cars.

## Bicycles

A bicycle can range from around $250 (a decent, basic mountain bike) to $4,500 (pro racing bike). There are many types of bikes to fit specific needs.

A commuter bike is used by students, professionals, and workers as a form of transportation. If you decide on this ecological and cost-effective mode of transportation, look for a bike with these features:

* Medium-width, strong, nonknobby street tires for a comfortable ride, even over potholes.
* Fenders (or the ability to have fenders added during the rainy season).
* Rear rack (to carry a set of bags or attach a plastic basket to carry items).
* Flashing rear red light and a good headlight.

You'll also need to budget for a helmet, a basket or saddlebags to carry your belongings, mirrors, and clothing to keep you safe, warm, and dry in different types of weather. In some areas, you are also required to buy a license for your bike.

## Cars

A car can be very convenient. You drive it in and out of your driveway, parking space, or garage to work or school. You can stop anywhere on the way home if you need to run errands. It can usually hold several other people. But, cars can cost a lot of money and can be expensive to insure, drive, park, and maintain.

### Bicycle Options

| Type of Bicycle | Characteristics |
| --- | --- |
| Commuter Bike | Made for easy, comfortable travel on paved city streets. |
| Travel Bike | Folds up to be carried in a suitcase or on an airplane. |
| Street-riding Bike | Grinds off curbs, jumps off walls; strong, heavy, 20-inch wheels. |
| Triathlon Bike | Very aerodynamic and streamlined, lightweight. |
| Mountain Bike | Cross-country racing model—for trail racing.<br><br>Downhill racing model—made to go downhill fast; full suspension bike with front and rear shocks. |
| Road-racing Bike | Dropped handlebars, skinny tires. |
| Tandem Bike | Made for 2 (tandem), 3 (triple), or 4 (quad) people. |
| Specialty Bike for People With Disabilities | Has three or four wheels for balance; can be pedaled with arms if legs are paralyzed. |

## Motorcycles and Electric Bikes

Motorcycles and electric bikes are primarily one-person vehicles. Several million motorcycles and motorbikes are registered in the U.S. You may find that a motorcycle or motorbike is the best option for you. Buying one costs far less than buying a car, and the costs of running and maintaining a bike are much less than most cars. You can set your own schedule, plan your own route, and take what you can hold.

Remember, you must pass a test in order to get a license to drive a motorcycle. Insuring a motorcycle can also be expensive—nearly as much as insuring a car. Motorcycles can be uncomfortable or unsafe in bad weather and limiting in what they can transport.

Chances of injury are much greater on a motorcycle or motorbike than in a car. These vehicles can be hard for other drivers to see. Unlike car drivers, motorcyclists don't have a frame surrounding them in case of an accident. Hospital emergency rooms see many young people with head injuries, some permanent, as a result of failing to wear a helmet. Helmet laws have been enacted in many states to try to decrease the number of deaths and head injuries from motorcycle accidents.

Don't forget to include the cost of a helmet and other safety and weather items when budgeting for a motorcycle.

## Renting a Car

If you don't have access to a car, it's possible to rent one for the day or week. When you travel, renting a car allows you to get to your destination and then pick up a rental car to use while you're there.

Many people take advantage of rental cars for vacation use.

**EXAMPLE:** A family visiting another part of the country can rent a car for the week. Having a car allows them to drive to other nearby destinations at less expense and with more flexibility than do other forms of transportation.

Although car rental dealers offer you the option of paying extra for insurance, most people don't need it. If you have personal car insurance, it often includes rental car coverage. If you pay with a credit card, car insurance is often a benefit of card use. When traveling for business, your company's insurance will provide coverage.

If you plan to rent a car in another country, check on the requirements and papers you will need before you go.

Beware! It often comes as a shock to many young adults that in many states you must be over the age of 25 to rent a car. You must also have a valid driver's license that has not expired.

## Alternative Transport

There are many unusual ways to get where you're going! One small-town teacher uses a scooter to get to work. Many students find skateboards or in-line skates perfect for getting to school. People in snowy areas sometimes cross-country ski or snow-shoe to work. If you live in a watery geographic area, you just might take a ferry, kayak, or small boat to work or school. Some ranchers use small planes to oversee their property, while people in rural Alaska may travel primarily by dogsled. Of course, there is always plain old-fashioned walking.

There are also innovative programs using familiar forms of transportation such as bikes and cars.

### Get Smart

**Riding Safely**

Besides a helmet, required by law in many states, serious motorcyclists recommend the following for safety:

* Goggles.
* Boots.
* A leather or other heavy jacket and pants.
* Gloves.
* Rear-view mirror.
* Windshield and roll-bar (for long trips).

| Pros and Cons of Carpools | |
|---|---|
| Advantages | Disadvantages |
| You save money because you pay only a share of gas, oil, repairs, and parking fees. | Requires you to stick to the group's agreed-upon schedule. |
| Lets you take advantage of carpool lanes for vehicles with one or more passengers, thus getting to work faster. | Leaves no room for spontaneity, such as stopping to run errands on the way home, unless everyone agrees. |
| Is better for the environment. | Depends on the habits of the others in the car pool. |

## Bikes for the Taking

Imagine walking a couple of blocks down the street to a rack of basic, no-frills bicycles. You take one and ride it to your destination, and then ride back. The bikes, hundreds of them, are free to everyone in the area on an as-needed basis. They are easily distinguishable and there is no reason to steal them.

In some cities in Europe and in this country, variations on this theme are taking place. The goal: to decrease pollution and traffic by keeping as many cars off city streets as possible.

## Carpools and Vanpools

With a carpool or vanpool, people take turns driving private cars with two or three other people to the same location at the same time each day.

**EXAMPLE:** Four people who work in the New Hampshire state capital all live one hour away in another town. They regularly carpool to work, which means three fewer cars on the road, five days a week.

## Case Study

### Car Sharing

Designed to help people who can't afford a car and to cut down on private car use and the frustration—and expense—of paying for parking, San Francisco's CarShare program began as a federally funded nonprofit organization in March 2001. Geared to big-city living, the program allows you to reserve a Volkswagen Golf, Jetta, or Beetle online for time periods as short as fifteen minutes.

You pick up your car from one of nine garages located in various parts of the city. A keychain attachment opens the garage, and a swipe card in the glove box allows you to get gas if needed. The swipe card electronically meters the time you use the car. At the end of the month, a bill neatly itemizes all your trips at a charge of $2.50 per hour plus 45 cents per mile plus the $10 monthly fee. One car owner's monthly bill was $71, far less than he would have spent driving and parking his own car. For people who don't have their own cars, CarShare can be an easy way to run errands.

Vanpools are groups of people who take turns driving a small van to the same business each day. The van aids workers in getting to work without having to drive and park private cars. Sometimes the vans are owned and maintained by the business. Of course, there are advantages and disadvantages to carpools and vanpools. Still, for many people, the advantages far outweigh the minor inconveniences.

## Owning Your Own Wheels

Even with all the alternative transportation options available, owning a car is still Americans' overwhelming first choice.

For all the independence and freedom car ownership can bring, it's important to make sure your decision to buy a car is a wise one. If not, your decision can leave you financially strapped and feeling anything but free.

### Selecting a Vehicle

What kind of vehicle do you want? What will be its primary use? Can you afford a new car? Will special requirements be necessary to drive in your climate? What options do you want or need? All of these questions and many more need to be asked and answered before you go shopping for a car. If you don't do your homework ahead of time, a car dealer may spot you coming and talk you into something you perhaps don't need and can't afford.

### New or Used?

Most people would pick a new car over a used car if they could afford it. But there are advantages and disadvantages to new cars and used cars.

New cars start to **depreciate**, or lose their value, as soon as you drive them off the lot, and they continue to lose resale value each year. You may be able to take advantage of depreciation by buying a used car in good condition. Look for one with very low miles on it.

The chief benefit of buying a new car is that just about nobody else has driven it. Certainly, nobody has driven it for any length of time or distance. It's never been in an accident or poorly maintained. Also, it may include safety features that older cars lack.

The chief benefit of buying a used car is that it will cost significantly less than a new one. But, you can never be sure of how it was cared for before it came to you. It's wise to choose a used car from a dealer or individual who can provide a repair record. Have a mechanic you trust check it out before you buy.

When looking for a good used car, think about what you can afford and what make and model of car you want. Are there specific features you want, such as **manual transmission**—a gear shift mounted on the steering column or on the floor that you operate by hand? Here are some helpful hints:

✱ If you go to a dealer, make sure it has a reputation for honesty. Talk to people who may have bought a car there. How long has the dealership been in business? Have complaints been filed against it with the Better Business Bureau in the last three years? How were they resolved?

Alabama Citizenship Workbook

* Research the make and model of car you want in consumer magazines and on the Internet to see the repair record and overall performance.
* Check the "For Sale" ads in places such as your local paper, weekly shopper ads, company newsletter, or credit union bulletin board.
* Test-drive the car. Ask to see the repair records. Ask every question you can think of. (Make a list ahead of time.)
* Have the car you like checked out by a mechanic of your choice. It may cost a little money, but it's worth it.
* Pay attention to the **odometer**, which measures the car's mileage. Dealers are required by law to give you the true mileage of the car. If the odometer has turned over at 100,000, the dealer is required to give you that information.
* What warranty, if any, does it have?
* Be willing to walk away if the price doesn't meet your expectations.

Beware of any used car with these telltale signs:

* Excessive rust.
* Drips of fluid on the pavement under the car.
* Brakes that pull or seem weak.
* Car that seems hard to steer or turn.
* The paint doesn't match (indicates the car has been in an accident). Some people suggest sliding a small magnet along the body. Wherever the magnet won't stick, it means plastic or epoxy body repair has been added—the car was in an accident.
* Moldy, wet odor inside the car.
* Blue smoke coming from the tailpipe (usually means the engine is burning oil).
* Lights that don't work, or only work sometimes.

## Good Sources of Car Information

Good information can come from many different sources, including:

* The first-hand experiences of family, friends, and neighbors.
* The Internet.
* Your insurance agent.
* A credit union car-buying service or recommended used-car-finding service.
* Daily newspaper columns that regularly review new cars.
* *Kelley Blue Book.*
* Magazines.

Your research should answer any questions about your year, make, and model of car related to:

* Overall performance.
* Gas mileage.
* Repair records.
* Safety.
* Comfort.
* Price, including new and used models and cost of options that interest you.

### Your Life

**Lemon Laws**

Every state has **lemon laws** to protect consumers. A "lemon" is a new car that:

* Can't be repaired after three or four tries.
* Can't be driven for one month out of one year (or the warranty period).
* Has one major problem after another.

Keep all receipts and service records for any car, but especially for one you think is a lemon. Lemon laws require manufacturers to either replace a lemon or refund money paid for the car and the repairs.

### Get Smart

#### Repossessions

Credit unions sometimes have repossessed vehicles for sale. These cars are often quite new with low mileage and are for sale at a reasonable price, since credit unions aren't in the car-selling business. Check them out!

### Makes and Models

Decisions regarding makes and models of cars may take some time to research. It's important not to have your heart set on one particular car. If you do, you might end up making a poorly informed purchase that you'll regret later. Keep your options open.

Your first decision may be about the size of car. If you regularly drive with kids you may want a minivan. If you take public transportation during the week, you may only need a mid-size car to take out of town on weekends. There are many categories of cars to choose from:

* Economy car.
* Mid-size car.
* Full-size car.
* Luxury car.
* Sports car.
* Sport Utility Vehicle (SUV).
* Minivan.
* Small or full-size pick-up.

### Standard Equipment

**Standard equipment** includes features that are part of the car's base price. You do not pay extra for them. They may include:

* AM/FM radio and cassette tape deck.
* Air conditioning.
* 6-cylinder engine.

It's important to know what features come with the car and which ones you will have to pay extra for.

### Options

There are many ways to increase the base price of a new car. One way is to add a lot of **options**, or added features, such as:

* Sunroof.
* CD player.
* Roof rack.
* Side airbags.
* An anti-theft package.
* Leather seats.

You can also pay extra for your car through dealer add-ons, options that come from the dealer's repair shop rather than from the manufacturer. These are not typically worth the extra money. Such add-ons include:

* Stain resistant spray for the upholstery.
* Rust-proofing.

Options are usually sold in sets, or packages, so in order to get, say, leather seats, you also have to get the more expensive sound system. Think carefully about the options you really want.

### Energy-Efficient Vehicles

Vehicles that use gasoline create carbon dioxide, a greenhouse gas. Scientific evidence suggests that the rapid buildup of greenhouse gases in the atmosphere raises the earth's temperature and changes the climate. According to the EPA, every gallon of gasoline your vehicle burns puts 20 pounds of carbon dioxide into the atmosphere.

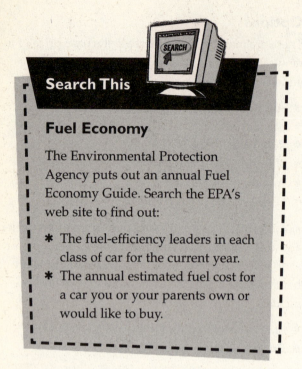

### Search This

**Fuel Economy**

The Environmental Protection Agency puts out an annual Fuel Economy Guide. Search the EPA's web site to find out:

* The fuel-efficiency leaders in each class of car for the current year.
* The annual estimated fuel cost for a car you or your parents own or would like to buy.

Buying a fuel-efficient vehicle can save you more than $1,500 per year in fuel costs! Not only that, over the lifetime of the vehicle, it will prevent more than 15 tons of greenhouse gases from polluting the air. You can save a lot of money and help protect the environment by investing in an energy-efficient car.

<u>Hybrid electric vehicles</u> (HEVs) are still new on the market but are beginning to catch the eye of consumers because of their fuel efficiency. They combine the best features of typical (internal combustion) gasoline engines and electric motors.

## Calculating Costs

It's very important to understand what you will pay for the car you desire. You may decide to lease, rather than buy a car. You may decide to save up for the down payment for six months in order to make a larger down payment and have a smaller loan. You may change your mind on the type of car you want because one car gets better mileage and seems to have fewer—and less expensive—repair costs.

## Owning vs. Leasing

When you own a car (meaning it has been paid in full), the pink slip, or title (proof of ownership) to the car, is yours. If you finance the vehicle through the dealership or through a bank or credit union, the pink slip remains in their possession until the loan is paid in full.

When you **lease** a car, it is like a long-term rental agreement. You make payments for two or three years, but at the end of the lease, the car goes back to the dealer. It is never yours. There are advantages and disadvantages to buying and leasing.

## Buying a Car

There are several ways to buy a car:

* You can save up the money and pay cash. For most people, it would take a long time to save this much money.
* You can trade in another car, which will help get the loan amount down.
* You can save up enough for a down payment. On a $20,000 car, the down payment might be one-fourth or one-fifth of the cost ($4,000 or $5,000). You will then get a loan for the remaining $15,000 or $16,000. The length of a car loan used to be two or three years tops, but cars have increased in price. Now, you can get car loans for 36, 48, or even 60 months, depending on the car and your financial situation. The longer the loan, the less the monthly payment, of course. But you will be making payments for a longer period of time and you will pay more because of the interest charges for carrying the loan a longer time. Consider carefully where you are in your life and the amount of stress you want. If it's a time of many changes, when your job or where you'll be living in six months is uncertain, it may not be a good time to saddle yourself with a big three- to five-year financial commitment.

The process of buying a car takes time and practice, but once you know the process, you'll be ready to go!

* Know the invoice price of the car. This is the price the dealer paid. You can find out the invoice price of any make and model of car on the Internet, from *Edmund's*, or from *Consumer Reports*. You can order a full report on a specific make and model of car, including each option, for a fee.

* Decide which options you want and find out the invoice price of each one. Then add up the invoice price of the car plus the options.
* Compare the invoice price with the **sticker price** on the car. This is the manufacturer's suggested retail price. It's usually around 10 percent above the invoice price. Subtract any dealer offers. Also subtract the value of your old car, the trade-in, if you have one. Subtract this amount at the end of the process, *never* at the beginning.
* Now, how much should go to the dealer as profit? Many people feel that around 3 percent is a fair profit. So you will be haggling over the 7 percent.
* What kind of warranty does the car have on the engine, transmission, and other parts?

There are many resources available to help you make a smart car purchase. The more knowledge you have, the better deal you'll be able to strike on the car of your dreams. Remember, be willing to walk away from that dream car if you can't reach a deal that feels right to you.

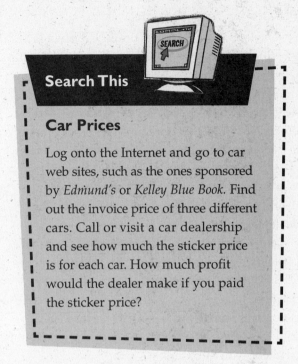

**Search This**

**Car Prices**

Log onto the Internet and go to car web sites, such as the ones sponsored by *Edmund's* or *Kelley Blue Book*. Find out the invoice price of three different cars. Call or visit a car dealership and see how much the sticker price is for each car. How much profit would the dealer make if you paid the sticker price?

## Leasing a Car

It's always important to compare the costs of buying and leasing a car. There are added leasing fees that must be calculated when comparing the two to see if you are getting the best possible deal. If you don't know the terminology or leasing process, it's easy to get stuck with a bad deal.

* The first step is to negotiate the price of the car until you agree on its cost, just as you would with a purchase. Say you arrive at a cost of $16,000.
* Next, you must know the amount you will need to pay. If the lease says that the car's value will be at least 65 percent of its current value at the end of the lease, then you will have to pay 35 percent of the $16,000, or $5,600.
* In addition, you will have to make a down payment. Often, it is equal to one month's payment plus a fee that includes a security deposit.
* If you make a down payment of, say, $1,000, you will be financing $5,600–$1,000, or $4,600, for 24 or 36 months. Remember, however, that you are making payments for two or three years on a car you will never own. Still, leasing may allow you to drive a car that you couldn't afford to buy.
* Watch the mileage restriction. You are usually allowed 12,000 miles per year. If you drive more than that, you will have to pay more—often a great deal more.
* At the end of the lease, you return the car and pay for any extra miles or needed repairs. At this point, there is often a large payment required, sometimes several months' worth of payments. Be sure to ask about these payments and factor that into your decision.

Leasing a car has definite pros and cons. Sometimes leasing makes good sense as a tax write-off for a small business. Often, people lease a car because it allows them to drive a fancier, more expensive car than they could afford to buy. This is because lease payments are lower than financing the purchase price of the car. However, it's important to remember that you never own the car. You continue to make car payments forever, unlike a car loan that eventually can be paid in full.

## Financing Your Vehicle

A vehicle may be financed through a savings and loan, the bank, a credit union, or the car dealership. Sometimes people decide to finance the loan through the dealership because they get special deals or **rebates** (money back). However, credit unions often have the best rates. Look for programs in your area that are partnerships between a credit union and participating dealerships. They let buyers take advantage of dealer rebates and still finance their car through the credit union—right at the dealership.

Banks, credit unions, and savings and loans have very different interest rates. It pays to shop around. Check the Internet as well. If you know the year, make, and model of car you want, you may be able to get pre-approved for a loan up to a certain dollar amount that is well within your budget with monthly payments you can afford.

## Operating Expenses

Buying the vehicle is just the beginning of the costs you must be prepared to pay for the privilege of car ownership. Do some research in your area to find out how much you will likely spend and calculate the monthly payment for the following items:

* License and registration fee (divide by 12).
* Car insurance (get the rate for 6 months and divide by 6).
* Gas and oil.
* Parking (lots, meters, and tickets).
* Car wash.
* Other maintenance.

When you finish, think about the amount of discretionary income you have each month. What percentage does the grand total for the car represent? Some consumer groups feel that 13 percent of your discretionary income is the maximum amount that should be spent on transportation.

## Maintenance

Like anything else you own, taking care of your car will make it last longer and require fewer major repairs. Here's the Big 10 of auto maintenance:

1. Check the owner's manual. Follow the maintenance schedule indicated for your car, or ask a mechanic for advice on a used car that's new to you.
2. Get regular lube and oil changes and tune-ups.
3. Wash the exterior and interior regularly.
4. Check all fluid levels and keep them filled.

### Search This

#### Calculate Your Car Payment

Find a source on the Internet that will calculate your car payment. You might try typing "car loan calculator" in a search engine.

Once you've found the web site, type in the number of months you want for the loan, the interest rate, and the loan amount. Then the program will compute your monthly payment. It's a good way to see what price of car is in your budget and the difference that interest rates can make.

200 Alabama Citizenship Workbook

### Role Model

**Parking Woes**

Angela had it all planned out. She figured it was a lot better to drive her car and park in the paid student parking lot than to ride the bus. She budgeted $3 per day times 12 days per month for a total of $36 for parking. It didn't work out quite that way.

Angela got five parking tickets last month, which she felt was unfair! They were 3-hour meters, and she only missed the expiration by 5 or 10 minutes, each time because the class ran a few minutes over.

Unfortunately, each ticket cost $16. She forgot to pay two of the five tickets within 30 days, so two of the fines doubled. Including the money she put into the parking meter to begin with, how much did Angela actually pay for parking last month? What would you do if you were Angela?

5. Open the hood and check all belts and hoses for signs of wear (frayed edges and tears).
6. Check tires for wear. Check tire pressure and rotate, balance, and align tires periodically.
7. Check paint. Touch up any scratches or nicks to prevent rusting.
8. Complete recommended preventive maintenance for cold winter (or hot summer) weather.
9. Check headlights, taillights, and brake lights.
10. Check brakes. If they feel low or if the car pulls to the left or right when you apply the brakes, get them checked right away.

Whether you buy a new or used car, you can save money by learning how to do some of the basic maintenance, such as oil changes, yourself.

### Insurance Coverage and Costs

The cost of insuring your vehicle is another major expense. Young people, especially, often pay high rates. You also pay more or less, depending on the vehicle you're insuring. Before you purchase any car, make sure you know how much it will cost to insure it.

Usually, insurance estimates are given on a six-month basis, so if the rate quoted is $450, that amount may only be for six months. You must divide by six to figure out how much you will have to put aside each month, so when the insurance premium comes due, the money will be there.

If you are in an accident or receive a moving violation of any kind that appears on your record, expect your insurance rates to go up even more.

### Get Smart

**Fluid Levels**

Just like people, cars need their fluids! Without the right levels, cars wear out more quickly and use fuel less efficiently. Check these vital fluid levels for your car regularly:

* Oil.
* Transmission fluid.
* Brake fluid.
* Windshield wiper fluid.
* Antifreeze.
* Water.

Alabama Citizenship Workbook

# Chapter 28 Wrap-up
## GETTING AROUND

There are many ways to get around. For some people, public transportation is an inexpensive, convenient option. For others, traveling by bike or motorcycle works well. Still others walk.

Many people choose to either buy or lease a new or used car. When purchasing a car, there are many things to consider, including financing, operating expenses, maintenance and repairs, and insurance.

New options in transportation are being developed, such as light rail systems and hybrid electric vehicles, which offer exciting new options to drivers.

Deciding on a means of transportation is a decision you'll make many times throughout your life. Each time, the conditions may be very different from the time before. It's important to establish a process for making such an important decision. The good news is, now is the perfect time to start.

**WORDS TO KNOW**

**depreciate**—lessen in value.

**hybrid electric vehicles (HEVs)**—energy-efficient vehicles that run by two sources of power, electric and gasoline.

**lease**—rent, usually for a long term.

**lemon laws**—consumer protection laws that require a car manufacturer to replace or repay the consumer for a defective new car that cannot be fixed after several tries.

**manual transmission**—on a car, gears that are shifted by hand with a gear shift mounted on the steering column or on the floor.

**mass transit**—public transportation in urban areas.

**odometer**—instrument on a car that measures the distance traveled in miles.

**options**—features added to a new car that cost extra and aren't included in the base price.

**rebates**—special bargains offered by a car dealership that return part of the price of a car.

**standard equipment**—car features that are included as part of the base price of the car.

**sticker price**—car manufacturer's recommended retail price, usually about 10 percent above the price the dealer paid the manufacturer.

Name _____

# 28. Getting Around

**After you read the chapter, write an answer to each question below.**

1. How can lifestyle and personal preferences influence the kind of transportation one chooses to take?
   _____
   _____
   _____

2. How do trolleys differ from light rail? Explain.
   _____
   _____
   _____

3. What are the advantages and disadvantages of owning a motorcycle rather than a car?
   _____
   _____
   _____

4. What sorts of things should you look for when shopping for a used car? Support your answer.
   _____
   _____
   _____

5. What are some differences between owning and leasing a car?
   _____
   _____
   _____

Name _____

## 28. Getting Around

**Circle the best answer for each item.**

1. What is another word for "lessen the value"?
   a. appreciate
   b. depreciate
   c. manipulate
   d. retaliate

2. What are energy-efficiency vehicles run by two sources of power, electric and gasoline?
   a. hybrid gas vehicles (HGVs)
   b. hybrid electric vehicles (HEVs)
   c. hybrid solar vehicles (HSVs)
   d. hybrid water vehicles (HWVs)

3. What is the term for features added to a new car that cost extra and aren't included in the base price?
   a. leases
   b. options
   c. meters
   d. tokens

4. What do you call car features that are included as part of the base price of the car?
   a. standard equipment
   b. special equipment
   c. luxury equipment
   d. base equipment

5. What is the manufacturer's recommended retail price, usually about 10 percent above the price the dealer paid the manufacturer?
   a. sticker price
   b. bumper price
   c. fair price
   d. invoice price

6. For many people, the primary purpose of transportation is to _____.
   a. make money
   b. run errands
   c. take vacations
   d. commute to work or school

7. _____ is/are the most important factor to consider when choosing any mode of transportation.
   a. Lifestyle
   b. Safety
   c. Personal preferences
   d. Cost

8. One disadvantage of mass transit is it _____.
   a. is more expensive than driving a car
   b. is more comfortable than driving a car
   c. allows less flexibility because of schedules
   d. cuts down on air pollution and saves energy

9. _____ is a type of bicycle that is made for two or more people.
   a. Commuter bike
   b. Travel bike
   c. Triathlon bike
   d. Tandem bike

10. _____ often offer the best terms on financing automobiles.
    a. Banks
    b. Dealerships
    c. Credit unions
    d. Savings and loans

CHAPTER 29

# How Insurance Can Protect You

**In this chapter, you will learn about:**

- different types of insurance
- how to choose the best insurance for you
- how to keep coverage once it's in place

It's enough to make anyone a little whiny. You save up all your money to buy a house or a car, and then you find out you have to pay more money to insure it! You're perfectly healthy, and yet people advise you to spend your hard-earned money on health insurance. What's the point?

Carla found out the hard way. "I didn't take the value of having insurance seriously until I suddenly got very ill. I was only twenty-two. How could this happen? It was not fair! Most unfair of all was how much I paid for not having health insurance. My hospital bills were staggering. Do you know I am still paying them off four years later? Check on me in six years. Trust me, I'll still be paying."

Alabama Citizenship Workbook 205

# Insurance Basics

If you lost your backpack, it would be frustrating and inconvenient, but it wouldn't cost much to replace it. However, if your car was totaled, or if you lost your house and all your belongings in a house fire, it would be devastating. There is probably no way you could simply write a check to replace what you lost. That's where insurance comes in.

You purchase insurance to help you pay for the things that could happen to you that you couldn't possibly afford.

Our laws say that if you cause damage to others, even without meaning to, you must pay to compensate them for their losses or injuries. Did a loose stair on your porch result in someone's falling and breaking a leg? You have to pay. Insurance can cover you against these kinds of expenses.

Insurance companies offer different **insurance policies**, or plans, for health, car, homeowner's, disability, and life insurance. The amounts of coverage may vary widely.

## How Does Insurance Work?

Let's say you pay $800 a year for your car insurance. You've had the insurance for two years, but you've never had to file a **claim**. (A claim is a request to your insurance company for payment of, or reimbursement for, losses for which you are insured.) You're a good, careful driver, but yesterday there was some unexpected ice on the road. You skidded, hit another car, and drove into a ditch. No one was hurt, but both cars were damaged. The cost for repairs will come to just over $6,000 dollars.

If you've only spent $1,600 on premiums (2 years x $800), how can the insurance company pay for the damages? It mixes your premiums with everyone else's premiums. Most people don't have accidents often, so the dollars in the pot are greater than the dollars needed to pay out claims.

When you buy insurance, you are sharing the risk with all the other **policy holders**—all the people who buy insurance, pay premiums, and are therefore eligible to file claims. Some of you will need to file claims. Others won't. Everyone, though, is protected *if* something bad happens. That is the value of having insurance and paying premiums, even when it's tempting to use the money for something else.

## Making it REAL

### What if Something Happened?

Imagine each situation below. What type of insurance would you need to protect you from the financial impact of these situations? Consider the consequences of *not* having insurance. What do you think might happen if you didn't have the money to handle these situations?

* You are injured and can't work for eight months.
* Your spouse dies, leaving you with two school-age children to raise alone.
* You accidentally rear-end another car, causing serious damage to both cars.
* You come home from a weekend away to find that a broken water pipe spilled hundreds of gallons of water into your house.
* You need emergency surgery to remove a tumor from your lung.
* You let a friend borrow your car, and he smashes your neighbor's garage door, fence, and prized rose bushes. It's your car, you have to pay.

## Buying Insurance

Insurance is complicated. When you buy insurance, you are entering into a legally binding contract with the insurance company. You are obligated to make your payments on time, and the company is obligated to pay certain amounts in the event of certain things happening. There are **three** important reasons why you should buy carefully:

1. You want to be sure the protection you believe you are buying will really be there when you need it.
2. You don't want to pay more for it than you must.
3. There is a lot of fine print.

## Insurance Agents and Salespeople

Get an insurance agent or sales person you can trust. An agent can explain exactly what you are buying. An agent can provide you with choices, and he or she can work with the company you choose to help you get prompt attention for your claims. It is wise to choose this agent with the same care you would use to choose any other professional. Ask friends, coworkers, your boss, and others. Who do they use? What have their experiences been?

## Keeping Costs Down

To some extent, you can control the cost of insurance by:

* Rechecking your needs and the prices of available coverage every year or so.
* Not insuring yourself against events you can afford to pay for on your own.
* Taking the highest deductible you can afford.

### Insurance Policies

| Type of Insurance | Purpose | Protection |
|---|---|---|
| Health Insurance | Protects in case of illness and other bodily injuries. | Pays for doctor or dental visits, prescriptions, hospital visits, and other illness or injury-related costs. |
| Car Insurance | Protects persons and vehicles in case of an accident or theft. | Protects against being sued; pays for damage to vehicles and property; may pay for towing and accident-related medical costs. |
| Homeowner's Insurance | Protects against damage to real property (structures or land) or damage, loss, or theft of personal property (items of value such as furniture, jewelry, or computer equipment). | * Pays for damage to a house and belongings due to fire, storms, wind or water damage, theft, or vandalism.<br>* May pay to rebuild a house similar to the one you had or to replace a stolen item.<br>* Separate policies can be purchased for each type of property or combined in one homeowner's insurance policy.<br>* Special insurance policies may be purchased to cover earthquakes or flood damage.<br>* Renter's (or tenant's) insurance covers personal property only. |
| Disability Insurance | Protects income when you are unable to work and earn a living. | Provides a percentage of income to insured when out of work due to injury or long-term illness. |
| Life Insurance | Protects the family in the event of the death of a wage-earning family member. | Provides money to the family of someone who has died to help the family pay bills related to the person's death and to help meet ongoing living expenses. |

## Individual Protection

Individual protection is designed to protect the assets, car, personal property, or home of an individual or family. It can also protect people in the event that they are unable to work, or a family in the event of a family member's death.

### Asset Protection

Insurance protects your **assets**—the things of monetary value that you own. Your assets may include items such as a car, house, and your electric guitar, as well as money you have in savings. If something should happen, you do not want anyone to take your assets in order to pay what can be overwhelming bills. Look around your room and house now. What items of value do you now own? What ones might you have in five years? In ten years?

### Car Insurance

Cars are not only expensive to buy, but are expensive to repair as well. If you are in an accident that is your fault, or if the accident is the fault of someone without insurance, it is up to you to pay. How will you do that? If you hit another car and no one is

A deductible is the amount you pay out of your own pocket before the insurance company pays. All policies assume you will pay some portion of the cost of your losses. Deductibles can range from as little as $100 to as much as $5000.

The higher the deductible you take, the lower your premiums will be. You should take the highest deductible you can afford. Over time, you will save a great deal more money in premiums than you will spend in deductibles.

### Get Smart

#### Irreplaceable Items

What items do you or your family own that absolutely could not be replaced? Even though your grandma's china and your grandfather's saxophone are valuable and important to you, many people put family photographs at the top of the list.

Losing a lifetime of photos is losing an important link to your own history. Here are some ways to ensure the safety of photos that can't be replaced no matter how much insurance you might have:

* Keep old family photos in a lockbox.
* Make copies of photos, and give them to other family members so no one family member has the only photos or family photo album.
* Put your photos on a CD or make a video slide show, so you have a record in more than one format.
* If you live in a location prone to forest fires or flooding, keep photos in a safe place away from home.

injured, you have the price of fixing one or more vehicles. On top of that, people may be injured or even killed. Property may be damaged if a car drives over a curb and hits a store. You should never drive a vehicle without knowing that there is insurance on the vehicle you're driving. The financial risks are too great.

Most states now have **financial responsibility laws** that require car owners to carry insurance unless they can prove that they are financially responsible up to a certain dollar amount. If you were extremely wealthy, it's possible you wouldn't need insurance. No matter what happened, you could just write a check to take care of it. Rest assured, however, that the other 99 percent of car owners need insurance.

You are required to keep proof of insurance in your car at all times. Keep it in the glove compartment or in a special clip attachment on your visor.

Car insurance covers:

* ***Your losses***—the costs to repair damages to your car or to replace it if it cannot be repaired. *Collision* coverage pays for damage caused by running into something or someone running into you. *Comprehensive* coverage pays for damages from other sources, such as hail or theft.
* ***Your obligations to others***—the cost to compensate others for injury or death or to repair or replace their property when anyone driving your car caused the damage or injury. This is **liability coverage**.
* ***Medical expenses***—the costs to care for both the occupants of your car and other people injured by your car as a result of a car accident.

Collision and comprehensive coverage are optional. There are times when you might choose to save money by not buying them. If you are driving an old beater, it may not be worth your insuring its replacement cost.

## By the Numbers

### When Not to Use Insurance

Say you get in your car one morning to find your case of 25 CDs was stolen during the night. You have insurance on your belongings, both as part of your car insurance and your homeowner's policy. Your car insurance deductible is $250. Your house insurance deductible is $500. How do you decide which insurance policy to use?

For small claims like this, it depends. How much would it cost to replace the CDs? If you use homeowner's insurance, you'll essentially replace all the CDs yourself, since the deductible (the amount you pay up front to file a claim) is $500, probably more than the replacement cost of the stolen items.

So, you figure using your car insurance is the best route to go, but first, ask yourself whether it's worth it. Remember, you must pay your $250 deductible up front, so the insurance will only pay the replacement costs above $250. Will your premiums go up if you file a claim? If so, it probably isn't worth it. Making matters more complicated, you may be required to prove the CDs were in your car.

In the end, you may decide you only really want to replace 10 or 12 of the 25 CDs that were stolen. How much would that cost?

It is necessary to determine who caused an accident, in order to figure out which insurance company should pay—yours or the other person's. However, suppose the other person doesn't have insurance? To protect against this eventuality, all states require people to carry at least a minimum amount of *uninsured motorist* protection. This is one time when you should consider buying more than the minimum.

Many states also require insurance companies to offer **no-fault auto insurance**. Under no-fault, your insurance company pays the medical bills of people injured in your car, no matter who was at fault.

## Coverage Costs and Requirements

Usually, car insurance policies are written on a six-month basis, so if the rate quoted is $450, that is only for six months. You must divide by six to figure out how much you will have to put aside each month so when the insurance premium comes due, the money will be there. If you are in an accident or receive a moving violation of any kind that appears on your record, expect your insurance rates to go up.

A new car will require insurance coverage that an older car will not. It's important to reevaluate your coverage to make sure that you're not paying for coverage you no longer need.

**EXAMPLE:** If you are driving an older car, the amount of collision and comprehensive coverage needed when it was new no longer applies. Now the dollar value of the car is worth very little, even though it's worth the world to you. The insurance company will not pay you more than its market value, no matter how much you originally insured it for.

## Problem Solving

If you find yourself in a position where you are denied coverage, here's what to do:

* Call your agent or the insurance company. Find out why you were denied coverage and request to see a copy of your file.
* Research other insurance companies. Even if you are denied coverage by one company, you may be accepted by another.

* If you know that your driving record is keeping you from getting car insurance, find out about special high-risk pools in your state. Such pools divide up all poor-risk applicants among many insurance companies so these high-risk people can continue to be insured. It will cost substantially more money to be insured in this way. Over time, as your driving record improves, you will qualify for lower-priced insurance. If it doesn't improve, you may find yourself unable to drive.

Insurance companies give discounts for car insurance under certain conditions. When purchasing car insurance, think about which of these apply to you and see how much you can save as a result!

* Completion of a driver education course.
* Good student discount.
* Nonsmoker.
* Nondrinker.
* Safe driving record.
* Low number of miles driven per year.
* Anti-lock brakes, airbags, security alarm.

### Get Smart

### Drive Safely

The best insurance against car accidents is the way you drive. Here are some tips for safe driving:

* Drive safely and defensively. Train yourself to be aware of what's happening around you so you have time to respond in order to prevent an accident before it happens.
* Pay attention. Keep distractions, such as conversations, music, or cell phone calls, to a minimum.
* Keep your car in good condition. Regularly check the brakes, lights, windshield wipers, fluid levels, and tires.

| Car Insurance Factors | |
|---|---|
| **Factors Involved in Cost** | **Explanation** |
| Age, type, and value of the car. | Newer cars and fast, sporty cars cost more to insure than a typical four-door sedan. |
| Cost to repair or replace the car. | Expensive cars will cost more to repair or replace. |
| Age of driver(s). | In general, older drivers pay less; teenage boys pay the most, based on insurance company accident statistics. Adding a teenage driver to a policy can increase rates by 75 percent or more. |
| Your marital status. | Married people often pay less than single adult drivers. |
| Your driving record. | If you have received tickets in the past few years or have been in one or more accidents, your insurance will cost more than insurance for someone with a clean driving record. You will also pay more if you have not been continuously insured in the last year. |
| Amount of driving you do and under what conditions. | Insurance companies factor in the amount of driving you do per year. If you have long commutes or drive under dangerous driving conditions, you will pay more for car insurance. |
| Your geographic location. | Rates differ from state to state and between urban, suburban, and rural areas. |
| Area of town in which you live and work. | It costs more to insure a car if you live or work in a high-crime area with lots of car thefts. |

## Homeowner's Insurance

Homeowner's (or house) insurance is designed to protect your **real property**—that is, your house, its contents, the land it is on, and any other structures on the property (a garage, barn, or workshop, for example). For many people, buying a house is the biggest financial investment they will ever make. It would be next to impossible to recover financially from the loss of this asset without the help of insurance. The savings institution that carries the mortgage on your house will require you to have homeowner's insurance to protect *its* investment.

## Personal Property Insurance

Personal property insurance covers all your personal belongings in case of theft, fire, or other disasters. **Personal property** is defined as all the items you own that can be moved. Personal property includes:

* Antiques.
* Appliances.
* Bicycles.
* Clothing.
* Computer equipment.
* Furnishings.
* Household items (bedding, dishes, books).
* Jewelry.

Personal property insurance is typically a part of any homeowner's policy. It covers losses at home and also items lost or damaged away from home (a camera lost on a river trip or golf clubs stolen from your car). **Renter's insurance** policies are designed to insure your personal belongings in a house you do not own.

Vehicle, homeowner's, renter's, and personal property policies combine to cover your possessions.

Imagine what it would be like to suffer the loss of all your belongings. Having insurance certainly doesn't make up for the terrible loss, but it can help you financially to begin to start over.

## Personal and Family Protection

Life and disability insurance policies protect you and your family in case you cannot earn an income due to death, injury, or illness. They are designed to protect people and lost income, rather than replacing possessions.

### Health Insurance

Health insurance is designed to protect you and your family in the event of illness or bodily injury. Medical costs can be overwhelming if you have to pay them all yourself. You may be lucky enough to have good medical insurance through your employer, but if not, you should purchase coverage yourself. (See pages 204–10 for more information about health insurances.)

### Life Insurance

<u>Life insurance</u> is designed to protect people left behind when someone dies. It provides survivors with money, which is called a "death benefit." Generally, life insurance is only needed by someone who has <u>dependents</u>—family members such as a spouse or children who rely on the person for financial support.

Life insurance can lessen the financial blow to the family in the event of the death of a wage-earning family member.

You buy life insurance for the amount it will pay in the event of the death of the insured individual.
**EXAMPLE:** Joe takes out a $100,000 policy.

There are **two** main types of life insurance:

1. Cash-value insurance.
2. Term insurance.

### Cash-Value Insurance

Cash-value insurance costs more than term insurance, but it has certain advantages. The policy grows in value over time as you pay into it. Should you decide for any reason to quit keeping it, you can cash out for the value you have accumulated. (This amount will be less than you've actually paid, because part of what you are paying for is protection.)

This kind of policy can reach a point in your life when it is fully paid up—often in 20 or 25 years. The protection and cash benefits continue, but you don't continue paying premiums.

The premium costs will not change as you grow older. If you are interested in this kind of insurance, you should compare the return on the savings part of it to other investment choices, such as bonds.

### When You Can't Afford Insurance

Health care and health insurance are expensive. There may be times when it is simply not affordable. At these times, do you have options? Fortunately, yes. There are government programs that can help, such as Medicaid. County health departments and state programs may also be able to help.

There are many free clinics around the country. One of these, Volunteers in Medicine (VIM), started with one clinic in South Carolina and now has 15 clinics nationwide. The brainchild of retired physician Jack McConnell, VIM clinics offer free or low-cost care to uninsured people, including doctor visits, prescriptions, and referrals to social service agencies and medical specialists when necessary. There have been cases of people with advanced cancer and other serious illnesses beating their diseases, thanks to the free treatment and surgery they received from physicians and other health-care providers.

In addition to volunteer physicians, VIM clinics rely on community volunteers to help keep clinic doors open evenings and weekends. These long hours and dedicated medical and community volunteers mean VIM's doors are always open to help the uninsured.

### Term Insurance

Term insurance is much cheaper than cash-value insurance, but it is only in force for the term of the policy—usually one year. It is never paid up. It has no cash value. Many individuals find it an excellent choice when they need coverage for only a few years. A spouse who stays home to care for children may want term insurance on the working spouse's life for the years when the children are small.

Term insurance policy costs go up as you get older. A 20-year-old can buy $100,000 worth of coverage for much less than a 50-year-old can. However, you can buy policies that guarantee not to raise your rates for as long as 20 years.

### Disability and Income-Protection Insurance

When an illness or accident prevents you from going to work, you have more than just medical bills to worry about. You lose your income. How will you pay your bills? How will you live?

Disability insurance both covers medical costs and provides you with income to pay the ordinary costs of living.

Disability insurance is often offered as a benefit by employers. Social Security, too, offers disability coverage to workers who have qualified by paying into the system for a certain amount of time. In addition, insurance companies sell this protection.

### Role Model

**Disability Insurance**

Greg was 33 years old. He had worked for nine years as a computer programmer, and he made a good salary that supported his two young daughters and his wife who stayed home to care for the girls. One day, he was diagnosed with a serious illness, and within six months, he could no longer work.

He had excellent medical insurance that paid the medical bills, but what about the loss of income? Suddenly, Greg's salary was not there, and he and his wife had house payments, food, utilities, a car payment, day care, and other monthly expenses. They did not have much money in savings and did not have family who could help them financially.

Luckily, Greg and his wife had disability insurance to fall back on. Without it, they probably would have had to sell their house.

You can get income protection in several ways:

* **Workers' compensation:** an employer program required by state governments and paid for by the employer. Workers' compensation provides income, medical-care expenses, and retraining for employees injured on the job.
* **Employer-sponsored coverage.** Premiums may be deducted from your paycheck. The employer may also cover part of the premium cost.
* **Individual disability policy,** for which you pay the entire premium.

When purchasing individual coverage, buy a policy that covers you for *no less than* 60 percent of your annual income. Review carefully any conditions that might be excluded from coverage. Also, check the <u>waiting period</u>—the amount of time you must wait after the disability or illness before you can collect benefits.

### Unemployment Compensation

There is one final avenue of protection against loss of income—<u>unemployment compensation</u>. This is a program administered through state governments and paid for with your payroll taxes. If you are released from your job through no fault of your own, you should contact your state unemployment office to learn for what benefits you qualify. You will be asked to complete certain forms. Your previous employer will be contacted. You will be expected to look for work and may be required to show evidence of your search.

### Maintaining Coverage

Insurance coverage is only there as long as your payments are up to date. You take a big risk when you pay late or skip a payment.

Imagine this. You're a careful driver and have never been in an accident. In fact, you don't drive all that much or very far. Now you're a little short on cash, so you've let the due date slip by without sending in your money. The company notified you that it would cancel if you didn't pay, but you didn't get around to it. Then, this morning as you turned a corner, a kid on a bike skidded in front of you. You hit her and knocked her down. She went to the hospital. You called your insurance agent and found you're no longer covered. Now what will you do? You could be looking at a fine for driving without coverage and huge expenses.

Don't make this kind of mistake. Make sure you are insured continuously by making timely payments. Also, if you change from one policy to another, make sure there are no days in between policies when you're not insured.

# Community Protection

*It can't happen here!* We humans have the ability to fool ourselves in the most amazing ways. We can't imagine anything really bad happening to us . . . until it happens. The news, however, is filled with examples of whole neighborhoods that were devastated by a tornado, natural gas explosion, or forest fire.

## When Disasters Strike

Throughout history, natural disasters of all kinds have occurred and will continue to occur. They include:

* Earthquakes.
* Forest fires.
* Tornadoes.
* Hurricanes.
* Windstorms.
* Floods.

Can you think of any more to add to the list? It is likely that you or someone you know has experienced one of these natural disasters.

Individuals can minimize the damage due to natural disasters to some degree by having some things in place (in addition to adequate insurance) before anything happens. For example:

* Think twice before building a house on the edge of an unstable hill, no matter how beautiful the view. The same is true of building a house right next to a river that regularly overflows its banks (in this case, flood insurance is very expensive).

### My Notebook

**Insurance Incidents**

Think back over the last year. Recall all the times when you might have benefited from insurance, and write them down.

* How often were you sick? Did you go to the doctor? Did you buy medicine?
* Did you have any injuries? Any trips to the emergency room?
* Were you involved in any bicycle or car accidents?
* Did you miss any income due to illness, accident, or injury?
* Was anything of yours stolen?
* Was your neighborhood damaged by any disasters, such as a tornado, earthquake, fire, or flood?

You may be surprised by how many things have happened that were easier to deal with by having insurance.

* If you live in an area where earthquakes occur, earthquake-proof your house. Bolt down your water heater. Secure your cupboard doors with child safety latches to help minimize loss due to breakage.
* Make a list of valuables to take upstairs if a flood occurs.
* Have all your important papers in one place to grab in case of evacuation.
* Keep important papers in a safety deposit box at a bank.
* Have a family evacuation plan in case of fire or other emergency.

* Keep a list of items to pack in the car if you leave your house due to the threat of a hurricane or other natural disaster.
* Make sure batteries in smoke alarms work. Experts recommend changing them twice a year, when we change the clocks for daylight savings time.
* Consider other alarms for your home, such as a carbon monoxide alarm.

Can you think of other ways to minimize the damage caused by natural disasters?

There are also disasters that are anything but natural. Terrorist attacks are an example. So are explosions at chemical processing plants or a dam that bursts. Can you think of other unnatural disasters?

These disasters—natural or unnatural—all have one thing in common: They affect more than one family. Sometimes an entire neighborhood or town is affected.

In addition to the loss of life and houses, public buildings and businesses may be lost with a resulting loss of jobs. In many cases, the damage may also have an impact on the area's **infrastructure**, which may include the roads, public utilities (including water and power), public transportation, emergency services, and public safety (including police, fire, and ambulance service).

In such cases, individuals cannot take care of the problem through their individual insurance policies alone. It is too enormous. Help must come from government at all levels and from relief organizations such as the Red Cross.

## Rebuilding

In the case of disasters that touch not just one house but an entire community, government steps in to help people. Agencies providing disaster relief go to work to provide temporary living quarters and food to people. Low-interest loans are made available for rebuilding. Procedures to quickly process insurance claims are initiated. Again, no one can sufficiently remove the pain and suffering of people who have experienced such devastation. But with the help of agencies, volunteers, and the government, people can slowly begin to put their lives back together again over time.

### Chapter 29 Wrap-up
#### HOW INSURANCE CAN PROTECT YOU

*Insurance protects you from the costs of major events you can't control and can't possibly pay for. Illness, death, injury, fire, car accidents—these are the kinds of events you buy insurance to cover. Insurance is complex, and you should find a professional—an agent or the sales person at a respected company—to help you.*

*At some time you may need car insurance, renter's or homeowner's insurance, life insurance, and disability insurance. Unemployment compensation is available through your state government. It is wise to have as much coverage as you can afford.*

**asset**—possession that has monetary value. (In the plural, *assets* are all the property owned by a person or business that could be used to pay debts.)

**claim**—request to your insurance company for payment of, or reimbursement for, losses for which you are insured.

**dependents**—people, usually family members, who rely on you for financial support.

**disability insurance**—coverage that helps with living and medical expenses if you cannot work due to injury or illness.

**financial responsibility laws**—laws requiring proof that you are financially responsible up to a certain dollar amount.

**infrastructure**—structure of a community or nation that includes the roads, public utilities (including water and power), public transportation, emergency services, and public safety (including police, fire, and ambulance service).

**insurance policy**—contract offered by an insurance company that details what kinds of events are covered, how the amount of payment will be calculated, and how much the insured will pay for the coverage.

**liability coverage**—type of insurance that pays the costs of your obligations to others for whose death, injury, or loss you are responsible.

**life insurance**—form of insurance that provides survivors with money, called a death benefit, if you die.

**no-fault auto insurance**—type of car insurance that pays medical expenses to policy holder and others injured in his or her car regardless of who caused the accident.

**personal property**—all the items you own that can be moved.

**policy holder**—person who buys insurance, pays premiums, and is therefore eligible to file claims if necessary.

**real property**—house, the land it is on, and any other structures on the property.

**renter's insurance**—property and liability insurance for people who live in a rented home.

**unemployment compensation**—government-run program operated by the states and paid for with payroll taxes. It provides cash benefits to people who have lost their jobs through no fault of their own.

**waiting period**—specified amount of time you must wait before collecting benefits.

Alabama Citizenship Workbook

Name _____

# 29. How Insurance Can Protect You

**After you read the chapter, write an answer to each question below.**

1. What types of things can an insurance agent do to help you?
_____
_____
_____

2. What can you do to control the cost of insurance?
_____
_____
_____

3. What happens, regarding insurance payment, if you are in an accident that is your fault? What happens if the accident is the fault of someone who doesn't have insurance?
_____
_____
_____

4. What happens to your insurance if you are in an accident, or receive a moving violation of any kind that appears on your record?
_____
_____
_____

5. If you bought a new car 10 years ago, how would you alter your insurance for it as it ages?
_____
_____
_____

Name _____

# 29. How Insurance Can Protect You

**Circle the best answer for each item.**

1. What is the request to your insurance company for payment of, or reimbursement for, losses for which you are insured?

    a. bill
    b. claim
    c. notice
    d. contract

2. What is the term for a clause, in an insurance policy, that exempts the insurer from paying a specified amount in the event of a claim?

    a. coverage
    b. premium
    c. deductible
    d. claimant

3. Who are the people, usually family members, who rely on you for financial support?

    a. deductibles
    b. claims
    c. riders
    d. dependents

4. What type of insurance pays the costs of your obligations to others for whose death, injury, or loss you are responsible?

    a. liability coverage
    b. disability insurance
    c. long-term care insurance
    d. riders' coverage

5. Who is the person who buys insurance, pays premiums, and is therefore eligible to file claims, if necessary?

    a. dependent
    b. rider
    c. policy holder
    d. premium holder

6. The higher the _____, the lower the _____.

    a. premium/claim
    b. deductible/assets
    c. deductible/premiums
    d. rider/deductible

7. You are required by law to keep _____ in your car.

    a. proof of insurance
    b. a copy of your policy
    c. previous claims
    d. your agent's name and address

8. You should never drive a vehicle without knowing that there _____ the vehicle you're driving.

    a. aren't any tickets on
    b. is insurance on
    c. haven't been any previous accidents in
    d. aren't any mechanical problems in

9. After a disaster, _____ are (is) made available by the government for rebuilding.

    a. free labor
    b. no-interest loans
    c. low-interest loans
    d. tools

10. All states require people to carry at least a minimum amount of _____.

    a. collision coverage
    b. property damage coverage
    c. uninsured motorist protection
    d. liability coverage

**Essay Question**

What types of insurance do you think you need now? What types will you need five years from now? 10 years? 20 years? Explain each.

CHAPTER 30

# How to Invest for Your Future

**In this chapter, you will learn about:**

- planning for your financial future
- the power of compound interest
- investing money

Sophie always loved animals, and from when she was 10 years old, she was sure she wanted to be a veterinarian. She knew that her parents would help her as much as they could but that she would need to pay for a large portion of her education expenses herself.

Sophie took every opportunity she could find to earn money and vowed to save one-third of everything she earned for the next eight years. Sophie's mom explained to her that there were better places than banks for saving toward a long-term goal. She steered Sophie to a mutual fund that invested conservatively. Although Sophie wanted her money to grow as much as it could, she didn't want to take big risks. She couldn't afford to lose any of it, if she was to reach her goal. Sophie's approach used the basic principles of investing—understanding about risks and returns.

## Long-Term Planning

Careful planning, budgeting, and smart shopping are just the beginning when it comes to securing your financial health. As you get more experienced with handling money in the short term, you also need to start thinking about your financial life in the long term. Saving and investing your money are the key to future financial well-being. When you save and **invest**, you put your money in stocks, bonds, or other instruments where it will grow for the future.

Financial planning sounds like a pretty serious and, let's face it, *challenging* topic. It conjures up visions of a large boardroom with lots of charts and graphs on the walls. Men and women sit at an enormous, long table looking at papers filled with numbers and dollar signs. But this is a misleading image, because financial planning isn't just important for businesses. It's essential for everyone.

Whether we're teenagers with a part-time job or multimillionaires in charge of a vast fortune, money is something that all of us must deal with in some way. Whether you have a lot or a little, you have to decide what you're going to do with it. So, why not be smart about your money?

Long-term planning involves investments that are focused on goals and needs that will arise many years in the future.

### Time Is Money

When it comes to saving and investing, time is on your side. No matter what your income level, starting to save when you're young makes an enormous difference. Not only do you develop good saving habits, but your money has more time to grow.

If you put your money in a safe deposit box, buried it like treasure in a hole beneath a tree, or hid it under your mattress, then it would not grow. But you know better. Your money is earning interest. And the interest is earning interest. We call that **compound interest**—interest earned on both your principal (the amount you invested) and on the interest it earns.

When asked if he could name the seven wonders of the world, Baron de Rothschild said, "I don't know what the first seven are, but the eighth wonder of the world is compound interest."

Albert Einstein called compound interest, "The most powerful invention of mankind."

Follow these **two** tips to reap the greatest benefit from compound interest:

1. Start to save and invest sooner rather than later.
2. Leave your money in as long as you can.

One easy-to-remember example of this is the following fact: *Money invested at seven percent interest will double in 10 years.* Notice there are two important parts to this equation: the percentage and the number of years. You need to know both to describe growth with compound interest.

### Basic Principles of Investment

When you have money to invest, you are faced with a variety of choices about what to do with your money.

You might buy a one-year bank certificate of deposit (a CD) paying $4\frac{1}{2}$ percent. This is a very safe way to invest. You know at the start the interest it will pay and how long it will go on paying it. You can be certain the money will be there (because of Federal insurance) at the end of that time.

On the other hand, you may want to get a higher rate of return on your money. You may have heard that people were getting a 15 percent return from investing in a certain stock, and you'd like to do that. Now, you can't be certain that because a stock paid 15 percent in the past it will continue to do so. Also, there is no certainty that the stock will bring the price you paid for it when you decide later to sell it. So, this stock investment is much riskier than the bank CD.

These examples demonstrate **one** basic principle of investing:

1. The greater the risk, the greater the return.

How do you choose which kind of investment to make? Your goals provide an important guide

# Long-Term Goals

When you save money for a vacation or to be able to pay the occasional major repair on your car, you have a short-term goal. You want to take that vacation later this year. You'll probably have to have new tires next year. For those purposes, you'll probably just put your money in a savings account at your bank, or buy a CD for the short term.

But when you save for something more than a couple of years off, then you have a long-term goal. Investing, rather than merely saving, is what you do to reach a long-term goal.

Long-term goals many people invest for include:

* College education.
* Buying a home.
* Retirement.

## Your College Education

A college education gives people experiences that improve their ability to appreciate life. It can also provide a network of friends who will support you in many ways through the years. A college degree also greatly improves your chances of finding work you enjoy and that pays a good salary. The more education you get, the more you qualify for jobs that pay the highest salaries.

Many colleges are very expensive. To attend one of these becomes a long-term goal because you need to save and invest over a long period of time to accumulate enough money to pay for it. Parents often start college saving plans when their children or grandchildren are quite young. If you have 18 years or so to save, you can afford to "ride out" some of the ups and downs of the economy, and you can accept a certain amount of risk.

## Buying a Home

A home is the most expensive purchase most people will make in their lives. However, to buy one, you do not need to save the full price. You need only save the down payment amount plus the additional percentage points and fees associated with the purchase. Depending on your income and the price of the house you're willing to start with, many careful people can save a down payment in under five years. It takes discipline.

## Retirement

Most people expect to live long enough to retire. Some people even make it a goal to retire early in order to pursue interests outside their work. But once you stop working, where will the money you need to live on come from?

* Social Security.
* Company retirement plan.
* Personal savings.

For most people, the answer is some combination of all three. Social Security is not enough for most people to live the way they have become accustomed to living. Some companies have good retirement plans for their workers, but you earn your retirement with them over many years of employment. Increasingly, people do not stay working for one company for long periods of time. So, it is wise to plan on having to fund much of your retirement yourself. As you have many, many years before you have to think about retirement, you should look at it as a *very* long-term goal.

Remember that time is money. If you save only $50 a week for 30 years, you'll have more than $307,000 at an 8 percent return. At 10 percent, you'd have over $450,000. Historically, the stock market has returned between 8 and 10 percent over the long term.

## Investment Tools

There are many ways to invest money. Some people buy land. Some people feel safest when they put their money in precious metals, buying gold and silver. Some invest in objects they expect to be able to sell later at a higher price—like fine art or rare stamps. These are unusual investments and require a great deal of specialized knowledge to earn any return. The basic tools for most investors include:

* Stocks.
* Bonds.
* Mutual funds.

These tools, composed of bond or stock certificates, are known as **securities**.

## Developing a Strategy

Your strategy for reaching long-term goals may be made up of different parts. It might look like this:

1. Commit to investing a certain amount of money regularly, perhaps $100 a month to start.
2. Use a savings account at the bank until you have the minimum amount needed to invest in a higher-yielding tool.
3. Make a minimum investment in a balanced mutual fund.
4. Continue to make regular contributions to that fund, perhaps through automatic withdrawals from your checking account.
5. Evaluate your goals and your investments periodically—once a year, for instance.
6. Make changes as needed.

## Stocks

Many Americans invest in **stocks**. A stock is a share of a company. When you buy a share, you actually become one of the owners. Here's how it works.

Large companies need a great deal of money to operate and grow, and so they seek investors. The investors give them money in exchange for stock certificates that prove they own a certain number of shares. The investors get a share of the profits and the right to make certain decisions about the company. The stock certificates themselves have value, and investors sell their certificates to each other. Every day, huge numbers of stock are bought and sold in the major stock markets of the world.

To watch how the stock certificates change in price, you can read the financial pages of any major newspaper or follow any of the financial channels on TV. Try it. Pick a company and keep track of its price for a month. Pretend that you had bought it on the first day you looked it up, at the price shown that day. What happened to it? Did the price stay steady?

### Get Smart

### Saving Strategies

One way to save money is to set aside a certain percentage of *every bit of money* that comes your way, whether it's from a part-time job or money from a family allowance. If you commit to saving 10 to 20 percent of all money you earn, without exception, you'll be amazed at how quickly it will grow. Put it in a savings account that pays a good rate of interest.

Some people save money by saving all their loose change. Whenever you have coins, just put them in a jar until it's full and then take it to the bank. This is a fairly painless way to save, because generally you won't even miss the small amount of change you set aside each day, but it will mount up over time. People have saved up for vacations to faraway places in this way!

### Your Life

**Stock Exchanges**

Most stocks are bought and sold on one of these major stock exchanges:

* New York Stock Exchange (NYSE).
* NASDAQ (National Association of Securities Dealers Automated Quote system).
* American Stock Exchange (Amex).
* Regional exchanges.

Stock indexes and averages measure and report how the prices of various groups of stock change. Their reports help us know how the economy is doing. The most frequently quoted indexes and averages are:

* *Dow Jones Industrial Average:* provides data on 30 actively traded blue chip stocks, such as industrial corporations, American Express, Walt Disney, and other service firms.
* *Standard and Poor's Composite Index:* rates 500 mostly NYSE-listed companies, along with some Amex and NASDAQ stocks.
* *NASDAQ Composite Index:* includes about 4,700 companies. The NASDAQ originally focused on small companies, but now includes many large, high-technology companies such as Microsoft.
* *Amex Market Value Index:* rates the performance of stocks listed on the American Stock Exchange.

If you sold it on the 10th day, would you have made a little money? How about at the end of the month?

People are interested in both the dividend a company pays (that's the share of profits distributed to investors) and the changing value of the stock.

Many different kinds of things can affect the day-to-day value of a stock, but over the long term, the guide to its value is the performance of the company. So, when you buy a stock, you should know as much as you can about the company. Investors ask these kinds of questions about a company before they invest in it:

* Does it make a product people want and will go on wanting?
* Is it financially strong? Or does it have more debt than it can handle?
* Does it make the kind of profit we expect in this market?
* Are the people at the top of the company honest, reliable, and good at what they do?

To learn the answers to such questions, investors read newspapers and business magazines. They talk to people who know or listen to them on the media. They also use their own good common sense. Some people form investment clubs and share the work of tracking stocks and researching companies. Use the search words "investment clubs" on the Web to find out more about these.

### Bonds

When you buy a **bond**, you are making a loan. (When you buy a stock, you are buying a part of a company.) Corporations, including governments, issue bonds to raise money. A bond is designed to pay a specified rate of interest at the end of a certain period of time. So, for example, you could buy a 10-year $100 bond guaranteed to pay six percent. It would pay six percent a year every year for the 10-year period. If you sold it to someone else, it would pay that person for the remaining years of the term.

Like stocks, investors are interested in both the interest that the bond will pay and its price.

## Government Bonds

Government bonds are issued by federal, state, and local governments as a means of raising money for government projects. Some are safer than others, depending on the financial health of the town or state. U.S. Savings bonds are among the safest securities instruments you can invest in because their value—the price they sell for—cannot change.

## Corporate Bonds

Corporate bonds are bonds issued by corporations. Their prices fluctuate. When interest rates fall, bond prices generally go up. Think about it. If you are holding a bond in a strong company that pays seven percent and the most anyone can get in a bank CD is $5\frac{1}{2}$ percent, wouldn't people want it? Your bond may be worth more than when you bought it.

As with stocks, you need to know the financial health of a company whose bonds interest you. You wouldn't loan money to someone without knowing you had a very good chance of getting it back. There are **two** major corporations that help investors in bonds:

1. Standard & Poor's.
2. Moody's.

These corporations rate bonds from AAA (the highest quality) to D (the bond will not pay any interest). Bonds with the highest ratings sell at the highest prices. You wouldn't be able to get anyone to buy a D-rated bond. It wouldn't be "iffy," it would be a bust!

## Mutual Funds

A <u>mutual fund</u> invests in a number of different tools. It sells you shares in itself. There are many different kinds of funds:

* Stock funds.
* Bond funds.
* Funds that invest only in foreign stocks.
* Funds managed to produce income.
* Funds that are managed to produce growth.

There are several others as well. You can pick a fund for almost any investment purpose you can think of.

The primary reason to purchase shares of a mutual fund is <u>diversification</u>. You don't have all your money in one place. Purchasing fund shares is generally less risky than purchasing individual stocks or bonds. It makes you less likely to lose money when one particular company is not doing well. Most retirement plans invest in mutual funds.

## Working With a Financial Advisor

In the beginning, you will need to make your investments and evaluate your plan by yourself. Over time, you may accumulate enough wealth (think of it, wealth!) to want the services of an investment counselor. When that time comes, he or she will ask you:

* What are your goals? What are you saving for?
* How much money do you have to invest?
* How long can you leave it invested before you want or need to take some of it out?
* Are you a risk-taker? Or are you fairly conservative? What is your comfort level for risk?

As you can see, these are the same questions you must be able to answer when you invest—at any level.

| Mutual Funds | | |
| --- | --- | --- |
| Type | Fund Composition | Characteristics |
| Stock Fund | Group of stocks with similar characteristics: type of product, company size, expectations for growth, high dividends. | Designed to meet investors' goals—growth (long-term) or income now—and level of risk. |
| Bond Fund | Group of bonds of similar corporations, including government corporations. | Like stock funds, but in general are less risky and grow more slowly. |
| Money-Market Fund | Group of financial institutions' plans for paying interest on cash deposits. | Are very safe, provide immediate access to your money, but pay a low return. |
| Mixed or Balanced Fund | Various mixes of stocks, bonds, and money market funds. | Like stock funds, but the greater variety gives the manager more flexibility to meet fund goals. |

## Retirement Plans

Because it is so important to have enough money to be able to retire comfortably, the government has provided tax breaks to corporations and individuals that set aside money for retirement. Some retirement savings plans include:

* Individual retirement accounts (IRAs).
* KEOGH plans.
* Employer-sponsored plans.

## Individual Retirement Accounts (IRAs)

Individual retirement accounts (IRAs) are personal retirement accounts. Some employers offer IRAs as part of their benefits package. However, anyone can open an IRA, even if you already participate in your company's plan. Funds from IRAs may be withdrawn without penalty as early as age 59 but not later than age 70.

If you withdraw funds from this kind of account before age 59, you will be charged a penalty, and the money you withdraw will be taxed as income for that year. There are a few exceptions to this rule.

**EXAMPLE:** You may withdraw money to help buy a first home, but the money must be repaid, usually within a year, to avoid penalties.

There are **two** basic types of IRAs:

* **Tax-deferred.** In these plans, the money you save grows tax-deferred. Tax-deferred means that the money saved will not be taxed until it is withdrawn many years in the future. Also, when an employee leaves a company, he or she may *rollover* the amount of his or her employer-sponsored plan into an IRA to continue saving for retirement. Tax-deferred IRAs include Traditional, SIMPLE, and SEP IRAs.
* **Non tax-deferred.** A Roth IRA is not tax deferred. Some people prefer to pay the taxes now, while they have a job. The benefit is that you pay no taxes when you withdraw the money after retirement, no matter how much interest has accrued.

## KEOGH Plans

KEOGH plans are tax-deferred pension accounts designed for employees of unincorporated businesses or for people who are self-employed, either full or part time. KEOGH assets may be placed in stocks, bonds, money-market funds, certificates of deposit, mutual funds, or limited partnerships. Like IRAs, KEOGH funds grow without being taxed until they are withdrawn as early as age 59, but not later than age 70.

## Search This

### Online Investment Simulation

One way to try your hand at buying and selling stock is to go on the Internet and experiment with some online investment simulations. Playing trading games online will give you a good feeling for how investing works without running the risk of losing any money!

One well known game is called the Stock Market Game. It's run by the education division of the Securities Industry Association. More than 700,000 kids played the game nationally in 1999 and interest in it continues to grow.

Since investing rules vary from state to state, you should go to the web site to find the online address of your state's Stock Market Game.

## Employer-sponsored Plans

Employer-sponsored savings plans are usually available from larger corporations. They are designed to help you save money toward your retirement. Currently, they include:

* **"401(k)" plans:** You can deduct a percentage of your salary to invest for retirement. Often, your employer will also contribute some portion of money to your 401(k) account. Non-profit organizations sometimes offer a similar plan, the 403(b). You can't withdraw money until age 59.
* **Stock ownership:** You can buy discounted stock in the company you work for.
* **Company pension plans:** Your employer puts money away in a variety of pension plans for your retirement.
* **Profit-sharing plans:** You have the opportunity to be paid dividends based on your company's earnings.

### Chapter 30 Wrap-up
#### HOW TO INVEST IN YOUR FUTURE

*Being a wise consumer goes a long way toward establishing your financial health. But planning for the future is also important.*

*The earlier you begin to save money, the faster it will grow, thanks to compound interest. Get in the habit of saving a percentage of your income now. Invest your savings wisely, and you will give yourself a financially secure future.*

**WORDS TO KNOW**

**bond**—interest-bearing instruments issued by government agencies or corporations. You are paid back within a specified period of time at a fixed rate of interest.

**compound interest**—interest paid on both the principal (the original amount invested) and the interest added to it.

**diversification**—reduction of investment risk by investing in several different stocks, bonds, or other securities so you don't have all your money invested in one place.

**Individual Retirement Accounts (IRAs)**—personal retirement accounts.

**invest**—put money in stocks, bonds, or other instruments that will allow it to grow.

**mutual fund**—large grouping of stocks, bonds, options, futures, currencies, or money-market securities managed by investment companies.

**securities**—stock and bond certificates.

**stock**—ownership shares in a company.

Name _____

## 30. How to Invest for Your Future

**After you read the chapter, write an answer to each question below.**

1. How should you save for a short-term and a long-term goal?

   _____
   _____
   _____

2. What are some things a college education can do for you?

   _____
   _____
   _____

3. Before someone invests in a company, there are a number of questions they should ask about that company. Where would someone find the answers to those questions?

   _____
   _____
   _____
   _____

4. What are government bonds, and upon what does their safety depend?

   _____
   _____
   _____

5. Why are traditional Individual Retirement Accounts (IRAs) tax deferred?

   _____
   _____
   _____

Alabama Citizenship Workbook

Name _____

## 30. How to Invest for Your Future

**Circle the best answer for each item.**

1. What are interest-bearing instruments issued by government agencies or corporations? You are paid back within a specified period of time at a fixed rate of interest.

   a. stocks
   b. bonds
   c. value funds
   d. CDs

2. Which term means interest that is earned on the principle and on interest that was earned earlier?

   a. growth funds
   b. diversification
   c. compound interest
   d. securities

3. What is a reduction of investment risk by investing in several different stocks, bonds, or other securities so you don't have all your money invested in one place?

   a. diversification
   b. growth funds
   c. securities
   d. value funds

4. Which of these is composed of riskier companies with potential for fast growth, and may be more or less aggressive?

   a. mutual funds
   b. value funds
   c. growth funds
   d. securities

5. What are personal retirement accounts, usually invested in mutual funds?

   a. Individual Retirement Securities
   b. Individual Retirement Mutual Funds
   c. Individual Retirement Plans
   d. Individual Retirement Accounts

6. Investors give companies money in exchange for _____ that prove they own a certain number of shares.

   a. stock certificates
   b. bonds
   c. bond certificates
   d. mutual funds

7. When you buy a stock, you should know as much as you can about _____.

   a. bonds
   b. mutual funds
   c. value funds
   d. the company

8. When you buy a _____, you are making a loan. When you buy a(n) _____, you are buying a part of a company.

   a. bond/stock
   b. mutual fund/value fund
   c. securities/futures
   d. growth funds/IRAs

9. Corporations rate bonds from _____ (the highest quality) to _____ (the bond will not pay any interest).

   a. AA/C
   b. A/F
   c. AAA/D
   d. BBB/DD

10. The government has provided _____ to corporations and individuals that set aside money for retirement.

    a. benefits
    b. more financial aid
    c. better health care
    d. tax breaks

# Chapter 1

## Review

1. A citizen is one who owes allegiance to a government; is entitled to government protection in exchange for that allegiance; and has certain rights, privileges, and responsibilities that come with citizenship.
2. The person must be: at least 18 years old; a lawful, permanent U.S. resident for five years (if not married to a citizen of at least three years); willing to swear loyalty to the U.S.; of good moral character; able to read, write, and speak simple English; and knowledgeable about U.S. government and history.
3. Besides establishing and organizing the policies, laws, and rules of a society, governments seek to protect and maintain the nation's security, law and order, public services, and other institutions necessary for the good of the society.
4. They protect the rights of citizens to a speedy and public trial; to have an attorney when accused of a crime; to have witnesses testify in court; to trial by jury in specific cases; and to protection from cruel punishment.

## Critical Thinking

1. Answers will vary, but responses should include examples both from the text and from their own experiences.
2. Some will assert that the native citizens' loyalty comes from their sense of home and lifelong identities as Americans. Naturalized citizens may value their citizenship because they've had to struggle to attain it.
3. Answers will vary, but students should give concrete reasons for their positions instead of supporting them with opinions. Encourage students to think about what life would be like for them without access to schooling and health care.
4. Though people would be free from constraints of law in anarchy, there would be no government to establish and maintain order. Social chaos and disorder would result, and daily life would become more dangerous and unpredictable. The economy would become corrupted, and armed militarism would arise to impose order and/or exploit the weak.
5. Answers will vary, but should be supported with concrete examples from their history studies and from the text. Students who say that citizens do not participate fully may cite racism and religious persecution as examples.

## Study Guide

1. Citizenship is similar to a contract or agreement in that citizens pledge their loyalty and assume certain responsibilities to the country in exchange for protection and certain rights and freedoms.
2. Most will prefer a monarchy because they're more likely to have basic rights and security than under a power-hungry, controlling dictatorship.
3. The "American Dream" is a common ideal or vision that unites all Americans. To many, it means having the freedom and opportunity, for example, to go to college, own a home, or become a public leader.
4. Answers will vary. Centuries of immigration have made America's population more and more racially diverse. Whites, blacks, Asians, Hispanics, and a variety of other ethnic groups in the U.S. continue to evolve and add color, depth, strength, and diversity to the nation's culture.
5. Duties that come from citizenship include: obeying government laws, defending the nation, paying taxes, serving on a jury, and attending school. Our responsibilities include: protecting each other's rights, voting, and helping to make society better.

## Vocabulary

Answers: 1. b, 2. b, 3. a, 4. d, 5. c, 6. a, 7. c, 8. d, 9. d, 10. a.

## Multiple Choice

Answers: 1. a, 2. d, 3. a, 4. d, 5. b, 6. c, 7. d, 8. c, 9. b, 10. c.

## Essay Question

Answers will vary. Students may point out that they are being good citizens by attending school and obeying laws. They should also note that they are too young to fulfill the obligations of paying taxes and defending their nation.

### Multiple Choice

1. d, 2. c, 3. d, 4. b, 5. c

Alabama Citizenship Workbook 231

# Chapter 2

## Review

1. They were (1) signing of the Magna Carta, (2) development of the English Bill of Rights, (3) development of England's unwritten constitution, and (4) use of common law.
2. They were (1) the right to vote, (2) freedom of religion, and (3) freedom of the press.
3. They were (1) the Boston Port Bill, (2) the Massachusetts Government Act, (3) the Administration of Justice Act, and (4) the Quartering Act.
4. (1) It had no taxation power; (2) it created no national court; (3) the states used different currencies; (4) there was no executive; (5) interstate commerce was not regulated; and (6) each state had veto power on amendments.

## Critical Thinking

1. Answers will vary. Students should suggest qualities of intelligence, honesty, etc. They should also give concrete examples of why they would want a representative to follow conscience or do as the voters wish. Encourage them to see the other side of the argument as well.
2. One view is that written constitutions made it very clear how the new governmental bodies were formed, how they functioned, and what powers they assumed—particularly in relation to citizens. Planning the government in writing also limited the kinds of abuses that could take place.
3. The only basic rights offered in many of the colonies were the right to vote and the freedoms of religion and the press. Since only male landowners could vote, most women could only exercise their religious beliefs without persecution in most regions and freely speak their minds in person or in print after 1735—if they were bold enough to do so in this male-dominated era.
4. The Boston Tea Party was a colorful act of defiance against English rule that triggered the Intolerable Acts, which unified the colonies and led to the Revolution.
5. Students should select examples from the colonial and Revolutionary periods that demonstrate the fear that the new nation would overwhelm the states and result in a government even worse than British rule.

## Study Guide

1. The direct democracy developed in ancient Greece was a system of government in which citizens voted directly for the laws they followed. In the ancient Roman republic, citizens elected representatives who convened in a legislature to make the rules and laws.
2. The advantages of a republic are: workability—it works for a large, widespread population; accountability—citizens only reelect effective, lawmaking representatives; expertise—citizens can elect well educated representatives, not just heirs in ruling families; participation—citizens take part in the system by voting and influencing leaders; and, leadership—citizens can work to become representatives themselves, if they so desire.
3. The Mayflower Compact of 1620—a governing plan for the Massachusetts colony—followed the Greek traditions of direct democracy and majority agreement in making laws. The House of Burgesses influenced the founders to establish a representative system of government that met to debate issues, make laws, and pass taxes.
4. Colonists reacted by protesting and petitioning, boycotting British goods, forming *Committees of Correspondence* to share information, and *Sons of Liberty* associations to frighten British officials.
5. Jefferson wrote the Declaration in three parts: (1) beliefs about government, including the social concept, (2) a list of grievances showing how the British king violated the social contract, and (3) a formal declaration stating that the colonies were now independent from Britain.

## Vocabulary

Answers: 1. d, 2. b, 3. a, 4. b, 5. d, 6. b, 7. c, 8. a, 9. d, 10. c.

## Multiple Choice

Answers: 1. a, 2. c, 3. a, 4. b, 5. b, 6. a, 7. b, 8. d, 9. b, 10. b.

## Essay Question

Answers will vary, but students should mention the principles of representation, having a voice in government, and valuing freedom. Encourage class discussion on this topic.

> **Short Answer:**
> The Founders of the U. S. Constitution were influence by John Locke's belief that human beings have "unalienable rights" that should not be threatened or taken away. These basic rights were spelled out as a basis for the writing of the U. S. Constitution.

# Chapter 3

## Review

1. They were (1) one state, one vote, (2) majority decides, and (3) keep the proceedings secret.
2. They were (1) popular sovereignty, (2) limited government, (3) federalism, (4) separation of powers, and (5) checks and balances.
3. They are (1) the legislative branch, (2) the executive branch, and (3) the judicial branch.
4. They are (1) to form a more perfect union, (2) to establish justice, (3) to ensure domestic tranquility or peace, (4) to provide for the common defense, (5) to promote the general welfare, and (6) to secure the blessings of liberty.

## Critical Thinking

1. Answers will vary. One view is that, had the public or press been informed of the kinds of issues and sacrifices the founders were considering, there would have been much less cooperation and compromise and much more strife and public posturing. A constitution would clearly have taken longer to create and perhaps the result would have been one that was not as well considered or effective.
2. Answers will vary. If a national legislature were based on proportional representation, in which each state's number of voting representatives is based on state populations, smaller states would have fewer votes and less power than larger states.
3. Answers will vary. Students may note that it was fair to count slaves for tax purposes, but may note that it was unfair to count them as people who would be represented in the government without the ability to vote and without being citizens.
4. Answers will vary, but students should note that a civil war would have been very likely.
5. Answers will vary. Encourage students to cite legal examples from their text rather than giving an opinion.

## Study Guide

1. The Virginia Plan was favored by the nationalists, who wanted a stronger central government and representation based on state populations. By contrast, the New Jersey Plan was favored by the confederationists, who sought to limit the central government's powers over the states and favored one-vote representation for all states.
2. The Great Compromise proposed a national Congress with both proportional and equal representation; that each state would elect representatives to the House of Representatives based on state populations; and that each state legislature would elect two people to represent its state in the Senate.
3. The Constitution is based on the principle of popular sovereignty, by which the people set the rules and give their consent to be governed. Similarly, as clearly spelled out in Article 1, the government has limited power to rule the people, who themselves have citizens' rights. The powers of governmental groups are limited further by the shared division of authority between state and federal governments. The federal government was divided into three branches and put under a system of checks and balances in order to further limit the authority of each.
4. The seven Articles, as listed in the Constitution, establish or have to deal with: (1) the legislative branch; (2) the executive branch; (3) the judicial branch; (4) relations among states; (5) amending the Constitution; (6) debts, federal supremacy, and oaths of office; and (7) ratifying the Constitution.
5. (1) Two-thirds of the members of Congress must vote to propose an amendment, or (2) two-thirds of state legislatures must vote to ask Congress to hold a special convention. For states to ratify an amendment, either (1) two-thirds of state legislators vote to approve it, or (2) three-fourths of states' conventions vote to approve the measure.

## Vocabulary

Answers: **1.** b, **2.** a, **3.** d, **4.** c, **5.** a, **6.** b, **7.** b, **8.** c, **9.** d, **10.** d.

## Multiple Choice

Answers: **1.** d, **2.** a, **3.** c, **4.** b, **5.** d, **6.** d, **7.** c, **8.** a, **9.** c, **10.** c.

## Essay Question

Answers will vary. Some will mention the Three Fifths Compromise as shortsighted, as well as the lack of an enumeration of freedoms, which was swiftly addressed by the Bill of Rights.

# Chapter 4

## Review
1. They are the Freedoms of (1) Religion, (2) Speech, (3) the Press, (4) Assembly, and (5) Petition.
2. They are (1) indictment by a grand jury, (2) protection against double jeopardy, (3) protection against self-incrimination, (4) due process of law, and (5) protection in cases of eminent domain.
3. People accused of crimes have the right to (1) know the nature of the charges, (2) know the witnesses, (3) a speedy public trial and impartial jury, and (4) a lawyer.
4. They are (1) protection against excessive bail, and (2) protection against cruel and unusual punishment.

## Critical Thinking
1. Answers will vary. Students should demonstrate knowledge of the various freedoms guaranteed by the Bill of Rights.
2. Answers will vary. Students should support their opinions with observations on the importance of the freedoms guaranteed by their chosen amendment.
3. Students may draw from their own experiences, but should demonstrate knowledge of both sides of the debate, and should note why church and state were expressly separated by our government.
4. Freedom of the press helps to keep government corruption at a minimum because media reporters have the right to investigate and publicize any possible wrongdoing. Other governments that lack this important freedom usually provide their citizens with only "official" news reports and are often riddled with corruption that goes unchecked.
5. Answers will vary. Students should discuss the effectiveness of background checks, registration, and a limit on the amount of weapons a person can own.

## Study Guide
1. Under the Declaration, people were ensured their rights to life, liberty, and the pursuit of happiness and safety. Other rights included the right of people accused of a crime to know who their accusers are; the right to trial by jury; and the freedom of press and religion.
2. The rights and freedoms extended in the Bill of Rights ensure that people are able to make informed decisions, which is critical to the success of a democracy. In order to do this, people need to have the freedom to attain reliable information, discuss their ideas freely, and communicate their ideas with their elected officials to improve our laws and systems on an ongoing basis.
3. People may be stopped from expressing their right to free speech when it involves: (1) slander, where lies are told to insure someone's reputation; (2) creating false panics in public; (3) encouraging riots or destroying property; and or (4) committing treason.
4. The Fourth Amendment prohibits authorities from (1) entering and searching a person's home without reason; (2) unreasonably taking a person's property, and (3) seizing or arresting a person without just cause.
5. The Ninth Amendment declares that people have rights beyond those mentioned in the Constitution. Though unlisted in the Constitution, all Americans are ensured other rights and freedoms like deciding: (1) where to live, (2) which school to attend, (3) which job to take, (4) whether to get married and have children, and (5) where to travel.

## Vocabulary
Answers: **1.** d, **2.** c, **3.** a, **4.** b, **5.** a, **6.** b, **7.** a, **8.** c, **9.** d, **10.** d.

## Multiple Choice
Answers: **1.** b, **2.** a, **3.** a, **4.** c, **5.** b, **6.** d, **7.** c, **8.** d, **9.** a, **10.** c.

## Essay Question
Answers will vary, but students should cite the freedoms that the Bill of Rights gives them, now and as adults.

# Chapter 5

## Review

1. The three parts include: (1) granting citizenship to anyone born in the U.S. or naturalized as a citizen, (2) ensuring due process of law for all citizens against state abuses, and (3) ensuring that states grant their citizens equal protection of the laws.
2. Among the many key suffragist leaders were Elizabeth Cady Stanton, Susan B. Anthony, Sojourner Truth, Lucy Stone, Mary Church Terrell, and Jeannette Rankin.
3. The legislation (1) guaranteed equal access to public places, (2) disallowed unfair voter registration practices, (3) challenged employers over discrimination in hiring, and (4) demanded that schools, unions, and employers that receive federal money stop discrimination.
4. They include: (1) senior citizens being allowed to work beyond the age of 65; (2) disabled people gaining access to public places; (3) female athletes gaining the right to participate in school sports; (4) Hispanics being taught in bilingual classrooms; and (5) limiting the practice of racial profiling by those in law enforcement.

## Critical Thinking

1. Answers will vary. Students may cite initiatives to give more people jobs, to help the homeless find housing, or to increase food subsidies to the needy.
2. Answers will vary. Students should support their response with facts rather than opinions.
3. Answers will vary. Many will assert that the states would divide into two countries, a free North and a slave South. War would likely result over territorial and asset claims. As a result, America as we know it today would not be the same.
4. Answers will vary, though most students will likely say that this amendment will never pass due to corporate influence in Washington.
5. Answers will vary. Students should use facts, not prejudice or hearsay, to support their views.

## Study Guide

1. Answers will vary. Among the key changes were: abolishing slavery; allowing women, young adults, and former slaves the right to vote; repealing the prohibition of liquor; abolishing poll taxes; and setting two-term limits for presidents.
2. The Northwest Ordinance banned slavery in this new region, but ensured that slaves who escaped there were returned. The Missouri Compromise maintained the balance between free and slave states by admitting Missouri (slave) and Maine (free) to the Union. The Supreme Court's Dred Scott decision ruled that Congress had no power to limit slavery in the territories and that slaves had no rights.
3. The Thirteenth Amendment (1865) abolished slavery in the U.S. The Fourteenth Amendment (1868) gave citizenship and civil rights to all citizens, including former slaves. The Fifteenth Amendment (1870) gave all citizens voting rights. Despite these changes, it would take a long time for equality to be enforced in the South.
4. Answers will vary. Though women had gained the right to vote in 10 states by 1914, they were not granted this right under the Constitution. Early suffragists like Elizabeth Cady Stanton and Susan B. Anthony helped to create an organized national movement to draw attention to their cause. Congress granted them the right to vote in 1920 under the Nineteenth Amendment.
5. Among the many key moments of the Civil Rights movement were: (1) Rosa Parks' 1955 arrest for sitting in the white section of an Alabama bus, (2) Martin Luther King, Jr.'s, efforts to boycott the Montgomery buses and, in 1963, his "I Have a Dream" speech in Washington, D.C.; and (3) the passing of the Civil Rights Act of 1964.

## Vocabulary

Answers: 1. a, 2. b, 3. d, 4. c, 5. a, 6. c, 7. b, 8. c, 9. d, 10. c.

## Multiple Choice

Answers: 1. d, 2. a, 3. d, 4. b, 5. c, 6. a, 7. d, 8. b, 9. d, 10. a.

## Essay Question

While our political process invites many groups and individuals to attempt to shape policy, the process is slow, in part to weed out laws which would not be workable. In the cases mentioned above, it took time to convince lawmakers that a majority of the population supported these amendments.

# Chapter 6

## Review
1. They are governed by: Article I of the Constitution; parliamentary procedure; the *House Rules and Manual*; the *Senate Manual*; precedents and past rulings; and specific laws.
2. The four types of congressional committees are (1) standing, (2) joint, (3) select, and (4) conference.
3. They (1) research subjects and hold hearings to get expert testimony, (2) write legislation related to their specific subject areas, and (3) decide whether to send legislation to the chamber for a vote.
4. Congress cannot (1) pass ex post facto laws, (2) pass bills of attainder, or (3) take away a prisoner's right to a writ of habeas corpus except during periods of civil war or invasion.

## Critical Thinking
1. Answers will vary. Students should demonstrate knowledge of both sides of the debate and observations on how citizen interests are best served.
2. Answers will vary. Students should demonstrate knowledge of the duties and responsibilities of a congressman or senator.
3. Answers will vary. Students should demonstrate awareness of the system of proportional representation, presenting thoughtful commentary on its merits and/or complications.
4. Answers will vary. Students should discuss the role of special interest groups in the election process.
5. Answers will vary. Students should demonstrate knowledge of the legislative process and present commentary on the protections and difficulties the system accords.

## Study Guide
1. The 435+ members of the House serve two-year terms and represent their districts in Congress. Representatives must be at least 25 years old, a citizen for at least seven years, and be a resident of the state. The 100 members of the Senate serve six-year terms to represent their states. Senators must be at least 30 years old, citizens for at least nine years, and be residents of the state.
2. While both houses of Congress do the same work in weighing issues and passing laws, the House is more strict and formal because of its larger size. House members are usually limited to five minutes or less of speaking time, as compared to more unlimited debate times for Senators.
3. In the House of Representatives, the Speaker of the House is the highest officer and is elected by members to run the chamber. The Senate's leader is the Vice President who, when unavailable, is replaced by the president pro tempore. Both houses are made up of majority and minority parties, which have floor leaders who set priorities on the kinds of laws their parties want to pass, and party whips who assist floor leaders in getting party members to help pass their prioritized laws.
4. Congress derives its powers from Article I of the Constitution and from specific amendments. These powers break down into "expressed" powers (collecting taxes, declaring war) and unwritten "implied" powers from the Elastic Clause of Section 8, which gives Congress the expanded powers make laws necessary to carry out its duties.
5. First, a bill needs to be introduced in the House or Senate. If first introduced into the House, it then is sent for further study before it could be debated and passed by the House. A passed bill needs to be introduced to the Senate, where it is sent to committee and debated before being passed and sent to a conference committee to unify both versions of the bill passed in Congress. The new bill that results undergoes a final vote by Congress before being sent on to the President for final, signed approval. The bill then becomes a law.

## Vocabulary
Answers: 1. b, 2. c, 3. b, 4. a, 5. b, 6. d, 7. a, 8. b, 9. b, 10. d.

## Multiple Choice
Answers: 1. b, 2. c, 3. b, 4. d, 5. a, 6. d, 7. a, 8. d, 9. c, 10. b.

## Essay Question
Answers will vary. Student responses should note both the speed with which some legislation can be passed and the slowness of most other bills. They should also note the small percentage of bills presented which become law.

# Chapter 7

## Review
1. They are: (1) transportation on the president's private jet, (2) Secret Service protection, (3) free housing in the White House, and (4) a pension after retirement.
2. They are to (1) replace the president if he dies or becomes disabled and (2) preside, or officiate, over the Senate. The vice president does not vote in the Senate unless there is a tie vote.
3. It would be (1) the Speaker of the House of Representatives, (2) the President pro tempore of the Senate, (3) the Secretary of State, and (4) the rest of the Cabinet members.
4. They are to (1) veto bills passed by Congress, (2) command the military forces of the country, (3) make treaties, (4) grant pardons, (5) enforce laws, and (6) appoint certain officials.

## Critical Thinking
1. Answers will vary, but are likely to include: college education or a military background, honesty, and integrity.
2. Answers will vary. Every state has a certain number of electoral votes, and typically all electoral votes from each state, except Maine and Nebraska, go to the candidates who get the most popular votes even if those candidates only win by a few votes or lack a clear majority of votes.
3. Answers will vary. Congress can (1) approve or reject programs or laws that the president recommends, (2) enact a law that the president has vetoed by a two-thirds vote of both houses, (3) set guidelines for how the president and the executive branch can implement policies, and (4) create or eliminate departments that the executive branch runs. They can also approve the people the president appoints.
4. Answers will vary by student, but should include concrete reasons for their choice.
5. Answers will vary. Students should demonstrate an awareness of the duties and responsibilities of the president, discussing the positive and negative aspects of holding such an important position.

## Study Guide
1. Bureaucracies resemble a pyramid. The president is at the top, senior managers and advisors are in the middle, and the millions of other employees are at the base. They have specific duties. They have rules so they can provide the same service, the same way, everywhere.
2. They are executive power, emergency powers, budgetary powers, and policy-making powers.
3. They've claimed it about military and diplomatic actions, arguing that the national security and the safety of the country required them to keep some things secret. It does not apply if a court requests evidence in an investigation or trial. The president must obey the court's request.
4. Among the most important are: National Aeronautics and Space Administration (NASA), the Environmental Protection Agency (EPA), the Civil Rights Commission, and the Peace Corps.
5. It is in charge of the nation's money. The Internal Revenue Service collects taxes. The U.S. Customs Service collects duties on goods entering the country and works to prevent smuggling. The Bureau of Engraving and Printing makes the country's paper money and coins. The Secret Service—which protects the president, vice president, and visiting foreign leaders—is part of the department.

## Vocabulary
Answers: 1. c, 2. b, 3. a, 4. c, 5. a, 6. d, 7. a, 8. b, 9. c, 10. d.

## Multiple Choice
Answers: 1. a, 2. b, 3. d, 4. b, 5. c, 6. c, 7. d, 8. a, 9. c, 10. b.

## Essay Question
Answers will vary. Students may suggest that coming to a consensus is easier if there is one person in charge instead of several. One person can make quicker decisions. This may or may not always be a good thing. One person can also ignore one viewpoint and act strictly on his own.

Alabama Citizenship Workbook

# Chapter 8

## Review
1. Federal judges are appointed for life and can only be removed through impeachment. The salaries of federal judges cannot be reduced by a president or Congress.
2. They are: bench trials where only a judge hears and decides the case, and jury trials where outcomes are decided by citizens.
3. They are: submit briefs and make oral arguments.
4. They are: (1) majority opinion, (2) concurring opinion, and (3) dissenting opinion.

## Critical Thinking
1. Answers will vary, but should note that the judicial branch must be free from the influence of the other branches in order to render fair and impartial decisions.
2. Answers will vary. People nominated are usually successful private industry figures or government lawyers, state court judges, magistrate or bankruptcy judges, or law professors.
3. Answers will vary. Students should demonstrate general knowledge of the duties of a Supreme Court justice and the system by which they are appointed, commenting on the difficulties that arise with respect to party politics, as well as the advantages unlimited terms for Court justices.
4. Answers will vary. Arguments for mandatory sentencing say for repeat offenders, "three strikes; you're out." Another argument is that judges are too lenient. Arguments against mandatory punishment say: Situations are unique. Should a 16-year-old acting as a lookout get life in prison because his older friend shot a police officer?
5. Answers will vary. Students should cite an example from the text and back it up with fact.

## Study Guide
1. Congress makes the laws. The president and the executive branch implement the laws. The federal courts say what the law means and say how the law applies to the facts in a particular dispute.
2. The president nominates people to become federal judges. The Senate must confirm anyone whom the president nominates to be a federal judge. The House can impeach judges and justices. Congress creates federal courts (other than the Supreme Court) and decides how many judges those courts need. Congress decides which types of cases the federal courts will hear and can amend the Constitution, with the approval of the states, to reverse a judicial ruling.
3. A person making an appeal usually asks the appeals court to review the process by which the trial was conducted, or how the law itself was applied. A three-judge panel reviews a transcript of the prior court's proceedings; listens to arguments from attorneys for both sides; and decides whether to uphold the trial judge's ruling, dismiss the case, or send the case back to the trial court so that it can be conducted properly. If a case is considered very important, all 12 judges will hear the case and make a ruling.
4. When any four justices feel a case is important enough for the Supreme Court to address, that case is added to the list of cases to be considered during that term, or session.
5. Justices who believe the Court should take an active role in policy-making and Constitutional interpretation are called judicial activists. They tend to interpret the Constitutional and federal laws broadly to achieve certain results. Justices who tend toward judicial restraint believe that policy decisions should be left to Congress and the president, not to the Court.

## Vocabulary
Answers: 1. c, 2. a, 3. d, 4. b, 5. c, 6. a, 7. d, 8. a, 9. b, 10. b.

## Multiple Choice
Answers: 1. b, 2. d, 3. c, 4. b, 5. a, 6. d, 7. c, 8. b, 9. c, 10. a.

## Essay Question
Answers will vary. Students may cite personal examples if they have any, but will likely cite famous court cases in their responses.

# Chapter 9

## Review
1. They are to (1) protect the states from foreign invasion with military action, (2) deal with foreign governments in issues of trade or disputes, (3) produce money used throughout the United States, and (4) make laws about the movement of goods and people between states.
2. They are (1) holding elections, (2) providing education, (3) regulating businesses, (4) passing laws that govern people's actions, and (5) providing and maintaining police forces, public buildings, and roads and highways.
3. They are (1) appropriations, (2) economic development, (3) commerce, (4) education, (5) natural resources, and (6) transportation.
4. They are (1) state board of education, (2) department of human services, (3) commerce department, (4) department of natural resources, and (5) transportation department.

## Critical Thinking
1. Answers will vary. In many states, symbols are nominated and voted on by school children.
2. Answers will vary. Some students may suggest that term limits keep fresh perspectives in our government, while others may suggest that long-term incumbents know their constituents better than any newcomer could.
3. Anarchy would b e the result. Students may suggest that rioting and looting would be rampant, schools would not exist, and life as they know it would cease to be.
4. Answers will vary. Citizens can propose a new law through this process starting a bill on their own. They ask voters to sign a petition to show their agreement. If the required number of voters signs the petition, it becomes a proposition or proposed law.
5. Students may suggest that those who came of age after the civil rights movement are just now becoming old enough to reach the level of governor. Prior to the civil rights movement, African Americans were not active in government in a way that would lead to high-level positions in state government.

## Study Guide
1. They are working together on projects, such as building or improving roads and bridges; providing support for poor people in the form of welfare services, such as food or health care that people get free or for a reduced cost; and taxing citizens to get money needed to pay for services.
2. Standing, or permanent, committees discuss bills dealing with ongoing issues, such as appropriations, economic development, commerce, education, natural resources and transportation. Interim, or temporary, committees are appointed to discuss short-term issues. For example, Iowa has used interim committees to study e-commerce, parking near the capitol building, and distance learning.
3. The governor often acts as the spokesperson for the state's goals and values. Some duties are ceremonial, such as awarding medals for heroism. The governor also meets with governors of other states to solve common problems.
4. The lieutenant governor presides over the senate and succeeds to governorship if the governor can't perform the duties of the office. The secretary of state supervises elections and is in charge of state records such as business licenses, births, deaths, and marriages.
5. State courts deal with everything from petty theft to cases involving the death penalty. Each type of court handles cases of a particular type or seriousness. Not all states are the same, but many state court systems include: State Supreme Court, Appeals Courts, General Trial Courts, and Lower Courts.

## Vocabulary
Answers: 1. c, 2. a, 3. b, 4. d, 5. c, 6. b, 7. b, 8. a, 9. d, 10. c.

## Multiple Choice
Answers: 1. b, 2. c, 3. b, 4. a, 5. d, 6. c, 7. b, 8. b, 9. c, 10. a.

## Essay Question
Answers will vary but should reflect a clear understanding of how state courts function.

### Short answer:
1. The executive branch, legislative branch, and judicial branch
2. This new foundation for Alabama's government didn't allow the state to engage in internal improvements. It also imposed suffrage on blacks, and power was limited to the white prperty owners and industrialists.

### Multiple Choice:
1. d, 2. a, 3. b, 4. b, 5. b, 6. c, 7. d, 8. b

# Chapter 10

## Review

1. They are (1) education, (2) public safety, (3) health and welfare, (4) environment and housing, (5) land use, and (6) utilities.
2. They are (1) the mayor-council plan, (2) the council-manager plan, and (3) the commission plan.
3. They are (1) commission, (2) commission-administrator, and (3) council-executive.
4. They are (1) water districts, (2) fire districts, (3) park districts, (4) library districts (5) insect control districts, and (6) metropolitan transit districts (for public transportation).

## Critical Thinking

1. Answers will vary. Many students will say that they didn't think about where those services came from before reading this chapter.
2. Answers will vary.
3. Answers will vary. The case was about a student who got caught smoking at school and the assistant principal searched her purse and found cigarettes and evidence of drug dealing. The family sued for unlawful search and the first court case found for the student. The appeal to the Supreme Court found the student's rights were not violated.
4. Answers will vary. Some of the arguments for limiting growth are: protecting the small-town quality of life, preserves green space, and keeps home prices low. Arguments against it are: improving the economy, that a real estate boom would benefit sellers, and higher tax revenues for more town services.
5. Answers will vary. Students should exhibit knowledge of some of the services for which tax money is allotted.

## Study Guide

1. They are city governments; county governments; town, township, and village governments; and special districts.
2. The charter form means that local government writes a charter to be approved by the state. This charter outlines the principles, functions, and organization of a local government. It serves as the government's "constitution" and defines the rights and powers of local government. The optional form means the state government provides specific choices of structures for local government, such as the council-manager form or the mayor-council form. Home rule does not give the local government absolute authority. The government will always be affected by state law.
3. English colonists established the county form of government when they came to America. Colonies were divided into counties to help carry out laws in rural areas.
4. It is known as the special district, units of local, special-purpose government set up to operate within specific limits. These are created to provide specific services to citizens that existing local governments do not provide.
5. Some metropolitan areas combine: the city government adds on or incorporates the suburbs. The entire area is governed as a whole by the city government. They cooperate: the city government handles problems affecting the entire metropolitan area and the individual government within the area deals with local issues.

## Vocabulary

Answers: 1. d, 2. c, 3. a, 4. b, 5. c, 6. d, 7. b, 8. a, 9. c, 10. b.

## Multiple Choice

Answers: 1. c, 2. b, 3. d, 4. a, 5. b, 6. c, 7. a, 8. c, 9. b, 10. a.

## Essay Question

Answers will vary. Students may suggest unlikely services like free ice cream, and no taxes to fund it.

# Chapter 11

## Review
1. They are: (1) choose and support candidates, (2) work to win elections, (3) act as watchdogs, (4) set policy, (5) communicate information, (6) lobby, and (7) provide leadership.
2. They are the following: (1) party loyalty is weaker, (2) there are more independent voters, and (3) more elections are nonpartisan.
3. They are: (1) direct mail campaigns; (2) bumper stickers, buttons, and posters; (3) fliers or small brochures; (4) speeches, political rallies, and personal appearances; (5) press conferences; (6) debates; and (7) television, radio, newspapers, magazines, and the Internet.
4. They include: (1) individual citizens, (2) political action committees (PACs), (3) Democratic and Republican national and state committees, and (4) the candidate.

## Critical Thinking
1. Answers will vary. Students should cite several examples where politicians supported or did not support their views.
2. Answers will vary. The chart depicts the 2000 Democratic and Republican sides of education reform.
3. Answers will vary. Among other arguments are the following. Those in favor of campaign finance reform believe that these groups are trying to buy the influence of the candidate. Those against it feel that that all groups have a right to express their opinions in a democracy.
4. Answers will vary. Some people don't vote because they feel their government is not effective; some don't trust the candidates; and some are turned off by negative campaigns and fighting.
5. Answers will vary. Some students will suggest it is a fair system, while others may say that it takes the power to elect the president away from the people and eliminates the principle of one citizen, one vote.

## Study Guide
1. They decide which issues are important, how to deal with those issues for the public good, which candidates and lawmakers should represent their views, how elected lawmakers should support the party's vision, and what laws should be proposed and passed.
2. First, they've influenced the outcome of elections. They can draw votes away from one major party, giving an advantage to the competing party. Second, they raise important issues. Many minor parties have been formed to support specific issues. Third, they get candidates elected to office.
3. In self-nomination, a person can declare that they are running for office in most local campaigns. Caucus (or meeting of party members) is sometimes used to select candidates and decide on policies. In a write-in, voters can write any name on a ballot in any election. A nominating petition is used in many places where a person needs a certain number of voter signatures on a petition. In a convention, some are chosen by vote of party members or delegates at a party meeting.
4. In a closed primary, voters must be registered as party members to vote in that party's primary. In an open primary, citizens can vote in either party's primary without stating their party affiliations.
5. You must be an American citizen, at least 18 years old, and a resident of the state in which you vote.

## Vocabulary
Answers: 1. d, 2. b, 3. a, 4. c, 5. b, 6. a, 7. d, 8. c, 9. d, 10. b.

## Multiple Choice
Answers: 1. c, 2. b, 3. c, 4. d, 5. b, 6. d, 7. a, 8. d, 9. a, 10. c.

## Essay Question
Answers will vary, but students will likely cite their parents as a big influence in their decision to choose one party or another.

# Chapter 12

## Review
1. They are (1) your family, (2) the schools, (3) your religion, (4) molders of public opinion, and (5) the mass media.
2. They are (1) how strongly people feel about an issue, (2) what people really want and need, (3) how public opinion is changing, and (4) how much the public is divided or unified in their feelings about an issue.
3. They are (1) forming small and large groups, (2) organizing, (3) operating, and (4) influencing and electing.
4. They are the facts that (1) they make issues known, (2) they help group members, (3) they support candidates, and (4) they use the courts.

## Critical Thinking
1. Answers will vary. The issues listed are the following? Should college athletes get paid? Is the president doing a good job? Should people be able to copy music from the Internet for free?
2. Answers will vary. Students may include mention of the fact that propaganda techniques often prevent the public from knowing all the facts of an issue because they are being hidden or skewed by propaganda techniques such as exaggeration and fear tactics.
3. Answers will vary. Students should exhibit an awareness of both sides of the issue. Voters deserve to know as much about a candidate as possible so that they are able to make a wise and informed decision. It is difficult, however, to find a person who hasn't made some mistakes. The risk of having their life exposed may prevent qualified people from running for office.
4. Answers will vary. Students should demonstrate a knowledge of some influential special interest groups (listed on pages 202–203) and how they operate.
5. Answers will vary. SADD mentions drug and alcohol use, underage drinking, impaired driving, and other health or life-endangering decisions.

## Study Guide
1. Governments, large businesses, and many other institutions today have public relations advisors who help them manage communications with the media. Some of them create spin—ways of talking about an organization's response to an issue that deliberately make the response appear positive in the media.
2. They are: region of the country, state, eligible voters, registered voters, likely voters, and ethnic and racial groups.
3. Special interest groups are organizations whose members share common concerns and who try to influence others to agree with them. Lobbyists are paid or unpaid professionals used by interest groups to try to influence the way legislators vote.
4. Grassroots campaigns go directly to the public by urging members and other citizens to write to their representatives or senators about issues coming up for a vote. They also send informational mailings to non-members, explaining their side of the issue.
5. They fear that they have too much wealth, power, and political influence; that they can corrupt individual politicians; and that they improperly impact voter choice and the democratic political process.

## Vocabulary
Answers: 1. b, 2. a, 3. b, 4. c, 5. d, 6. c, 7. b, 8. a, 9. c, 10. d.

## Multiple Choice
Answers: 1. a, 2. c, 3. b, 4. b, 5. d, 6. a, 7. c, 8. d, 9. b, 10. a.

## Essay Question
Answers will vary. Students may note that ordinary people have fewer opportunities to interact with legislators than corporations and lobbyists do. Suggestions may deal with how to change that situation.

# Chapter 13

## Review
1. The four main reasons we need laws are to keep order, to ensure safety, to protect property, and to protect freedoms.
2. The four main characteristics of good laws is that they should be fair, as in treating all offenders equally for the same offence; reasonable in that they make sense to people; understandable in terms of knowing what one must do and not do; and be enforceable (i.e., making people obey) by law enforcement personnel.
3. Unlike criminal law, civil law holds that (1) the impact of an action is limited to an individual, not society; (2) that in most cases the individuals and their lawyers should solve their dispute (mostly without a judge); and (3) that a guilty party should not be punished by imprisonment, but by paying fines.
4. Constitutional law is based on the Constitution of the United States of America. It ensures that (1) the federal branches of government will remain balanced; (2) power will be properly divided between federal and state governments; and (3) the individual rights of citizens will be protected.

## Critical Thinking
1. Answers will vary. Students should defend their opinions with fact.
2. Sometimes citizens who believe a law is unjust practice civil disobedience—the breaking of a law to express their opposition to it. By doing so they hope to draw attention to their view in hopes that the law to be changed.
3. For many people, moral laws are the basic beliefs that determine good and bad personal behavior—or the basic difference between right and wrong. Many people agree that, for example, murder is wrong and that charity is helpful, so laws that reflect those universal beliefs are generally considered fair and correct.
4. Paying taxes provides money for the government to use for the common good of society. It pays for things like military protection, Social Security for those who can't work, public parks, and the like. Such things make life safer and better for society.
5. Answers will vary. Some will see Ali's action as brave, while others will characterize it as cowardly.

## Study Guide
1. Protected property includes (1) something you can touch, (2) something you create, and (3) the right to do something. Something you can touch includes physical property like an automobile or pet; something created could be a song or story; the right to do something would include the right to live on rented property or occupy a paid seat at a baseball game.
2. Copyright law protects a copyright-holder's original works. The holder of a copyright has the exclusive right to reproduce the work, distribute it, and perform or display it in public.
3. Minors who commit offenses are often treated differently than an adult would be treated. This is because the law assumes that minors are less aware of, and able to take responsibility for, their actions. Students should offer and support their views.
4. Answers will vary, though most students will note that the system seems extremely harsh when compared to modern U.S. laws.
5. Answers will vary. Students may say their main responsibility is going to school, and that they are contributing by striving to become productive members of society.

## Vocabulary
Answers: 1. b, 2. b, 3. a, 4. d, 5. c, 6. a, 7. c, 8. d, 9. d, 10. a.

## Multiple Choice
Answers: 1. b, 2. c, 3. d, 4. d, 5. c, 6. b, 7. d, 8. a, 9. c, 10. c.

## Essay Question
Answers will vary, but students should note that having a code of conduct in a society helps everyone by outlining what behaviors are expected and condoned. Without these boundaries, society would operate with significantly more chaos.

 **Multiple Choice:** d

**Essay**
Student answers will vary, but they should mention the words fair, reasonable, understandable, and enforceable in their evaluation of the rule.

# Chapter 14

## Review
1. A judge in a civil suit can remedy the dispute in terms of (1) compensation and (2) equity. For example, compensation would be payment for lost wages. Stopping a party from repeating the offense for which they are liable is an example of equity.
2. The five categories include: (1) contracts and private agreement disputes, (2) personal injury or property damage issues, (3) property disputes, (4) consumer protection issues, and (5) domestic relation disputes.
3. Unlike civil law, criminal law (1) punishes offenders by sending them to prison, (2) requires a higher level of proven guilt, and (3) considers society also to be the victim of the offense.
4. The corrections system punishes offenders by (1) granting probation, or limited return to the community; (2) levying fines; (3) forcing the offender to do community service; (4) sending the guilty person to jail; and, in some states, (5) allowing the death sentence for offenders who commit very serious crimes.

## Critical Thinking
1. Answers will vary, but students should show an understanding of the damage slander and libel can do, as well as the ways in which these statutes can be misused.
2. A plea bargain occurs when a prosecutor and defendant make an agreement and avoid trial. To avoid trial, the defendant pleads guilty to a less serious charge and, in return, gets a lighter sentence and may have other charges dropped. Students should offer their views of this practice.
3. Some students may point out that all citizens should be able to exercise these basic rights, but others may argue that one earns these rights by obeying the laws of the nation.
4. An innocence project often comprises a group of students working to reopen cases where the defendant may have been wrongly convicted. It is a response to a system that can mistakenly convict innocent people for the crimes of others.
5. Answers will vary. Students may point to lack of parental supervision, the personality of the juvenile, peer pressure, drugs, or other causes. Encourage discussion.

## Study Guide
1. A civil trial procedure begins with (1) the court pleadings, or the submission of written explanations of the opposing cases. Then, both parties (2) gather evidence to support their cases. Finally, (3) a trial takes place in which the sides try to convince a judge or jury that the other side is wrong. Unlike a criminal trial, a jury in a civil trial has to be 51 percent convinced that a particular party is right.
2. Often, the parties in a civil suit choose to avoid the money and time costs of going to trial. Lawyers cost money and the trial process can take years to complete. Many choose one of two forms of arbitration: (1) mediation, or the choice to allow an unbiased person to offer solutions; or (2) arbitration, the process in which one or more people review the case and decide an outcome.
3. A typical trial has four main stages: (1) jury selection, in which a jury of 12 citizens is chosen; (2) the trial, where the burden is on the prosecution to prove the defendant's guilt; (3) the verdict, or the decision of guilt or innocence; and (4) the sentencing of punishment for those found guilty.
4. When dealing with juveniles, courts try to help them avoid further criminal behavior, treat and rehabilitate offenders, and punish the guilty.
5. Answers will vary, but student responses should rely on rational reasons, especially those in their text, rather than emotional reactions.

## Vocabulary
Answers: 1. b, 2. a, 3. d, 4. b, 5. c, 6. d, 7. a, 8. c, 9. a, 10. d.

## Multiple Choice
Answers: 1. a, 2. c, 3. c, 4. d, 5. a, 6. d, 7. d, 8. b, 9. a, 10. d.

## Essay Question
Answers will vary. Some students will suggest that the system works if it keeps dangerous offenders off the streets. Others may question its success given the high rate of recidivism.

# Chapter 15

## Review
1. The U.S. economy is based on capitalism, a system in which individuals and business can create wealth with little government interference. In the U.S., this system allows the freedom to buy and sell services, compete, work, make a profit, and own property.
2. Most countries today have replaced the barter system with one of the following: (1) a command economy, (2) a market economy, or (3) a mixed economy. A command economy has the central government making most of the economic decisions. A market economy relies on natural market forces—and not the government—to control the market. A mixed economy includes a combination of market-driven forces and central government control.
3. U.S. business organizations include: (1) sole proprietorships, (2) partnerships, (3) corporations, and (4) not-for-profit organizations.
4. The three main factors of production include: (1) capital (money, tools, machinery), (2) land (including natural resources), and (3) labor (human work and people employed in production).

## Critical Thinking
1. Answers will vary. Most students will say it's unfair based on their own experience asking their parents for things, but others may point out that it's smart to set the price as high as you can to make more money.
2. When a company has a monopoly, it controls the sales of a good or service in a market—which is dangerous, in that it can raise prices as high as it pleases since there is no competition available. In a mixed economy (like that of the U.S.), the government will likely take steps to end the company's dominance and introduce competition.
3. Answers will vary. Student responses should reflect a clear understanding of the text and present realistic solutions. This exercise can also be used as a group activity.
4. When investors put money into stocks, the stock market goes up. When investors sell their shares, the market goes down
5. Answers will vary based on your location and the local economy.

## Study Guide
1. While capitalism is based on an open market-driven economy, communism does the opposite—the government makes economic decisions, controls property, and shares profit with the community. Socialism includes limited private ownership and control of production and profits.
2. A free market economy is free because the market allows private businesses and individuals to buy and sell as they wish with little government interference. They are not forced to sell or buy at a price determined by the government. Most Americans don't like the economy to be totally free (laissez-faire) because they want protection from economic conditions that would restrict or end their freedoms.
3. The supply of something is the amount of a good or service that producers are willing and able to supply at a certain price. Demand is the amount of a good or service that people are willing and able to buy at various prices. When supply is greater than demand, prices tend to go down. When demand is greater than supply, prices tend to go up.
4. The barter system is the exchange of one kind of good or service for another. Students should describe their personal use of this system.
5. Answers will vary, but should utilize information from the text and be presented clearly.

## Vocabulary
Answers: **1.** a, **2.** c, **3.** d, **4.** b, **5.** a, **6.** b, **7.** b, **8.** d, **9.** a, **10.** c.

## Multiple Choice
Answers: **1.** a, **2.** c, **3.** b, **4.** d, **5.** a, **6.** b, **7.** c, **8.** d, **9.** b, **10.** d.

## Essay Question
Churchill meant that in capitalism not all share in the wealth of the nation, while in socialism the miseries are shared equally, thus not felt as strongly as if they were concentrated among one class.

**1.** a, **2.** c, **3.** Alabama will have the greatest production increase between 2002 and 2005 by 530,000 vehicles. **4.** b, **5.** d

# Chapter 16

## Review

1. The Constitution gives Congress the power to (1) collect taxes, (2) borrow money, (3) regulate commerce domestically and abroad, and (4) coin money.
2. Business cycles through four stages: (1) expansion (growth), (2) peak (highest growth), (3) recession (slowing of growth), and (4) depression (a recession that lasts more than six months).
3. The government measures economic performance by using the following indicators: (1) Gross Domestic Product (GDP), (2) Consumer Price Index (CPI), (3) inflation, (4) deflation, and (5) the unemployment rate.
4. The Federal Reserve's four main duties are (1) to carry out the federal government's monetary policy; (2) to make and enforce rules for banking institutions (and protect consumers' credit rights); (3) to keep the banking system stable; and (4) to serve the U.S. government, the public, financial institutions, and foreign official institutions in financial matters.

## Critical Thinking

1. The Great Depression happened in the 1930s after a period of expansion in the previous decade. It was a very severe recession that closed a lot of businesses. During this period, one quarter of the U.S. workforce was out of work and many people suffered.
2. Students may suggest that the American economy is critical to the world economy, and hence the Fed chairman would be second to the president in importance to the world.
3. First, Standard Oil bought smaller competitors and then used its size to make its suppliers charge lower prices for what they needed. With lower costs, Standard Oil could charge lower prices than its competitors, which it then bought or forced out of business.
4. The Federal Trade Commission is an independent commission that protects consumers and smaller businesses. It (1) enforces antitrust laws, (2) eliminates false or deceptive advertising, (3) investigates suspicious business practices, and (4) informs the government and public about antitrust laws.
5. Answers will vary, but students should give a concrete example to back up their opinion.

## Study Guide

1. The government uses (1) fiscal and (2) monetary policy as its most important tools to improve the economy. Fiscal policy is the plan for how much government plans to collect and spend; monetary policy is the plan for how much the money and credit the government will make available. Adjustments in either can help improve the health of the economy.
2. The federal agencies that protect consumers are (1) the Consumer Product Safety Commission that focuses on product safety; (2) the Food and Drug Administration that focuses on food and drug safety; and (3) the Department of Agriculture that focuses on food safety.
3. The EPA is the Environmental Protection Agency, a government agency that protects the environment. It does so by enforcing environmental laws, protecting air quality, monitoring businesses so they don't pollute, and overseeing the disposal of hazardous waste.
4. Unions use tactics like boycotting their company products, picketing in protest, or striking—stopping work until the problem is resolved. Many people feel that unions are responsible for the high prices of American products compared to European and other products, and for the difficulty some businesses have removing incompetent workers.
5. Answers will vary, but should take into account the effect carrying a national debt has on our economy.

## Vocabulary

Answers: 1. b, 2. c, 3. c, 4. a, 5. d, 6. a, 7. c, 8. d, 9. a, 10. b.

## Multiple Choice

Answers: 1. a, 2. d, 3. a, 4. c, 5. d, 6. c, 7. c, 8. b, 9. d, 10. b.

## Essay Question

Answers will vary, but should use information given in the text to formulate a response.

1. Student answers will vary. Possible answers are Microsoft Corporation, AT & T, IBM Corporation. Possible reasons: The controlled the production and sale of the product or service. The company is located in all cities and/or towns and states. As a result, they set prices as they pleased and adjust prices to squeeze out competition. 2. b 3. Mixed economy, Central Government and market forces. Market economy, Natural market forces. Command Economy, The central government. Market economy, Natural market forces. 4. b, 5. a, 6. d, 7. c, 8. b, 9. The Primary Source Document on page 260 should be used as reference. 10. Government can raise interest rates to make money too expensive to borrow. Therefore, economic activity will slow down. Government can also raise taxes and cut its own spending. Citizens can save more money than they spend. This reduces the demand for goods and services and force prices down. Businesses can help improve the economy by producing more goods and services. This way supply will be greater than demand and prices will drop. 11. corporation, 12. partnership, 13. not-for-profit organization, 14. corporation, 15. sole proprietorship 16. corporation, 17. d

# Chapter 17

## Review
1. United States foreign policy is designed to (1) protect American citizens, (2) work for world peace, (3) support democracy, and (4) provide humanitarian assistance.
2. The president relies on advisors from (1) the State Department, (2) the National Security Council (NSC), (3) the Central Intelligence Agency (CIA), and (4) the Department of Defense.
3. In determining foreign policy, only Congress can (1) declare war, (2) approve treaties, (3) ratify appointments, and (4) approve funds needed for foreign policy-related activities.
4. The UN charter goals are (1) to maintain peace and international security, (2) to develop friendly relations among nations, (3) to cooperate in solving international problems and in promoting respect for human rights, and (4) to coordinate the actions of the member nations in securing peace.

## Critical Thinking
1. Students should note that the same powerful new weapons that protect us can also be used against us. For example, the U.S. was the first to drop the atomic bomb, but others quickly gained the technology.
2. The War Powers Act was passed in 1973 as a means to limit the president's extended use of military power. It holds that the president must notify Congress with 48 hours of sending troops into a dangerous situation. Congress then has 60 days to approve the operation; if they do not, the troops must return home.
3. Answers will vary. Students should cite examples of media coverage in foreign conflicts such as Bosnia or Somalia.
4. Citizens can influence foreign policy by (1) making a career choice that would include international government or business work, (2) electing particular officials, (3) joining with others to influence government, and (4) boycotting foreign products to show discontent.
5. The four tools of foreign policy are (1) diplomacy, (2) alliances, (3) foreign aid, and (4) intelligence.

## Study Guide
1. The U.S. government's humanitarian assistance includes (1) providing disaster relief, (2) protecting the global environment, (3) improving health in other nations, and (4) providing food to combat hunger.
2. The domestic groups that influence foreign policy include farmers, labor unions, manufacturers, and think tanks. The farmers want to sell crops to foreign countries and be protected from domestic competition. Labor unions want to protect domestic jobs, keep manufactured foreign goods from being less expensive than American goods, and obtain trade agreements with other countries. Manufacturers want safely to make and sell goods overseas and be protected from lower-priced foreign goods. Think tanks use scholars and researchers to influence policy decisions.
3. The U.S. changed forever from its isolationist policy after World War II. It then took a more active role by creating the United Nations (1945) and helping in the founding of the North Atlantic Treaty Organization (NATO) to protect against communism.
4. The four non-UN international organizations include: (1) the North Atlantic Treaty Organization (NATO), (2) the Organization of American States, (3) the World Bank, and (4) the World Trade Organization (WTO).
5. Answers will vary. Students may cite the varying forms of government and economy, as well as differences in natural resources, technological development, environment, and military power.

## Vocabulary
Answers: 1. b, 2. a, 3. c, 4. a, 5. b, 6. a, 7. d, 8. b, 9. a, 10. c.

## Multiple Choice
Answers: 1. d, 2. c, 3. d, 4. d, 5. d, 6. c, 7. b, 8. d, 9. c, 10. b.

## Essay Question
Answers will vary. Students should use of facts and arguments given in the text as a basis for their response.

# Chapter 18

## Review
1. The world is divided into (1) wealthier, more developed, industrialized nations (24 countries) and (2) poorer, developing nations (165 countries).
2. A transnational company expects the host country to provide (1) infrastructure, (2) natural resources, and (3) a trained or trainable workforce.
3. Terrorists threaten (1) the security of nations and their citizens, (2) ways of life in civilized nations, and (3) life on earth with weapons of mass destruction.
4. The three main areas of focus include: (1) hunger and nutrition, (2) infectious diseases, and (3) drug use and abuse.

## Critical Thinking
1. Answers will vary, though most students will identify their lifestyle as superior. They may cite material wealth. Encourage them to consider their homes, food, and clothing instead of toys and games.
2. The four factors include the subjects of (1) tariffs on imported goods, (2) open markets, (3) jobs and competition, and (4) costs (of business).
3. The main nonrenewable fuels are oil, natural gas, and coal. The oil supply will be depleted in 40 years, natural gas will last 60 years, and the supply of coal will be used up in 200 years.
4. Refugees in a host country can create ethnic and political tensions and resource shortages as well as a larger international crisis. Student answers will vary on the question of what should be done with refugees.
5. Answers will vary. Encourage students to think of the many volunteer organizations they can participate in through their school and community.

## Study Guide
1. Unlike poorer, developing countries, industrialized nations tend to have a higher GDP, lower birth rates, higher literacy rates, a smaller percentage of agricultural workers, longer life spans, lower child labor rates, and more technology.
2. Western, consumerist culture tends to value (1) material wealth, (2) modernization, and (3) profit-making. In some developing nations, the people value (1) being satisfied with what they have; (2) knowing that owning things won't make anyone better or happier; and that (3) modernization tends to destroy traditional culture, and make poor people poorer and rich people richer.
3. The three problems that contribute to world hunger are (1) population growth vs. food production, (2) food distribution, and (3) land use. Rising populations may create more demand for food than the world can satisfy. Food distribution is difficult in many nations that lack the necessary infrastructure or money to buy food in the first place. Land is sometimes used for more profitable cash crops or factories, leaving less land for food.
4. Drug abuse (1) ruins human lives and health (especially among the poor), (2) causes crime and conflict (especially among the poor), (3) supports terrorists and criminal organizations, and (4) costs every citizen money by using up government funds in treatment and prevention.
5. Answers will vary. Students should suggest that legalizing some drugs would decrease their popularity if they are no longer taboo. They should, however, note that these substances are dangerous, which is why they are illegal. Encourage discuss about how to curtail drug use.

## Vocabulary
Answers: 1. a, 2. c, 3. b, 4. d, 5. d, 6. b, 7. a, 8. c, 9. a, 10. b.

## Multiple Choice
Answers: 1. d, 2. d, 3. c, 4. b, 5. b, 6. d, 7. d, 8. a, 9. d, 10. a.

## Essay Question
Answers will vary, but should cite examples from the text feature.

# Chapter 19

## Review
1. They are (1) decide on things you want to accomplish that require money, (2) come up with a plan for earning and saving the money, and (3) stick to the plan.
2. They are (1) your income and (2) your expenses.
3. They are (1) your filing status and (2) the amount you earn.

## Critical Thinking
1. Answers will vary. Students will probably cite overspending, either on gifts for others or on things for themselves. They may also mention underestimating the true price of living on their own, a new car, or another major purchase.
2. Answers will vary. Students should discuss setting up a savings plan and consider their living expenses and changes, such as rent increases, that may happen in the meantime. They should also mention the costs of gas, maintenance, insurance, and registration.
3. Answers will vary. Students may mention: required local taxes, contribution toward health insurance, retirement plan contribution, charitable contribution, union dues, and savings.

## Study Guide
1. (1) Housing: about 32%; (2) food: about 13%; (3) clothing: about 5%; (4) health care: 5%; (5) entertainment: a little less than 5%.
2. It allows you to organize long and short term savings plans, adjust your expenses and savings if you have a change in income, and adjust flexible and discretionary expenses over a number of months in case of emergencies that require more than your savings plan allows.
3. It is: (1) reduce discretionary expenses, (2) reduce flexible expenses, and (3) reduce fixed expenses.
4. They are: (1) large envelopes labeled by category, (2) file folders labeled by category in a file drawer or box, and (3) an accordion folder and labels for identifying each pocket.
5. They are: (1) federal taxes, (2) FICA (Federal Insurance Contribution Act), (3) worker's compensation or disability programs, and (4) state taxes.

## Multiple Choice
**pg. 82**
Answers: 1. c, 2. a, 3. d, 4. a, 5. d

**pg. 83**
Answers: 1. d, 2. c, 3. a, 4. c, 5. c, 6. c

# Chapter 20

## Review
1. These are: providing loans and charging for financial services.
2. These are: (1) fill in all the information, (2) complete the check register, and (3) figure your balance.
3. They are: (1) statement period, (2) ending balance, (3) checks deducted, (4) deposits credited, (5) fees or charges deducted, and (6) interest earned.

## Critical Thinking
1. Answers will vary. Some students may be somewhat confused by these money management tools, and others may feel proud that they can handle this grown-up task.
2. Answers will vary. Students may mention that there might be a temptation to spend the money because it is very accessible.

## Study Guide
You need: (1) your signature, (2) "For deposit only," and (3) the account number to which you want the check deposited.

## Multiple Choice
Answers: 1. a, 2. c, 3. a, 4. d, 5. b, 6. c, 7. b, 8. c, 9. b, 10. b

# Chapter 21

## Review
1. These are: a person's character, capacity, and capital.
2. These are: fraud by credit card companies, fraud by sellers, and fraud by other people.
3. These are: (1) employment and income, (2) housing, (3) assets, and (4) credit history.
4. (1) Your property may be repossessed; (2) your wages may be garnished; and (3) you may be forced into bankruptcy.

## Critical Thinking
1. Answers will vary, but should show understanding of the concepts.
2. Answers will vary.
3. Answers will vary. Some students may say they'd be scared by the responsibility, others may suggest they'd feel successful and adult.
4. The advantages are: (1) if you don't have ready cash, you don't have to wait to buy something, (2) using credit will help you save money because you can catch good sales, and (3) credit comes in handy for emergencies. The disadvantages are: (1) credit makes it easy to overspend, (2) you have to pay it back with interest, and (3) when you buy a lot on credit, payments pile up and can leave you with little for the essentials.
5. Answers will vary. (1) Look at your budget. Can it handle a new expense? If not, create options. (2) Make sure your paycheck isn't all going toward paying off credit card debt. (3) Save some emergency money. (4) If you charge a new item set a payment schedule for yourself and stick to it.

## Study Guide
1. The principal is the amount charged or borrowed, and the fee that is paid for the use of the money is called the interest.
2. When a business wants to expand or increase its inventory, it gets a loan, called commercial credit, to cover the costs. Credit used by individuals is called personal credit.
3. They could: (1) quote a low APR in conversation and then sneak a higher APR into the written contract; (2) say the customer must buy a service contract or extended warranty in order to get financing; and (3) say the customer must buy all kinds of insurance from the dealer.
4. There are relatively low-cost loans to help with college expenses. Depending on which school you attend, you may borrow from the federal government, from your state government, or from a private lender. If you can prove financial need based upon your and your parents' finances, you may qualify for a subsidized loan. The government pays off part of the amount borrowed, so you won't have to pay back the full amount.
5. (1) A person may snoop in your wallet to get your credit card number. (2) A restaurant server or store clerk may discreetly copy your credit card information. (3) Someone may steal your wallet.

## Multiple Choice
Answers: 1. d, 2. a, 3. a, 4. d, 5. c, 6. a, 7. c, 8. a, 9. d, 10. a.

# Chapter 22

## Review
1. They are: psychological, sociological, and economic.
2. They are: two-for-one sales, coupons, contests, and rebates
3. They are: bait and switch, phone fraud, pyramid schemes, contests and sweepstakes, loss leaders.
4. They are: to buy products that are safe, be informed, have a choice, and be heard.

## Critical Thinking
1. Answers will vary. Students who have always had their needs provided may cite their wants as more important.
2. Answers will vary. Students may object to such a fine distinction. As examples, they may cite new car ads that proclaim "0% interest" but the small print tells you that only some customers will qualify for that rate.
3. Answers will vary. Students will likely cite brand loyalty in clothes, shoes, and some food items such as cookies or soda.
4. Answers will vary. Many students will say they like online ordering, but may suggest it's not worth it for large purchases with big shipping costs or that food may spoil in shipping.
5. Answers will vary. Some students may boycott based on environmental or employment practices, or perhaps based on price.

## Study Guide
1. Market research studies people to understand their buying behavior. Advertising is the business act of attracting attention to products or services with information designed to stimulate consumer buying. What is found from the market research is what helps the companies in determining how to approach the advertisement.
2. The informational ad describes features to convince consumers to buy the product. The persuasive ad tries to create desire by giving the impression the buyer will feel fulfilled, satisfied, or happy if he or she has this product. Image enhancing ads try to make consumers feel like they will belong to a special group if they buy the service or product. Brand ads reassure consumers that they can count on the quality because it comes from a well known, reputable manufacturer.
3. Answers will vary. Compare student responses and encourage discussion.
4. Feedback from consumers is critical for all businesses and service industries. It helps them with their short-term and long-term planning. It helps them to know how to improve their product development, service, and ultimately, their sales.

## Vocabulary
Answers: 1. d, 2. b, 3. c, 4. a, 5. d, 6. c, 7. a, 8. c, 9. d, 10. d

# Chapter 23

### Review
They are: reputation, stability, and ease.

### Critical Thinking
Answers will vary. Some students may be willing to pay a shipping charge to avoid going to a store. Others may cite deals that make it just as cost effective to order online.

### Study Guide
1. Answers will vary.
2. Shopping in a store requires that you get there and have some means of purchasing items, such as cash, credit cards, or checks. Shopping online requires a personal computer with a web browser, an online connection, an online connector, an account with an Internet service provider, and a credit card or debit card.

### Multiple Choice
Answers: **3.** b, **4.** a

# Chapter 24

## Review
They are: (1) always shop from a list, (2) shop on a full stomach, (3) compare prices, and (4) buy what you like to eat.

## Critical Thinking
1. Answers will vary. Students may note that their diet has been largely controlled by their parents' preferences. Some will have simple diets, others more varied. Some may prefer more variety than is available to them in their parents' home.
2. Answers will vary. Compare answers and discuss with students.

## Study Guide
1. Most vegetables—fresh, frozen, and canned—are grown with fertilizers and pesticides created in laboratories. Most meat and dairy products come from animals that have been fed hormones and antibiotics, as well as commercially grown feed.
2. Food prices are influenced by many of the same factors that affect other commodities: Supply—an early frost in Florida may kill much of the orange crop, making oranges more expensive country-wide. Demand—a surge in the popularity of a certain kind of food will mean suppliers can, and will, charge more for it. Transportation costs—imported foods generally cost more.
3. Bulk buying means buying items in large quantities, which generally means that a person pays a lower price per unit. Bulk buying can save money, but it doesn't make sense unless a person has a lot of storage space and a large enough family to eat the food before it gets too old and goes bad.

## Multiple Choice
Answers: 1. a, 2. b, 3. a

# Chapter 25

## Critical Thinking

1. Answers will vary. Students may mention that natural fibers come from plant and animal sources. Many people prefer fabrics made with natural fibers because they allow your body to breathe and they feel good to the touch. Synthetic fibers are man-made and people are often attracted by their ease of care and their lower cost. Many can be machine washed and dried and can be ready to wear without ironing.

2. Answers will vary. Some students will buy clothing that doesn't fit properly because the store doesn't have the proper size or because fashion dictates wearing something which is too big or too small.

3. Answers will vary.

## Study Guide

1. Designer clothes are created by well known fashion designers. They almost always cost more than department store brands. Sometimes it's because they use high-quality fabrics and have a superior cut. Often, it's because the manufacturers spend more on marketing and merchandising. Department stores often have their own special brand names. Clothing with their labels is sold only in their own stores. It is usually of decent quality, because the store would not put its name on an inferior product. They sometimes sell "designer labels" alongside their own brands as well.

2. Look at the labels to see what they are made of. Look at the hems to make sure they are not visible on the outside of a garment, aren't close to unraveling. Check the buttons to see if they are tight or loose. Check clothes for linings, since if they are lined, they last longer. Is a sweater starting to "pill" from people trying it on? Learn about fabrics and what to expect from them.

3. Because of international commerce, visual symbols have been developed to explain fabric care to people who speak many different languages.

## Vocabulary

Answers: 1. c, 2. a, 3. d, 4. b, 5. c, 6. b, 7. a, 8. b, 9. a.

## Essay Question

Answers will vary, but you really can't be sure you got the very best deal. Comparing prices at several places and researching your purchase will ensure a good deal.

# Chapter 26

## Review
1. The plans are: (1) HMOs, (2) PPOs, and (3) POSs.
2. They are: (1) consider a short-term policy, (2) evaluate your health status, (3) evaluate how often you visit a doctor, (4) comparison shop for good premium prices, and (5) check on the rating of the insurance company.

## Study Guide
1. Traditional medicine treats specific diseases and conditions mostly with medication and surgery. Physicians often specialize in a particular field. Options for diagnosis can vary, and preventative medicine is often used. Alternative medicine is made up of chiropractic, acupuncture, relaxation, vitamin, and herbal forms of treatment, and is used often to supplement traditional approaches.
2. Answers will vary. Among other measures, it is important to (1) research the physician, facility, or health subject thoroughly; (2) get trustworthy recommendations; (3) use only licensed health-care practitioners; (4) ask for references; and (5) prepare questions to ask your physician about his or her background and your medical needs.
3. They are: (1) one doctor is responsible for all of a patient's care, (2) expensive procedures are not performed unnecessarily, and (3) the insurance company must approve any nonroutine care procedures that your doctor orders.

## Multiple Choice
Answers: 1. b, 2. c, 3. b, 4. d, 5. c, 6. d, 7. a, 8. c, 9. d, 10. d.

# Chapter 27

## Review
1. They are: study newspaper ads, narrow down neighborhoods, and visit apartments for rent.
2. They are: compatibility, reliability, and willingness to communicate.
3. They are: apartments, condominiums, co-ops, co-houses, houses, and low-income housing.
4. They are: your down payment; a mortgage; and points, fees, and other charges.

## Critical Thinking
1. Answers will vary.
2. Answers will vary.
3. Answers will vary. Students may suggest that it can be easier for someone else to be in charge of maintenance, repairs, homeowner's insurance, garbage pickup, etc., but that there are great financial advantages to owning in the long term.

## Study Guide
1. It is a nonprofit organization. With volunteer labor and donations, houses are refurbished or constructed. The prospective homeowner that helped build the house then buys the house through a no-interest loan. Habitat for Humanity makes no profit on the house. A committee selects potential homeowners, based on their need, their willingness to participate in the building project, and their ability to repay the no-interest loan.
2. Look for "For Rent" signs in windows; check the classified rental ads every day for your desired part of town; let coworkers, friends, and family members know you're looking for something; visit or call the property managers of apartment complexes in which you would like to live; attend open houses; and contact property management firms.
3. You do not own the property until the loan is repaid. You are buying the property from the mortgage holder and securing the loan with the property. This means the mortgage holder can take the property if you default or don't make your payments.

## Multiple Choice
Answers: 1. d, 2. b, 3. a, 4. c, 5. b, 6. a, 7. c, 8. b, 9. c.

# Chapter 28

## Review
1. Questions include: (1) How far away do you live from school or work? (2) What convenient and reliable transportation options are there?; (3) How long does it take to get there by the transportation options you've considered?; and, (4) What are the advantages or disadvantages or each option?
2. Eight forms of mass transit are: subways, trolleys, buses, light rail, streetcars, trains, ferries, and taxis.
3. They include: bicycles, cars, motorcycles and electric bikes, and rental cars.
4. The Big 10 are: (1) follow the maintenance schedule in the owner's manual, (2) get regular tune-ups and oil changes, (3) wash the car regularly, (4) check and maintain all fluid levels, (5) check all belts and hoses for signs of wear, (6) check and maintain tires and mechanization, (7) touch up paint when needed, (8) do preventative maintenance in hot/cold seasons, (9) check all lights regularly, and (10) check and maintain brakes regularly.

## Critical Thinking
1. Answers will vary. Students should note the environmental, financial, and health benefits of riding a bike instead of driving.
2. Taxis differ from other forms of mass transit in that (1) they are often the most expensive option, (2) they drop people off at specific destinations, unlike others, and (3) passengers pay a metered fee and are expected to tip. Taxis can be a bad choice to take when there is bad weather, or during a busy part of the day, because they are often unavailable.
3. Many students will say they prefer to drive; others may say they will walk if their destination is close by.
4. Answers will vary. Students may cite concerns about cost, convenience, and other factors.
5. Answers will vary. Students may note that at least one major carmaker has introduced a hybrid vehicle for sale.

## Study Guide
1. Answers will vary. Lifestyle is an important deciding factor. One person may have a very busy life, which would make a car the best choice. Another person may value exercise or protecting the environment, so a bicycle may work best. Personal preferences about comfort and convenience also matter; some might take the bus because they dislike driving, or ride a motorcycle because of the freedom it offers.
2. Trolleys are old-fashioned, electric cars that run on tracks, usually transporting people on circular routes around popular urban areas. Light rail are new, quiet, and nonpolluting trains that quickly transport people down city streets.
3. Motorcycles cost less to buy, repair, and, in some cases, insure than cars; they also give the driver a feeling of independence. Among the disadvantages are that motorcycles are more dangerous, harder to see, and less comfortable than cars.
4. When shopping for a used car, one should look for one from an honest dealer or seller offering a car in good shape, with low miles and a good repair record. It is also a good idea to inquire about a warranty and have a mechanic look over the vehicle before deciding to buy.
5. Answers will vary. Owning a car means that you will pay for the car in full, possess the title, and have the option to resell it. Leasing a car is the equivalent of renting a car long term; you make lower monthly payments to use temporarily a car that you do not own.

## Vocabulary
Answers: 1. b, 2. b, 3. b, 4. a, 5. a, 6. d, 7. b, 8. c, 9. d, 10. c

# Chapter 29

## Review

1. They are: (1) that you want to be sure the protection you believe you are buying will really be there when you need it; (2) that you don't want to pay more for it than you have to; and (3) that there is a lot of fine print.
2. They are: (1) earthquakes, (2) forest fires, (3) tornadoes, (4) hurricanes, (5) windstorms, and (6) floods.
3. It covers your losses, your obligation to others, and your medical expenses.
4. They are homeowner's insurance, renter's insurance, and personal property insurance.

## Critical Thinking

1. Answers will vary. Students may cite family heirlooms or photographs.
2. Some students may say they will never need it. Others may cite family history of debilitating illness as a good reason to obtain it.
3. Answers will vary. Insurance does not cover all the costs associated with a natural disaster.
4. Some students will cite wanting a higher deductible to create lower payments, while others prefer to make higher payments in return for a lower deductible in case of a crash or needed repair.
5. Answers will vary. Students may mention that cash-value costs more than term, but it has advantages. The policy grows in value over time as you pay into it. You can also cash out at any time for the value you have accumulated (less the amount used for protection). It can also reach a point where the policy is fully paid up—often in 20–25 years. The protection and cash benefits continue, but the premium payments don't. The premium costs will not change as you age. Term is much cheaper and is only in force for the term of the policy—usually one year. It is never paid up. Costs go up as you get older, but there are policies available where the rates won't go up for as long as 20 years.

## Study Guide

1. An agent can explain exactly what you are buying, can provide you with choices, and can work with the company you choose to help you get prompt attention for your claims.
2. Answers will vary. Some ways to control costs are: rechecking your needs and the prices of available coverage every year or so, not insuring yourself against events for which you can afford to pay on your own, and taking the highest deductible you can afford.
3. It is up to you to pay.
4. Expect your insurance rates to go up.
5. The amount of collision and comprehensive coverage needed when the car was new no longer applies. Now the dollar value of the car is lower.

## Multiple Choice

Answers: 1. b, 2. c, 3. d, 4. a, 5. c, 6. c, 7. a, 8. b, 9. c

## Essay Question

Answers will vary. Most students will mention only health insurance and car insurance as current needs. In five years, they might want renter's insurance and other types, as well. Later on, they'll add life insurance, homeowner's insurance, property insurance, and possibly others, such as disability insurance and long-term care insurance.

# Chapter 30

## Review
1. Start to save and invest sooner rather than later, and leave your money in as long as you can.
2. They are: (1) stocks, (2) bonds, and (3) mutual funds.
3. They are: Standard & Poor's and Moody's.
4. They are: Traditional IRAs and Roth IRAs.

## Critical Thinking
1. Answers will vary. Students will likely consider a CD or bond a conservative investment, while stocks are more risky.
2. Answers will vary. Students may mention college education, buying a home, and retirement.
3. Answers will vary. Students may mention stocks, bonds, and mutual funds as the common investment tools. More unusual investment tools are land, precious metals, fine art, and rare stamps.
4. Answers will vary. Students may mention that, over time, a person may accumulate enough wealth that they want the services of an advisor.
5. Answers will vary. Some students will not want their employer running their retirement fund, but others may welcome sponsored programs, especially those in which the employer also contributes.

## Study Guide
1. Short-term goals are things like an upcoming vacation, a major repair on your car, or needing new tires next year. For these goals, students probably would just put money in a savings account or buy a CD for the short term. Long-term goals are those things people save for that are more than a couple of years off, such as a college education, buying a home, or retirement. For a long-term goal, it's wise to invest, rather than save.
2. A college education gives people experiences that improve their ability to appreciate life. It can also provide a network of friends who will support you in many ways through the years. It greatly improves your chances of doing high-paying work that you enjoy. The more education you get, the more you qualify for jobs that pay the highest salary.
3. Investors read newspapers and business magazines. They use common sense, talk to people who know, or listen to them on the media. Some people form investment clubs and share the work of tracking stocks and researching companies. Students can use the search words "investment clubs" on the Internet to find out more about these.
4. Government bonds are issued by federal, state, and local governments as a means of raising money for government projects. Some are safer than others, depending on the financial health of the town or state.
5. IRAs are tax deferred because they allow the individual to put away a certain amount of money each year (maximum amount varies) that will not be taxed until the money is withdrawn many years into the future. The individual may withdraw the money without penalty as early as at age 59 but not later than at age 70.

## Vocabulary
Answers: 1. b, 2. c, 3. a, 4. c, 5. d, 6. a, 7. d, 8. a, 9. d, 10. d.

## Essay Question
Answers will vary. Students may present their plans to the class to compare different strategies for achieving similar goals.